To Barry: and a ___ in the Cowbri ___ Company, who look after my welfare so well!

From: Ian, the ancient mariner author of these salty stories plus others for all ages.

Best wishes & happy reading to you all. This is a gift with no obligations.

Ian K Bryce

22nd March 2007

2, Cae Stumpie,
Cowbridge,
Vale of Glamorgan. CF71 7DL

Tel: 01446 772080.

SHIPMATES AND MISTRESSES –
BYE AND LARGE

Shipmates and Mistresses – Bye and Large

by

IAN KINLOCH BRYCE

The Memoir Club

First published in 2005 by
The Memoir Club
Stanhope Old Hall
Stanhope
Weardale
County Durham

British Library Cataloguing in
Publication Data.
A catalogue record for this book
is available from the
British Library.

ISBN: 1 84104 043 6

Typeset by TW Typesetting, Plymouth, Devon
Printed by CPI Bath

*Dedicated to my family and friends –
wherever they may be – and especially daughter PETA
who persuaded me*

I have chosen a title for the story of my life, that I believe will allow me freedom to create 'episodes', containing related subjects, regardless of time or place, and might therefore reflect my frequent changing attitudes to people, institutions, ideas and things. This also, I believe, should avoid the possibility of a boring chronology of events, many of which are not worth recording.

Definition: 'Bye and large', is to take a broad view of things; to take everything into consideration. An old naval expression from the days when ships were sailed 'bye and large' – just off the wind and with every sail doing its share.

Quote: 'We don't see the world as it is. We see it as we are.' And sometimes the faculty of serendipity helps us to make fortunate discoveries by accident. I believe it will happen often in this book. I hope so.

Contents

List of Illustrations

Foreword

Sir Neil Jephcott Bt. M.A., M.I. Mech.E.

Ian has rung down on the telegraph 'stand by' and as Chief I'd better warm through the main engine and prepare for movements, and plenty of movements there are in this autobiography. Such has been my relationship with Ian – he has always been a bit ahead of me – which is right and proper as the senior by some years, although we both left the Merchant Navy about the same time, he from the glamorous cruise liners, and they were glamorous in those days, myself from dreary tankers. So in this respect his background before we met up in Warsash was very different.

It was not long after that that Denny, my first wife, and Brandy, Ian's first wife, became friends as did the children, and when tragedy struck we were in a position to help, as Ian records in his book. So started an association which has continued happily to this day.

I have occasionally had Ian as a crew whilst sailing – i.e. with the roles reversed, and on one particular occasion he was of dubious assistance! However, there were mitigating circumstances: since his attention was totally absorbed by the third member of the crew, not only did he not help, but also he deprived me of the help of the third member (who subsequently became his wife). So I sailed single-handed!

Thanks to a prodigious memory, frequent reunions and his old navigation notebooks (he told me that he'd got a record of every sight he'd ever taken!), Ian has been able to recount a brilliant description of the notorious 'Russian' Convoys. He is also quite unusual in that his traditional Merchant Navy background gives a very different slant to the Royal Navy's role. The admiration that the Royal Navy's personnel had for the MN is well recorded, and particularly how badly they felt about being ordered to leave the merchant-men to fend for themselves in the appalling PQ17 incident. Stirring days, only alleviated by his description of the 'heads' in Murmansk whilst *Oribi* was in dry dock. They will be all too familiar to anyone who has dry-docked on the North East coast during winter at that period! Ian's on the spot description of Dunkirk and its evacuation is a fine corollary to John Masefield's 'The Nine Days Wonder' and those traumatic few days.

It was not until 1969 that the average person travelled, until then only those on business or the very wealthy were so privileged. His cruising around the world with American ladies aboard obviously had its compensations unknown to tanker engineers! It also allowed him to see a lot of the world which was unknown to most people at that time. Tourism is now so popular, with the UK population being so much better off – not only in financial terms, but also with longer holidays, and has made most of these places widely and commonly visited by air. Cruising is another popular facility, usually of much shorter duration than in those early days.

Ian's sudden and traumatic introduction to shore side showed his flexibility and personal drive. 'Deck' Officers had always had problems in finding work ashore and adjusting to civilian life. There are few traditional appointments available as Harbour Masters and the like, and few have use for their navigational skills, so they are obliged to break into some new shore-based field. In this respect Merchant Navy engineers are much luckier than their Deck counterparts. Ian on coming ashore experienced for a number of years the hazards of marketing. His leadership skills together with his enthusiasm in development and training of staff led him to the adoption of techniques largely emanating from America and the oil industry into establishing his own business. It is strange to think in those early days that management training was initially largely restricted to the Administrative Staff College at Henley and Cranfield.

His depth of character is also clearly shown in the way he tackled the loss of Brandy, subsequently having a second family with Susan. I shall always remember his advice to me on my second marriage, nominally a quiet wedding until I received Ian's telephone message. He said 'don't make it too quiet, it's probably your Bride's only marriage!'

Autobiographies are always a balancing act between fact and truth as remembered, and very often it is impossible to establish which. With the author's memory of incidents, (which inevitably becomes reminiscence) I believe Ian has carried out this balancing act to perfection, allowing his readers rapidly to become his friends as bystanders, be it on an ice cold bridge in an Arctic gale, or on a warmer site with female company.

Acknowledgements

'Come on Dad, write a book' said my elder daughter, Peta, many times towards the end of the last century. 'You've related so many stories that I think would be of interest to our youngsters, which would be impractical for us to pass on verbally. So, get cracking!' And I did in 2001, having contacted the 'Memoir Club'.

I am indebted to Peta for suggesting it, and to my wife, Susan, for supporting the idea by giving me the benefit of her expertise on the computer, quite beyond my comprehension, and acting as the most efficient sub-editor of my manuscript throughout the four-year process. I am grateful to all other members of the family and many past shipmates and colleagues ashore, too numerous to mention individually, for their helpful jogging of my memory.

The Memoir Club guidance and teamwork have been greatly appreciated and my particular thanks to Sheila Seacroft, whose editorial energy and efficiency inspired me to achieve even greater personal expectations.

Most of my written memories have come from direct, personal experience, but I have to thank many books and their authors for providing details, read subsequently, that have improved my narrative, and the chief ones I want to list here:

HMS Thetis by David Roberts
The History of the Worcester 1862–1929 by Frederick H. Stafford
The Story of the Worcester 1862–1962 by Commander Gordon Steele VC, RN
Dunkirk by A.D. Divine
The Nine Days Wonder by John Masefield
BEF Ships before, at and after Dunkirk by John de S. Winser
Commando by Peter Young
Convoys to Russia, 1941–1945 by Bob Ruegg and Arnold Hague
The Russian Convoys by B.B. Schofield
Dönitz by Peter Padfield
Autumn of the U-boats by Geoffrey Jones
Maritime Strategy by Vice-Admiral Sir Peter Gretton
Life Line: the Merchant Navy at War by Peter Elphick
The Fourth Service: Merchantmen at War by John Slader
Heroes of the Fourth Service by Frank Pearce
Upon Their Lawful Occasions: Reflections of a Merchant Navy Officer During Peace and War by Vernon G.A. Upton

Details from RNLI, Poole, by Brian J. Wead, which enriched my Chapter 12 in Cardigan Bay.
The North Atlantic Run by John Maxtone-Graham
Great Leaders by Professor John Adair
Management Teams, Why They Succeed or Fail by Meredith Belbin
Use Your Head by Tony Buzan
What Do You Say After You Say Hello? by Eric Berne
I'm OK You're OK by Thomas A. Harris.
Don't Say 'YES' When You Want To Say 'NO' by Herbert Fensterheim and Jean Baer
All in the Mind by Ludovic Kennedy
The Age of Reason by Thomas Paine

If anyone reading the above feels left out, then I'm sorry.

Thanks Peta for pushing your parent along the path of a lifetime, and thanks to Tony (Harry) North for encouraging me with his rousing reviews.

Finally, to the Engine Room, thank you Chief, Neil Jephcott, for providing my 'Foreword'.

CHAPTER 1

My musical momentum (an overview of my life) – 1922–2001

'IF MUSIC BE THE FOOD OF LOVE, play on,' said Orsino in the play, *Twelfth Night*, by William Shakespeare. In echoing his sentiment I would add that music has always been one of the greatest loves throughout my life and I am still 'playing on'. I believe that a preview pleases an audience or readers by providing sign-posts showing the way ahead. Therefore, I have chosen music and the pleasure it has given me in all its moods, from classical to jazz, to relate this, the story of my life.

I start naturally enough with my mother and father. My mother, born Zillah Florence Musitano in 1891, was a skilled, versatile amateur pianist, and my father, Laurence Leslie Bryce, whose date of origin was 1885, sang as a boy chorister and later in life performed a variety of songs and monologues for friends at private parties, often accompanied by my mother.

It was my mother who maintained that my ear for music started in the womb. During the period of my gestation, from autumn 1921 to summer 1922, I must have listened to countless Chopin compositions from mazurkas to nocturnes and remember well the daily rendering of 'Rondo Capriccioso' by Mendelssohn, a great favourite, which undoubtedly caused my first vigorous movements within and told my mother how much her efforts were being appreciated.

At the age of five, in 1927, it was thought timely to sit me on the piano stool, where under the tuition of Miss Watson, I started on Middle C and went CDE, CDE, CDEFEDC, to which I was encouraged to sing the words, 'Here I go, here I go, here I go all in a row'. Watty, my name for my tutor, was tall and slim, with hair piled on top, surmounted by a boater type hat with an enormous hatpin for security. Her tight skirt reached the ground in Edwardian fashion and with her parasol and pince-nez glasses perched on her nose, she appeared, to me, to be terribly old. Probably she was only in her thirties or forties. Next came the left hand doing the CDE routine and of course soon I learnt the never to be forgotten difference between treble and bass clefs. I have wondered since why Mum didn't teach me, but reasoned she was too impatient and busy with her Townswomen's Guild, tennis, bridge and other pursuits. With tongue stuck out of the corner of her mouth, she could transpose from key to key instantly, quite beyond me.

I was born at 7 a.m. on 9 June, 1922 at 99 Stanhope Road, Darlington and at the age of eight, in 1930, went to the Queen Elizabeth Grammar

School, just five minutes walk away. It was then that the round football interfered with my piano practising. I became something of a show-off as centre forward for my Form team and, between games, dribbled a tennis ball along the pavement, to and from school, to improve my ball control. This neglectful approach to my music continued when the family moved to Cardiff in 1934. Then, it was the oval shaped rugby ball, introduced to me at Monkton House School, as a priority in any Welsh school, that caused further neglect of practice. I still had piano lessons from Mary Evans, a friend of my sister Betty and of similar age, some eight years older than me, but a lot younger than old Watty in Darlington. I still didn't practise enough, but Mary, on my weekly visit to the Evans' house, was lenient and allowed me to play more modern music of my choice.

Having decided on a sea career, I went away to the Thames Nautical Training College HMS *Worcester*, moored off Greenhithe, Kent, from 1936 to 38, as a cadet preparing to become a Deck Officer in the Merchant Navy. My only contact with a keyboard, in this 19th Century Ship of the Line, was a ropey old untuned upright piano in the bowels of the ship, on which I would bash out the popular tunes of the day, The Astaire/Rogers films were plentiful in the thirties, so I would play for my shipmates to sing, 'They all laughed at Christopher Columbus, when he said the world was round', a popular song, to which some tried tap-dancing, just like Fred!

After a year on the Atlantic in Canadian Pacific cargo ships, without a piano, we were at war. I was called up as a Midshipman Royal Naval Reserve and reported to Chatham Barracks on 28 August 1939. My first ship was HMS *Kittiwake*, mined in the Dover Straits on 20 September, followed by HMS *Fitzroy* minesweeping in the North Sea and at Dunkirk during 1940. Returning from a run ashore in Grimsby, I helped Stoker Fitzroy (Heavy-weight Boxing Champion of the Navy pre-war) to regain his feet and return on board the *Fitzroy* (a coal burning Sweeper) without fuss or further reference, which endeared me to the stokers, who invited me to become an honorary member of their Mouth-Organ Band. I accepted gladly and later when on leave, joined them for an evening at the Fitzroy Tavern in Fitzroy Street, Soho, during the Blitz. We played merrily through the Red Alert until the All Clear in the small hours, with the occasional crump crump far away and drinks on the house throughout. Music from my harmonica compensated for the lack of a piano in those days. Still a Midshipman aged nineteen, I was appointed to HMS *Oribi*, a brand new fleet destroyer, on my birthday in 1941. I spent the next three years in *Oribi* (until after D-Day 1944) on the Arctic and Atlantic oceans, escorting convoys and getting home on leave to Cardiff on average about twice a year.

It is during this wartime period that piano playing meant so much to me. When on leave, I would have breakfast and then, still in pyjamas and dressing gown, sit at my mother's lovely, overstrung upright and play lots of Chopin plus Billy Mayerl's syncopated 'Marigold' (Mum's favourite colour was orange), with bits of boogie, all day. I can see my mother's head coming round the door in the late afternoon as she said 'Are you going to get dressed before your father comes home?' What wisdom she had, to let me be and allow me infinite time to unwind and through the solace of a Chopin nocturne or maybe the stimulation of his 'Revolutionary Study', escape from and counterbalance the stress and horrors of war. I don't think I appreciated it so much at that time, after all, war was still something of an adventure to a seventeen rising twenty-two year-old, but I understood later what therapy it must have been.

On board the *Oribi* we had fun with music in many ways. I was Navigator (Pilot or Vasco for short) and had as my Yeoman an excellent and talented man called Bill Goodacre (or Goody for short). Goody was a master on the fiddle, straight or syncopated like Stephane Grappelli, and we found players of drums, banjo, accordion and trombone amongst the crew. My forte was on keyboard and this was a folding foot-pumped harmonium intended for hymns at Church Services, but sounded OK when emitting Miller big-band music. The band assembled in the SDO (Signal Distribution Office) from where we could broadcast throughout the ship, and we would begin with our signature tune, Tommy Dorsey's 'Song of India'. This became a popular evening entertainment when in harbour, from Scapa Flow to Iceland and North Russia, with many volunteers from the ship's company to sing songs, with requests. One number asked for by the Seamen's Messdeck, especially for the Pilot (me), was 'Let's get Lost', a hit on BBC radio at that time. When in Boston, Mass, having a new bow fitted after ramming U-531 in May 1943, I heard my first car radio, in the leafy lanes near Groton, and it was Duke Ellington's 'Don't get around much anymore'. Goody and I still meet at Harry's or the Garibaldi, in St Albans.

Our Captain was an 'upper yard man', meaning he had been promoted through the ranks, much decorated in previous destroyers and well liked by all. He was aware and very proud of his ship's band and on one occasion did a most unusual thing which was applauded in a big way. VA2 (Second in Command Home Fleet) Vice-Admiral Sir Bruce Fraser was flying his flag in the battleship HMS *Anson* at anchor in Hvalfjord, Iceland, when ordered to return to Scapa in a hurry and we *Oribi* were commissioned to give him passage. This meant we flew the flag of Vice-Admiral at the masthead when we entered the main fleet anchorage at Scapa and all ships with captains junior to VA2 (which meant all except C in C Admiral Tovey in HMS *King George V*, our destination) would have to 'sound the still' on bugle or pipe and salute us as we passed. The big ships always had a Marine Band on the fo'c'sle entering harbour, so our Captain, Lieut-Cdr J.E.H. McBeath DSO, DSC, RN turned to me on the bridge and said 'Ian, muster the ship's band on the fo'c'sle and tell them what to play.' 'Aye, aye sir.' Of course Mc took the longest route possible through the anchorage, he and the Admiral enjoying every moment, as we received recognition from the battleships, aircraft-carriers and cruisers we passed, with Goody on the fiddle leading the band playing Glenn Miller's 'In the Mood'.

VE Day, 8 May 1945, saw me dancing in the streets of Birkenhead, close to my ship HMS *Wild Goose*. Music blared from everywhere, as anyone grabbed anyone else, to dance in and out of the terraced houses, just like the Cornish Floral Dance. Three months later I was up to similar antics on VJ Day in Barrow-in-Furness, whilst putting a frigate into the Reserve Fleet. It came as a pleasant surprise when I was drafted as Lieutenant RNR to HMS *Vanguard* for the Royal Tour to South Africa in 1947. Happily, there was a piano in the Wardroom of Britain's last battleship, which I played occasionally, when not making up a foursome at bridge with the Surgeon, Paymaster and Constructor Commanders. In November I was demobbed and returned to Cardiff, to live with my parents while studying for my 'Master's' Certificate, which I got in February 1948. When not studying, I was having fun on Mum's piano again and liked accompanying records on the radiogram, especially Litolf's Piano Concerto. My father also enjoyed listening and would often pop a request my way. Esme and Pat, girlfriends in Cardiff, were also pianists and we frequently got together during the war years for musical sessions.

In the spring of 1948, I rejoined Canadian Pacific Steamships and a year later, Brenda Pearce and I got married. For our wedding in 1949 at Llanishen Church and afterwards at the Royal Hotel, Cardiff, I had composed a parody of 'Much-Binding-in-the-Marsh' — the signature tune of Kenneth Horne and Richard Murdoch, ex RAF types, in their popular radio show after WW2. Many relatives and guests got a mention and the last verse went like this:

> Much-Splicing-in the-Church,
> Our mothers hats are causing a sensation.
> Much splicing in the church
> As they circulate from friend to fond relation.
> Telling of the match they made
> With ingenuity,
> 'My girl was in the WRNS you know
> And my son goes to sea,
> So we thought', said Zill and Elsie,
> 'How suited they would be
> For much splicing in the church.'

Brenda and I sang this at the reception to great applause. A year later, I switched to Cunard White Star Line and we set up home in Warsash on the Hamble river. My first Cunarder was *Caronia* sailing from Southampton, and after three Atlantic crossings to New York and back, we set off on a World Cruise, the first of three for me. Quickly realizing that a radiogram in the Wardroom was a very good reason to embark with a selection of my own music, all 78s in those days, I took three or four albums of Beethoven Symphonies (which weighed a ton) in my baggage. The 'Green Goddess', as she was called, had a grand piano in the First and Cabin Class lounges, which I played often when in port between voyages. There were moments of melodic delight when, on West Indies cruises out of New York over Xmas and New Year, I heard calypso rhythm coming across the water from local boats. One year we had Geraldo on board who conducted the ship's 'Steel Band', with oil drums and other weird instruments, on the promenade deck. After twenty years afloat, I swallowed the hook finally in 1956, in order to make a happier family life ashore.

So, here I am in 1957, a Sales Representative in Regent Oil Company, adapting and enjoying my new career, being promoted to Sales Superin-tendent and Depot Manager in Woolston, Southampton, until 1962, when Brenda died, I ventured into Motor Factoring as a Co-Director with a solicitor friend, to avoid being moved about in Oil as a single parent, with daughter Peta, eleven and son Charles, aged five. Two years later, economic circumstances caused me to go back into the oil industry and just prior to this, in 1964, I married Sue Balkwill. Once again I was a Sales Representative, this time with Conoco/Jet Petroleum, living in Malvern, with no piano meantime. It was a sensible decision for Sue to sell her Solo dinghy, only used on hols when staying at her parents' house on the Salcombe estuary, maybe twice a year, and buy a piano with the proceeds. We were fortunate to find a Barratt & Robinson mini-piano (one octave less than usual) prior to a local auction sale. It was agreed that I would return from business to join Sue in time for the bidding, but when we met, Sue said our doctor's wife was there and might be joining in, so to avoid a silly situation with her friend, it would be better if I did the bidding for us from the other side of the hall, which I did. We agreed a ceiling of £50 and got it for £47.

Sue had sung in many Cathedral Bach Choirs such as St Albans, Llandaff and now Worcester. It was she who introduced me to the splendour and delight of choral music. When, in 1968, we lived at The Barn in Stourport-on-Severn, she held madrigal parties with me as butler and a happy listener, plus Charles and Andrew, our one-year-old. I revived my affection for Fats Waller and started to compose parodies on his tunes drawn from my marketing experiences in 1969/70, and these I sang at the piano onto a big-reel tape recorder. Happily, our marriage survived, despite my hour by hour, day after day cacophony, until eventually I was satisfied and got a company in Birmingham to produce a 'single' disc from the tape, comprising four songs, copies of which I sent to my friends and colleagues in Conoco Head Office and other Districts as Christmas presents. Now, I was District Manager in the Midlands, with a favourite pub called the Mug House at Claines, near Worcester. My latest parody prank was about my fellow DMs in the UK, which I wanted to sing at a Sales Conference in Dublin shortly, so I thought the 'Mountains O' Mourne' melody would be suitable. I searched for the sheet music everywhere but failed to get a copy. When I told John Trow, landlord of the Mug House, who spoke like Walter in 'The Archers', he said 'Ah, well, the pianist from Powick Mental Hospital comes in about now and e'll give it 'e'. Sure enough, a man with a massive mop of hair arrived. John told him about me and without any hesitation he pulled a sheet of manuscript from his pocket and said 'What key do you want it in?' 'Oh,' said I, 'E flat will do nicely thank you,' and to my amazement I had it in no time at all for the price of a pint. And we tried it out on the pub piano much to John's delight. Elgar, as a young man, conducted an orchestra at Powick.

In 1970 Fiona was born in Stourport and a year later I was promoted to Head Office in London, as Manager of the Industrial Market throughout the UK, known as D to C (Direct to Consumer) to distinguish it from the Retail market (Jet Petroleum). Peta married Derek Ball in 1973, when Sue's parents Alan and Ella (Mrs B) stayed at 'Halyards', 37 King Harry Lane, St Albans and Mrs B realized that we had room in this large family house to accommodate a bigger piano. Thus, about a year or two later, she offered us her boudoir grand, saying she no longer played because of arthritic hands. We thanked her, but said play on for the pleasure and exercise. The formidable Mrs B said 'If you won't accept it, I'll give it to Andrew!' which she did, and the Chappell grand was delivered promptly and we sent our mini-piano to 'The Port', East Portlemouth. Ella gave me the invoice dated 1917, which showed that her father, F.J.Harding, purchased the Rosewood Mignon Grand Pianoforte by Chappell in Bond Street for £123. He did well, because the list price was 147 guineas (£154), so he got a 20% discount. Terms stated at the foot of the invoice: £10 deposit, balance in cash. Even nowadays, when playing The Port piano, I hear Mrs B's voice from the grave saying 'Ian, you must read music more.'

Andrew took Suzuki violin lessons from Brenda our neighbour and showed great prowess, while Fiona had flute lessons from Jenny for many years and achieved a high standard. With the gift grand piano in our house, Sue and I played much more and even tried Beethoven's Turkische Marche duet. Sue resumed Bach Choir at St Albans Abbey/Cathedral and I became a patron, attending their excellent concerts. Grand-daughter, Joanna, was born in 1979 and has become a very good pianist. I took early retirement from Conoco in 1980 and formed my own Company, Kinloch Bryce Associates, Management Consultants. Running Courses in hotels, away from home, meant I would miss the piano, so Sue gave me a classical guitar to take with me. Brad Knowles, of the Spanish Guitar Centre in London, gave me lessons at his house, near Muswell Hill, for seven years. I still enjoy the instrument very much, especially playing Gershwin melodies and Xmas Carols.

'Halyards' was ideal for parties, so we had many good ones in the 80s and 90s. For the 1920s Style Party in 1983, we asked our guests to dress appropriately as flappers and boyfriends in beads and boaters. Impersonating Noel Coward came naturally to my friend and business colleague Tony Dixon, so I composed lots of nonsense verses about the guests which he monologued, with me on piano, and everyone joined in the chorus after each verse to the melody of the Master's 'I Went to a Marvellous Party', ending with 'I couldn't have liked it more.' We two wore monocles for the occasion.

When a friend or relative dies, I close up at the piano and play Chopin's Sonata Op. 35, which includes the famous 'Marche funebre'. This is my own personal way of grieving, going from 'pp' to 'ff' as my feelings move me and singing a spontaneous, celebratory tribute to the one who has just 'crossed the bar'. I would love some people, from the past and present, to attend a fantasy party right now, such as – Louis Armstrong, Bach, Maria Callas, Ella Fitzgerald, Scott Joplin, Liszt, Glenn Miller, Mozart, Verdi and Fats Waller; with Acker Bilk playing 'Stranger on the Shore', on his clarinet, in the background (our tune, back in 1963/64). Then I would introduce Kirsty MacColl singing her 'Tropical Brainstorm' (2000). All these well known characters have enriched my life enormously and still do, plus two lesser known guys called Mack Gordon and Harry Warren. 'Who are they?' sez you. Well, I've only become aware of them in recent years, although their names have been staring me in the face for fifty or more. They created words and music for 'Chattanooga Choo Choo' and 'Kalamazoo', and I delight in playing these two tunes regularly to this day. They were most popular during the war years and especially appropriate when going on leave. Dick and Eleanor Harding, Canadian cousins, came over in 1997 and Eleanor was skilfully tickling the ivories, when I asked her if she knew Kalamazoo. 'You bet I do,' she said. 'An aunt took me from Windsor, Ontario, in Canada, to Kalamazoo, Michigan, in the USA and bought me my first party dress. Guess I was fourteen at the time.' 'At last!' I cried, 'You're the gal I've been singing about since 1941!'

The greatest musical event in 1999 was nephew William Balkwill getting into the National Youth Orchestra with his trumpet. Amongst many family members, we attended the concert in the Albert Hall in 2000 on the Queen Mother's 100th birthday to hear him perform. He was accepted for a second year and promoted to principal trumpeter in charge of eight others and on 26 May, 2001 he played a fanfare in St Albans Abbey when Fiona and Craig Robson were married. It was exciting escorting the bride, my daughter Fiona, to such a splendid sound.

When we downsized house last year, staying in St Albans, accommodating the piano was a major factor. Happily, we found 19 Antonine Gate, nearby, with large living and dining room combined and so the Chappell sits comfortably in its corner. In 2001, whilst in Australia, we had it restrung and polished and for my 79th birthday Sue gave me a card which said 'Ian's loo pot' (your present) will follow later. It took me ages to crack the anagram, for that's what it was, and realize that a substantial 'piano stool' was coming my way.

A happy musical moment in my life was provided recently by my second grand-daughter, Scarlet Kiki Kinloch, born on Halloween 2000 to son Charles and Malindi Duncan. Now as a one-year-old toddler she danced with a great sense of rhythm to the music of Carroll Gibbons – one of my favourite pianists – with his Savoy Hotel Orpheans. Being able to reach the piano keyboard on her own now, rather than banging away and making a din, as most kids do, she selected a note, paused to listen, then toddled along to try another one and so on, which caused proud grandpa to think that here we had a natural inherited talent and who knows what potential. This feeling was enhanced when we shared the melody from *Mister Cinders* 1928, as I swung into a favourite tune of my Mum's 'Spread a little happiness' – and she danced away.

Music being the international and ageless language of love that it is, what better way to end this episode than with a line from a favourite sheet of music, like 'Kalamazoo', which is – 'A B C D E F G H I got a gal, in Kalamazoo. Don't wanna boast but I know she's the toast . . .' and so on.

Of course Kalamazoo can be any old place you're heading for, with a certain lady-friend in mind – such as Glasgow-on-Clyde, London-on-Thames or Cardiff-on-Taff from a sailor's point of view. The piano is good for my morale, keeps me young and happy, day in and day out, and to think it all started with CDE, CDE, CDEFEDC – Here I go again!

CHAPTER 2

Darlington – 1922–1934

'CARRY ON, ADMIRAL' SAID MY MOTHER, as she returned to the bathroom with my night-shirt; saluting me, as I sat in the bath surrounded by my floating fleet. This made me feel important and very much in charge, before being scrubbed and put to bed, aged two or three. Now, in my seventies, living in St Albans, I am still called 'Admiral' for fun and get piped aboard my two favourite watering holes, Harry Smith's Bar and the Garibaldi. I guess it's because of my 'blow me down' attitude and 'rig of the day' always ship-shape, if not exactly Bristol fashion.

I have had my bedtime story, mother has departed, and suddenly I hear a deep, sonorous voice saying 'Fee-Fie-Fo-Fum, I smell the breath of an Englishman.' This must be my visiting god-father from Gosforth, Uncle Fred Fleming, coming to say goodnight. I dive under the bedclothes and pretend not to be there, while he sits on the bed, talks to himself and says 'That's funny! I wonder where Ian can be?', and so on; shifting his position until he lands on me, then with tickles and much laughter, that is the end of a frequent happy childhood game. This must have helped me realize 'who I was' and 'where I was' as a human being. Twilight was often frightening, the walnut grain of the wardrobe by my bed forming fearful figures in my mind, so, when I shouted, Mum put the light on until I fell asleep. My birthplace, 99 Stanhope Road, was a large Victorian terraced house with five bedrooms, kitchen and scullery and two scary dark places, the cellar and from my playroom, the attic, a space under the eaves, where lived a wicked witch, or so my step-sister Betty said, when I was being disagreeable.

A regular ritual in the nursery/bedroom scene, each evening, was me saying my prayers, as prescribed thus: 'Gentle Jesus, meek and mild, Look upon a little child; Pity my simplicity, Suffer me to come to thee.' Charles Wesley 1707–88. That was my first ever prayer, followed by a list of people and creatures, such as family, friends and pets, that I would ask God to bless, with monotonous regularity. It was mumbo jumbo to me then and meant very little to me when grown-up, because I then considered Jesus to be an assertive man, with a strong message and certainly not submissive, as implied by the words 'meek and mild'.

Another early memory is being taken out in my pushchair, often by Annie the maid, but sometimes by sister Betty, eight years older than me, with her school friend Dorothy Redfern in company. The game, for that's

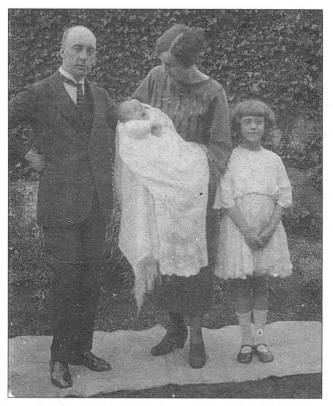

Ian as an infant in his mother's arms, with his father and sister Betty

what it was, went like this. When I had dozed off, they would park me round a corner and disappear. I would wake up and after looking for them in all directions, let out a bellow and start to cry. This was the signal they had been waiting for. Back they came to cuddle and make a great fuss of me saying 'Diddums then'. I suppose there was some early learning in all this, telling me that life then, now and in the future, was, is, and always will be, full of ups and downs.

As a family in 1925 we attended the centenary of the Darlington to Stockton railway and had a ride on the original train, in an open truck, with a man walking in front waving a red flag; the first efficient 'Railtrack' indeed! Road traffic was very little in the twenties, but increasing, with the arrival of the 'Baby Austin' in the year I was born. Mum had some money of her own, so she bought a family car, which Dad drove; Mum never did. Advised by a rally-driving friend, we got a Rhode (unusual), a sporty, open, four-seater with portable windows and a manual pull-over hood. This took us (plus Olive, the maid and Spot, our fox-terrier) on week-end picnics to the seaside — Whitby, Saltburn, Redcar, and the Yorkshire dales —

Richmond, Reeth and Grinton, for summer hols in a cottage. Seeing grouse shot by men in butts made me cry.

When I was about four, I heard Mum say to Dad 'You must dash down to the mortuary immediately. I've just read about the death of an old man in the paper, unidentified, it sounds like old Plumpton, and with no relatives, we must be sure he has a decent funeral.' 'Of course, my dear, I'll go at once to identify him', said Dad, and off he rushed. 'Old Plumpton' was the man who came to clean our drains regularly. A fine upstanding figure, who like many at that time, was out of work, so my parents did what they could to help him and usually gave him a big meal on Sunday, in the kitchen, with Olive, where he would tell me lots of stories about his life in the army with Kitchener in the Sudan. Everyone looked very old to me, but I suppose, with his grey hair and waxed moustache, he would have been in his late sixties. He always wore his medals on Sunday, when he took Spot for a walk, feeding him ice-cream, which we never did. 'I was a lucky blighter,' he would say, 'not to lose a leg or an arm – like those poor devils from the Great War, who you see squatting on the pavement in town, collecting pennies in a line, from passers-by.' I knew what he meant because I had asked Mummy why they were doing that and she said there was no work for them to do. This memory lingered on through life and I feel contributed to my shift in political attitude after WW2.

About twenty minutes after Dad's departure, the front door bell rang. When Mum opened the door, who should be standing there? None other than 'Old Plumpton'. Well, my Mum looked as though she had seen a ghost, but I was 'over the moon' that the old boy was still alive. You see, a few weeks before, I had dropped my weekly pocket-money, a silver threepenny-bit, in Stanhope Road and it had rolled into the gutter and down the drain. I was almost in tears, but suddenly remembered my old pal 'Plumpton' and knowing where he lodged, I went straight there. 'Of course I'll come, just show me where' – and grabbing his bag of tools, we set off for the scene of the tragedy. My coin was back in my hand in no time and never will I forget 'Money Down the Drain' rescued by my good old friend Plumpton.

Another good friend of mature years was Mrs Morrison, our next-door neighbour, wife of a Methodist Minister, who made her own bread every Friday. Knowing this, I would call about 11 a.m. each week, to be welcomed with 'Come in Ian, I've got your cottage loaf hot and ready for you' and I would sit and eat it with butter and jam in a kitchen filled with that evocative smell of freshly baked bread. What a lot of friendly adults I can recall from those days. Two doors away was the Barclays Bank Manager, whom my father called Lionel Clark, but to me was Uncle Proxy, and only years later did I discover that 'proxy' meant he stood-in for an

Ian in early childhood,
outside 99 Stanhope Road, Darlington

absent godfather at my christening. Then there was Mrs Eshelby, a plump lady, from a farm in the country, who called each Wednesday in a big Austin car, with a large wicker basket containing fresh farm produce such as butter and eggs, her perks as a farmer's wife no doubt.

Most afternoons, I was put in a front bedroom to rest and my mother would pay a barrel-organ man, with monkey, to play me to sleep. In 1926 there was a 'General Strike', in support of the miners, but it didn't last long, because the wealthier middle-class did working-class jobs to keep vital services going. I don't think Mum bothered about politics, but Dad was Conservative and said nasty things about Labour. In Hintons, the grocers, the staff fed me broken biscuits behind the counter whilst my Mum placed her order; much more fun than sitting unfed in a supermarket trolley nowadays. In the summer of 1927, we went by car to somewhere near Giggleswick in the Dales at 5 a.m., with shaded specs, to witness a total eclipse of the sun. It was dark for a few minutes and I remember seeing the cows lie down.

Some years later, the Cuthberts took over from the Morrisons in the Methodist house next door and there were two sons much older than me. The elder had a new sports car, an 'SS Swallow' parked in the road and he would sit me in the driving seat, where I made engine noises as I clutched the wheel and went on fast fantasy journeys. Younger brother, about twice my age, set me up with my first mobile phone in the shape of a cocoa tin. Because our terraced houses extended out at the back, his bedroom faced mine over the garden wall. When we were armed with a cocoa tin each and a taut piece of string in between we could communicate on our own 'hot line' without parental interference.

My father was a Commercial Traveller with W.D & H.O. Wills, Imperial Tobacco Company of Great Britain and Ireland Ltd, with head office and factory in Bristol. His business was to sell cigarettes, from the humble Woodbine (that reputedly won the First World War!), Gold Flake and Three Castles to the oval shaped posh Passing Cloud; cigars of all shapes and sizes, plus Cut Golden Bar pipe tobacco. Our house always had lots of such products, free of course, and his was a busy, popular, well paid, job, because the majority of people smoked at that time. Grandpa Bryce, who died in 1913, was Customs & Excise in Bristol, and when Dad, Laurence Leslie, left the Grammar School, he joined Wills as an apprentice in the factory. As a member of the Gloucestershire Yeomanry (Hussars) – Territorial Army – he was called up in 1914, switched to Royal Field Artillery (RFA) and spent the whole war in Flanders, near Ypres, as a signalman/gunner promoted to Subaltern (one pip on the shoulder) in 1917. He never talked about the war, but I learnt years later, that he had been badly gassed in 1915 and later had neurasthenia (a nervous breakdown – so called for officers – shell-shock for the troops and what would now be known as Post Traumatic Stress Syndrome for all ranks). For this he had a war pension, but as it meant having a medical every year, which recalled ugly memories, he decided to chuck it in the mid twenties. After being demobbed in 1919, he returned to Wills, retrained at the factory, met and married my Mum, Zillah Hammond (née Musitano) who had been widowed in 1917, with daughter Betty, now five, before being promoted to Representative for the Firm in County Durham and north Yorkshire. He preferred train travel and walking, although used the car for remote places, to fulfil his monthly schedule around the area. Thus, we settled in the market-town of Darlington with much happiness.

In September, aged five and a bit, I started at Claremont Preparatory School, about ten minutes walk from home. It was small, about twenty to thirty pupils and run by Mr and Mrs Blain, a Scottish pair; he with his hot milk and brandy each morning! and a deterrent cane in the corner which I never saw used, and she seen frequently, in felt hat with feather, on her bicycle, provided with cords from hub to rear-mudguard to prevent her tartan skirt getting in the spokes. They had a large house with plenty of space for a playground, two junior teachers and a few boarders, two of whom were Germans called Joachim and Eckard von something (I forget), and who became great chums of mine, often coming on picnics with us at week-ends. Their dress and manners were immaculate and my mother was most impressed, when, on a Sunday morning outside St Cuthbert's Church, they would stand to attention, click their heels, remove their school caps and bow to her from the waist. I was christened at that church by the Vicar, the Rev. Drury, whose vicarage was opposite us, a keen horseman and renowned for getting to matins at the last minute, clad in frock coat and gaiters, at high speed on his bicycle, waving to one and all.

Once when I was ill in bed, Joachim and Eckard called to cheer me up. Examining the pictures, mostly of ships, even in those days, they paused in front of RMS *Berengaria*, looked at me and said 'That was our Kaiser's *Imperator*, and only then did I realize it had been given to the Cunard White Star Line as compensation for losses during WW1. I had a feeling then that they would follow their father into the German Navy, but never knew. However, sometimes at sea in WW2, I would wonder if, perhaps, one or the other was looking at my destroyer through a periscope, or maybe, if I had just dropped a pattern of depth charges on one or the other of them in a U-boat; sad if either were so? J and E talked of freezing winters in Germany and we always had a few weeks of snow in Darlington each year when I was a kid. Mum always took us to a field near Carmel Road with a big wooden toboggan seating six, where we joined in the local winter sports.

1930 was packed with events. Amy Johnson, a twenty-six-year-old airwoman from Hull, flew a Gypsy Moth, solo, from Croydon to Australia (Port Darwin) in 19½ days. Aged eight, I was going through a period of walking in my sleep and talking at the same time. My parents told me afterwards how I would descend to the lounge, after bedtime, and hold forth about my heroine, Amy; since when, through life, it's no wonder I've often fancied older women! The Indian sage Gandhi's name and picture was in the papers a lot, as he protested against the Salt Tax as part of his Civil Disobedience campaign. His appearance fascinated me, perpetually wearing nothing but a 'loin cloth', even in the UK, when visiting the King at Buckingham Palace. When Gandhi was asked what he thought of western civilization, he replied 'It would be a good idea', a remark that has lived on and I think is appropriate to this day.

Airships were another form of transport, liners in the sky with a future, it was thought. This idea was abandoned, when R101, which I saw flying low over Darlington in the summer of 1930, hit a French hillside on her first journey to India, causing a hydrogen explosion which killed 44 people and left only eight survivors, saved by a water tank drenching them from above. Aeroplanes were still a novelty and people would stop in the street and look up with curiosity, when one flew overhead. Howard Hughes, the Hollywood film magnate, produced the movie *Hell's Angels* in 1930 about Royal Flying Corps (RFC) dog-fights in WW1, starring Ben Lyon and Jean Harlow, the blonde bombshell, who later became my first teenage pin-up – an older woman again! With arms outstretched, I would weave about, making noises like a Sopwith Camel in a dogfight over the trenches. Dad got me to show-off doing this in front of his friend Captain Percy Wood, who lost a leg in Flanders and who had witnessed the scene many times. Sir Alan Cobham, a pioneer in long distance flying, toured the country with his circus, giving flights to the public. Dad paid for Betty and me to go up, for ten minutes, with other passengers, in a biplane. I can close my eyes and still see Mum and Dad below us on the tarmac.

The most important move for me that year was leaving Claremont and going to the Queen Elizabeth Grammar School, only five minutes walk from home. Also about then I joined the Wolf Cubs, who met weekly, to encourage skills such as knots, signalling, first aid and other benign activities, in an Army Drill Hall nearby, under the guidance of Mrs Lee, a large maternal figure, called Akela after the caring wolf in Kipling. From these new environments a gang was formed, and because age enhances early memories, I can recall the names clearly and without hesitation.

Our gang, in alphabetical sequence consisted of (1) Ian Bryce (me), (2) Tom Carrick (younger son of the Grammar School's 2nd Headmaster), (3) Bill Glover (freckles, with an amusing pretty sister Mary), (4) Geoff Gould (with a more mature, *Sun* page 3, sister Mary), (5) Graham Joyce (affectionately called 'fairy feet' because of his physical antics, but good fun and with a widowed mother who was generous with her home-made cakes), (6) Walter Ryder (son of the Vet in Stanhope Road), (7) Neville Varley (looked – with specs – and was – more intelligent than most) and (8) Maurice Zissler, who lived opposite Graham (small and dynamic, descended from 19th century mid-European refugees) whose wealthy father ran a large pork-butcher's shop in town. I saw Maurice in Darlington not long ago, after about sixty years. It was just like yesterday, and now he has retired, with the next generation still running the Zissler business.

We all dressed alike at nine and ten years of age with short trousers and long woollen socks held up by elastic bands, exposing knees often covered with scabs from frequent falls, picked as a pastime, which naturally delayed healing. These were topped by a grey shirt and woollen tie, under a V-necked pullover. Hair was short and smoothed down with Brylcreem, the popular dressing of the thirties. Most of the time we wore our school caps, dark blue with four coloured stripes showing which House we were in, depending on where the initial letters of our surnames came in the alphabet. The four Houses were Britons – green, Danes – red, Normans – blue and Saxons – yellow. Our gang consisted of two Britons, three Danes, one Norman and two Saxons, so whatever the activity, it was usual for the Britons and Saxons to take on the Danes and Normans, making four a side.

The gang really took shape within the QE Grammar School, which we all attended. During the holidays we met daily, outdoors, usually in Stanhope Park, opposite the school, and did a lot of good deeds for parents, like running errands, bits of shopping, clearing gardens and so on, invariably rewarded with eats and drinks. Never carted about by our parents in cars, we moved on foot or bike in what was then a safe environment. A popular

Ian aged 11. Christmas 1933

pastime was dividing into two small groups, one tracking the other at a distance, guided by natural clues, and practising Wolf Cub skills like First Aid, carrying one of us around on a made-up stretcher with one arm in a sling and splints on both legs, to prevent the fake casualty running away. During term time, on occasions, Graham was bullied in the playground and we gang members, keeping a lookout, would look tough and shape up to one or more of the persecutors. I never recall any physical violence, just loud verbal abuse, though sometimes, our presence with the words 'give over', a popular northern expression, would be enough.

A sweet shop near the park was a good outlet for our pocket-money, with wine gums at 1d or ½d tubes, aniseed balls about ten in a bag for 1d and a cardboard container full of sherbet with a liquorice stick to suck through, then consume, for a similar price. When at Claremont I had *Bubbles* and *Tiger Tim* as weekly comics and it was my habit to run round to the paper shop, just round the corner in Verity Street, at 7 a.m. to collect on the day it came out. Now, at Grammar School, I moved on to *Sexton Blake*, a 4d thriller and *Boys Own Paper*, containing Billy Bunter and his gang in the Remove, at Greyfriars: So far as daily newspapers went, apart from the *Northern Echo* in the evening, my father read the *Daily Telegraph & Morning Post* and my mother the *Daily Mirror* with its cartoon strip of the penguins, 'Pip, Squeak and Wilfred', much loved by Betty and me, who joined their club called the 'Gug Nuncs' and pinned their badges on our blazers.

I became a keen, serious, reader at QE's school, especially of history, and would show off my knowledge in front of family and friends. My sister was very good for me then, whispering 'Stop being a know-all, Bunny' (her nickname for me). In 1932 I was awarded *The Three Musketeers*, by Alexandre Dumas, as a prize for reading. Betty was a day-girl at Polam Hall, which was mostly boarders, and she would invite her school friends to tea-parties at our house, including a Siamese girl with a pet monkey on a lead which sat on her shoulder and was friendly when I fed him nuts. They were all about sixteen and one, Nan Walmsley, would delight the group by telling ghost stories, in the dark of our lounge. I remember her well because she always let me sit in, even when others said 'Don't you think Ian will be too frightened?' She made me feel very grown up, listening to her spooky tales – an older woman again! Sister Betty was developing her talent for acting and I went with Mum and Dad to see her play Theseus, Duke of Athens in *Midsummer Night's Dream* in the spacious grounds of Polam Hall. Film actress Elizabeth Allen had been taught at posh Polam and that proved an incentive to others, in the thirties.

In 1927, Al Jolson not only sang, but actually spoke from the screen in *The Jazz Singer*. By 1930, with few exceptions, like Charlie Chaplin, silent films were a thing of the past. So, in 1932, we had Greta Garbo in *Grand Hotel* and *Mata Hari*; Johnny Weissmuller (Olympic swimming champion) as Tarzan in *The Ape Man* and Shirley Temple, aged three, appeared. For me, the big movie event was in the Court Cinema, seeing Joel McCrea and Dolores Del Rio in *Bird of Paradise*. I suppose as a naive ten-year-old voyeur, I was suddenly aware of sexy feelings as I watched exciting embraces under water in tropical seas – wow!

As regards religion we were nominally Church of England (C of E). Much later in life, I was told that Mum (Zillah) had been christened a Roman Catholic in Chepstow in 1891, having an Italian father, William Musitano (Accountant) and Welsh mother (Fanny Williams). Her father died when Mum was four, with brother Don, two, and Fanny switched the family to Congregational Chapel. Then when Mum married Dad in 1919, she changed to C of E and remained thus until he died in 1967, when she reverted to being Congregational, all changes under the Christian umbrella.

I got my first long trousers in 1932 in the form of a black suit, worn on Sundays with black tie and Eton collar, to the 11 a.m. Service and Sunday School in the afternoon, with Harry Bentley, similarly attired and being jeered at by street hooligans en route. I chewed gum in church unobtrusively and stuck it under the ledge meant for hymn books in our regular pew for use the following week. Thus did I start tastefully along the path of righteousness.

I think it was the move into an adult suit that made me more aware of how my parents looked and what clothes they were wearing. Mother was a lovely looking person with poise and a slim figure which she retained through life and which showed off her fashionable garments to great advantage. She looked Italian, with dark brown flashing eyes, inherited by our youngsters and always dressed in colours which suited her, orange and brown in particular, her favourites. For accessories she liked a snake-skin handbag, crocodile shoes, a fox-fur stole around her neck and gold bracelets, on one of which I had cut my teeth. Hats with her were an obsession and she had a vast collection, many of which were made by her with whatever suitable materials came to hand. She was a vivacious, talkative, fun character with many friends who played whist, bridge and tennis. They called themselves, most aptly, the 'Chinwaggers Club'. She joined in lots of Church activities, such as Sales-of-Work and charities like Dr Barnardo's.

My Father I would describe as a kind-hearted disciplinarian who led by example in actions and speech. Brought up in the last decade of the nineteenth century, he was immaculate in his toilet and dress with well manicured hands and a fortnightly visit to the barber for his hair to be cut, singed and shampooed, even though he was ninety per cent bald. He always wore a hand-tailored suit with waistcoat, a handkerchief tucked up the left sleeve of his jacket and spats over his shoes in cold weather. A stickler for changing into house slippers, which were kept in a copper sheeted box by the dining-room fire, he regularly cleaned his leather shoes with Properts Saddle Soap, no doubt a hangover from his youth in the Cavalry. He was short in stature, a slim, fit and fast walker. Also, a heavy smoker, as was the fashion in those days, he would puff cigars and cigarettes, mostly indoors, and a pipe when out and about. His glasses were pince-nez when I was little, but he switched to the comfort of a frame in the thirties.

Dad took me to Feethams Ground on Saturday afternoons to see either cricket or football. I first got the lovely smell of embrocation at the football, sitting in the Stand, above the passage from the dressing rooms as the players returned after half-time. He also introduced me to Rugby Union with a trip to Murrayfield, Edinburgh, to see Scotland play England in the Calcutta Cup, but soccer was my favourite then. Newcastle, Sunderland and Middlesbrough were all doing well in the 1st Division, and therefore had most of my attention. It was Saturday, 5 November (Guy Fawkes day) and I was playing football about 11 a.m., on the school playing field. 'Head it Brasso!' (my nickname) shouted the outside-right as he swung the ball in my direction, and as centre-forward, I jumped in the air to do his bidding. However, in going for a goal, I ended up in a heap, clutching my stomach in great pain. The referee, also sports master, was greatly concerned, put me in his Austin Seven and rushed me home. My parents called in Dr Chalmers, who said an appendix operation was necessary, immediately. A second opinion confirmed this diagnosis, so I was taken to Coniscliffe Nursing Home and operated upon that afternoon. On coming out of the anaesthetic, I was furious at having missed my fireworks.

I went home after two weeks for another two weeks in bed before the stitches were removed. Mum and Dad put me in their room with its large double bed which caught the afternoon sun. I never missed an opportunity to show visitors my four inch scar and said – 'Don't make me laugh, please – 'cos it hurts so!' Betty and Olive played board games with me and I read *Chums Annual*, containing a serial throughout on the Scarlet Pimpernel. Spot wuffed in now and then and Dad put the wireless speaker in my room. He would tune in to the BBC Home Service, but because the receiving equipment was in the dining-room, downstairs, we had to shout 'How's that?' 'Too loud!' 'That better?' 'Yes, OK!' At five o'clock every day a voice from BBC HQ in Portland Place would say 'This is the BBC Dance Orchestra and this is Henry Hall speaking'. After half-an-hour of popular music, known to me, the same voice would say 'Goodbye everybody and here's to the next time', which was the cue for their signature tune 'Here's to the next time' with me knowing the words and joining in.

After a few days at home, Mum and Dad said 'We think you deserve a present now, before Christmas. What would you like?' and I replied 'A canary please.' And so, a canary it was; in golden cage on tall stand for constant company. I asked Betty what she thought him or her (we never knew which) should be called and she suggested Dix after the appenDIX I had no more. Dix sang beautifully, perched on the bed and even my finger, after being trained to fly around the bedroom and return to the cage for food. Now we had another member of the family to sing along with Henry.

Looking back to those days, I realize that I was a fortunate child, not made to feel privileged, because my parents tried, and succeeded somewhat, to give me a reasonable sense of values. Yet here I was being well fed and educated when the majority of people in the UK were unemployed and uncared for. 1931 was a year of terrible economic depression and I heard Dad mention names like Ramsay MacDonald and Stanley Baldwin, but I was unaware of the 'Hunger Marchers' from everywhere, in their thousands, especially from Jarrow, who passed close to us, converging on London in October 1932. My father was promoted to South Wales in 1934. Betty had left Polam; we had sold No 99 and lived in cabbage smelling digs until the summer hols when we moved to Cardiff. In those hols, I camped in Jersey as a 2nd Class Scout promoted from Senior Sixer in the Cubs.

It was during our time in digs and my last term at the Grammar School that I fell in love with a blonde girl who walked along the pavement on the opposite side of the road in her High School blazer. It was a distant relationship, we never spoke or touched, just an occasional admiring glance, and once I heard a friend call her Marjorie, so at last I knew her name. I was just twelve at the time and remember well that missing her was a major source of sadness when we said goodbye to Darlington.

CHAPTER 3

Cardiff – 1934–1936

FOR ME, THE MOST MEMORABLE THING about the move to Cardiff in August '34 was how it affected the shape of my balls! You see, in Darlington, at the Grammar School, soccer with the round ball was my obsession, but now, in Welsh Wales, the oval ball took precedence and rugby reigned supreme. I discovered this on joining Monkton House School in September, about twenty minutes bike ride towards the city centre from our new home. This was a semidetached house, 141 Lake Road West, facing Roath Park lake, with its swans, ducks and rowing boats for hire.

Our neighbours, on the open side, were Bill and Joy James with son Tony, two years my junior, who remained a lifelong friend until his death in 1999. The first Welsh word I noticed, on the front of a 28 bus, was 'Rhwbina', its destination a few miles to the north, after passing our house, and Tony told me how to pronounce it, Roo-by-nar. Years later, he told me that when we arrived his mother had said 'I can't understand a word that little boy next door says.' My parents spoke without accents and father most grammatically, as did Betty, who had studied elocution and began teaching from home. I had quite a strong north country accent with idioms of speech which I soon converted into a Welsh lilt. Dad often helped to sort out my expressions. When I knocked on the door of the study, which he used as his office, and said 'Can I come in please?' he would reply 'I know you are capable of coming in, what you mean to say is "may I", you are seeking permission.' Without being too pedantic, he did teach me to speak correctly, which gave me confidence in whatever company I found myself throughout life. Similarly, with table manners, he was very strict and this I have never regretted.

Monkton House, an independent day-school, for about a hundred boys in my day, was founded in 1870 by Henry Shewbrooks, of Monkton in Pembrokeshire, as 'An Academy for Young Gentlemen', which established a strong rugby football tradition in the area. As Queen Street railway station was only ten minutes walk away, many boys came down the valleys from Aberdare and Rhymney, as well as from coastal towns nearby, to be taught by headmaster C.A. Williams, MA (Oxon) and his staff. There were so many boys with the same surname, such as Davies, Evans, Griffiths, Jones, Lewis, Thomas and Williams, that each had a number for roll call, for example, Davies say up to 10, Jones to 15 and Williams maybe up to 12 or whatever.

Misbehaviour was dealt with by masters giving 'cubes', not 'lines' as was customary in most schools. The numbers for the first 'cube' were taken from the day and month of the current date, say 511 (Guy Fawkes Day) multiplied by 511 and again by 511 and because they were given in multiples of 5, the next 'cube' had one added, 512 and so on. Any number of 'cubes' more than 20 was considered 'over the mark' and meant the cane, one stroke on the hand for every 5 cubes, administered by the Maths master, who no doubt invented the system. There was a time limit for handing in 'cubes' to prefects to be marked and I expect they just checked samples and probably used log tables or slide-rules anyway (no calculators then). I recall some 'tough guys' went over the mark deliberately to have the lot caned off. The standard of behaviour was good so 'cubes' must have had some effect and probably sharpened my mind for the calculations needed in astro-navigation a few years later.

Naughty as I may have been, I did get a book prize in Form 3a for 'General Proficiency' and it was *Twenty Thousand Miles in a Flying-boat* by my first flight acquaintance in Darlington, Sir Alan Cobham. My school uniform came from Jothams, the appointed suppliers, in the Duke St Arcade. We got to know the staff well and I remember Dad at his desk, faced with the bill, deducting 5% for cash by immediate payment. He did this with all bills in those days before credit cards. It set me an example that I abide by to this day, using the convenience of credit cards, who now deduct the 5% and me, later, paying up the full amount and avoiding interest.

Two assembly points became popular for 12 to 14-year-old girls and boys during the hols and at week-ends. One was at the east end of the promenade, which ran across Roath Park on the south side of the lake and where, on the edge of deep water, changing huts and diving boards were provided for swimmers. The other place was the Kardomah Cafe in Queen Street, to drink milk-shakes and start a life of flirting with the opposite sex. Dad arranged swimming lessons for me by a Police Instructor in the public baths and then I was able to use the lake, not only with the gang during the day, restricted in area by a ring of buoys, but early morning from 7 o'clock, when I could swim round the clock tower out in the middle, a memorial to Scott's 1912 Antarctic Expedition, with swans hissing their annoyance at my intrusion on their territory.

Trams on tracks still ran from Pier Head through Bute St, St Mary's St, Queen St, City Rd, Albany Rd and Ninian Rd to the terminus at the bottom of Lake Roads West and East and of course on other routes, whereas in Darlington trams had been superceded by trackless trolley buses a few years before we left. On Thursdays Queen St was jammed with people from the valleys to shop and visit the five cinemas – Capitol, Olympia, Park, Odeon and Empire. The Capitol had a massive Hammond organ with flashing lights and an arm-waving organist in tails, rising from the depths at the interval, playing 'Oh I do like to be beside the seaside' or some such tune, which always got us to sing along. Not knowing where I was a lot of the time, Mum and Dad hoped I wasn't becoming a 'corner boy', one of those supposed delinquent youths who loitered on pavements particularly at street corners. I wasn't one of those, even though I might have been persuaded to be, by acting out the words of that well known George Formby song, 'I'm leaning on a lamp post at the corner of the street, in case a certain little lady comes by'.

Friendships developed at school: Dickie Davies whose parents allowed us to caddy for them at Whitchurch Golf Club; Jack Tyrell of Shirley Rd whose father was an Engineer Officer in the Merchant Navy, and mostly away from home; Winter Lates whose family owned a Men's Outfitters in St Mary St Arcade, usually good for a bargain, and Derek Williams who played his own set of drums, at home in the garage and the envy of us all, when he let us have a go. Around the lake: Pat Jones, a tall blonde jazz pianist who inspired me on the keyboard and whose father played the fiddle; Jean Arthur, an early steady whose father had an MC from WW1; Pam Williams and Stephanie Elms from Cyncoed – fun in and out of the water; Paul Whiteman whose father was a Senior Civil Servant, and near him lived Joan Wellington, a budding actress with an eccentric widowed mother, always said to be ailing, which caused her curtains to be drawn and the doctor present most afternoons.

The closest of my chums was Bill Griffiths, just yards away in Lake Road West, whose father was a Rep for Bearbrand stockings (loved by the ladies for his samples), Mum plump and jolly, sister stunning redhead, Betty, same age as mine and housemaid who with boyfriend told us lots about sex. Bill was a boarder at Sebright School near Kidderminster, so we only met in the hols. He was mad keen on Army goings-on in the OTC (Officers' Training Corp) which got me involved in mock military actions in the field at the back of our house. This was no-mans-land, like WW1, between us and the Jewish Cemetery with its wailing burials, where we dug a trench with dug-out and chimney to smoke our pipes and prepare for battle. We used air-guns with Woolworth's goggles to protect our eyes and a rusty old boiler as a tank for a rolling downhill attack. Being inside this vehicle was the roughest ride ever. J Richmal Crompton's books about 'William' were known to most about now and our sisters likened us to William and his mate Ginger – usually up to no good. Sitting at tea one day at home, Bill casually opened his jacket and a number of lead slugs fell out on the table, causing a curious expression on my Mother's face.

Pa Griffiths was given 'Trade Show' tickets by his customers, which admitted him and a friend to cinemas in the forenoon to preview forthcoming films. He seldom used them, so Bill and I did. We saw *Evergreen* with Jessie Matthews, who later in life became Mrs Dale of the Diary fame, Will Hay as headmaster trying to control his unruly scholars and lots of Fred Astaire, Ginger Rogers musicals. It was during my summer hols from the *Worcester* in '37, that we got parental permission to stay up all night and listen on the wireless to the world heavyweight fight, in New York, between the world champion Joe Louis (known as the 'Brown Bomber') and Tommy Farr, a Welsh lad from Tonypandy who lasted all fifteen rounds and almost won the title. Some weekends in summer I would go for picnics with the Griffiths family to those beauty spots Ogmore and Southerndown on the coast of South Wales, noted for miles of sand dunes and very few people. Years passed, I went to sea and my Dad wanted to help Bill join W.D. & H.O. Wills in Bristol, but WW2 started and Bill joined the Infantry. We never met again and one of the saddest moments of that bloody war was in '43 when Mum greeted me, arriving home on leave, with the news 'You'll be sad to hear that Bill has been killed in Italy.'

Dad joined Glamorgan County Cricket Club, then situated opposite the Angel Hotel in Westgate Street with J.C. Clay as captain. He also joined Cardiff Athletic Rugby Club, the other side of the big high stand from the cricket ground in what was The Arms Park. On Saturday afternoons we sat in the low stand on the south side to enjoy the fast, side-stepping skills of Cliff Jones as stand-off and Wilf Wooller as centre three-quarter, a combination that put Wales top of the four UK nations. Monkton House, called Monkey House by boys of other schools, played its rugby in Sophia Gardens, off Cathedral Road. Because of my speed and agility (I had been good in the 100 yards race, on Sports Day, in Darlington) I was placed as outside-half (stand-off) or centre three-quarter, which allowed me to emulate my heroes Cliff and Wilf.

I went to Cardiff City's ground, Ninian Park, to see Wales play England and learned the words in welsh of 'Mae Hen Wlad Fy Nhadau', the Welsh National Anthem, from a hand-out, which I have used as a reference ever since. Singing this following the British National Anthem, within minutes of one another, left me in no doubt about which I preferred in all respects. The Welsh Anthem is truly glorious, especially when performed in The Arms Park, now called the Millennium Stadium. Its words uplift the spirit, I found out from a translation, years later: 'Foremost comes the land, part of our planet earth, in which poets and minstrels rejoice, commendable, peaceful pursuits and music flows in the freedom of her streams.' The other anthem, which is sung in the UK as a matter of tradition and has never been proclaimed as national by an Act of Parliament or a Royal Proclamation, focuses attention on glorifying an individual, whose enemies should be scattered and their politics confounded.

With this memory in mind, I want to say, here and now, that for many decades I have considered our British National Anthem with despair, as a total anachronism, and would like to see it changed. I cannot subscribe to a God who singles out monarchs for saving and sending victorious, over whom I wonder? Numerous monarchs were saved and one sent victorious at the end of the 1914–18 war. Meantime 8½ million subjects were not saved by God or any of those monarchs, many of whom were related. I believe that the words of anthems such as ours can breed a narrow, tribal patriotism of self-interest and independence as opposed to a wider one of multinational welfare and interdependence. Therefore, I declare myself in harmony with citizen Thomas Paine (1737–1809), who declared in his book *The Rights of Man*, 'My country is the world, and my religion is to do good'. Enough said for the time being.

Now, living in the sea-port of Cardiff during this two year period, I sailed on many short voyages round the Severn Estuary and two foreign trips in coal tramps, in the summers of '35 and '36. This fitted in with my growing desire, over the last few years, to go to sea and happily had the support of Mum and Dad (Zill and Les as I now called them to my chums). Glyn Jones our semi-detached neighbour worked for a shipping company in Cardiff docks and arranged for Dad and me to spend a month of the summer hols aboard one of their ships. One voyage was from Barry to Nantes, Oporto in Portugal and back; uneventful except for Dad sampling the vintage port and educating me with an occasional sip. The other trip was to Nantes, then on to Santander in Spain, during the civil war, and back to Port Talbot. Details of this voyage are told in Chapter 4. Cardiff has featured a lot in my life and I have a great affection for this cultural, capital city. Little did I think then, that I would qualify for my Master Mariner's Certificate of Competency at the Pier Head, Cardiff, twelve years later, in 1948.

At other leisure moments in summertime we went on many trips aboard Campbell's Paddle Steamers, sailing from the Pier Head at the bottom of Bute Street, Cardiff to Bristol, Portishead, Clevedon, Weston-super-Mare (some said super-mud), Minehead, Ilfracombe, Lundy Island, Porthcawl, Barry and Penarth. The busiest and most popular was the shortest, about an hour, crossing to Weston, with its long pier and lengthy promenade. Weston was a favourite place for Mum because she and brother Don grew up there when my widowed Welsh Granny ran a boarding-house on the front called 'Atlantic View'. Dad preferred a longer day out, say up to Bristol under the suspension bridge or down to Ilfracombe, feasting on the cold buffet, silverside of beef in particular and enjoying a bar, open from cast-off to berthing on return. Living in Cardiff put us closer to Mum's relatives in Bristol: cousin Cath with daughters Ann (Dinks), Cecily and son Beresford Lowther; Uncle 'Taff' Evans at the Corn Exchange; sometimes his son Teds with wife Margaret, and Don Musitano, with wife Doll, sons Bill, Peter and Michael from Par in Cornwall staying at the Grand Hotel. On Dad's side of the family there was his sister Barbara in Bristol, much troubled with rheumatoid arthritis, nursed by her daughter, young Babs and his brother Harry with wife Dorcas (Darkie) whom we would visit in Clevedon and with whom I would stay for a week or two during the hols, as convenient.

Dad didn't really like driving and Mum wasn't interested in learning, so the Rhode car was sold and Mum bought a fur-coat with the proceeds. I refrain from recording Dad's reaction! He continued using trains and had a large chauffeur-driven car to meet him at Pontypridd to take him on business up the valleys. This did not mean the family was now without wheels because Betty bought a Bantam Singer for £120 with part of her inheritance from her Grandpa Hammond. I must declare that Mum was not selfish, far from it, she would give away almost everything, most generous in the extreme; she was extravagant when purchasing clothes, though it could be said her figure justified it. Hats were economic – she made her own with great flair from bits of fur, feathers and almost anything handy. One day walking with my sister she saw a piece of fur poking out of a stranger's dust-bin on the pavement. Mum stopped, lifted the lid, removed the fur and said 'Just what I've been looking for to finish my new hat'. Betty was horrified and exclaimed 'Mother how can you do such a thing, in a public place like this, too?' 'Well, they obviously don't want it do they?' she replied. 'Good old Zill' sez I, when Betty told me, a phrase picked up from Mum's cousin Teds and her brother Don.

To my benefit Mum was always keen for me to have girl-friends from an early age, but more of that as we go along. Words flowed naturally from her almost without stopping. She would talk to anyone and everyone wherever she was which also got her listening to many tales of woe and brought out her helpful compassionate side – listening, empathizing and advising – called counselling today. For us her continuous chat was a source of amusement; she would say the funniest things and end up with 'Oh my god what have I said?' Betty was a wonderful sister, making my birthday cakes like ships, mostly of marzipan and boosting my pocket money with the odd 6d or more. She was very good to me despite my teasing impersonations of her posh, elocuted voice on the landing outside her bedroom door, when she was rehearsing.

I was fortunate to have such good parents and admired each for their individual qualities. There were times when they had rows, quite frequently, actually, but always reconciled and Betty and I believed that it was this alternating 'love–hate' relationship that kept them together. It seemed they just couldn't manage without each other. At times in our presence Mum would refer to him as 'that silly old bugger' and he would say of her 'that stupid woman', but very soon they would be in harmony again at the piano, which was a great bond. Mum would play for him to sing a favourite song or monologue, such as 'Ol' Man River' from Showboat or maybe 'Ain't it grand to be bloomin' well dead'. Music was still mainly self-made, which helped unite families, despite wireless being commonplace now and us having a tall mahogany cabinet containing an HMV wind-up gramophone to play our collection of 78 rpm records of classical and dance music. My school days in the port of Cardiff are remembered as happy and adventurous, providing an appropriate environment as a prelude to my sea-going career.

CHAPTER 4

My many mistresses: part 1 – 1934–1941

To BEGIN WITH, IT WAS A CASUAL FLIRTATION with a Princess called Ena, when I was twelve, in 1934. Having been a Wolf Cub in Darlington for many years, as a Senior Sixer, at the age of twelve, I was promoted to Second Class Scout, and went camping in Jersey, taking passage from Southampton to St Helier in the crosschannel paddle steamer *Princess Ena*. A card was sent to my parents on arrival, expressing great pride at not being sea-sick. This was my first deep-sea voyage after small boat trips in Torbay to watch the J Class yachts race in 1932. Staying at Paignton with my Uncle Harry, a retired Master with the Bibby Line and listening to his stories about the Middle and Far East I became aware of salt in my blood and wanted to be a Master Mariner myself one day. Also, hearing about another sailor uncle, Willie, a Chief Engineer in the Merchant Navy, who died in West Africa in 1904 from malarial fever at the age of thirty, further increased my urge to go to sea.

My godfather Fred Fleming had a son-in-law, Ben Grant, who was Staff Captain of the *Empress of Britain* in 1935 and my father took me to Southampton to meet him on board this famous flagship of Canadian Pacific Steamships. We dined at the Dolphin Hotel, where Captain Grant told me about life in liners, the good points but also about long periods away from home which, at my age then, did nothing to deter me. Aboard the *Empress*, we met Bill Mayne, Third Officer, who came from Cardiff, where his father managed the dry-dock, and he gave us some idea of life as a junior watchkeeping officer world cruising and on the Atlantic service to Canada. I was to sail with both Grant and Mayne in CPS ships after WW2.

In 1936, I was accepted as a cadet to join the training ship HMS *Worcester*, moored in the Thames, off Greenhithe, Kent, that year in mid-September. Meantime, in the summer holidays of July and August, Dad took me aboard the coal tramp *Wrotham*, out of Port Talbot bound for Nantes, with coal, and Santander, to pick up iron ore, before returning to South Wales. We signed on articles as Supernumaries, with Captain Sheasby, an experienced seaman, fluent in French, for whom we formed a high regard. We had free run of the ship, so I felt like one of the crew, painting, scrubbing and taking tricks at the wheel. The Spanish Civil War had started in mid-July, but there wasn't any sign of fighting in Santander, just armed troops and frightened civilians in the streets. We covertly took some refugees on board before we sailed. I think Dad was pleased to witness me coping well with the worst of weather in the Bay of Biscay, so both of us felt the sea was for me, rather than following my father into W.D. & H.O. Wills, Imperial Tobacco Company of Great Britain and Ireland Ltd, which had been mentioned often by my parents, and which, in that era, could easily have been arranged. 'Just a word my son, before we get home,' said Dad. 'Forget some of the language we have heard and even used aboard this ship, because I don't think your mother would appreciate it!' 'OK Dad, understood.' I replied.

The *Worcester* I regarded more as a new parent, even grandparent, than a mistress, because she introduced me to a very different way of life and discipline. Therefore, I shall deal with this period separately in Chapter 5; except for the reference, I make now, to the *Cutty Sark*. It was during my last term in the *Worcester*, in June 1938, that I sailed from Falmouth to the Thames, in the fastest lady of her time, the *Cutty Sark*. Launched in 1869, as a tea-clipper for the China trade, she would often overtake steamships doing 17 knots. Talk about sexy! That she was, with her slim lines, streaming aft from a beautiful figurehead in decolletage and short chemise (cutty sark) providing a stimulating sight for sex-starved sailors working on the bowsprit. However, in the 1890s steam was overtaking sail and she was sold to the Portuguese, under whose flag she sailed until the 1920s, when, taking shelter in Falmouth, she was seen by Captain Dowman. He bought and reconditioned her as a training ship for boys which continued until his death in 1936. His widow, Mrs Dowman, kept the ship open for thousands of visitors every year, but wanted to see the famous old clipper put to some real use again.

On 16 February, 1938 she offered her to the Thames Nautical Training College as an additional ship to the *Worcester* for training cadets, and her generous offer was accepted. So it was that on 11 June, ten cadets, plus bags and hammocks, with me as Cadet Captain, boarded the Watkins tug *Muria* at Gravesend for Falmouth, to form part of the crew of the *Cutty Sark* under tow, working in pairs at the wheel. We left Falmouth to cheering crowds and blaring sirens on the evening of 15 June and arrived at the Nore early on Saturday, 18, having been saluted en route by the P&O liners *Corfu* and *Rawalpindi*, and also the Finnish four-masted barque *Passat*, anchored off Dungeness. The RAF also turned out a flying boat, containing Air Marshall Sir Frederick Bowhill (Old *Worcester* who later headed up Coastal Command in WW2), which circled and signalled us on the aldis lamp. Admiral Sir Edward Evans, C in C Nore (another OW, more about him in Chapter 5), came aboard off Chatham. The *Cutty Sark* proceeded up the Thames to her moorings close to the *Worcester*. There she remained throughout WW2, until, in the 1950s, she was given to the National Maritime Museum and taken to Greenwich. There she is, in dry dock, open to visitors and flying the Red Ensign; a fitting reminder of how much

Worcester cadets aboard Cutty Sark *passing the grain-ship* Passat *in the English channel.*
Ian is third from the left

the Merchant Navy meant to our welfare in the past, and particularly our survival throughout two world wars. The name is from Robbie Burns' Tam O'Shanter, who, prone to drunkenness, had his mare's tail clipped by wags in Ayr, but told his wife it was seized by the witch Cutty Sark.

My next love affair afloat was with the Beaver sisters, Dale and Burn, general cargo liners in Canadian Pacific Steamships. The SS *Beaverdale* was my first ocean-going ship, as a cadet. I joined her in Surrey Commercial Docks on 19 August 1938 (Discharge No. R179047), and after six voyages across the Atlantic, switched to the *Beaverburn* in March 1939, where I remained for five crossings, until war was imminent and I was called up as a Midshipman RNR in August. The voyage of a Beaver was London, Hamburg, Antwerp, Montreal and back to London for a Monday morning each month (good marketing)! When the St Lawrence froze from November to April, we went to St Johns, New Brunswick and Halifax,

Nova Scotia. It was during this year that I took sights with a sextant of sun, moon, planets and stars at noon, dawn and dusk each day, weather permitting. This gave me the practical back-up to the theory of astro-navigation learnt in the *Worcester* and made me the confident navigator of a wartime destroyer and so on throughout my post war career in the Merchant Navy.

The sisters wisely thought I needed more than offshore skills and sent me onshore to develop other, more intimate, skills, on the waterfronts of Europe and Canada. Each Beaver, and there were four pre-war, had two cadets, and the senior one was responsible for showing junior the way around. In Hamburg we walked through Ten Mark Alley, screened from public view at each end, where small boys flogged condoms and tried to persuade us that their sisters, in windows nearby, were waiting only for us. 'No port of call here, just look,' said Senior. At the end was a VD Museum, displaying the ghastly results of loose living, with a commissionaire who said 'Now boys, back to your ship, Ja?' Not bloody likely said we, and headed for the Cafe Blue Grotto. With our girl-friends there, we exchanged cuddles and paper marks, brought from London in our sweaty jock straps, illegally, for coins, to our mutual advantage. Then, on we went to imbibe steins of beer and meet frauleins in the cafes of the Reeperbahn.

It was there I met Irene, she aged twenty-one and me sixteen, the first girl in my life to take me to bed for the night and give me the low down on what a lady really likes. After one all-night session she said 'Promise to contact me whenever you dock in Hamburg and I'll always see you. My boy-friend can wait.' This was a happy prospect for me, so on Valentine's Day, 14 February 1939, I watched Hitler launch the battleship *Bismarck* through binoculars from the bridge of the *Beaverdale* in Hamburg docks and then did as Irene had suggested, steered a course for her place.

I returned on-board next morning feeling more mature, even, than the *Bismarck*, for not only had I, also, been launched in Hamburg, but commissioned as well! My magic mentor taught me the sincere preferment of shared delights over selfish, solo satisfaction and, when feeling like it, how to have fun at the same time. Happily, this initiation shaped my attitude then and has remained with me ever since. *Danke schoen* Irene.

Occasionally I had met Irene's mother, who liked a game of cards and seemed to approve of our closeness. I believe Irene's father was at sea with the German Navy, I knew not where. Years later, after WW2, I didn't know whether Irene was still alive, because Hamburg had been bombed mercilessly and I never went back. However, my memories often went back and still do, so I composed a few lines, which I thought summed up the situation way back in 1939:

> Irene Worlein, my fraulein in the Reeperbahn,
> Said 'Ian, you sure have a heap to larn

About sexy deutsch stuff,
Diving down on my muff
Before Hitler shouts *achtung, auf wiedersehen*.'

My teenage sex education continued, when one or other of the Beaver sisters took me to Antwerp, alongside a berth in the main tidal stream of the river Schelde, with cafes close by on the waterfront, all playing *'J'attendrai'*, top of the pops on the continent in 39. Senior cadet said 'Follow me and I'll show you a thing or two.' First we went to Skipper St and dropped in the Café Lighthouse, full of gays in drag. 'Just be polite, say little and take in the scene.' I had never seen such a group of gorgeous girls (I mean boys) before, but they were well mannered and treated us heteros without prejudice. 'You won't see anything like this back home,' said Senior and when I told my sister later, she wouldn't believe me.

It was with dismay that I got nowhere with a girl I fancied in a cafe opposite the ship, until the 4th Engineer told me 'You're wasting your time mate. She's a lesbian.' 'What's that?' I said. 'Don't you know? She only goes with other girls,' said he, to which I reacted with typical male egotism, 'She must be crazy with guys like me around.' We visited sleazy night-clubs with sexy floor-shows in downtown Montreal, but nothing much developed. As for London, we berthed in Surrey Docks, and I had a girlfriend in the baker's shop on the corner of Plough Lane. I took her to the pictures, back row of course, but because I had been on the Middle Watch at sea the night before, I fell asleep, so, it was a non-event.

My mistresses in wartime were all dressed alike in grey, before camouflage and Mountbatten Pink became the marine cat walk fashion. The Beaver sisters, Dale and Burn, sadly, were torpedoed and sunk in the Atlantic by U-boats, in 1940. By then I was in the Royal Navy as a Reserve Midshipman. It was on 29 August 1939 that I entered the Wardroom of Chatham Barracks, aged 17 years 2½ months, and a Commander looked at my lapels and said 'What are you?' 'A cadet from Canadian Pacific, Sir,' said I. 'Glad you're here,' said he. 'It doesn't really matter what you wear.' Silvers put on Mid RNR blue patches next day. My parents came up to the Sun Hotel and Dad, a most law-abiding citizen, asked 'What will you drink my son?' 'I'll have a pint of bitter please Dad,' was my provocative reply. 'And indeed you will,' he nodded, with a smile. 'If you're old enough to fight for your country, you're old enough to drink in it!'

The *Kittiwake*, an Anti-Submarine Sloop, was at Holyhead when I joined her on the day war with Germany was declared, 3 September 1939. I had chased her by train from Chatham through London, where baggage was searched for IRA bombs, then Milford Haven and Liverpool on the night of the 2nd, where a Commander got the Guard to lock me in a carriage with despatches, to be let out when met by a senior staff officer in Holyhead. A most memorable introduction to the Senior Service!

A few days later, we sent a working party to help remove bodies from the submarine HMS *Thetis*, beached in a bay nearby. *Thetis*, on trials in Liverpool Bay, sank on 1 June 1939, when only 4 escaped and 99 perished; a tragic event, which has always been surrounded in controversy. Did salvage of sub take priority over rescue of crew, and who was in charge? Churchill said in February 1940 'All interest in this tragedy has now been submerged by the war'. To the Admiralty maybe, but not to survivors and next of kin. It transpired that there was a Trinity House Vessel, berthed in Holyhead, whose purpose was servicing the moorings of lightships and buoys and which was fitted with equipment capable of cutting into the hull of the submarine, but her services were not commandeered. Were 'Their Lordships' aware of her presence nearby, and if not, why not?

We sailed for Dover, to start patrolling the Straits for U-boats, our main armament being depth charges. On 20 September, ten miles off Dover, a big bang blew the middle out of the ship, killing six men in the Engine and Boiler Rooms, leaving us with a thirty degree list to port, but staying afloat and wondering was it a torpedo or a mine? (later, it proved to be the latter). The First Lieutenant (No. 1, a Lieut-Cdr in those days!) shouted 'Follow me Mid. We must get the CBs (Confidential Books) over the side.' 'Aye aye sir!' from me; then to myself 'You must be mad; what . . . go below in this state?' Thoughts of *Thetis* flooded my mind. We were close to Dover, little risk of the enemy getting our CBs; and with the books down aft in the Wardroom safe, whilst bagging them up in the dark with torches, there was every possibility of a capsize, trapping us in a watery grave. Anyway, we did it, as per the book, KR&AI (Kings Regulations and Admiralty Instructions).

Later I was chuffed when the captain, Commander E.R. Condor (who distinguished himself in HMS *Whitshed* at Boulogne and Dunkirk in 1940) wrote in my RNR Officers Training Book Conduct – 'Superior. When ship was mined, carried out his duties with marked coolness and ability.' Little did he know how scared I felt at the time. Thus it was, the bird *Kittiwake* supported me under tow into Dover harbour. Here, in the cliff tunnels beneath the Castle, where Operation Dynamo (named after the room), the Dunkirk evacuation, would be controlled eight months later, Admiral Ramsay, one of our best Admirals from Dunkirk through to D-Day, sent us on survivors' leave. My next appointment was five months later, so I was lucky to be on paid leave during this so called phoney war period; far from phoney for ships of the Merchant and Royal Navies, it should be noted!

During this leave I became friendly with many young doctors and medical students at Cardiff Infirmary. This meant a lot of social activity between the Angel Hotel, opposite the castle, and the Blue Horizon Club in St Mellons, made possible by doctors having a petrol allowance. One night in the Infirmary, I asked to see an operation live, so they dressed me up in a white smock, with mask, and stood me behind the anaesthetist to watch some old boy have his stomach opened up by one of my friends who was duty surgeon and so had not been out on the booze with the rest of us. It was fascinating being a spectator and of course I had no idea that about a year later I would be a young man, as opposed to an old boy, on that operating table.

In February 1940, I joined *Fitzroy*, Fleet Minesweeper (ex Survey Ship), at Sheerness. A mistress with appalling arms; a four-inch forward with maximum elevation of forty degrees, a twelve-pounder (breech block stamped 1898) on the poop and four Lewis (WW1 vintage) machine guns on the boat deck, for air defence, but, with astonishing accommodation. No hammock slinging here, but a commodious cabin with bunk, down aft, in a flat near the Wardroom for me, the only Midshipman in the 4th Minesweeping Flotilla, as I was to discover when we joined the other ships in the North Sea. We worked with Oropesa sweeps (long wires with cutters to floats towed on each quarter) out of Grimsby, Harwich and Sheerness, keeping channels clear for our shipping, through the minefields on the east coast.

My job was varied, from watch-keeping on the bridge, to working with the Chief Buffer (Chief Bosun's Mate) on the sweeping deck and sometimes closing up on a Lewis gun, to fire at a floating mine or enemy aircraft. The Buffer sharpened my seamanship no end as he rolled the same hand-made cigarette, hour after hour, from one corner of his mouth to the other, relighting it every now and then. He also advised me what to do on a run ashore! 'Catch em while they're carrying, Mid,' he would say. The captain, Reggie Forbes (Lieut-Cdr) had a ready wit. When avoiding dive-bombers and ordering the wheel hard-over, he would shout from the bridge, 'Don't worry, my monk brother at Ampleforth is praying like a dynamo for us.'

The Admiral at Harwich thought we should know what a gas attack was like if it ever happened, so as a ship's company, with gas masks on, we were ushered into a warehouse on Parkestone Quay and the doors firmly closed. Some cylinders of tear gas were let off as we waited in the dark and after a few minutes we were ordered to remove our gas masks. It was indeed a moving experience in many ways as we staggered about weeping, coughing and gasping for breath until the doors were flung open and we were allowed to go in search of fresh air. Oh yes, I remember it well. Not the sort of thing you forget in a lifetime and I had heard Dad say that in 1915, before masks were issued and when gas was smelt in the trenches, they peed in their socks and covered their faces with them. At least we were spared that expediency. Our drill made sense at that early stage of the war, although, mercifully, gas was never used.

In Grimsby, I bought a bicycle for 30/- (£1.50) from the police lost property, which got me to the Officers' Club, on the edge of town, in ten minutes. At sea, it was lashed to stanchions on the sweeping deck and when invasion was thought imminent in July and August 1940, I rode ashore with webbing equipment carrying ammunition and a Webley 45 on the hip. A local girl-friend would take me home after the Club and Mummy would shout from upstairs, no doubt with food and drink in mind, I hope you're looking after Ian and giving him what he wants? She was, in all respects, and it was mutual, if only Mummy had known, thanks to my Teutonic training in enemy territory.

We met local fishermen for drinks at the Pestle and Mortar pub in Grimsby and did a deal, which was, when at sea, to lift pots, remove lobsters or crabs and leave money and tins of Pussers tobacco, in lieu. A lobster was half-a-crown then (12 ½p). The flotilla went to Dunkirk and we did four trips from Dover before bomb splinters, from near misses, put us out of action. The Dunkirk tale is told in Chapter 6. After the fall of France, there was a buzz (navalese for rumour) that fire ships would be sent to Calais to burn Hitler's invasion fleet (as Drake did to the Spaniards long ago) and we sweepers would precede them, to clear the way, regardless of German coastal batteries and Stukas. Happily, it was abandoned and we continued sweeping off our own coast.

Reggie granted me permission to grow a beard and approved its appearance when big and black, a few weeks later. The Admiral came aboard *Fitzroy* to welcome us back to Harwich by inspecting the ship's company on the sweeping deck and he paused in front of me, with an amused look in his eyes. Turning to the Captain, 'Reggie,' he said, 'the three most abominable sights aboard a naval ship are, one, a bearded midshipman, two, a pregnant Wren – and three, a hat-stand in a Wardroom's lobby and I see you have one them here.' He then laughed at his joke, as I did, and he shook me, warmly, by the hand. The Lady Fitzroy rented an allotment, for a peppercorn, on the north side of the estuary and as Mid, in charge of the motor-boat, I would land the gardening party – fell in on the upper deck, a motley bunch from all ranks with sacks, buckets, spades and forks; to be picked up later with their produce, and provide our vegetables for the rest of the year.

MT (Motor Transport) Wrens were a great attraction, women with wheels, and the Surgeon Lieut and I visited London for a day, in August, with Diana and Rosemary, in an RN Vauxhall (the old type, with fluted bonnet), getting out of town before the blitz started, after sunset. The girls were still in civilian clothes, because uniforms had not yet been issued. It was in the winter of 1940, when Wrens were buying up all available serge to make trousers, that a Commander-in-Chief made the following signal: 'Wrens' clothing is to be held up until the needs of seagoing personnel have been satisfied.' Rosemary and I, on the back seat of the car, with rug cover, showed our Identity Cards at an Army Check Point, whilst retaining our intimate posture, acknowledged with a friendly 'Carry on' from the Corporal, which we certainly did.

WRNS Quarters were at Dovercourt nearby, and one evening in the dark, I shinned up the drainpipe and in through the bathroom window to rendezvous Rosemary. There were knocks on the door and voices saying 'Come on Rosemary, hurry up!' – to which she replied, quite sincerely, 'I'm sure I'll be coming soon.' Down the pipe I went, on the bike to Parkstone Quay and in the motor-boat back to the ship, to find Reggie with Wren guests waiting to go ashore. 'Sorry sir, had a bit of engine trouble inshore, but it's OK now.' Reggie was always reasonable, often inviting me to parties and praising me for being young in years yet old in discretion.

Sadly, Reggie's other brother, Jock, was killed in command of the submarine *Spearfish* during the summer of 1940. It so happened that the Cameronian Regiment was stationed at Harwich and when a few officers came to dinner, including Bruce Seton, film actor (the Sergeant in *Whisky Galore*), they brought a piper with them. It was a moving event, after the port was passed and we sat around the table listening to a lament on the pipes for Jock, coming from the cabin flat, just outside the Wardroom. The *Fitzroy* was a happy ship, a binding factor being operation 'coal ship', with all hands turning to, regardless of rank. As one of two coal burners in a flotilla of oil ships we gained an extra day in port, refuelling. However, we were not popular at sea, emitting flames from our funnel, trying to achieve 15 knots flat out. Oil ships, in company at night, would signal 'Put out that fire!'

Had I had enough of a slow coal burning ship I asked myself? I read an AFO (Admiralty Fleet Order) saying Observers (navigators) were needed for the Fleet Air Arm, training in the West Indies, and I wondered if my future would be better in the air? When back in the MN, I could fly Canadian Pacific Airliners across the Pacific. I even phoned their Head Office, but they were non-commital. Reggie suggested I consult 'Blood' Ede, Commander, ex-FAA in *Salamander*, which I did, and he said 'Mid, with your training and experience, you'll do better down here, they can train them quickly for up there; that's my advice.' And I took it.

During my time in *Fitzroy* I solved a most pressing economic and social problem. You see, Midshipmen in big ship Gun Rooms were permitted to drink beer, wine and sherry only, spirits being forbidden. Beer and/or sherry was 4d to 6d a glass, whereas a gimlet (gin and lime) or a pink gin (i.e. with angostura bitters) was only 2d a tot. The answer was obvious; I reached agreement with the Surgeon Lieut and Lieut RNVR Dan-buoy Davies (always the first to sight such buoys, marking the swept channel), to drink on their accounts and settle up at the end of each month. Thus I was able to live in a manner to which I was accustomed, and entertain guests, on my pay, 5/- (25p) a day! The old girl ended her days touching off an acoustic mine and being beached on the mud at Harwich in February 1941; there were no casualties. After that she was scrapped, and once again I went home to Cardiff on survivor's leave.

CHAPTER 5

HMS *Worcester* (training ship on the Thames) – 1936–1938

J OINING THE SHIP'S COMPANY of the *Worcester* as a cadet, aged 14, was a monumental step for me in human relations. Instead of pedalling my bike to and from a day school, going home for lunch, I was now, day and night, either up aloft or in my hammock, alongside boys who were my 'shipmates', not just occasional school friends. I felt my attitude changed from one of selfish individual care, to one of interdependence with my shipmates, having a common purpose, manning the ship, on a watery element that at times could be a threat to all of us. The word 'shipmate' came into my life then and is still one of the most treasured words in my vocabulary to this day as I communicate often with many old shipmates from the past, in both Merchant and Royal Navies.

A school ship on the Thames had its beginnings in London Street, a turning off Fenchurch Street when a man of vision, William Munton Bullivant, merchant and one time seaman, met an old friend Richard Green, a Blackwall shipbuilder and owner, and discussed the institution of a Nautical Training Ship to improve the character and knowledge of Mercantile Marine Officers. In 1861, Bullivant wrote on the subject in the *Shipping and Mercantile Gazette*, which caused considerable support from other shipowners and merchants who formed a Committee of Manage-ment. The Admiralty agreed to lend a 50-gun frigate of 1,500 tons. She was moored at Blackwall Reach and handed over to the Committee in May 1862, to be fitted out at the latter's cost. At this time, 1863, the Board of Trade at the request of the Committee, granted certificates to cadets who had been two years in the *Worcester*, which allowed the possessor to count the two years on board as one year's sea time, thus reducing the term of apprenticeship from four to three years. Bill Bullivant invented flexible wire rope to replace the long-standing hemp, a tremendous improvement in standing and running gear, afloat and ashore. Richard Green and his brother Henry were leading men of high repute in shipping, with a fine fleet of thirty sailing vessels, some of them known as 'Green clippers', on the Far East trade.

In 1875, with an increasing number of cadets, the frigate became inadequate, so the Committee turned to the Admiralty, who agreed to lend in exchange the *Frederick William*, a screw line-of-battle ship, re-named the *Worcester* and in future the Institution would be known as 'The Thames

Nautical Training College HMS *Worcester*. At this time the ship was moved to a mooring off Greenhithe, which was the centre of many social activities in Victorian days. The Royal Thames Yacht Club, of which Richard Green was Commodore for many years, held its sailing matches in this reach of the Thames and it was at the White Hart Inn that the Club made its headquarters on shore. The First Sea Lord agreed to make cadets members of the RNR (Royal Naval Reserve) and also the Admiralty permitted the Blue Ensign to be flown by ships where captain and a proportion of officers and crew were RNR. The Admiralty, in 1895, granted eleven naval cadetships for competition between the *Worcester* and HMS *Conway* — a similar, friendly rival, training ship, which had been moored on the Mersey off Birkenhead since 1859.

In 1929, the Secretary of the Training College, Fred Stafford, wrote *The History of the Worcester*, with a foreword by The Earl of Inchcape, then Chairman of the P&O Company and many times Chairman of the Worcester Committee, who said that during the past sixty seven years the *Worcester* had done great work — he went so far as to say, performed a 'national service' — in the training of youths to become officers in the Royal Navy, and more particularly in the Merchant Navy and other maritime services, at home and abroad. He referred to P&O in 1907, providing scholarships which halved the fees for selected candidates and this probably encouraged other major shipping companies to employ Worcester cadets.

In 1904, the Prince and Princess of Wales (later King George V and Queen Mary) distributed the prizes aboard the *Worcester* and awarded the Gold Medal, initiated by Queen Victoria in 1867, to be given to the boy who displayed the qualities likely to make the finest sailor. They were rowed out to the ship from the village causeway (jetty) in the six-oared gig, which had been presented to the ship by members of the London Stock Exchange and aptly named 'Bull and Bear'. Thirty-three years later, in 1937, Queen Mary, as Queen Mother, attended the Annual Seafarers' Service at St Paul's Cathedral, which was inaugurated in the *Worcester* way back in 1890. A party of cadets plus band had attended every October since then and I was lucky to be included this time. It was a great thrill marching from Charing Cross Station, up the Strand, Fleet Street and Ludgate Hill to St Paul's and being cheered from crowded pavements. When a bystander was asked for an opinion, he said 'The Worcester band is definitely the "loudest" band that has ever played in the City of London.'

The annual visit to Lloyds in '37 was an interesting event for me. After a conducted tour and seeing the 'Lutine Bell', only struck to announce a maritime disaster, a special Worcester tea was laid on in the Captain's Room. On being shown where the records were kept, one cadet, son of a sea captain, said 'May I take a look at my father's record?' 'No, you may not,' smiled the guide. Another significant occasion, in April 1937, was the opening of the Greenwich Maritime Museum, by the King and Queen, when Worcester cadets and those from the Royal Naval College lined the route to the Main Hall. Now, this is known as the National Maritime Museum, close to the Royal Observatory, on the dateline, and I have been a 'Friend' for many years.

For the Coronation Naval Review at Spithead in the summer of 1937, I was in the party that stayed in HMS *Vernon*, Portsmouth, for three days, a 'stone frigate', or shore establishment. We went afloat by motor launch to HMS *Frobisher*, where we lined the ship's side as the Royal Yacht *Victoria and Albert* passed by, in procession, and a Lieutenant removed his 'cocked hat', the only time I had ever seen one worn, never since, before waving it in the air and shouting 'Three cheers for Their Majesties, Hip, Hip, Hip, Hurrah!' Full dress never came back after WW2, maybe because of the prohibitive cost and maybe a square-jacket in lieu of a frock-coat was considered sufficiently sophisticated for special occasions, after a war wearing battle-dress most of the time.

A few distinguished 'Old Worcesters' deserve a mention – so here goes. In 1875 young Heihachiro Togo left the ship after two years training. Thirty years later in 1905 as Admiral in command of the Japanese fleet he defeated the Russians at the battle of Tsushima in the Sea of Japan. In 1906 he received the OM (Order of Merit) from the hands of Prince Arthur of Connaught, and was created a Count by the Emperor of Japan. In 1911 he came to England to represent his Emperor at the Coronation of King George V and revisited the *Worcester*, after which he was wined and dined by the OW's Association. When aboard his old training ship, no doubt he recalled that as a cadet he was teased by his shipmates, when his leave was stopped for a week, by them saying 'For the present "Togo" you are "Nogo" as regards the shore.'

Among British officers of high rank trained in the *Worcester* one of the most distinguished was Admiral Sir Edward Ratcliffe Garth Russell Evans, KCB, DSO, LLD (later Lord Mountevans). I have spelt out the Admiral's forenames in full for any students of genealogy who may read this. From the *Worcester* he joined the Navy in 1897 and went on his first Antarctic experience as a lieutenant from 1902–04. Seven years later he sailed with Captain Scott on board the *Terra Nova* to take part in the Antarctic expedition, as second-in-command. When Scott died returning from that dramatic dash to the South Pole, Evans took charge and brought the ship home. During the Great War (1914–18), E.R.G.R. Evans had many exploits to his credit, the most notable being when in command of the destroyer *Broke* in the English Channel. With another destroyer *Swift* in company he engaged and defeated six German destroyers and thereafter was known in the Navy as 'Evans of the *Broke*'. For his services in action Evans was promoted to captain.

After the war Captain Evans was dispatched to the China Station in command of the light cruiser *Carlisle* and while there rendered heroic service to the steamship *Hong Moh*, wrecked on the rocks in the Formosa (Taiwan) Straits with eleven hundred Chinese coolies on board. Other ships stood by, but the real rescue began when the *Carlisle* arrived and Evans himself from the cruiser's motor-boat swam to the wreck with a life-line. Always a powerful swimmer (he was famous at Dover for his winter swims) he performed this difficult task in very rough seas. Lloyds gave Silver Medals, their highest award then for saving of life at sea, to many others involved, but to Captain Evans it was decided to present a Gold Medal, the first of its kind to be struck. In the 1920s he was seconded for a time to the Australian Navy as Commander-in-Chief.

Admiral Evans was probably the most decorated officer in the Royal Navy. His thirty or more medals and awards included the King Edward VII and King George V medals for Antarctic exploration, plus French, Italian, Portuguese, Norwegian, Belgian and USA Orders and other decorations. In recognition of his scientific attainments, geographical societies showered honours upon him. For me personally it is a fantastic memory actually meeting him as I did when he was Commander-in-Chief The Nore in 1938. The *Cutty Sark* was under tow by the tug *Muria* on her last voyage from Falmouth to the Thames, having been presented to the *Worcester* by the last owner, Captain Dowman's widow. He came aboard off Chatham and as Cadet Captain I presented my nine shipmates, the crew of *Worcester* cadets. He and Lady Evans stayed about an hour chatting and before leaving he gave each of us a signed copy of his book *South with Scott*. The Marine Band remained aboard to play us all the way up the Thames to his old training ship the *Worcester* at Greenhithe.

The previous year, in 1937, he had presented the prizes and we dressed ship (flags overall) and manned the yards for his arrival aboard a destroyer. I was the end man on the port lower Main yard-arm and that view from aloft I shall never forget. We were dressed in bum freezers (jackets like page boys with white waistcoats and gloves. Before going aloft we were told to turn our white gloves inside out and on returning to the deck, turn them back again. This was in order that any tar from the rigging would be on our hands and not transferred to those of the Admiral when shaking his.

In 1894 the Jackson-Harmsworth Expedition to the Antarctic sailed from Greenhithe with Lieut. Albert Armitage RNR (OW) second in command. In 1901 when Scott sailed south for the first time in the *Discovery*, Armitage was his second in command, navigator and ice pilot, one of a few onboard with previous experience in the Antarctic. Later in life as a retired Commodore of the P&O Line, he talked to cadets about his favourite topic, etiquette, especially to boats crews who were responsible for ensuring that ladies never slipped on the causeway, although he said 'You should stop short of actually hugging them.' Along with E.R.G.R. Evans (OW) and J. Doorly (OW), there was a third 'Old Worcester', Lieut. H.R. Bowers RIM (Royal Indian Marine) — nicknamed 'Birdie', who accompanied Scott in 1912 and died with him. On the quarter-deck of *Worcester* (2) under the

Prize day aboard HMS Worcester, *30 July 1937, when Admiral Evans presented the prizes. The cadets are manning the yards, and Ian is at the end of the port main lower yard-arm (i.e. ½ in left of smoking chimney)*

bell, in my day, was a memorial to Bowers saying 'OW 1897–99, one of Captain R.F. Scott's party of five who perished in the Antarctic March 1912 on the return journey from the Pole to their base.' Petty Officer Evans and Titus Oates had died previously but the tent containing Scott, Wilson and Bowers was discovered eight months later and after diaries and belongings were removed the three were left, where they lay, in peace, covered with snow and a cairn erected above them. It is apparent that many cadets, trained in the old ship, went on polar expeditions.

Now let me tell you about an old Worcester I was very close to during my two years training, Commander Gordon C. Steele VC, RN. In WW1, after service in submarines, 'Q' ships and in the battleship HMS *Royal Oak* at the battle of Jutland, Steele was appointed as First Lieutenant of Coastal Motor Boat (CMB) 88 in the Baltic Campaign in 1919. He was awarded the Victoria Cross (VC), when in the harbour of Kronstadt, his captain was killed, he took over command of the CMB and succeeded in torpedoing a Russian battleship and a battle-cruiser, before escaping from the harbour.

Steele was a cadet from 1907–9, one of the first to have a P&O scholarship in the *Worcester* and this entitled him to serve his apprenticeship in that Line. He joined the Navy in 1914 as a Sub-Lieutenant RNR and was transferred to the RN in 1915. After WW1 he specialized in anti-submarine duties, and was serving as First Lieutenant-Commander of HMS *Cornwall* on the China Station, when he applied for command of the *Worcester* in 1929, at the age of 38. Ten years later, Captain Steele was required for naval service at the very outbreak of WW2. I feel sure that when he rejoined, to become Commander NS Northern Area and subsequently, Inspector of Anti-Submarine Equipment from 1940–45, he contributed greatly to our victory in the Battle of the Atlantic. Gordon Steele was appointed Captain-Superintendent on 1 August 1929 and because he was under the normal age for retirement, the Admiralty agreed to keep him on half-pay for two years. He was Captain when I did my training from 1936 to 38 and therefore I benefited from the many good changes he initiated. GCVC, as he was affectionately nicknamed by us cadets, was an active man, full of new ideas and many improvements took place. The first, a simple one, was to convert a deckhouse on the fo'c'sle into 'a modern liner's chart house' by installing a steering-wheel, engine telegraph and a gyro-compass (ex *Discovery*). This helped me to win a prize, in my last term, for 'Practical Navigation', a pair of binoculars given by Sperry Gyroscopes Ltd. The ship's library was stocked with modern books and a supply of daily papers and periodicals introduced. The tuck shop, on the Main deck, was enlarged, a very big plus, and a Science Laboratory was established below decks with a Science Master appointed to the staff.

In my time, Mr Fogg, one of the Seamanship Instructors, ran the tuck shop, with a sliding window which was closed when and for as long as Mr F thought fit. For instance, if the window was slammed shut and Mr Fogg was seen sniffing a bar of soap, we all knew that someone had farted. Rarely could we discover who was to blame for this delay, the length of which depended on when Mr F, by sliding and sniffing, thought the atmosphere was clear enough to resume. The Science Master was Mr Smith, a burly figure, whom we nick-named 'Bruiser', remembered kindly by me for an incident on an away cricket match. On the way back, our bus parked and we were given twenty minutes freedom. Off we went to a nearby pub and ordered a pint. I was about to take a gulp when an arm came over my shoulder, seized my pint and a gruff voice, Bruiser's, said 'I'll take care of that Mr Bryce, thank you.' Back on the bus, he did have the decency to hand me the price of a pint, whatever it was then, plus a necessary reprimand to a fifteen-year-old, for under-age drinking. Years later, during the war, I met 'Bruiser', in the Wardroom of a battleship, anchored near my destroyer in Hvalfjord, Iceland, prior to a Russian convoy. He was then a Lieut-Commander (Schoolmaster) and when I reminded him about 'pinching my pint', he enjoyed a moment of reflection, laughed heartily and without hesitation stood me a large pink gin, but of course, I was then a twenty-year-old Sub-lieut RNR.

On shore many improvements went ahead. Ingress Abbey, a grand historic building, built in the reign of Edward III and recently the family home of Mr Houlder, Acting Chairman of the Worcester Committee, became part of the College. It was set back on the shore, opposite the ship, with three or four rugby fields between and surrounded by six grass tennis courts. Behind the Abbey in a former conservatory, with one side removed, stood a Bristol Fighter two-seater training model, kindly loaned by the RAF, for the benefit of the Air Cadets. A flying instructor from Gravesend Civil Air Port visited weekly and when the cadets became more advanced, he took them for flights at Gravesend. The number of Air Cadets increased in the thirties to about a dozen and the RAF sent Air Commodore Tedder (later Marshal of the RAF Lord Tedder of D-Day fame in 1944) to inspect and encourage. The Senior Pilot of Imperial Airways paid frequent visits to see his son, O.P. Jones, Air Cadet (Cox of Worcester Crew '38) and gave a boost to air training. Many Air Cadets, of my time, flew in the RAF during WW2 and one, 'Fanny' Fisher, I know, was an early Pathfinder, over Germany, in a Mosquito. Also, Chris Roncoroni (Worcester Crew 1938) and L.M.S. Holmes (Euston to Glasgow, as some said) amongst many others, were in the Fleet Air Arm.

The mansion itself provided oak-panelled reading rooms, a splendid old-fashioned library and in the basement, a laundry, which coped with some two thousand items a week. The entire vast estate was levelled extensively and surrounded by an iron fence, to keep out the public and to keep in four wallaby pets, who leapt about everywhere and were, presumably, a gift from an OW 'down under'. Before my time, in 1933, the College Offices were moved from Mark Lane, London, to Ingress Abbey and Fred Stafford, Secretary since 1905, was succeeded by Ian Borland, his Head Clerk, who had been with him since 1922.

In addition to being Secretary to the Committee, Borland did many duties normally done by a school Bursar, established excellent local relations 'twixt ship and shore and was a tremendous support to Steele. During WW2, when the College was evacuated from the ship to Foots Cray Place, he held the fort at Greenhithe, single-handed, absolutely indispensable and the future of the *Worcester*, after the war, would have been a matter of conjecture but for his presence, living with his family at Ingress Abbey. His son Malcolm, born in '34, was a Worcester Cadet from 1949 to '51, in HMS *Worcester* (3) (ex HMS *Exmouth*, Schoolship) and became an Extra Master Mariner at the early age of 26. He is now, in the 21st century, Chairman of the Old Worcesters Association.

Captain Steele's disciplinary reforms were carried out tactfully and with a view to reduce fagging and stop bullying. He introduced the Divisional system, so successful in the Royal Navy, and this led to the formation of three Divisions, named and situated around the three masts, Fore, Main, and Mizzen. Each Division was made up of fifty to sixty cadets of similar seniority, age and muscle. This determined our personal space on the Lower Deck, where we kept our sea-chests, containing all our clothes, a book-box, full of school and seamanship literature and where we slept in our hammocks. The line of the masts down the middle of the ship decided who was port and starboard. Thus we ended up with six sub-divisions, parts of ship, or tops as they were called: for example, Fore Port, Fore Starb'd, Main Port and so on. In games and rowing, competitions developed, usually, between the three tops on each side of the ship, known as the Port Watch and Starb'd Watch.

The great thing about any cadet's sea-chest, was what was displayed under the lid, when he opened it, photos of family or film stars, usually, depending on maturity I guess. For me it was Jean Harlow, the blonde bombshell, and a picture of the family wire-haired terrier, Mickey. When a lid was opened and the pin-ups seen showed a family, including an attractive sister, cadets nearby would take an interest, more so prior to a half-term dance, when relatives were invited on board. A voice might be heard saying 'Give you six Milk Flakes if you introduce me to your sister.' Other bids might well be forthcoming, but sisters never knew. Part of our social training, to prepare us for dancing as ships' officers, in later life, was dancing with each other in the Games Room. What a lark that was, but seriously, I met a First Lieutenant in destroyers, years later, when I was a Mid, whose proud boast was that he had danced with the late Duke of Kent, when a cadet at Dartmouth Naval College, so obviously they did likewise.

The four continuous decks from stem to stern and bottom to top, were Tier Deck, mainly storerooms, first above the keel and on a level with the boat platform along the port side, then Lower Deck, as already described, next came Main Deck with eating section for'd, staff cabins aft and space amidships, which would be rigged as classrooms with tables, benches and canvas screens, as and when required. Finally the Upper Deck, used for falling-in by Divisions, exercise and many drills in seamanship.

At the forward end of the Upper Deck was a raised half-deck, called the Fo'c'sle leading to the 'heads' (toilets). Cadet Captains and Senior Badge Cadets only could loiter on the Fo'c'sle at their leisure, but juniors had to hurry across, whether their mission was urgent or not. The heads, at the sharp end, consisted of six cubicles either side of a horizontal spar called the bowsprit, and senior cadets used the side that had won the boat race, that particular year, Port or Starb'd Watch. Junior cadets were often ordered to sing a song, standing on the bowsprit, to entertain their seniors, enthroned as they were, before being given permission to depart.

At the after end of the Upper Deck was another raised half-deck, called the Poop, under which was spacious accommodation, occupied by the Captain, a bachelor, and his mother. In my last term, in '38, I was Cadet Captain in charge of cadets cleaning the Poop and remember, often, Mother

Steele, probably in her late sixties at that time, opening a window of the Poop deckhouse and handing me a handsome bowl of mixed fruit for myself and the boys, bless her.

During our period of training we all had a turn, first, at being Deputy and then Mate of the Upper Deck, which entailed being on watch, armed with telescope, on the Quarterdeck, just for'd of the Poop, from 8 a.m. to p.m. The day started with Divisions' fallen in and prayers at 8, followed by a very superior breakfast with the Captain in the Poop. The rest of the day, I recall, was occupied, mostly, in dipping the ensign, in reply to passing merchant ships.

There were two gangway ladders from the boat platform up the port side to the Upper Deck. The ship's company one was forward, between Fore and Main masts and the Captain's aft, abreast the Mizzen mast with his gig moored below. Entrance to the ship after sunset was through doors in the ship's side, from platform to Tier Deck and then up companionways inboard. The *Worcester* was moored, fore and aft, facing up river, with the causeway about 1.4 miles away on the port bow. The boat traffic 'twixt ship and shore was all propelled by oars, except a motor boat, driven by a Seamanship Instructor, to handle stores. All boats were coxed by Cadet Captains with cadets producing the power, twelve oars in a cutter, six in a gig and four in the jolly, or tier boat. This gave us great experience in handling boats in a tidal river, and I must mention 'slewing', which was judging when to turn a quick half-circle, by backing port oars and heaving hard with starb'd, on an ebb tide, to come alongside the platform, rather than ram it head-on and tossing the starb'd oars upright at precisely the right moment, to avoid trapping them under the platform. What fun it was.

Similar oarsmanship was being practised in the *Conway*, which led to them challenging *Worcester* to a gig race in 1890. This became an annual event, rowed alternately on the Thames and Mersey, for two miles over a straight course, discontinued in 1906, revived in 1929 and ending in 1939. *Worcester* won 18, *Conway* 9 and there was 1 dead-heat in 1905. In 1935, Mr Davis of Durban issued a challenge to the *Worcester* and *Conway* on behalf of the *General Botha*, the training ship he founded in South Africa, in 1920. The race took place in the Royal Albert Docks, on 5 June, in three cutters, on loan from Chatham Dockyard. Mr Davis was present and provided a silver cup in memory of his son Howard, an 'Old Worcester', who was killed in WW1. *Worcester* won by two lengths ahead of *Botha* and about four ahead of *Conway*. The crews and other guests were entertained to tea aboard the *Rangitata*, New Zealand Shipping Company.

Let's go back to my space on the Lower Deck, in Fore Port, the year being 1937. Headroom under the deckhead beams was about 5½ feet, so the majority of people had to duck. About 8 feet in from ship's side was a strong, continuous wooden rack, under the deck-head, running fore and aft and about 1½ feet in depth, to accommodate our book boxes on top and fitted with metal brackets underneath, which when released, provided hooks for one end of our hammocks. The other end was lashed by rope through a ring in ship's side, to whatever tautness desired. My sea-chest, measuring about $4 \times 2 \times 2$ feet, sat on the deck, under my book box and in line with my hammock. Therefore, allowing for one foot between hammocks, my personal square footage was about $12 \times 3 = 36$ and that goes for each of my 24 shipmates, berthed alongside me in Fore Port. Cadet Captains were different and had plenty of space, slinging in amidships.

Now, having set the scene, let me reflect on my most vivid memories of incidents in my time as a cadet. Asleep in my hammock at 6.30 a.m., I am awakened by the shrill sound of a Bosun's whistle, coming from Mizzen Division. I turn out, lash-up my hammock and go to the wash-place. There are lots of basins around the sides and a large bucket in the middle containing antiseptic fluid, supervised by 'Tecus' Reid, a short, thick-set, Seamanship Instructor, ex Petty Officer in the Navy, armed with a 'tweaker' (short stick). I can hear his voice now, as I feel a tweak on the bum, saying 'Come on lad, get gargling!' so I dip my enamel mug in the bucket and comply over a basin. After PT at 7.00, we dress and at 8.00, fall-in by Divisions, Port and Starb'd, on the Upper Deck. Then appears from aft to stand in our midst, the most important person in our lives, Mr A.F. Jackson, Chief Officer. He is a tall, alert, figure with chiselled chin, a stern expression, but a twinkle in his eyes, who demands a high standard of efficiency in everything we do. 'Fore Port,' says 'J', our nick-name for him, 'you all look a bit dozy this morning, so away aloft, over the Foremast fighting top and back (a platform, halfway up the mast).' Off we go, up the starb'd rigging and down the port, feeling far from dozy on return.

At 11 a.m. and 1.30 p.m. we go 'slewing' on the Upper Deck. Slewing is an outward and visible sign of comradeship and a good way of getting exercise aboard ship. It is done by linking arms in twos or threes and walking round the Mainmast on the Upper Deck in a clockwise or anticlockwise direction, depending upon which crew won the last Port v Starb'd boat race. I link in with shipmates such as Ted Burnham, Bill Orriss, Nigel Rhodes, Chris Roncoroni, Ashdown from Portadown, Mike Wallrock, 'Cutie' Birch, 'Bird' Snow and 'Cow' Luard, the nick-names of the last three indicating how they looked and behaved to the rest of us. When my sister Betty and godmother, Aunt Nora, came aboard for my Confirmation by the Bishop of Rochester and witnessed this procedure, Nora turned to Betty and said 'Good gracious, how very peculiar, what are they doing?'

At 8.30 p.m. I hear the Bosun's whistle again, sounding the 'still' for three minutes private prayers. After slinging my hammock, I am kneeling under it, beside my sea-chest, with one eye on my Cadet Captain, who doesn't pray, but parades up and down, to make sure that I do. At one time, when I was a third termer, my good friend to this day, Pete Heywood, was

Worcester *chums. Back row, l. to r.: Pete Luard, Friend, Rhodes*
Front row, l. to r.: Ian Bryce, Birch, Snow. Looking through life-belt: Ted Burnham

Cadet Captain of Fore Port and when I met him in Falmouth, a few years ago, we shared that funny old memory of spying on each other. I am aware, as is everyone, that when the 'carry on' is sounded, we all undress at high speed, place our clothes neatly on our sea-chests, before jumping into our hammocks, the last two in, being detailed off as 'hammock hands' for tomorrow. This task means, after we lash-up our own, in the morning, they stow them all in a netting and place them out again in the evening, for us to sling, before prayers. Therefore, as my Cadet Captain looks away from me, I undo shoe-laces, fly-buttons and shirt buttons after loosening tie. Slip off shoes and socks if possible. This is an exciting exercise that I am good at and I have never been a 'hammock hand'. If anyone gets caught by the Cadet Captain undressing rather than praying, he is automatically detailed as one of the two.

When I was promoted to Cadet Captain, in spring term '38, I was in charge of Main Port, making sure my lot prayed and also I became a coxswain in charge of boats. As cox of a cutter, picking up cadets on the causeway, I remember, sometimes local girls would try to make the younger new cadets blush, by coming close and whispering rude words to them, such as 'arseholes'. There was an embarrassing moment when I was cox of 2nd gig, conveying the parents and sister of a fellow cadet from shore to ship. One of my crew got a used condom stuck on the blade of his oar and tried to shake it off discreetly, but with difficulty, whilst I tried to distract the passengers by pointing out sights ashore. The Tier boat made the last trip of the day, regularly, at 9.30 p.m. to ferry the Masters back from the pub. A popular story, undoubtedly apocryphal, was about Luly, our excellent Headmaster, sitting on the side of the boat with his feet outboard, in the River Thames and saying 'Cadet Captain, why hasn't your crew baled the boat out?'

It was about mid-term that I became coxswain of the Tier boat. On this particular night, we secured the boat and wended our way, myself and four crew, up the companionways in the stern, which took us past the Captain's pantry. Suddenly, the smell of freshly cooked sausage rolls assailed our nostrils. We looked in and saw about fifty on a tray, so, with quizzical looks from my crew, I said 'OK chaps, one each and shuffle them around.' Stupidly, we started munching, there and then, which meant our mouths were full when we rounded the corner of a bulkhead and bumped into 'J', who, quickly appreciated the situation, paused and said 'Ah, Mr Bryce I see. Report to my cabin at eight tomorrow morning.' 'Aye, aye sir.' from me. When I entered his cabin next day, 'J' said 'Bryce, you were responsible for stealing sausage rolls, were you not?' 'Well sir, we didn't think five less would be noticed . . . But, yes sir'.

'J' continued with 'You must learn that when in charge, as leader, you are responsible for the conduct of those under you at all times, wherever you are, in or out of the boat.' ('Yes sir') 'So, I am going to disrate you, one rank, to Badge Cadet, for the rest of this term. Now you may carry on.' ('Aye, aye sir'). As I opened the door to depart, he called out 'Oh, by the way Bryce, I shall not be telling your parents.' 'Thank you sir.' from me. Undoubtedly 'J' was right, in doing what he did. I always had a high regard for him and this episode was probably the high spot of my disciplined learning in the *Worcester*. A lesson in 'leadership' that helped me two years later, when as a Midshipman on the beach at Dunkirk, evacuating the army in boats, I had to deal firmly with two truculent army Captains in the RASC.

I left the *Worcester* with two First-Class Extra Certificates, one for scholastic achievement and one for seamanship. My thanks go to all the staff, but particularly to Messrs Mulhall, Hopkins and Wakeford, for introducing me to spherical trigonometry and the art of astro-navigation, in the Third, Second and First Nautical Forms respectively. Also 'J', for the oral sessions on Rule of the Road at Sea, as stated in 31 Articles. A mistake could mean an hour's hammock drill, carrying it over the shoulders, facing the 'Ten Commandments' on the Main Deck and repeating the misquoted Article over and over again, with the biblical articles as an inspiration. It certainly got us to prepare well and there were very few errors, which hopefully meant none, at sea, later in life. Most important, I've just remembered, 'Dappy' Windsor, our Signals Instructor, so called because he always wore plimsolls. He it was, who taught me semaphore and the morse code, by flags and lights, remembered and used, occasionally, to this day. Summing up, overall, my *Worcester* training gave me a sense of responsibility, to use my initiative and take risks with limitations, to comply with discipline from others, in order to develop my own self-discipline and to be aware of situations and the appropriate action needed for leadership and team work. I feel today, that all these qualities and attitudes have stood me in good stead throughout my life and are still hanging around in my subconscious. How often I draw upon these resources nowadays, is another matter.

When I came to London in 1971, promoted by Conoco from the Midlands Head Office, I picked up the threads and became more involved with old Worcesters. The College had ceased to exist in 1968, but the Association of Old Worcesters was going strong under dedicated guidance of Chris Willis, Honorary Secretary, with changeable Presidents and Chairmen alongside. Every year, Sue and I, on Remembrance Sundays, sometimes with son Andrew and daughter Fiona, have attended the special service at our two *Worcester* war memorials in the Undercroft of All Hallows by the Tower, taken for us by the Vicar, The Venerable Archdeacon Peter Delaney. The simple, sincere gathering of thirty or forty, means a lot to me, as I pause and scan the names of WW2 casualties, about 150, of whom some thirty (20%) are names I remember during my time. It was a pleasure to meet Jan Bezant, OW again, a friendship going back to 1939, when we went from Canadian Pacific Steamships to Chatham Barracks as RNRs. He, now an Elder Brother of Trinity House (opposite All Hallows), asked us in for a sherry after the Merchant Navy Service at 11 a.m. in the sunken memorial garden, where every name, some 30,000, in every ship, some 2,500, is displayed. Recently, on 30 June 2000, we had a Celebratory Dinner in the Great Hall of the Merchant Taylor's Company, attended by OWs from all over the world. I sat next to Brian Smith from Auckland, NZ (Worcester 1933) whose splendid model, which took him 15 years to build, was on display. I heard later that probably it will end up in the London Docks Museum.

In 1998 a National Memorial Arboretum was established and dedicated at Alrewas in Staffordshire, halfway between Lichfield and Burton-on-Trent. The biggest feature honours the memory of the ships and men of the Merchant Navy and Fishing Fleets lost in the Second World War. 2,535 trees have been planted as a 'Merchant Navy Convoy', each tree representing a ship lost. In 2001 it was agreed that former cadets from

Ian at the National Memorial Arboretum at Alrewas, Staffs. He is talking to the Rev. Simon Douglas-Lane, Hon. Chaplain to the Conway club, having just unveiled a plaque in memory of the staff and former cadets of the Worcester. *Each of the trees planted behind him represents a ship sunk by enemy action*

training ships should be remembered and a gathering was arranged in April to plant a tree, with a plaque placed nearby, to be unveiled by an 'old boy' from *Worcester, Conway, Pangbourne, General Botha, Mercury* and *Indefatigable.* More than 200 came to the service in the beautiful, wooden Millennium Chapel of Peace and Forgiveness which stands within the Arboretum. Sue and I discovered that one of the hassocks had been worked and presented by Chris Willis. The most modest Hon Sec told us so, when we met him, as we browsed around admiring the chapel and its contents beforehand. It was only then that I realized he must have made the hassock, with Worcester Crest, presented to Peter Delaney, of All Hallows, on a previous occasion. This goes to show, anyone trained in the *Worcester* can accomplish anything.

I felt most honoured being asked to unveil the *Worcester* plaque, whilst old shipmate (1937) and President of the OWs, David Matthews, planted the tree behind me. Ted Burnham and Angus Baber, both of my time, were also present and we all happily, with many others scattered worldwide, continue the shipmate theme, which means so much to me and with which I began this chapter, sixty-five years ago.

CHAPTER 6

Dunkirk – May–June 1940

THIS IS MY STORY ABOUT THE EVACUATION of the British and French troops from Dunkirk, the beaches to the east and the harbour, in the summer of 1940, relying mainly on my memory to describe events as seen and experienced by me. I was seventeen at the time, a Midshipman RNR in the Fleet Minesweeper HMS *Fitzroy* and I have extended my tale with relevant details researched during the sixty years since, in order to give a more complete picture and link with personalities known to me, before and after this historic happening..

The Norwegian campaign, in the spring of 1940, had been a disaster for the Allies. We were not involved, but between February and May, whilst sweeping channels in the North Sea, we had been attacked by Stuka dive-bombers (JU 87s) and machine gunned by Messerschmitts many times, with our air escort, an RAF Anson, circling on the horizon and incapable of defending us against this latest blitz technology. On 10 May the Germans attacked in Europe, quickly overwhelming the Dutch and Belgians and sending panzer tank divisions through the Ardennes, which were supposed to be impassable and therefore not covered by the heavily fortified Maginot Line, built by the French between the wars from Switzerland to the Belgium border, especially to stop any future attack by Germany. It proved worthless.

The 'blitzkrieg' tactics employed by tanks, with Stukas, not artillery, now providing the forward bombardment and supported by masses of infantry, to occupy and hold territory as usual, moved rapidly to the coast at Abbeville, on the Somme estuary. It took them only ten days. They then headed north up the coast to capture Boulogne and Calais. This completely encircled the BEF (British Expeditionary Force) and part of the French Army, both ill-equipped to fight a modern war, who began a retreat on Dunkirk, only 25 miles east of Calais. It soon became apparent that the troops couldn't hold a bridgehead and would have to be evacuated by sea. At 1530 on Tuesday 28 May, *Fitzroy* sailed from the 'Downs' (between the east Kent coast and the Goodwin Sands) with the 4th and 5th Minesweeping Flotillas, bound for the beaches near Dunkirk, to join in the evacuation. We were now part of operation 'Dynamo', being master-minded by Admiral Ramsay, in the cliffs under Dover Castle.

We sweepers, with say a speed of 15 knots, were best employed lifting men off the beaches with boats, whereas destroyers, capable of 30 knots plus, were dashing to and fro between jetties in Dover and Dunkirk harbours. They uplifted more men than any other class of vessel. Cross channel steamers, paddle steamers, tugs and lifeboats from all round the British Isles, together with all suitable merchant ships, were employed in the evacuation and eventually hundreds of small boats, manned by civilians, rallied round. The first estimated figure for possible rescue was put at 45,000, but this as we know was vastly exceeded and a total of some 338,000 troops was returned to the UK, the nucleus of an Army to continue the war against Nazi terrorism spreading over Europe. At the time of departure for the Dunkirk beaches, we were ignorant of all the background details I have just described. All we knew was that since 10 May things had not been going too well for us and having Norway in the back of our minds, it seemed that the Army needed our assistance once again.

The shortest distance to Dunkirk was 39 miles from Dover, known as Route Z, running parallel to the French coast and only a few miles out, but on 27 May several ships were hit by shells from German shore batteries and it was necessary, therefore, to establish two circuitous channels much further off shore. This meant ships steaming greater distances, by Route X, 55, or Route V, 87 sea miles. We went out by Route X and at 2010, when 4 miles off Dunkirk, *Fitzroy* was ordered to investigate a fishing smack and small motor-boat flying Belgian colours. From these vessels we embarked 8 Belgian army officers, 2 French soldiers and 2 Jewish refugees. The boat was hoisted inboard and the smack taken in tow, but her stern pulled out and she was abandoned. The Belgian officers surprised us with the news that King Leopold had capitulated to the Germans that very morning and they had been ordered to lay down their arms and surrender. Feeling frustrated and wanting to fight on, they got together and appropriated a fishing smack lying in the fairway at Nieuport and here they were. One of them, over-loaded with souvenirs, off-loaded to me a German Mauser pistol plus 200 rounds of ammunition, which I treasured secretly until many years after the war, but more about that in due course. As we approached the coast, we saw the town of Dunkirk covered by dense black smoke streaming from oil tanks, which had been bombed, to the westward. For a few days this gave partial cover against air attack, when embarking troops in the docks.

The *Fitzroy* anchored off La Panne beach, about 9 miles east of Dunkirk, at sunset, 2130, with about 1 ½ hours of twilight to go at that time of year. I was called to the bridge by my captain, Lieut-Cdr Forbes RN and No. 1, Lieutenant Freeman RNR, to be given my orders for immediate action. Reggie Forbes, with his usual wit, said 'Mid, I want you to go ashore with the boats and bring off the British Army, got it?' 'Aye aye sir.' said I, saluting. The First Lieutenant was then more specific: I would have Ordinary Seaman Hawkins and Signalman Minter with me in the ship's motor boat, towing the whaler and so on. The Belgian motor boat was found to be useless. Both crew members were lively lads about my age and well known me, Minter when watchkeeping on the bridge and Hawkins when running the boats in harbour. Minter carried a small handy Aldis Signal lamp, with battery, to maintain constant communication with the ship and Hawkins was just the man for the job, having received his early training, like me, on the waters of the river Thames. Descended from a family of London lightermen for generations back and being involved afloat from an early age, his seamanship, ropework and towing skills were excellent.

We found the sandy beach shallow and shelving and large numbers of support troops were assembling in groups, wondering what to do and where to go. The Midshipman's insignia on my jacket meant nothing to them, but they recognized a naval officer, regardless of rank, and so army officers from Majors down saluted me and said, 'Sir, tell us what to do.' This was very agreeable to me, so I sent lots of them further east along the beach to form groups opposite the other sweepers, keeping a suitable number in my presence to take aboard *Fitzroy*. I got an officer or NCO to gather men around the whaler, about ten each side and, with bow to seaward, keep launching forwards into deeper water, to keep the boat afloat, as men got into the boat in pairs up forward. It was tedious and difficult at first, with a bunch of land-lubbers, or pongos, as we affectionately called our army mates, but they improved with practice. Of course this required men in the water up to their waists, but it was warm enough. When twenty or so were in the whaler, still afloat, we put ten men in the motor boat with Hawkins and he took both boats, whaler under tow, out to the *Fitzroy*. Minter flashed his Aldis frequently to tell the ship the situation, usually with his mate, Signalman Froggatt, at the receiving end, on the bridge.

If, in those days, as a third party, I had studied my behaviour, I feel sure I would have described myself thus: rather fancies himself, strutting about on shore as a midshipman boasting a silver knobbed black cane, which makes him mildly insufferable and he has quite a lot to say for himself over a gin and lime, which he shouldn't be drinking anyway. In my favour, I would say I had developed a greater degree of confidence, helped by a Warrant Officer's good advice. He said 'Mid, when you inspect this lot, your first group of libertymen, find something to say to one of them, if not finding fault, and they'll all take heed and respect you for it. I know 'cos I've been one of them. Don't just say "Carry on".' I always appreciated being called Mid, never 'snottie', a word I detested and a hangover from history, when it was alleged midshipmen wiped their noses on their sleeves, hence the three buttons placed on each arm of a mess jacket to prevent such obnoxious behaviour. I belief the word 'snottie' was perpetuated in some ships, as a put-down, by senior officers. This brief appraisal, exposing my feelings about myself, was thought appropriate to express before recalling the next incident in my life.

Ian on Fitzroy *between trips to Dunkirk*

It was getting dark, about 2300, when I was approached by two officers, sporting three pips on each of their shoulders, indicating they were Army Captains (equivalent to Lieutenants in the Navy) and I also noticed that they were in the RASC (Royal Army Service Corps), responsible mainly for transport behind the lines. They had, between them, a large suitcase and one of them said, 'We want to put this in the boat, it has some valuable gear in it.' 'What sort of gear?' I asked. 'Oh, personal stuff, belonging to us both,' was all they said. 'In that case, no, you can't take it with you.' I said 'Only men and small-arm weapons go in the boat.' At first they were polite, but then became more objectionable, trying to pull rank a bit and even suggesting they would give me a share of the contents if I gave my permission. This confirmed in my mind that it was loot in the suitcase, so I raised my level of assertiveness said 'I repeat, "no" is the answer to your request, I'm in charge here and I say what goes in the boat, so don't forget it.' Enough said for the time being. The weather worsened and at midnight we stopped ferrying off because of surf and tidal conditions. Sleep was a good idea, so Minter, Hawkins and I went into one hour watches and I enjoyed two hours sleep on the sand dunes under army greatcoats provided by a group of officers.

At 0300 conditions improved and we resumed traffic off shore. The two Captains with the suitcase tried it on once again, but this time I turned aggressive and patting the Webley 45 on my hip (they were unarmed) I said most emphatically 'You can both bugger off, with your bloody suitcase, because you won't take it off here.' They disappeared somewhere promptly, probably along the beach, to try their luck elsewhere and I've wondered ever since, what was in that suitcase? I felt afterwards that the spirit of 'J', Chief Officer of the *Worcester*, had been with me and later I remembered his words of wisdom, way back, after catching me and my Tier Boat's crew pinching sausage rolls. 'Bryce,' he said 'you must learn that when in charge as leader, you are responsible for the conduct of those under you at all times, wherever you are, in or out of the boat' Thank you 'J'. At 0350 on the 29th, the boats were hoisted inboard and *Fitzroy* proceeded back to Dover where we disembarked 109 British troops, 8 Belgian Officers, 2 French soldiers and 2 Jewish refugees, but no bloody suitcase!

At 2230 that day, we sailed again, but this time, at daybreak on the 30th, we anchored closer to Dunkirk harbour, only about 3 miles to the east, off Malo beach. The shore was swarming with soldiers, khaki everywhere and many of them wading out to sea in columns, hoping to improve their chances of rescue. A very different scene from last time. A greater variety of craft were gathering all the time and a clever expedient drill was developing between Malo and La Panne. Dutch skoots (small flat bottomed coasters), some commanded by British naval officers, were running up on the beach at low water, taking on a full load of troops and floating off on the flood tide. They would then transfer their human cargo to larger ships in deeper water. This improved the troop-flow considerably and two skoots off-loaded into *Fitzroy* that forenoon. We three, Hawkins, Minter and self, headed for the beach with the boats, but now we had acquired a second whaler and so a shuttle service was possible, with one whaler loading and one in transit, thus doubling our somewhat smaller, but none the less valuable, troop-flow.

Soon after dawn, the air became alive with German aircraft, fighters firing tracer bullets at the troops on the beaches and dive-bombers going for the ships off shore. We know now that Hitler called a halt to his panzer divisions for three days, just short of Dunkirk, to consolidate, and told Herr Goering to destroy what was left of the British Army, with his supposedly superior 'Luftwaffe'. In hindsight, many think that this decision cost him the war. The air attacks on us came, every now and then, throughout the day, but somehow we got used to them, only falling flat when they came very close, being determined to carry on with our boat routine. One of the troops said that if you saw the tracer coming at you, then it wasn't going to hit you, a consoling thought maybe.

Most attitudes were positive, with comrades helping the 'walking wounded' and there were plenty of those, mostly ill clad. They were all extremely weary, having had little or no sleep for days on end. Occasionally there would be a selfish surge of men, regardless of rank, who might threaten to swamp the boat, but only once did I feel it necessary to fire my Webley over their heads in order to restore order and discipline. It could be said, using naval parlance, that it had a similar effect to firing a shot across the bow of a ship to make it stop.

Later in the day, some troops who had been fighting a rear-guard action arrived on the beach and in my section, they happened to be Scots Guards. The procedure smartened up immediately and dramatically, because a Regimental-Sergeant-Major (RSM) had arrived and took charge, under my guidance and with my approval. The whole process accelerated, when the RSM (wish I knew his name) said, at the salute, 'Sir, tell me what you want and I shall see it is done'. His men, with boots lashed round their necks and rifles held high overhead, got the boat drill buttoned in no time and speeded up the loading, with officers and NCOs, waist-deep in the water, making sure their men got into the boat first. I was mightily impressed and found the RSM's presence an inspiration. His attitude made me feel almost impregnable, just ignore the enemy fire and carry on the good work. Of course, we were lucky not to be hit. This RSM was the first I'd ever met, but Dad, who served throughout the '14–'18 had told me what a 'tour de force' they were and now I had proof of that. Back onboard later, my captain, Reggie of the Forbes Clan, Aberdeenshire, was pleased we had embarked some Scots and said 'Well done Kinloch Bryce', as though I had arranged it. On party nights in the Wardroom, Reggie, with his highland upbringing, would give a skilful performance of the 'Sword Dance' with other officers providing cacophonous bagpipe noises.

Some men had come back through Ypres (Wipers to the troops of WW1) and I remembered how Dad, a gunner in the Royal Field Artillery (RFA), spent four years in the Ypres salient, just twenty miles up the road, being gassed and shell-shocked, but preventing the place being occupied by the enemy. He started as a Private in 1914 and in 1917 received his Commission as Second Lieutenant in the Special Reserve of Officers. I felt sad for Dad, knowing how he would feel when he heard about the present situation. We returned to the ship about mid-day and sailed for Dover. As we steamed away, I looked back and with emotion, saw signal lights flashing from the beach, SOS (Save Our Souls), the international appeal for help from peril. The ship was crowded and we had to keep them well distributed and stationary to avoid the ship listing over, especially on sighting the white cliffs to starboard and the temptation to rush to that side. Wounded were everywhere, being cared for by our Doc. One soldier, hit in the arms and chest and bandaged up, was in my cabin bunk. His uniform was ripped and bloody, so I gave him some of my clothes, shirt and trousers to wear before landing at Dover. This time, we disembarked 678 British troops and sailed for Dunkirk again at 2000 that evening.

Out by Route X as usual, we anchored off Bray beach, midway between La Panne and Malo and about 6 miles east of Dunkirk, in the dark at 0200 on 31 May. Looking back now, it seems ludicrous, but it is a fact, borne out by records at the National Maritime Museum, that when we went ashore, we found only 3 men on the beach. They didn't know what was going on and neither did we. However, it is most likely that just before our

Ian's bike and army rifles on the deck of Fitzroy, *returning from Dunkirk*

arrival, Captain Tennant RN, Ramsay's Senior Naval Officer (SNO) in charge at Dunkirk, ordered troops, already assembled on the beaches, to go to Dunkirk harbour, where he thought it safe to embark troops by night from the Eastern Mole, now considered fit for use. We went back to Dover an hour later and at 0830 disembarked three British troops. Let us not ridicule this minuscule rescue by comparison with the others, for we all know a similar number of men, wiser maybe, gave perpetuity to another critical and spiritual, moment in history. The Dunkirk spirit also lives on.

After a day in Dover, we sailed again at 1930 and arrived off the beaches in the middle of the night, about 0100 on the 'not so glorious' 1st of June. It was obviously sensible to search along the coast for any troops coming from the hinterland and unaware of current naval strategy. We went ashore with the boats and found groups of 'Tommies' hiding in the dunes. At dawn, the dive-bombers arrived and concentrated their attention on the ships off shore. I recall a ghastly moment when I saw splashes from a stick of bombs blot out my view of the *Fitzroy* and thought that's it, she's been hit, guess I'm one of them now, hoping to be rescued. Happily, when the splashes subsided, there she was, my floating home, flashing a signal, to my delight, answered by Minter, which said 'Rejoin ship now.'

When aboard, we were told that splinters from the near-misses by Stukas had shattered our de-gaussing gear, rendering it useless. This meant we were no longer protected from magnetic mines laid on the sea-bed. De-gaussing is another word for demagnetizing and that was the navy's answer to the German magnetic mine, introduced soon after the outbreak of the war. All ships were fitted with coils running round them, outside the hull at upper deck level. A current was then passed through the coil, which neutralized the magnetic field of a ship's hull by producing an opposing magnetic field. With our DG gear out of action, we were now vulnerable, but fortunately returned to Dover without mishap, taking Route Y, the furthest off shore and probably the safest. We saw a ship being heavily bombed on the southern horizon, enveloped in red flames and then disappear completely. Later, we discovered it was the Fleet Minesweeper HMS *Skipjack*, not so fortunate and one of many ships sunk during the evacuation. Alongside in Dover, we disembarked 67 troops and then, because of our damage, we were withdrawn from Operation 'Dynamo'.

Waking up on 2 June, after a good night's sleep, the buzz went round that volunteers were needed to make up crews in ships which had suffered losses, so the navigator in *Fitzroy*, David Shaw, Sub-Lieut RN, and I, made ourselves available. At first, we were sent to the Fleet Minesweeper HMS *Hebe*, back, the previous day, from serving as a sort of command ship off-shore, for General Gort (C in C of the BEF) and his staff. She was now berthed alongside in Dover. For about two hours in the forenoon, David and I sat in the Wardroom of *Hebe* under very strange conditions, sipping coffee and waiting for decisions to be taken in other parts of the ship. Officers would come and go, exchanging a friendly word, but behaving in a withdrawn and fearful manner. I now know a lot more about post-traumatic stress, but I barely recognized it then.

The Junker JU 87 Stuka had an air-activated siren fitted to each wing, causing an increasing scream as it plummeted from the sky. This deafening din during the Stuka's dive added a new and more terrifying dimension to bombing. Having experienced Stuka attacks, albeit infrequently, I could understand why the *Hebe*'s crew felt devastated, after being subjected, as they had been, over many days, to such terror tactics. Being aware of their recent ordeal, I realized that these men were shocked beyond belief and I want to show my understanding and sympathy now, by quoting from what I read forty years later.

In their capacity as command ship off Bray-Dunes, few of the crew had slept for five days. On the evening of the 31st the ship's Sub-Lieutenant collapsed, going into fits and convulsions. Next day, 27 members of the crew came down the same way. Finally, as *Hebe* returned to Dover on the morning of June 1, the ship's surgeon collapsed too, mumbling that he could not face another trip to Dunkirk. Under these sad circumstances, *Hebe* was ordered to rest, the only cure, and proceeded down channel to Portsmouth. David and I went aboard HMS *Winchelsea*, a V & W destroyer, in need of two deck officers.

This was my first experience sailing in a destroyer at the incredibly high speed of 35 knots (about 40 mph) and I liked it. Speed was obviously our main safety factor against anything, being able to weave and dodge, providing the weather, and particularly sea conditions, were good. They were ideal then and we had a clear run on the shortest Route Z, reaching Dunkirk harbour after sunset on 2 June and securing alongside the Eastern Mole at about 2300. The German land forces had resumed their attack and we came under mortar fire, which happily, either fell short or whistled overhead.

Morale was high and we encouraged those courageous troops, who had been fighting the last rear-guard action, as they marched in good order, along a somewhat shattered wooden jetty, to come aboard. They were mostly French Poilus (infantrymen) being hastened by our captain, Lieut-Cdr Hawkins, shouting 'Vivement, vivement mes amis, vivement', from the bridge and 'Jolly Jack' joining in, from the fo'c'sle, with 'Wakey, wakey, get a move on, you fucking frogs.' It had the desired effect.

Little did I know at the time, but became aware later, that I was in spitting distance of a previous captain (E.R. Condor in the *Kittiwake*) and now in the destroyer *Whitshed* and a future captain (J.E.H. McBeath, with whom I would sail in the *Oribi*, a year hence) and now in the destroyer *Venemous*. Just before midnight, after embarking 152 French troops, *Winchelsea* sailed from Dunkirk, following in the wakes of *Whitshed* and *Venemous*. This was the last night of Operation 'Dynamo' and Ramsay received a signal from Tennant saying, succinctly, 'BEF evacuated'.

When France surrendered on 22 June, we stood alone. About that time I went on leave and was astonished to hear some people say 'Let's do a deal with Hitler now, we don't want a long bloody war like the last one and they look like winning anyway.' Happily, this was not the view of the majority, who were well aware of the evil nature of Nazi occupation. My life had been threatened many times, already, by those bastards and I was horrified to hear a young army officer on the Home Front say 'We've got the answer to those Stuka dive-bombers you know.' 'Really,' said I, 'tell me more.' 'Well, you take cover by diving into a ditch and bring 'em down with accurate rifle fire.' I did not respond, but was glad that this absurd attitude was adjusted to one closer to reality, after the Dunkirk veterans had related their experiences.

On 16 August, the Central Chancery of the Orders of Knighthood at St James's Palace, was pleased to Publish by Authority, *The London Gazette*, which read:

> The KING has been graciously pleased to give orders for the following Appointments to the Most Excellent Order of the British Empire, for good services in organizing the withdrawal to England, under fire and in the face of many and great difficulties, of 335,490 Officers and Men of the Allied Armies, in about one thousand of His Majesty's Ships and other craft between the 27th of May and the 4th of June, 1940:

D.S.C. AT 18

Aged only 18 years, Midshipmaı I. K. Bryce, R.N.R., of H.M.S. Fitzroy, son of Mr and Mrs. L. L Bryce, 141 Lake - roac West, Cardiff has been awarded the Distinguished Service Cross for his work in connection with the Dunkirk evacuation.

He was formerly a pupil of Darlington Grammar School and Monkton House, Cardiff, Midshipman Bryce and was trained on H.M.S. Worcester. He was a cadet with the Canadian Pacific Steamship Co. when he was called up.

The DSC at 18

followed by the names of those considered to be most deserving of recognition, the CBEs, OBEs and MBEs. After their priority, followed the awards for service in action and *Fitzroy* received 1 Distinguished Service Cross (DSC), 4 Distinguished Service Medals (DSM) and 2 Mentions in Dispatches. I feel it appropriate now to name the recipients.

DSC . . . Midshipman Ian Kinloch Bryce, R.N.R.
DSM . . . Signalman Frederick Froggatt, C/JX 144084.
Signalman Dick Minter, C/JX 155114.
Stoker First Class Walter Albert Worman Ward, C/JX 97894.
Ordinary Seaman Gordon Harry Hawkins, C/JX 168509.
Mention in Dispatches . . Lieutenant-Commander Reginald Arthur Forbes, R.N.
Sub-Lieutenant David Alexander Shaw, R.N.

I have wondered ever since, why give a Cross to those with a Commission, or on their way towards one, as I was then as a Midshipman, and a Medal to the men, in other ranks? It made me think what Queen Victoria might have said when creating her Cross, the VC, during the Crimean War, in 1856. Did she perchance say, 'I want my Victoria Cross to be regardless of rank,' because that's what it was and has been ever since? I believe she was a socially adaptable woman like the Mrs Brown, portrayed so well by that astute actress, Judi Dench, in the film of that name.

My present day feelings are, that many with authority talk a lot about democracy, but act with very little humility. To me, the recurrence, twice a year, of an honours list, suggests that we subjects are still supposed to adapt and conform to what those in power think our places should be, in a social hierarchy of Empire that no longer exists, yet gives its members an assumed superiority. Dad comes back into my mind again and again, because he often said 'My son, there were far more VCs won in the trenches than were ever awarded.' And he witnessed such, I've no doubt.

An investiture was arranged at Buckingham Palace on 15 October, with relations and friends, but because of the London blitz it was postponed and never did happen. Good old Zill was so looking forward to buying, or maybe making, a special hat for the occasion and that would have been a happy conclusion to my efforts at Dunkirk. However, it was not to be and I got my gong in Scapa Flow a year later, aboard the battleship HMS *Anson*, when KG VI was visiting the Home Fleet. This enigmatic fellow officer, by rank an Admiral of the Fleet now, didn't say anything to me, even though he had been a Midshipman, at a similar age, in WW1. He just pinned the ribbon on my chest as though it was a flag-day in a market-place.

I am not an aggressive person by nature, but after this first hostile year, I felt totally committed to fighting an evil, threatening bully, in a war for humanity in general and not solely motivated by a patriotic fervour for 'King and Country'. KG VI was actually a shipmate, in a remote sort of way, aboard HMS *Vanguard*, after the war, in 1947, on the Royal Tour to South Africa. I did admire him as a person in many respects, for fighting to overcome his speech difficulty and for being a conscientious monarch under circumstances he would rather not have endured. David Shaw was also in *Vanguard* as a Lieutenant, but I'll tell you about that later in Chapter 11. Bumped into Reggie Forbes again, at sometime during the war, in the Central Hotel, Glasgow and before the 50th anniversary of Dunkirk, in 1990, I contacted the Thames Watermen, hoping to get news of shipmate Hawkins to celebrate the occasion. They knew about him and the family, but Gordon Harry had gone away and we never did find him.

CHAPTER 7

Cardiff blitz: Infirmary and Mountain Ash Hospital – February–May 1941

I T WAS DURING THE LAST WEEK in February, 1941, Wednesday, 26th, about two hours after sunset, say 1930, when my piano playing in our house, 141 Lake Road West, was interrupted by the air-raid sirens sounding a red alert. Being in uniform as always in wartime, I donned great-coat and tin-hat, slung my gas-mask across the right shoulder and went outside. As I joined neighbour Bill James, who was an Air-Raid Warden, on the pavement, the hill on the other side of the lake became lit-up from end to end, accompanied by a distinctive sound like masses of pebbles being dumped on a promenade. It soon became apparent that hundreds of incendiary bombs had been dropped on the high ground of Cyncoed to start fires and guide in the heavy bombers, so we hastened to get members of our families into the concrete shelter in Bill's garden, which he was happy to share with us.

There followed a lull in which my mind went back over the past nine months. After Dunkirk the threat of invasion loomed large and over Grimsby there were times when we thought we saw paratroops in the searchlight beams but they turned out to be aircrews baling out. Then when the Famous Few had won the Battle of Britain, in September, invasion was discounted and the Germans began their fearful blitz on London each night. My thoughts moved on to November when one night Londoners didn't hear the sirens after two months of nightly bombing and wondered what could have gone wrong. Goering had changed his tactics again and bombers were attacking cities and towns in the provinces. It started with a devastating blitz on Coventry by dropping 600 tons of high explosives and thousands of incendiaries. Birmingham, Sheffield, Manchester and Glasgow were next. After these, the ports came under attack from the 400 bombers sent over Britain each night.

The lull ended to the droning sound of heavily laden bombers overhead and Bill and I presumed they would be trying to identify the docks to the south of us. So now it was Cardiff's turn, I thought. Suddenly I heard the familiar sound of a diving aircraft, not a Stuka this time, something bigger, probably a Heinkel or Dornier, and I shouted 'Get down'. We both flattened out on the pavement and I counted a stick of four bombs exploding further down the road. Bill and I stood up and moved towards the noise to see what damage had been done. It was when I tried to walk,

63

that I was forced into a limp and realized my left foot was squelching in my leather half-wellington boot. A hand to the back of my left thigh felt sticky and I knew it was blood, which meant I had been hit. No immediate pain, just a feeling of numbness. Bill was OK and helped me back to his shelter before returning outside. Bill's wife, Joy, plus Mum and Dad with grand-daughter Christine, Betty's daughter aged 18 months, and Mrs Jones were all safe and sound. Mum was marvellous and calmly applied a tourniquet to the top of my thigh, as best she could, to stem the flow of blood.

Bill came back eventually and put us in the picture. Of the stick of four dropped, the first went in the lake, the second on this side of the lake, blowing the park railings across the road and killing Harry Davies on the pavement about 100 yards from us and wounding Glyn Jones in the arm. Davies and Jones were also Air-Raid Wardens. The third bomb fell on the Jenkins' house, 135 and three doors down from us. Happily Mr and Mrs were in their shelter with Mrs Davies, whose husband had just been killed, and the fourth fell, harmlessly, in the field at the back. This was war on our door-step and rather than terrify us into submission, as the Nazis hoped, made us even more determined to hit back. Was it our misfortune that this bomber maybe mistook the lake as being part of the docks, considered to be a legitimate target? Maybe it was, but, with Coventry in mind, I must not invent navigational errors as an excuse for those bullying, belligerent bastards.

Bill phoned for an ambulance and after a shot of morphia I was put on a stretcher and with Glyn in company driven off to the Cardiff Infirmary. The blitz was still going on but we got there alright and were lined up with lots of other casualties on the ground floor, to be examined by the staff. Naturally, my thoughts went back to previous visits with my friends the medics, but never had I been carried in horizontal. The morphia was doing a good job, I felt no pain, just happy and dozy and remember thinking how lucky I was. Once again I had survived, but had I been hit a few inches to the right the family jewels might not have had such good fortune. All of a sudden I heard a familiar voice say 'Good God it's Ian!' and I opened my eyes to see the friendly face of the young duty surgeon, known to me, but whose name I cannot remember. 'You shouldn't be here,' he said. 'Only last week we were celebrating your coming on survivor's leave.' I realized he had recognized me by my uncommon black beard and said something like 'I know, stupid sailor ashore, but still surviving, I guess. Glad you're here tonight 'cos I've seen you in action, remember?' 'Yes of course, we'll take care of you and I'll see you tomorrow,' he said as he departed. Full of confidence after this exchange, I just passed out and have no memories of going through the operating theatre and being put in a ward on the first floor afterwards.

It was in the forenoon that I came round, to find myself on my back in bed, with a large curved basket taking the weight of the bed clothes off my legs and two lovely nurses to nurture me. One of them told me about my op; removing a piece of bomb splinter from my bum, which had penetrated about six inches through muscle and fat, to lodge against the thigh bone without fracturing it, fortunately, and this would mean daily dressing treatment for some time, allowing the wound to heal from inside out, to prevent gangrene. At this time penicillin had been discovered, but was not in general use. About midday, my surgeon chum looked in as promised and said 'Here you are Ian. Please allow me to return to you your rightful property, a personal gift from the Third Reich.' He placed in my hand the bomb splinter that I treasure to this day (irregular in shape $1\frac{1}{2} \times \frac{1}{2} \times \frac{1}{2}$ inches, weighing $1\frac{1}{2}$ ounces) and confirmed what the nurse had told me, adding 'I think you deserve a rest, anyway, after so many survivals.'

Mum and Dad came to see me in the afternoon and they told me that sister Betty, returning from rehearsing with the Cardiff Little Theatre last night, was alarmed and frustrated at being stopped and not allowed to proceed down Lake Road West, until she explained her concern for parents and daughter Christine at 141, when she was granted permission to pass. This was after the 'all clear' and she found them safely back in the house, which had only suffered window damage. Dix the canary was singing away and Mickey, our wire-haired fox terrier, was back in his basket asleep, having been in the shelter with everyone else. So, life at home had returned to normal. Dad gave me his sweet ration, a tin of Parkinson's Humbugs to keep on the locker beside my bed. What a blessing those humbugs proved to be.

Soon after sunset the sirens emitted their mournful wail and the sound of incendiaries was close. Some of my medic friends were roof-spotting because of this and came down frequently to keep me informed with remarks like 'Got 'em in the searchlights, Ian and shot two down already'. This helped a bit, but not a lot. The church opposite the Infirmary was on fire, lighting up the ward through half-shattered windows, and I have never been so frightened in my life. I suggested the nurses take cover under my bed in case the ceiling collapsed and they said 'What about you?' 'I'm OK,' said I, pulling the sheet over my head for psychological protection and until the 'all clear' sounded. I nourished the nurses with humbugs whenever their heads appeared from under my bed, with open mouths like chicks in a nest.

Next morning a most sensible decision was made to evacuate all patients from the Infirmary to hospitals up the valleys and this was arranged in accordance with seafaring tradition, women and children first. So it was, in the afternoon, I was transported in an ambulance to the hospital at Mountain Ash, about 18 miles north of Cardiff, between Pontypridd and Aberdare in the valley of the river Cynon, a tributary joining the Taff at Abercynon, 3 miles to the south. I kissed the nurses in Cardiff goodbye and gave them what was left in the tin of humbugs.

Now, I had to adapt to my new surroundings for some time, a hospital as opposed to a ship, and found to my surprise over the next two to three months that they had many things in common. The first and most noticeable of these was that the Matron of a hospital was commanding an isolated unit in a Health Service, very similar to the Master of a ship in the Merchant Service. The Matron, I soon discovered, by her very presence, was the driving force for loyalty, discipline and the setting and maintenance of standards. In her presence, patients, sisters, nurses and senior experts, both surgical and medical, stood to attention, metaphorically. I thought this formed an analogy with seafaring: where Nelson still inspired the Naval Service so, it seemed to me, did Florence Nightingale still inspire the Nursing Service. As long as Matron was in charge, accepting advice, but brooking no interference, as a patient I felt that the 'lady with lamp' would get me well again, not just being part of a countrywide system. Another similarity was the Matron doing rounds, inspecting for cleanliness and like a Captain doing rounds at sea, demanding that everything was 'shipshape and Bristol fashion'. Writing up the log book was important, but secondary. Pity that the role of Matron went away a few decades ago, but now there is talk of bringing her back again and who better to administer what is needed most, a competent, decentralized authoritarian person to act.

I had a warm welcome into the ward from about ten Welsh miners in their beds recovering from various physical injuries incurred down the pit. 'Where did you get that beard from, boyo?' said one of them. 'I grew it at sea,' said I. 'Oh, it's a sailor you are, is it?' said another, followed by a loud, raucous voice, from behind a screen, saying 'Where's your ship then boyo, up the Taff is it?' This had us all laughing with each other and we were wardmates, similar to shipmates, from then on. The river Taff ran down the next valley to the east, only a few miles away over the mountain, past Merthyr Tydfil and thence to its estuary in the Bristol Channel at Cardiff. So, the inquiry was natural enough, had I sailed my ship, whatever it was, up the river into Taff Vale? It was apparent to me immediately that the spirit amongst miners, no doubt engendered in the pits, was very like that amidst sailors in a ship. The job in both cases was frequently perilous, working in a hazardous environment which made comradeship and interdependence essential qualities in all members of the team, whether called crew or shift.

Having discovered these happy similarities, I then discovered that the man in the next bed on my right was a crane driver from Cardiff docks, who had broken his leg. We shook hands and got into a conversation about Tiger Bay (a notorious area at the bottom of Bute Street), cargoes and ships, mainly coal tramps, and pubs down the docks. He knew the 'Six Bells', run by three well endowed sisters and therefore popularly known as the 'Six Swingers'.

'Do you play cribbage?' he said. 'No, 'fraid I don't . . . but I'd like to learn,' I replied. That was it, for the next few weeks, until he had repaired enough to go home, we played crib, hour upon hour, day after day and I loved it. I have a lot to thank him for (wish I could remember his name) because I played a lot at sea later and still enjoy a game to this day. All my kids play crib as a result of my tuition. Frank, father-in-law Mark I, my first wife's father, was also a keen crib player, but the circular pegging board I brought back from Canada confused him.

Obviously the word had got around about my misfortune, even as far as Grimsby, because I received a lovely letter from the Jeffers family, trawler owners and people I had met in the Officers' Club. Mrs J, who was Irish, had a cousin in the Navy, Captain Fogarty Fegen, often talked about since his heroic action in the autumn of 1940, when he commanded the *Jervis Bay*, armed merchant cruiser (AMC) and went into action against the pocket battleship *Admiral Scheer* to protect an Atlantic convoy. The convoy scattered and was saved. Sadly, but inevitably, the *Jervis Bay* was sunk with all hands (including some OWs). Fegen was awarded the VC posthumously and it was intended to include all the crew, I feel sure. In addition to the letter, the Jeffers gave me an enormous tome, *The Herries Chronicle* by Hugh Walpole, comprising four books, *Rogue Herries*, *Judith Paris*, *The Fortress* and *Vanessa* and running to 1,500 pages overall. This book was my closest and much loved companion for 2½ months, 75 days, which averaged out at 20 pages per day and suited my pace of reading, between games of cribbage. It all happened in the Lake District, known to me since childhood.

The Herries Chronicle was published in 1939 and the Foreword written by Hugh Walpole on 19 September that year must have had current appeal to a public so recently at war. For that reason I'm quoting a few chosen words from the Foreword here and now. Hugh Walpole said, firstly, 'In the middle of the last war, sitting in the mud in trenches, I comforted my soul with visions of an "English Chronicle" that would stretch, without break, from the days of Elizabeth to our modern time.' And secondly, he said 'If the historical novel can show that human beings have always suffered, known happiness, needed love, displayed fortitude, trembled and prayed very much as they do today, a fine sense of the continuity of the brotherhood of man can be emphasized.' I know now, even more so, after living through the last sixty tumultuous years, why this tome was much beloved by me then and, I believe, aided my recovery.

Visitors were always fun, as expected to be, coming to cheer me up. Mum, bless her, came up on the bus from Cardiff every week and Dad, doing his business up the valleys, looked in whenever he could. Dad's car-hire chauffeur, Dai Davies, a large lovable Special Constable, with whom any sensible person would not pick a quarrel, lived in Ynysybwl (quite my favourite Welsh word, pronounced 'unisibool), about five miles away and he with his son would look in now and then. For a few years after, when on leave from my destroyer in the Home Fleet, I would accompany Dad up the valleys for a day out and Dai, whom I got to know and liked well, would take me into a cafe whilst Dad did his business in the tobacco shops nearby. History more or less repeated itself verbally, because I was still in uniform and so, some wag always said 'Where's your ship then boyo?' But this time I replied 'Up the Taff of course, anchored off Pontypridd, where do you think?' The wit of miners and me, a sailor, I found complementary, with many mutual laughs to endorse this feeling at the end of any dialogue.

Mum's excursions on the bus were devoted to conversations with whoever was adjacent. Over a period the chat became regular with a little flat-capped Welshman who said 'Once a week to see your son is not enough, I'll visit him between times.' This little man did just that and was amusing company for half-an-hour or so, giving me the local gossip and a hot tip for the 2.30 at Chepstow or wherever and I always gave him a bob or two to put on the certainty, but wasn't bothered when I got no return. It was a friendly human gesture, much appreciated at the time. Good old Zill, my Mum, would always bring a cake and usually said it had been baked in rather a hurry. On one occasion she produced a large three tiered sponge cake and confided to me that she had lost a small saucer in the cooking process. After giving half the cake to my crane driver chum in the next bed, I was not too surprised when he took a bite, paused and then handed me a piece of china that had almost cracked his dentures.

Two staff visitors must go on record. The visit of the Matron, a tall dignified figure in navy blue with white accessories, whose face, from a look of stern appraisal, went easily into one of warm smiling approval, was enjoyed each day. The better she knew a person, the sooner the change took place. At first, not surprisingly, the arrival of a bearded midshipman, only eighteen years of age, probably made her wonder how this obscure off-shore creature would behave. Men from under the ground, miners, she knew all about, but wasn't it said that sailors had a girl in every port and might not this bearded monster consider her hospital to be one such place? I must warn my nurses and keep an eye on him, was the likely thought that crossed her mind. However, it seems she approved of my behaviour, because the warm friendly smile got ever sooner as the weeks went by. There came a time when her smile seemed to suggest that even a kiss and cuddle with one of her nurses would come within the limits of her approval. This was just as well, because it was already happening. After all there was a war on.

The happenings were with Pat, the night nurse. She was my other staff visitor, lovely to look at, with flashing brown eyes, long auburn hair, piled up under her nurse's cap and the slimmest waist I'd ever seen. Between rounds, she would sit, in the dark, by my bed, on the opposite side to the crane driver, who snored, which told us we were not being observed. We held hands and chatted in hushed tones, with a snog and a squeeze and after her last round, she'd let her hair down. Looking back on boy meets girl in wartime, I found that comfort and support, in the form of love, was a need that most people desired and for me the word 'friendship' fully embraced those feelings. I find the present day overuse of the word 'relationship', to describe every occasion that a male comes alongside a female, to form an item or otherwise, is both unattractive and totally lacking in emotional expression. In wartime, it seemed to me, lots of barriers came down between the sexes and most people were happier as a result. It didn't always include sex, nice if it did, but invariably it extended friendship, regardless of sex.

The time came for me to walk about with crutches. As I staggered round the ward, chatting to an ever changing group of miners, injured doing their bit for the war effort underground, the cry was 'Put a parrot on your shoulder boyo and it's Long John Silver you are.' It was an unforgettable social experience for a young seaman like me, to have shared this part of my life with mine-mates. Soon I was walking with a stick, so home I was sent in mid-May. I kissed Pat and Matron goodbye, then went on leave before joining my next grey mistress.

CHAPTER 8

HMS *Oribi*: part 1 – 1941–1942

TWO HAPPY AND MOST MEMORABLE EVENTS took place in the month of June 1941 and both of them in Glasgow, on my nineteenth birthday, the 9th. The first was when I arrived by train from Cardiff, clean-shaven once again and reported to the Naval HQ, situated in St Enoch's Hotel, to receive guidance about joining my third mistress in grey, the destroyer, HMS *Oribi*. Across the foyer I saw a face I thought I knew and within a flash realized it was the film actor Ronald Colman, in a lieutenant's uniform, no mistake. Another lieutenant told me I would stay one night in hotel and the next day go to digs in Paisley Road West before reporting aboard *Oribi* in Fairfields shipyard, Govan. He confirmed my recognition as correct and said that RC had come back from Hollywood to do his bit for his country and with some amateur sailing experience had become an officer in the RNVR (Royal Naval Volunteer Reserve).

The second was to phone Aunt Jean Massie in Falkirk, as suggested by Dad, and she, in her distinct Scottish voice, said she would come down by car and take me out for the day and to let her know when it would be convenient. This contact was going back down the Kinloch side of the family and for the sake of any genealogical readers I feel I must explain. My granny, on father's side, was Annie Kinloch of Bo'ness. She was the youngest of ten, with a sister Janet, three years her senior, who married a Jeffery and they had a daughter Jean, who married a Massie. Dad, quite rightly called her 'cousin Jean', she was a first cousin to him, but I think the simplest way to state my relationship with Jean Massie is to say that her mother was my granny's sister, QED. This was an exciting start to tracing roots north of the border and this year, in 2002, I'm happy to say, the roots have spread worldwide, particularly in the USA, but we won't go into that, right now.

Next day, my landlady greeted me at the digs and told me all about the black-out routine. Glasgow had been heavily bombed, like other ports, but was quiet just now, she told me. About 1100 hours I reported to the First Lieutenant (No.1) aboard *Oribi*, one Benjie McLeod, married to a glamorous blonde Swedish lady and whose daughter was christened in the *Oribi*'s bell six months later with god-parents Jack McBeath and Prince Bertil of Sweden. Just thought I'd start a bit of name dropping, for what it's worth? No.1 gave me some papers to sort out and an hour later sent me ashore to get some lunch, suggesting I find a pub near the dockyard. I shall never forget this lunchtime, for what I saw in the manner of drinking. I

HMS Oribi *at sea*

stood at the bar, munching a sandwich and sipping a pint next to two dockyard mateys who took it in turn to call for 'chasers', at least two each within half-an-hour. For the uninitiated, a chaser consists of Scotch, usually large, in a small glass and a pint of ale, the procedure being to down the Scotch in one, warm the glass by rolling in the hands and shake the drops into the pint, which is then taken more slowly. It was an education and I watched with respect. Not for me at lunchtime, but I might try one in the evening sometime, why not?

Returning on board, I met 'Jimmy' Nimmins, Lieut (E), in charge of the engineering department and standing-by, with No.1, during the construction stage. A year later, he and I would perform in a ship's concert in Murmansk, he in uniform and me in drag, singing 'There's a Small Hotel', a popular tune in the thirties, to whistles and suggestive shouts from our salty audience. Also, in the basic team was 'Claude' Stacey, Warrant Officer, Gunner (T), for torpedoes, which he claimed was the ship's main armament, but he would, wouldn't he? We had four 'tin fish', which we never used in anger, but his domain included depth charges, handled, fused and fired, in patterns, by his torpedo-men and used frequently, often with success, against U-boats. So Stacey was a very important member of the team.

Oribi had started life as ship J1112 in January 1940, the first emergency class fleet destroyer, the 'O' Class, with the intended name of 'Observer', but when the South African Government sponsored the ship it was changed to

Oribi, the name of an attractive species of South African antelope. Launched a year later by Lady Dollan, wife of Sir Patrick, Lord Provost of Glasgow, she was completed and commissioned on 5 July, when Lady D presented a super radiogram to the Wardroom at the party therein. Before the commissioning, Aunt Jean, as promised, came to Glasgow in a chauffeur driven car and took me back to her home in Falkirk, where the dining table groaned under the weight of food laid on for cousin Ian. A Scottish high-tea, no doubt, and I loved every minute. Aunt Jean said 'Ian, I was pleased to hear from cousin Leslie, your father, that your sister Betty had married a man with the good Scots name of Malcolm.' She had a son Charles and a daughter Jean and in the 'fifties, about twelve years later, when I was ADC at Holyrood Palace in Edinburgh, Brenda, my wife, stayed with Charles Massie, his wife and family in Costorphine and I saw Aunt Jean again, plus many more Massie cousins.

Lieutenant-Commander J.E.H. McBeath DSO, DSC, RN (of *Venemous* renown at Dunkirk a year earlier) commissioned the ship and after trials accepted it on behalf of the Admiralty. In doing so, he persuaded the Fairfield's Dockyard Manager to swap hats, giving him his naval cap and taking in exchange a splendid black 'bowler hat'. This was kept on the bridge and when we went to action stations Mac would don the bowler, to the delight of the ship's company. He was certainly a captain with a difference. Being born in South Africa and educated in Massachusetts had given him a wider, more worldly vision than the usual RN personality in command, whose original entry to the Navy was either 'Dart', indicating Dartmouth, or 'Pub', for Public School. Mac called all his officers by their first names, most times, although naturally he was always 'Sir' to us. This in no way diminished the sense of discipline, rather did it increase the feeling of being in a close-knit personal team. He was a teetotaller, but didn't mind us drinking, within limits and having fun, when in port, with Wardroom parties, some of which he would attend.

My fast lady's figure, with a displacement tonnage of 1540, was 345 ft, stem to stern by 35 ft beam and a draft of 9 ft approx. Her skin was welded, smooth and rather delicate, being less than ¼ of an inch thick, with no armoured corsets on her sides or deck to protect her from those predatory rapists, U-boats eager to penetrate her hull with their phallic weapons, torpedoes, or from attacks by their bully-boy brothers with bombs. Moving and manoeuvring at variable speeds up to a maximum of 35 knots (40 mph) was her best defence, provided by two steam turbines producing 40,000 SHP (shaft horse power). Also, in such a confined space, between decks, she created and cared for about 200 shipmates, on average, her floating family, of which I was happy to be one.

Shipmates accumulated fast before we went down the Clyde, to the Tail of the Bank between Greenock, Gourock and Helensburgh, to carry out trials, testing all the ship's equipment. As regards officers, St Leger Moore, Sub-Lieut RN and chain smoker, shared a cabin with me. He being senior had the lower bunk and me the upper, which meant I awoke each day in a thick choking cloud, when he lit up as our servant (same as batman in the army) produced our morning tea. No thought of cancer then, but to deal with any current disease, such as VD, we had Surgeon Lieut Bob Swan, RCNVR, from Winnipeg, Canada. Doug Little, a very large, slaphappy Lieut RNVR from a wealthy 'cotton' family on the Wirral in Lancashire and with a gorgeous actress wife called Annie living in London, became GCO (Gunnery Control Officer). Percy Bugle, Lieut RN, next senior to Benjie, fulfilled the role of navigator (Pilot) with me as his assistant, which suited me well. Percy said he was OK with coastal navigation, but admitted he was a bit lacking in experience off-shore and this was where my skills developed in merchant ships would prove handy. Our centre of operations was the charthouse, a small compartment, under the bridge, starboard side and alongside the captain's sea cabin, of similar size, on the port side. We had a chart table, with lots of chart folios in drawers underneath and a settee, used as a bunk by the Pilot when at sea. There were voice pipes from both captain's sea cabin and the charthouse to the bridge, which could be heard in common, sometimes helpful, but at other times an intrusion on a well deserved rest.

Senior ratings, standing-by in the early days, were 'Paddy' Bourke, CERA (Chief Engine Room Artificer), 'Jock' Graham, Chief Stoker, George Turnbull, OA (Ordnance Artificer), responsible for guns and Willis, the Chief Boatswain's Mate (Senior Seaman Petty Officer), the Buffer, so called because as his right-hand man, he came between No.1 and the seamen, for work to be done about the ship. All other ratings joined when the ship commissioned, including AB (Able Seaman) Bill Goodacre, an HO (Hostilities Only – rating in for 'duration of war' only) with 1½ years service already and who was made a Quartermaster. He was one of about eight ABs, whose duty on watch, at sea, was at the wheel steering the ship. With a Bosun's Mate (Assistant) to operate engine-room telegraphs and pipe orders, by walking round the ship, he was in charge of the wheelhouse, under the bridge, just for'd of the SDO (Signal Distribution Office). In harbour they were stationed on the quarter-deck, aft, by the gangway, aware of boat traffic, the comings and goings of personnel and responsible for piping the ship's routine, as ordered by No.1 through the OOD (Officer of the Day).

Watches at sea went thus, from midnight, 0000 to 0400 (the Middle), 0400 to 0800 (the Morning), 0800 to 1200 (the Forenoon), 1200 to 1600 (the Afternoon), 1600 to 1800 (the 'First Dog'), 1800 to 2000 (the 'Last Dog'), 2000 to 2400/0000 (the First) and so on. Dog-watches date back to days

Oribi. *Bill Goodacre ('Goody') in the chart-room*

of sail, when dog-days were lazy ones and the same applied to the ship's company's idle hours between tea and supper. The operation of two dog-watches made it possible, in a three watch ship, to have a three-day watch-cycle, giving everyone a change. A watch consisted of a group of men detailed off for such duty. Three watches at sea, maybe, but in harbour the ship's company was in two watches, Port and Starboard. When a man referred to his 'oppo', he meant his opposite number doing the same job in the other watch, as shown on the Watch and Quarters Bill, drawn up by No.1 and the Coxswain with the cooperation of heads of departments. Quartermasters came directly under the Coxswain, whose action station was on the wheel, a senior petty officer responsible for regulating disciplinary procedures overall, which entailed setting up, on separate occasions, the 1st Lieut's and Captain's tables, on the quarter-deck, to deal with Request Men and Defaulters, as and when required.

Dennis Easom joined as an OS (Ordinary Seaman) HO, having had basic training at HMS *Collingwood*, a 'stone frigate' (shore establishment). In the early days of the commission an interesting exchange took place on the upper deck of the *Oribi* between the most senior seaman, the Buffer and the most junior, OS Easom, when some seamanlike action was required. The Buffer turned to Easom and said 'Right lad, cut that rope.' Easom had to admit that his knife was down below in his locker, so the Buffer said 'Go get it lad' and when he returned, continued with this memorable piece of advice, 'Remember this lad, a seaman without his knife is about as useful as a bull without bollocks, so never forget it.' Dennis never did and in fact told me this story at a re-union in the nineties, all of fifty years after the event. He said recently, that to this day, when he puts a hand in his pocket to see if he has remembered something, not necessarily a knife, he always thinks of the Buffer. Within two years, in *Oribi*, Dennis went from OS to Leading Seaman, then was selected as CW candidate (Commissioned and Warrants Branch to become an officer). He finished the war as an RNVR officer in command of an 'X' Craft, one of our midget submarines.

As Assistant Pilot to Percy, the tedious part of the job was correcting charts, in the charthouse, from frequent issues of Notices to Mariners, but this was offset by exercises and quite often, the excitement of real action against the enemy, working on the ARL (Admiralty Research Laboratory) plot. The plot was in the SDO, directly under the bridge, with communication by voice pipe, its shape being four feet by three at table top height, with a glass, transparent surface, under which moved an illuminated compass rose driven on lateral and vertical cogs by the gyro compass, giving direction and the ship's log, protruding from under the hull, giving speed. A blank chart covered the glass surface, through which the light, indicating the ship's position, could be seen. A jointed arm, pivoted from the top right corner of the table, fitted at its free end with a circle, graduated in degrees with ruler attached, allowed *Oribi*'s course to be plotted. The position and movements of other vessels, relative to *Oribi*, could then be plotted by bearing and distance. Scales on the plot could be varied according to the situation. A small scale would be used to keep track of the ship's position, in latitude and longitude (by transferring the course and distance steamed to the navigational chart on the bridge) and also the ship's position relative to a convoy when screening at a distance and zig-zagging in order to confuse any U-boat commander who might be observing us through his periscope.

There was also a direct voice pipe to a hut on the port side of the bridge containing the Asdic equipment. This was a submarine detecting device based on the reflection of a sound-transmission from an object in the water. An operator, in head-phones, swept with his Asdic dome, also protruding from under the hull, from 80 degrees on each bow, alternately, to ahead, in 5 degree steps, transmitting (ping) at each step and pausing in case an echo (wop) was heard, which might indicate a U-boat, or maybe just a shoal of fish. The sound was 'ping', fading away, until suddenly, 'ping – wop' and so on. If the wop was lower than the ping, then it was opening doppler, target going away, but if the wop was higher, then it was closing doppler, target coming towards. With the plot in a larger, attacking, scale, this information could be plotted and after a short time, the course and speed of a U-boat could be determined. On hearing an echo, the operator would shout out, for example 'Echo bearing red four-five, range six thousand', meaning he had detected something at 45 degrees on the port bow, 6,000 yards (3 miles) away. This was heard by the Officer of the Watch (OOW) on the bridge and whoever was keeping watch on the plot. Whenever at sea acting as a convoy escort, or screening fleet units such as battleships and/or aircraft-carriers, the Asdic transmissions would be broadcast through a loudspeaker on the bridge to make the OOW immediately aware of any echos. The sound comes easily to me even now, having lived with it, on and off, for three years in *Oribi*.

The focal point of the ship was the bridge and the lay-out as follows: on a raised platform, in the middle were two compass binnacles. The gyro was dominant, about five feet tall, topped with a rotating ring, fitted with prism for taking horizontal bearings and commanding an all round view of the horizon except for a narrow arc of about thirty degrees, obscured by the tripod mast and funnel, abaft the bridge. The master gyro was suspended by a wire, in the bowels of the ship and controlled the gyro compass card in the bridge binnacle, one of many links to repeaters throughout the ship. A few feet behind, was the solid wooden magnetic binnacle with its compensating magnets, acting as a check on the gyro and available for navigation and steering, should the gyro fail. A similar arrangement was in the wheelhouse, except the gyro repeater was a magnified, illuminated band at eye level, over the magnetic compass, in front of the helmsman.

Stepping down to a level two feet below and for'd of the bridge compass platform, enabled the OOW to work on the chart table, recessed into forward side of the bridge, with a canvas screen to drop for black-out. Over this area, from port to starb'd, was a metal canopy about a foot in width from fore to aft and on the vertical forward support side it had windows right across allowing a clear view ahead. In heavy weather, when she shipped it green over the fo'c'sle, the thing to do was dash under the canopy and with luck escape any spray going down your neck as it lashed across the bridge. On each side of the bridge was a large fixed signal lantern, with shutters worked by a bar handle, used for long distance morse signalling by light and giving out a cheerful clapping sound as it spelt out the message. The flag deck was close behind the bridge, with halyards up to the mast-head and yard-arms and all the signalmen, including the Yeoman were called 'bunting tossers' by their shipmates. Finally, the two most important items on the bridge were the captain's high-chair, solidly made of wood for long periods at 'action stations' and of course the distinguished black 'bowler hat' from Govan.

It was essential that a new ship should work-up for a few weeks to reach a high standard of efficiency before going on active service. This required masses of exercises for the crew to become familiar with the ship and the effective operation of everything onboard, carried out in a reasonably safe area. So, off we went to Scapa Flow in the Orkney Islands, base of the Home Fleet, anchored in Hoxa Sound. We set off south through the Cumbraes, round the Mull of Kintyre, north through the Minches, round Cape Wrath and due east (090 by gyro) to the petulant Pentland Firth, that stretch of turbulent water between Scotland and the Orkneys. Hard a'port and in through the boom defence gate to Gutter Sound on south-east side of the Island of Hoy, which was the destroyer haven with lots of buoys for berths and our depot ship HMS *Tyne*, with ex-merchantman *Dunluce Castle*, nearby, providing accommodation for relief crews and transfers. Lyness, a few scattered buildings ashore, one of which was a Church of Scotland tea-hut, surrounded by sheep, was the only sign of habitation. There was little incentive to go ashore, except for a good long walk, with trees conspicuous by their absence. We were told that the only tree in the Orkneys was in the graveyard of capital, Kirkwall, on the north side of the Flow. Our lifestyle improved considerably when the WRNS came to Scapa a year or two later!

The first exercise, I recall, was not self-motivated shipwise, but came from higher authority in the Flow. One day, about 0900, the Yeoman of Signals, Munroe (brought with Mac from *Venemous*) told Percy that a visual signal from C-in-C Home Fleet in KG V (HMS *King George the Fifth*) seen from the anchorage over the island of Hoxa, said there was to be a mock fleet exercise for all ships in harbour, conducted by flags and visual lamp signals, because of W/T (Wireless Telegraphy) silence, usually imposed, simulating a fleet action at sea against similar enemy forces. Percy said 'Ian, I'll be on the bridge with the Yeoman and with you on the plot, we shall distinguish ourselves, no doubt.' 'Aye, aye Percy, but isn't this a bit "old hat"? an anachronism, surely? I know our destroyers didn't do too well in their torpedo attack against the *Bismarck* in May this year, and I suppose they're thinking of the *Tirpitz* now, but, well (with *Jervis Bay* in mind), isn't the real battle out in the Atlantic, protecting our merchant shipping, our very life-line for food, fuel and all other commodities to enable us to continue this war?' Percy agreed, but of course we did the exercise, successfully sinking an imaginary battleship with our torpedoes, which we never did in reality. Most of our time was spent screening convoys. We wondered whether 'Their Lordships', with their assumed Whitehall wisdom, were quite 'with it'. More comment on such personal views, in the light of experience, throughout this book.

We had four 4.7-inch guns: A on the fo'c'sle, B one deck up, in front of and just below the bridge, X down aft on super-structure, with Y further aft on the quarter-deck, all with a maximum elevation of 45 degrees, would you believe it, after Dunkirk and all that? We did have a 4-inch A/A (anti-aircraft) gun, just for'd of X gun, in the space intended for four torpedoes, which reduced our complement from eight to four of those things amidships. Abaft the funnel on a platform we had a 4-barrelled (two-pounder) Pom pom, handy against aircraft and also 4 single-barrel 20 mm-Oerlikons were placed strategically round the ship, fore and aft, two on each side. The Director, for controlling the guns, was like a big basin between the back of the bridge and the mast, at a higher level to give an unobstructed view and built to contain four to six operators with Doug Little (GCO) in the middle and fitted with a large visual rangefinder and also radar antennae projecting horizontally forward above their heads.

Whatever the Director did was relayed to the TS (Transmitting Station) in the superstructure below, where it was transposed into instructions to the guns. I mustn't get too involved here because I'm not a gunnery man, but basically, at each gun, on bucket seats either side of the breech, was a Layer (for elevation) and a Trainer (for direction), each following a pointer on a dial, controlled from the TS, by turning handles this way and that, in order to stay spot-on. When *Oribi* rolled and pitched during a shoot, in the days before stabilizers, this was a tricky business, but practice improved standards. Many a day when berthed in Gutter Sound we sent TS and guns crews to exercises on simulators aboard the *Tyne*, and this was much easier and more economical than going to sea each time.

When we did go to sea for a practice shoot, it was many miles to the west of the 'Old Man of Hoy', a conspicuous pillar of rock on the coast, very like Nelson's Column in Trafalgar Square, and way out there we used two small, uninhabited, rocky islets as targets. Sometimes we used a moving surface target, towed at a safe distance by a tug. Other times, we exercised our 4-inch A-A gun by shooting at a sleeve towed by a Fleet Air Arm Swordfish biplane. On one such occasion a shell burst slightly closer to the aircraft than the sleeve and quick as a flash the Observer in the Swordfish flashed a signal on his Aldis-lamp, 'For your information, we're pulling this bloody thing, not pushing it!'

Throughout the exercises off-shore we were becoming more familiar, day by day, with the latest technology, Radar, the official name for the principle of radio-location. In addition to the one for gunnery, we had radar mounted on the mast, with an all round sweep to detect objects on the surface and in the air, with a range of about 20 miles. The four Seaman Radar Ratings operated the radar from within the SDO, alongside the plot, sitting on a stool, facing a 12-inch monitor which indicated distance-off and relative bearing of an object as directed by the operator. A black canvas curtain hung from the deckhead, to surround him and help his vision and concentration, with a voice-pipe to report direct to the bridge above. In those early days of radar the operators, and they were all Scottish, had faith in their equipment, which is more than Mac and most of us had. They realized that they had to build up our confidence by showing it in operation

successfully on the high seas. To prove their case, an operator on the
monitor would shout up the voice pipe to his mate on the bridge armed
with binoculars 'Ahoy Jimmy, I've got a wee object on the port bow, red
50 at 4000 yards. Can you see anything out there?' 'Aye, indeed I can Jack,
there's a trawler on that bearing about 2 miles away,' and this was in hearing
distance of the captain. It took a little time, but gradually we all realized
that this latest toy was invaluable, especially as an aid to navigation. Soon,
I was working closely with the radar boys in fog and at night, when they
could give me distance and bearing on an edge of land and Mac, from his
great height, stopped looking down his nose and ridiculing them.

It must be mentioned that in many situations the ship had to conceal its
presence from the enemy and this required radar to remain switched off as
well as maintaining W/T (Wireless/Telegraphy) silence. Therefore, the
presence of land, surface or aircraft in the ship's vicinity had to be detected
by look-outs. There were two on each side, below bridge level, within
shouting range of the OOW, each responsible for 90 degrees from abeam
to ahead and abeam to astern, sitting in bucket seats with binoculars
mounted on a post between their legs. They were trained to be aware of
peripheral vision, seeing something on the horizon or in the sky, out of the
side of the eye and then amplifying with the glasses. It worked well, but as
their main problem was staying awake, the OOW or a signalman would
lean outboard and have a chat occasionally.

On Monday 4 August, at the crack of dawn, we were despatched to the
mainland of Scotland to meet a VIP plus staff arriving by train at Thurso in
the forenoon. We anchored in Scrabster Bay and about 0930 a drifter
named *Smiling Morn* came alongside and discharged Winston Churchill, his
Chiefs of Staff and a few others. When offered shelter from the drizzle that
had set in, the Prime Minister said 'No, the place for action is the bridge.'
There he stood on the compass platform, cigar in mouth, collar up and with
eyes screwed against the wind and driving rain. Mac was in charge at the
gyro binnacle, not in bowler hat I hasten to say, surrounded by Admiral Sir
Dudley Pound, the First Sea Lord, General Sir John Dill, Chief of Imperial
General Staff, Air-Chief Marshal Sir Wilfrid Freeman, Vice-Chief of the Air
Staff, Sir Alexander Cadogan of the Foreign Office and a tall unsmiling
man, Lord Cherwell (until recently Professor Lindemann), friend and
confidant of the Prime Minister. Owzat, for a name-dropping exercise?

Two of the others who came onboard were H.V. Morton (travel author)
and Howard Spring (journalist/novelist) whom we entertained in the
Wardroom. Their destination was still a well kept secret, although we
guessed, as did others, that it was a rendezvous with President Roosevelt,
recently reported by the US Press as going on a fishing holiday off New
England. As we went alongside the *Prince of Wales*, we could almost hear a

whisper go round the battleship – 'It's Winston!' Later in August, after Winston had returned home, it was made known that on 12 August 'The Atlantic Charter' was agreed in Placentia Bay, Newfoundland stating new hopes for a future world. Morton wrote *Atlantic Meeting*, given to me by my father for Xmas in 1943 and I met Spring's son, Lieut RNVR, in Portsmouth Dockyard, 1945, putting ships into Reserve Fleet after VJ Day. In fact, over a gin or two, we swapped a blanket for a duffel coat to balance our respective audits. After the war I read, with great interest, Howard Spring's autobiography and the title, I think, was *Fame is the Spur*. Born and brought up in the Splott area of Cardiff, the quotation at the front of his book said everything about the tough struggle he had in his early years. I remember it well as:

> Fame is the spur that the clear spirit doth raise
> To scorn delights and live laborious days.
>
> *Milton*

Come the third week in August it was decided we were 'worked up' sufficiently and we returned to the Clyde for Fairfields Shipyard to deal with minor repairs. Leave was given, a few days to each watch, and most people took advantage. I think it was because of my pre-war experience in Canadian Pacific Steamships, running to Canada and becoming what I called a mid-Atlantic character, that I established a really good rapport with Bob Swan, the 'Doc' as he was called. Bob said to me 'Gee Ian, how about a night out in London?' Well naturally, it appealed, but on my pay of five shillings (25p) a day, the idea seemed absurd until he followed up with 'Of course, I'll pick up the bills on my pay (whatever it was as a Canadian Lieutenant) and besides, I've just got to visit the Ritz Hotel.' Why, he never explained, but maybe the folks in Winnipeg expected it of him and would be impressed. Railway vouchers were supplied to forces personnel in wartime, so that helped and we got them from the Writer in the ship's office.

We went to the Ritz to satisfy Bob's desire, but it was almost empty and we moved on to the Embassy Club, where as officers we were made honorary members. The calypso music by Edmundo Ross was great, but the atmosphere was frightfully formal and nothing like the Boogie Club in Denman St, discovered by me, later, in '42, run by black guys and dolls and which, as a member, was my favourite port of call when passing through London on leave throughout the rest of the war. A knock opened a sliding slot on the door, revealing a cheerful Caribbean grin and when I showed my member's card, a welcoming voice said 'You back on leave again Boss? Well, come right in.' Inside this dusky, colourful, jitterbugging joint, anyone danced with anyone else and Fats Waller, had he been there, would surely have played 'Jumpin Jive'. It seemed my mid-Atlantic, merchantman, upbringing was asserting itself in the heart of Soho. Pity about the Ritz in '41.

We had booked in to a twin-bedded double room, to cut the cost, at the Green Park Hotel in Half Moon Street, so back there we went to pass out, peacefully, assisted by a bottle of Canadian Club Whisky. In the early hours I got the urge to pee and as we were not en suite, I wandered along the landing to the loo. On the return journey, I heaved a sigh of relief in my half-asleep state, opened a door and entered a room I thought was ours just as the air-raid sirens sounded a 'red alert'. Imagine my surprise when a figure sat up in bed and it wasn't Bob. At a glance, I appreciated the figure of a gorgeous young lady in a state of fright, understandably. 'Where's the shelter?' she said, hoisting a sheet in front of her for modesty. Rather than answer her question, I acted with chivalrous initiative, jumped into bed beside her and said 'I'm here to shelter you,' whereupon, I was rewarded with a warm welcoming hug, which smothered the sound of the sirens. About five hours later I slipped away quietly from my loved one, we never did exchange names, leaving her to snooze on, with a satisfied smile and thinking to myself 'What a blitz that was!' 'Where the hell have you been buddy?' said Bob, when I found our room. 'I'll tell you in the train on the way back to Glasgow,' I said and as we checked out at reception I glanced towards the stairs and there she was. A wave and a blown kiss ended our brief, but mutually supportive, wartime friendship.

Back aboard *Oribi* we were greeted by a new shipmate with four legs answering to the name of 'Bastard'. Apparently, the day before, Jock Graham had ascended from the boiler room and was wiping his oily hands with cotton waste, on the upper deck, when up the gangway walked a fellow Glaswegian in the shape of a handsome black and white fox terrier. 'Come 'ere you young bastard,' said Jock and a patting hand with a wagging tail reaction ensured that he was now a member of the crew. 'How did you know his name Jock, is he your dog?' said a seaman standing nearby. 'No, he's not, but he is now and his name's Bastard from now on.' For the next two years this four-legged friend was loved and cared for by everyone onboard. Never at a loss for food he got assistance at all ship's ladders which were very steep and almost vertical. He could scramble up OK, but soon learned to wait at the top, for the next person along to carry him down. Also, he was quick to learn that a sea-dog had a bitch in every port, but more about that later.

Oribi was the only 'O' Class destroyer operational, because the remaining seven ships, which would form the 17th Destroyer Flotilla, 17th DF, had not yet been completed. Being ready for action, we sailed from Greenock on 17 September as part of the 19th Destroyer Flotilla, under the command

Oribi. *'Bastard'*.
An important member of the crew

of HMS *Laforey*, Captain D's ship, known as D19, in company with the Dutch destroyer *Isaac Sweers*. We were on Operation 'Halberd', the passage of convoy WS11 X from Gibraltar through to Malta. The island of Malta had been under siege since Italy entered the war, when France fell to the Nazis in 1940, but air attacks had intensified recently, with German bombers joining in, to support their life-line to Rommel's Afrika Korps in Libya. The fourteen superior merchant ships, reasonably fast, say 15 knots, drawn from such Companies as Blue Star, Clan Line, Ellerman City and Union Castle, sailed out north of Ireland where we were joined by a larger group of ships from Liverpool, to form an Atlantic convoy. The majority, of about 40 in total, were destined for somewhere beyond the Cape of Good Hope and as mid-Atlantic was the safest area in which to head south, we did that, until in the latitude of Gibraltar, we peeled off with the WS11 X ships and headed east for the Mediterranean.

Some of us destroyers detached from this convoy and went ahead at high speed to enter Gib at night on 23rd in order to refuel the next day. There we were, doing 25 knots, blacked out, in a very dark night and sensibly closed up at 'Relaxed Action Stations', which meant Coxswain on the wheel and Captain Mac directing the ship at the gyro on the bridge, with me alongside him. Suddenly, a shout from both starboard look-outs 'Ship green 90 close.' Mac and I saw on the starboard beam the knife-edge bow of a destroyer coming at us fast. 'Hard a' starboard,' shouted Mac down the voice-pipe. 'Hard a'starboard sir,' replied the Coxs'n, spinning the wheel rapidly to the right. We hoped the other ship would go hard a'port to clear our stern and that she did. Our bow went to the right and our stern, from about the mast aft, swung away from the would have been intrusive bow, missing us by inches all the way down the side until this unknown vessel disappeared into the night astern. 'Midships, meet 'er,' said Mac, which the Coxs'n repeated, followed by 'Bring 'er back to 090, then steady as you go.' 'Well' said our captain to those present 'after that close shave I think we all deserve a cup of Kie [ship's cocoa], signalman, knock-up a brew.' About a year later, we were having a joint Wardroom party with a chummy destroyer on the Russian run, HMS *Fury*, in Murmansk, and talking about near-misses, when their No.1, Ian Clegg, told us about some daft bugger crossing their bow when they were patrolling the Straits of Gib. Having swapped dates and times our No.1, Benjie McLeod, responded typically 'Oh, so it was you stupid sods, not keeping a look-out, that almost chopped us in two.' We remained chummy ships regardless.

Berthed in Gib for the day, Percy stood me lunch, way up high, in the Rock Hotel, the closest I ever got to those Barbary Apes who live on the top of the rock. During the night 24/25, to avoid spying Italian eyes from the Spanish mainland opposite, we sailed away to the east and into the Med. Here we joined the Malta bound merchant ships who had come through the Straits in the dark hours and were now supported by a huge naval force for operation 'Halberd'. It included the battleships *Prince of Wales*, *Nelson* and *Rodney*, the cruisers *Edinburgh*, *Kenya* and *Sheffield*, with about 20 destroyers, including 3 Tribal Class, *Cossack*, *Zulu* and *Gurkha*, plus we three of the 19th DF, providing an outer A/S (anti-submarine) screen. Also present was the aircraft-carrier *Ark Royal*, which had been sunk many times by Lord Haw-haw on his propaganda radio station 'Gairmany Calling' and which provided Fulmar fighter cover for the convoy for the next three days. Owzat for notable naval ship name dropping? Sadly, *Ark Royal* was in fact sunk in the Med, by an Italian sub, two months later, in November '41.

In daylight on 27th we had three attacks pressed home by Italian torpedo bombers, coming in low to drop their fish, two of which came close to us, but we dodged them. Flak from the big ships aimed at these aircraft was bursting over our heads and we had two guns' crew wounded by falling shrapnel. That evening, four more attacks took place, on the last of which a torpedo was dropped just abaft our port beam, which we avoided by turning stern-on and increasing to full speed. This aircraft was shot down by our pom-pom and Oerlikon guns. The MV (Motor vessel) *Imperial Star*, of 10,000 gross tons, was less fortunate, being hit port side aft by a torpedo which damaged her rudder and propeller, causing her to remain stopped and helpless at 2030 hours. *Heythrop*, a smaller Hunt Class destroyer was ordered by the Convoy Commodore to take off *Imperial Star*'s passengers and rejoin the convoy. *Oribi* was told to take the only casualty of the convoy in tow to Malta.

We got a tow going, even working up to 8 knots, but her flooded compartments, giving her a draft of 38 ft aft and her jammed rudder, made her sheer off, dragging us round in circles, stern first and forcing us to slip the tow. On this fine moonlit night we tried for four hours without success and reluctantly had to remove the persons aboard and attempt to scuttle her. Because her valves were jammed scuttling was impossible, so we lashed three depth charges together below the waterline, fired by a safety fuse. We shelled her and left her on fire and sinking at 0500. Happily, no lives were lost, but I shall never forget her Master's face, standing near me on the bridge of *Oribi*, with tears in his eyes as he watched his lovely mistress being put to death. My eyes were moist too. With 220 miles to go to Malta, mostly in daylight, Mac wisely decided to sail close to the Sicilian coast, about 7 miles off, and fly the Italian flag. All guns were trained fore and aft to indicate no action was expected and crew kept off the upper deck. We were circled by Stukas and Heinkels but left alone and being first of a new Class probably helped. They would have recognized a Tribal any day by its distinctive silhouette.

We arrived, with the convoy, at Malta just after noon and berthed alongside a cruiser in Valetta harbour. Within the hour the air-raid sirens sounded and the OOW on the cruiser's quarterdeck looked down from a great height on ours below, where Quartermaster Bill Goodacre and his Bosun's Mate Harry Dempster (a lively, lovable, cockney shipmate) were on watch. 'Don't worry, they always do a bit of air reconnaisance at this time of day' shouted the OOW, followed by a whistling noise and a loud bang nearby, as a bomb fell in the harbour. Harry's quick response to the advice from above, was 'Quite right sir, but I think 'e must 'ave dropped 'is bleedin' camera!'

Hugging the North African coast the 19th DF got back to Gib on 30 Sept and to the UK by 6 October. In April 1942 King George VI awarded the Island Fortress of Malta the George Cross and in 1992 a fiftieth anniversary medal was granted by the President of Malta to all people involved with the island's battle between 1940 and '43. A Presentation Ceremony was held at the Malta High Commission, London, in January '94, when Bill and I received our gongs from the High Commissioner Salv. J. Stellini. He spoke sincerely and ended most humorously when he said he remembered nothing about the war himself, as he was only one year old in '42, but his mother had told him years later that for her the most important piece of cargo carried by a convoy to Malta was a case of Johnson's Baby Powder. He thanked us now, personally, for the creature comfort we had brought to him at that time in his life.

During our absence two more 'O' Class destroyers had completed on the Clyde and were 'working up' at Scapa Flow when we returned in mid–October. They were *Offa* and *Onslow*, the latter being our Captain (D) of the 17th Destroyer Flotilla, who in person was Captain (4 rings by rank) H.T. Armstrong DSC, affectionately called 'Beaky' because of his notice-able nose. Apart from captaining *Onslow* with its normal complement of officers and crew, Beaky had about six or seven Staff Officers, specialists in such things as torpedoes, guns, Asdics and so on, who operated throughout the flotilla. The Specialist (N), for navigation, was Peter Wyatt, a large jovial Lieutenant RN, with a big black beard, with whom Percy and I soon became friendly. Also, we got to know the officers of the *Offa*: Bill O'Brien, No.1, David Unwin, the navigator, Gilbert Forsyth, the Doc from Fife, two Sub-Lieuts, Arthur Power RN and Dennis Earle RNVR from New Zealand, all captained by Alastair Ewing, a Lieut-Cdr like Mac.

CHAPTER 9

HMS *Oribi*: part 2

W HEN HITLER ATTACKED THE USSR in June '41, he turned a dubious neutral into our immediate Ally and no longer did we stand and fight alone. The first convoy sailed from Liverpool to North Russia in August. The first of our many trips on the 'Russian Run' was to provide an escort for PQ 5, a convoy consisting of 5 British and 2 Russian merchant ships, in company with the cruiser *Sheffield* and three minesweepers, on 1 December. There was no enemy activity this time, but the future was very different. We detached on the 7th to enter the Kola Inlet and the convoy went on to Archangel. The Kola Inlet runs north and south in the latitude of 69 N, with Polyarnoe, HQ of the Russian Northern Fleet, about 5 miles inside on the western shore. SBNONR, Senior British Naval Officer, North Russia (a Rear-Admiral later) was also stationed there. Vaenga Bay was a large anchorage, with a signal station, opposite Polyarnoe. The landscape surrounding the Kola Inlet was bleak, snow-covered tundra. Murmansk, the main port for merchant ships to unload, was a further 25 miles up the creek on the eastern shore. We berthed alongside the Russian destroyer *Kuibyshev* on the jetty at Polyarnoe, where we received a warm welcome, along with much swallowing hospitality, in between air-raids from German occupied Finland, 30 miles away. We heard later that the Japs had bombed Pearl Harbour that very day, 7 December, and that the US was now at war with the Axis Powers.

The scene was set for a Russian party, the like of which I have never known since and it was between us seamen, who have a lot in common the world over. Soviet ships had not yet been contaminated by Political Commissars, which included minimizing fraternization, but their presence was being felt, when next we visited Murmansk in March '42. On this occasion, in December '41, the captain and officers of the *Kuibyshev* invited their opposite numbers in the *Oribi* to a meal in mid-afternoon. It was eight a side sitting alternately, Russki, Brit, around the outside of a long U-shaped table, with both captains and an interpreter at the short top table. The space in the centre was for numerous stewards with large carafes to distribute vodka. There was a deathly hush in their warm friendly Wardroom as we sat, each with a small glass, about 2 inches high by 1 inch in diameter, which was replenished frequently with neat vodka. Then tap tap from a gavel and up stood the Russian Captain who said 'To Churchill'. We all stood and repeated 'To Churchill,' followed by someone saying 'To bottom,' which we again repeated and downed the vodka in one gulp,

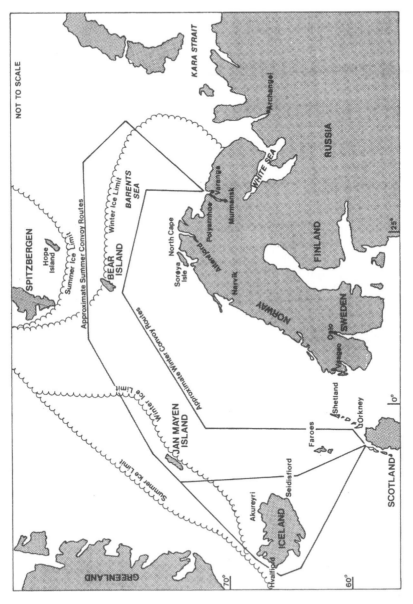

Approximate summer and winter convoy routes from the United Kingdom and Iceland to Murmansk, North Russia

leaving an empty glass, but not for long. We sat down and the Russki on my right thrust a plate of black bread in my direction, making encouraging eating signs, which I interpreted as 'you'll need this between toasts, to stay in touch'. A few minutes elapsed, then tap tap and Mac was on his feet saying 'To Stalin.' 'To Stalin' and 'To bottom' from everyone, with more black bread. People began chattering now as we toasted Anthony Eden and Molotov, the Foreign Secretaries, before moving on to Generals Wavell and Voroshilov and almost any Russian or British that came to their minds.

The decibels increased as neighbours talked to each other in whatever language suited them best and indulged in some friendly back-slapping. My Russki friend said 'Where your home?' to which I replied 'Cardiff' and this meant 'Da, da – To Cardiff! – To bottom.' Then from me to him 'And your home is?' Back came 'Sevastopol,' leading to 'Yes, yes – To Sevastopol! – To bottom.' I forgot to say that whilst all this was going on, we consumed large platefuls of exquisite caviar, a first time for me. After about two hours of vodka-induced chat, with a shanty or two thrown in, Mac beckoned to me and said 'Ian, go back and tell Percy (who was OOD in *Oribi*) that we have been invited to stay on and see a film.' Taking great care I negotiated the cold upper decks, descended to a sober Percy in our own warm Wardroom Mess and delivered Mac's message coherently. All I remember after that, is feeling very happy about our new Ally, leaving the Mess, turning right into the nearest cabin, which happened to be the Doc's, climbing into the bunk and passing out until 0500 hours next morning. Doc slept on the Wardroom settee that night and I believe only two from each ship were capable of watching the film. We had a return match a few days later, offering them trayloads of neat duty-free brandy, gin, rum and whisky, in sherry glasses. Then it was agreed that the honour of becoming allies had been satisfied and both ships resumed normal social behaviour.

We sailed back to Scapa independently before Christmas, where it was all go, preparing for Operation 'Archery', the Commando Raid on Vaagso in Norway. A.D. Hunt (Mike), Sub-Lieut RNR, ex-Union Castle Line, trained at Pangbourne Nautical College and who became a lifelong friend, joined *Oribi* on our return. We left Scapa, for Sollum Voe in the Shetland Islands, on Christmas Eve and endured a westerly gale Force 8, which caused damage to some ships on passage. The joint force commanders Rear-Admiral Burrough and Brigadier Haydon, together in the former's flagship, the cruiser, HMS *Kenya*, decided to postpone the raid for twenty-four hours. With Mountbatten at the helm, cutting through red-tape and improving inter-service cooperation, Combined Operations developed a new sense of urgency. Within two months he was ready for Vaagso, his first big raid, which was to have a subtle influence on the whole future course of the war. The objective was to destroy the German garrison in the little Norwegian port of South Vaagso, blow up the fish-oil factories, sink shipping, bring back volunteers to Britain, capture code-books and round up Quislings, so named after the prime Nazi collaborator in Norway. The more Germans defending the European coast, the fewer would be available to fight in Russia and North Africa.

Vaagso Island was on the tip of Norway's elbow shaped coastline, about 100 miles north of Bergen in latitude 62 N. It lay on the north-west side of Vaagsfjord, the largest of several snow-covered, mountainous islands, with the village ports of South and North Vaagso at each end of Ulvesund, a narrow channel on its eastern sheltered side. The garrison was estimated at 150 infantry plus 100 Labour Corps, with gun batteries covering the fjord on two other islands, further in. Our force consisted of *Kenya* (HQ ship), *Onslow*, *Oribi*, *Offa* and *Chiddingfold* (Hunt Class destroyer), escorting two infantry assault ships, *Prince Charles* and *Prince Leopold* carrying the Commandos (51 officers and 525 other ranks). The RAF had two bases within operational range, at Sumburgh in the Shetlands and Wick in the north of Scotland, 250 and 400 miles respectively from Vaagso. Bombing missions were assigned to Hampdens and continuous fighter cover was provided by Beaufighters and Blenheims of Coastal Command.

The force sailed from Sollum Voe on Boxing Day afternoon and on the bitterly cold, clear, dawn of the 27th we saw the snowclad land of Norway ahead rising out of the sea, with a pin-prick of light in our direction from the conning tower of HM Submarine *Tuna* indicating our landfall was spot on. Closed up at action stations, there came a cry from the GCO in our Director 'Go on Jimmy bomb the bastards' coinciding with the Hampdens delivering a low level bombing attack on the gun emplacements and dropping smoke bombs where the commandos were going to land. We had a grandstand view of Doug's elder brother Jimmy, a Wing Commander in the RAF, leading the squadron in, which gave it the feel of a family party. At the same time, about 0850 hours, *Kenya* opened fire with her 6-inch guns on the shore batteries. It was a complete surprise to the enemy who thought we were one of their convoys coming down the coast. As we ran into the fjord I saw lots of them leaping out of lavatories with trousers literally round their ankles as we increased their speed of progress with our small arms. We had 100 commandos aboard, to land round the corner, past Maaloy Island, in Ulvesund, between South and North Vaagso, to prevent reinforcements coming south. This we did without difficulty and as the operation progressed, the skirling of Major Jack Churchill's bagpipes could be heard playing 'The March of the Cameron Men', somewhere in the fjord, to inspire the natives as well as the invading troops.

German merchant ships came merrily down the Ulvesund channel thinking we were one of their destroyers, but when getting the message with a shell or two from our guns, they ran themselves aground. That was a pity because Mac had told Mike and me that as RNRs, who better to take prizes back across the North Sea. However, we did take a lot of prisoners, merchantmen and Quislings, plus a large group of free-Norwegians who wished to resume fighting with us. It was a glorious happy day and everything went our way. A few ME 109s and Heinkels showed up in the afternoon but were soon seen off, before we departed to the west at sunset. When we had moored to the buoy in Gutter Sound, Scapa, I had a memorable few words with one of our prisoners, a middle aged merchantman. Looking to the north he saw the bottom of an upturned hull and said 'Vot is that please?' I replied that it was the cruiser *Derfflinger*, one of the their High Seas Fleet scuttled in June 1919 and recently salvaged. Then he amazed me by saying sadly, 'I once served as a seaman in *Derfflinger*.' I nodded with nautical nous and thought to myself, he's probably thinking about the happy times with his shipmates in those days, and why not?

Hitler was furious with our audacity and not being satisfied with the advice he received from the military, delivered his own verdict in the month of January 1942. He said 'Norway is the zone of destiny in this war. I demand unconditional obedience to my commands and directives concerning the defence of this area.' His statement resulted in many big ship moves. The battleship *Tirpitz* sailed from the Baltic and reached Norway in safety. Then on 11 February '42 *Scharnhorst*, *Gneisenau* and *Prinz Eugen* broke out of Brest and made their successful dash up the English Channel, under the command of Admiral Otto Ciliax, ultimately to reach Trondheim in Norway. Then in March *Hipper* and *Lutzow* joined them. Apparently, Hitler just sent for Grand Admiral Raeder and told him that the German fleet must now use all its forces for the defence of Norway. It was said soon after the Vaagso raid that seldom in the history of warfare has so much been gained strategically by so small a force. The code name 'Archery' was most appropriate, the arrow having certainly struck the gold.

In January St Leger Moore left and my new cabin-mate was Sub-Lieut John W. (Spud) Murphy, RNVR. A Classics Master at a Public School in peacetime he had been AB then CW rating in a Tribal destroyer before training at King Alfred in Brighton. Six years older than me, of similar build with most expressive face, a natural wit with flexible voice, he could mimic anyone in any dialect, his favourite being Irish, inherited from his mother. Definitely a great asset to the Wardroom Mess and we formed a friendship which generated a lot of fun for us and for our messmates in *Oribi*. The Admiralty said that Navigators could appoint a suitable seaman as Yeoman, so AB Bill Goodacre was offered the job by Percy and accepted. He was ideal, being of superior intelligence, bags of initiative and with immaculate skills on the plot and correcting charts. He was called 'Goody' from then on by everyone, including Mac. Also he was made Ship's Musician and Ship's Librarian, each new job worth 3d (1 ¼p) per day extra on his pay.

Mac introduced a blue battle-dress to destroyers in Scapa. His, tailored at Gieves Ltd (the naval tailors in London and Portsmouth), was of very superior cloth, but he suggested that we officers got army ones and had them dyed because it was OK with him for us to wear them at sea instead of reefers. Early in February we went to the Clyde for a boiler clean, which allowed four days leave for each watch, so home I went to Cardiff and swapped some duty-free fags with a friend for a Home Guard khaki battledress, which Achille Serres dyed navy blue overnight. What a sensible garment, with plenty of pockets and lots of space for sweaters and the Mae West inflatable life belt. When at sea this was always worn, in a deflated condition, tied under the arms, round the chest and held up by a canvas strap around the neck. So called because when inflated, we resembled that well endowed lady film star of the 30s. When she heard about it she said, figuratively speaking, 'Gee that's great, to know that my personal contribution to the war effort is keeping the boys afloat.'

Later in February captain Mac granted my request to start growing a second beard and we sailed to Iceland where we met our latest allies in the US Navy. We British had occupied this strategic place in mid-Atlantic during the summer of 1940, to forestall any possible German ideas and the US, in the summer of '41 had taken over the occupation to release our forces to fight elsewhere. Iceland had three ports: Reykjavik, in the south-west corner, having a large anchorage for merchantmen with Hvalfjord, a big, long fjord branching off it to the north for use by naval ships; Akureyri, in the middle of the north coast and Seydisfjordur on the east coast. We used all three at various times, but mostly Hvalfjord (Reykjavik). The US boys were pleased to welcome us and being 'dry' (no booze) in their Wardrooms, a good deal of bartering went on, such as a bottle of Gordon's gin for two cartons of Lucky Strike or Camels. Also, later, we organized silk stockings from them for our girl friends and wore them under our 'long johns', on the Russian run, to keep warm, before presenting them back home.

By weird coincidence I am writing this on St David's Day 2002, exactly 60 years, to the day, after the Russian Convoy PQ 12 sailed from Reykjavik, on 1 March 1942. The convoy consisted of 18 merchant ships, 7 British, 7 American and 4 Russian and another bizarre fact has just become apparent. The convoy Commodore (Captain H.T. Hudson RNR), with his communications staff of four, flew his flag in *Llandaff*, named after an ancient cathedral village on the Banks of the River Taff, now part of the City of Cardiff. Commodores of convoys if not RNR were usually retired Admirals RN recalled as experienced, professional resources.

Before this and many other Russian sorties, I want to create a picture in the mind of what a convoy looked like at sea. The standard form for all convoys was rectangular, with a 'broad front' of numbered short columns, the port (left) hand one being 1 so on. For example PQ 12 had 6 columns, suitably spaced with 3 ships in each column. The *Llandaff* was No. 31, which meant she was in column 3, in the front as 1, which was a good position for the Commodore to exercise control. Convoy size varied vastly and our next one, PQ 16 in May, had 36 ships, which disposed itself as 9 columns of 4, with the Commodore in *Ocean Prince* as No. 51, but more about that convoy later. The close escort surrounded the convoy to protect it from enemy attacks by U-boat, surface ship or aircraft and consisted of destroyers, minesweepers, corvettes, trawlers and sometimes whalers, the last two named usually astern to act as rescue ships.

Because of the recent concentration of Kriegsmarine battleships and cruisers in Norwegian fjords, the Commander-in-Chief (C-in-C) Home Fleet, Admiral Jack Tovey provided a distant covering force, to close the convoy in the event of surface attack, but meantime, to keep about 100 to 200 miles away to the west. This routine started in March '42 with PQ 12 and continued thereafter, with all outward-bound convoys. On this occasion it was composed of the battleships *King George V*, *Duke of York*, battlecruiser *Renown*, aircraft carrier *Victorious*, cruisers *Berwick* and *Kenya* (sent to join us later when we were threatened by *Tirpitz*), with an A/S screen of six or more fleet destroyers. As a close escort we always called this distant force, irreverently and with a sense of inverted snobbery, 'the slugs', implying, would they ever get to us in time?

Four trawlers escorted the convoy along the south coast from Reykjavik and after *Oribi* and *Offa* had refueled in Seidisfjordur we joined PQ 12 as part of the close escort, with two whalers, off the east coast of Iceland, on 4 March. I feel everyone should be told that it is memories combined with much reading, between now and then, that makes relating the events of the next few days far more exciting, or should I say frightening, than they seemed at the time. At about noon on the 5th, some seventy miles south of Jan Mayen island, we were spotted by a long range German reconnaissance plane. This Focke-Wulf Condor circled us, out of gun range and reported our position, course (NE'ly) and estimated speed back to base in Norway. So now the Kriegsmarine, including U-boats (there were 4 ahead) and the Luftwaffe knew about us and our intentions. Admiral Otto Ciliax had hoisted his flag in *Tirpitz* commanded by Kapitan Karl Topp and he decided to put to sea from Aasfjord at 1100 hours on the 6th with 4 destroyers. His quarry was PQ 12, which he assumed would be surprised and destroyed quite easily. However, at 1800, Lieut Raikes in Submarine *Seawolf* sighted *Tirpitz*, dived to avoid detection and surfaced two hours later to transmit this intelligence to Admiralty. That same evening PQ 12 ran into loose pack-ice and *Oribi* suffered considerable damage to her bows, affecting her value as a fighting escort. With shored-up collision bulkhead, her maximum possible speed was reduced from 35 to 15 knots.

Admiralty passed on *Seawolf's* news to C-in-C first, then to the Commodore of PQ 12 and escorts, before the cruiser *Kenya* (Captain Denny) joined, to take command of the close escort. Throughout the night, fortunately, the weather got worse and dawn broke to thick fog patches, drizzle and snow squalls over a lumpy sea. Icing up made flying operations impossible, which prevented Fairey Albacores leaving *Victorious*, but also made Otto and Karl feel frustrated aboard *Tirpitz*, not being able to use their Arado seaplane to find us. Another convoy QP 8 was returning from Murmansk in ballast (empty), scheduled to pass close to PQ 12 between Bear Island and the North Cape of Norway on the 8th.

It is astonishing to record our good fortune against Otto's misfortune on 7 and 8 March. Both convoys crossed over safely whilst *Tirpitz*, with 4 destroyers spread ahead, on a northerly course, passed about 50 miles away in murky weather, ahead of QP 8 and astern of PQ 12. Otto and Karl then altered to an easterly course, roughly parallel to ours and steamed at high speed for a few hours before turning south. Their plan was to intercept the laden convoy, PQ 12, between where they thought it was and its destination. They got our speed of advance wrong and once again missed us by about 50 miles although the destroyer *Friedrich Ihn* came across *Ijora*, a Russian straggler, from QP 8 and sank her by gunfire. Meantime, at noon, a signal from Admiralty ordered the convoy to go north of Bear Island, but Commodore Hudson and Captain Denny agreed that ice conditions to the north were appalling and decided to 'do a Nelson' (turn a deaf ear as opposed to a blind eye) and hold on to the south-east in snow squalls. Their, on the spot, judgment was superior to Whitehall's and probably helped our luck to hold. Also, we must remember that radar, in both navies, was still in its infancy.

Ciliax had been ordered by Raeder not to get involved in a fleet action with an aircraft carrier present. During the afternoon of the 8th, having been told about the Home Fleet at sea with *Victorious* and no chance now of finding the convoy, he decided to give up and headed south for Vestfjord (Narvik). This was the one and only time *Tirpitz* went to sea aggressively and she failed to achieve her objective. She visited Spitsbergen in Sept '43 to shell the surface coal-fields and harass the Norwegian weather station, but that was a fairly benign mission for a battleship of her calibre. We were there a month later, with USS *Tuscaloosa*, to appraise the scene, the closest I've ever been to landing on the moon! It is my opinion that Otto's natural initiative was handicapped by restrictive superiors, thank God. Denny detached the damaged *Oribi* to proceed independently and we reached Murmansk on the 10th. The convoy PQ 12 got in, without loss, on the 12th. I believe this episode can best be described as a very lucky survival situation, except for the poor souls lost in the *Ijora*.

Oribi in Rosta Dock, showing her bow, damaged by ice, and ice on the upper deck

In Kola Inlet, the first priority was getting our bashed-in bow temporarily repaired and for this we entered Rosta Dry Dock at Polyarnoe. The dockyard workers, mostly women, did the job, but before setting about the hull, they built a house-like structure around the stem of the ship, in order to work round the clock without showing any lights to attract enemy bombers. It all happened very smoothly and within two weeks a replacement bow had been fitted with great efficiency. Going into dry dock meant that the heads (lavatories) were out of action and we had to go ashore to perform the most fundamental function. The facility ashore was a fragile hut, built on and projecting slightly over a low cliff, facing north, with an icy surface about six feet below. Inside was a low-slung plank with 8 holes admitting an arctic bum-blasting breeze. To give you a real feel for the place, I am printing a ballad composed by 'Paddy' Bourke, CERA, who was a worthy bard in a basic, bawdy way, so here it is, called 'Rosta Dock'

You can talk of the trail of the Yukon,
And its hell of ice and snow,
But how about Rosta Dock shithouse
Where it's 40 degrees below?

Think of the heads in West Country
And of those in the RNB,
Then think of those at Rosta Dock,
Where the shit flows down to the sea.

We've convoyed some shiploads to Russia,
To help carry on with the fight,
But I guess when we get out of Rosta
We'll be carrying a few gutfuls of shite.

The seats reach up to your ankles,
And shit bespatters the walls.
One slip and you're bang thru' the shithole,
Or stood on the next bloke's balls.

Slipping, sliding and swearing,
To the shithouse we wend our way,
One look and sniff at the fragrant pit
And the shit's put off for the day.

We've cancelled our shits so often,
Just hoping the urge would depart,
If we don't hurry up and get out in the stream
We'll be turd-bound and unable to fart.

There's just one of the crew enjoys it,
His name 'The Bastard' to wit,
He can't find a tree or a lamp-post,
So he uses the column of shit.

So roll on the day of refloating,
When our own shithouse doors open wide;
The queue will reach from fore to aft,
Four deep and up each side.

And next time you're sitting pretty,
With the seat all cosy and tight,
Just think of the shithouse at Rosta,
You'll want to stay there all night.

Then sing of your 'Vulgar' boatman
Or any other old dit,
But never forget the '*Oribi*'s' crew,
Who go down to the sea – JUST TO SHIT!

When out of dry-dock, alongside the quay in Polyarnoe, a Ship's Concert was organized with the appropriate title 'Jack in Joe's Land'. Such concerts are common throughout the navy and usually lots of fun, with rank and seniority ignored and contributions from people in most parts of ship. Paddy presented 'Rosta Dock' in monologue style and now that we were 'out in the stream' again, feeling greatly relieved, there was thunderous applause from the audience and much barking from Bastard. Commissars were around now, but they avoided drawing attention to themselves by interfering and rather used their presence to act as a restraint on east-west fraternization. There were exceptions, however, and we teamed up with a group of Russian Submariners, who spoke good English, finding that we shared a similar sense of humour. One said to me 'My friend here was going to torpedo you coming in, as a German, but I pushed him from the periscope, then shouted "*neat, neat* [no, no] that is a British destroyer". So you see, it is me you have to thank for being alive. Yes please, I would like a large – what do say – pink gin? Thank you.'

On 29 March we put to sea, with the Russian destroyers *Gremyaschi* and *Sokrushitelny* to meet Convoy PQ 13 coming in. Also with us were three British minesweepers, *Gossamer, Hussar* and *Speedwell*, stationed in North Russia and old friends of mine in the North Sea two years ago. The cruiser *Trinidad* was with the convoy and as we rendezvoused, three German destroyers attacked in the half-light dawn on the 30th. One was badly damaged and *Trinidad* fired a torpedo to finish her off, but it malfunctioned, turned and came back to hit *Trinidad* herself, who then had to limp into Murmansk for repairs. The rest of the convoy arrived safely.

Back alongside in Polyarnoe, our social life continued when Submariners invited us to a dance at Red Navy House. To hell with the Commissars, it seemed. My beard was good and thick by this time and I was unique amongst Russians because they didn't grow them. Very few ladies were present, about four or five, to cope with twenty to thirty rampant Russian and British nautical gentlemen. The ladies were dressed in field-grey army uniforms with six-shooters on their hips. The only really sexy feature about them was their boots, felt and to knee height with raised heels, twenty years ahead of our 'kinky boots' fashion in the UK. My Russki shoremates grabbed a tall, slim lady and lifted her hand to touch my beard. And we were off, dancing round in circles with her fingers stroking my whiskers and her voice saying '*boreda, boreda*' (Russian for beard). She seemed happy

Oribi. *The bearded midshipman*

and I was delighted because that word, in my limited Welsh, meant 'good morning'. We had found something in common and what lovely musical languages they both are, Welsh and Russian.

On the quayside, a four-legged form of fraternization was going on. In the absence of a canine commissar, Bastard had decided to do his bit, as it were, by conducting a communist courtship which his human shipmates seemed unable to achieve. This seadog's run ashore soon fulfilled his faith in finding a bitch in every port and after some sensitive, soviet sniffing, courtship rapidly developed into coupling. Their natural, 'doggie style', performance was cheered on by Brits and Russkis alike and their mutual message, to us all, was loud and clear, 'Isn't this what life's about?'

After a month exactly in Kola inlet, on 10 April, we sailed as Senior Officer of the escort to the westbound convoy QP 10 (22 ships in ballast) with *Punjabi*, *Marne*, *Fury* and *Eclipse* as our fellow destroyer escorts, the minesweeper *Speedwell* and trawlers *Blackfly* and *Paynter*. Air and U-boat attacks were constant, 4 merchant ship casualties, 2 to each form of attack, but with a probable U-boat kill by *Oribi* as some compensation. The two victims of U-435, *Kiev* and *El Occidente*, had been with us on the lucky PQ 12. The 18 ships of the convoy reached Iceland on the 21st and we got to Scapa on the 24th.

PQ 15 was different because (a) of the loaded merchantships, 16 were American, 9 British with just 1 Russian and (b) it was the first Russian convoy in which a Catapult Aircraft Merchantship (CAM) sailed, the *Empire Morn*. A 'Hurricane' fighter was mounted on her fo'c'sle ready to be catapulted off, get amongst enemy bombers and shoot down as many as possible before running out of fuel. It was a 'one-off' event, at the end of which the pilot would pancake on the sea astern of the convoy, bale out with Mae West inflated and wait to be picked up by the rescue trawler. The convoy sailed from Reykjavik on 26 April and arrived in Murmansk on 5 May, with the loss of 3 ships, all British, bombed by aircraft.

We were part of the Home Fleet's distant covering force, which for the first time included the American battleship *Washington*, 2 cruisers, USS *Tuscaloosa* and USS *Wichita*, plus 4 American destroyers. The British ships present were *King George V*, *Duke of York*, *Kenya* and *Victorious*, plus 11 destroyers, including *Oribi* and the ill-fated *Punjabi*, making a total A/S screen of 15 to protect the 'slugs'. It was on 1 May, in low visibility, east of Iceland, that *King George V* was in collision with *Punjabi*. Somehow, the Tribal destroyer crossed ahead of the battleship, was rammed amidships and cut in two. The front section containing most of the crew remained afloat, fortunately, but the stern half sank immediately, with a few survivors in the water, until the depth-charges exploded deep down, with fatal results for most of them. I do believe we met a Lieut RNVR from New Zealand later, whose guts were tough enough to withstand the shocks in the water. In Seidisfjordur, two days before, we had fuelled from the oil-tanker, alongside *Punjabi*, and now were next to them on the screen. We heard ships' sirens blowing and shouts coming out of the fog, but had no idea of the disaster that had taken place so close, on our port side. Wartime security prevented this mishap being made public knowledge. We were sad for all the *Punjabi*'s crew and we realized how grief-stricken their captain, Lieut-Cdr, The Hon. J.M. Waldgrave, must have been, as a survivor, on his bridge, seeing half his ship sink, with so many shipmates, in such tragic circumstances. We and other destroyers rescued him and 206 shipmates from the front half before it sank.

Back in Scapa by mid-May, I paused to reflect. It was a year ago that I cast aside my crutches without falling flat on my face, and I had not felt the slightest pain or discomfort from my bumbombed leg in the meantime. Well done the team at Mountain Ash. Since then I'd been to Scotland, Malta, Norway, Iceland and Russia, with lots of near-misses but no hits happily. Sub- Lieut Dicky Gardner RN joined *Oribi* and Mike left, heading south by train from Thurso to marry Margaret. Mike had been Fo'c'sle Officer when it came to Stations for Entering and Leaving Harbour and Mac gave me that job now, saying 'With 4 years at sea, as a Midshipman, you're more qualified than any Subs coming aboard.' I remember this move causing a few raised eyebrows on the fo'c'sles of other destroyers, coming alongside with Lieutenants in charge. Jock Graham was always working the capstans, wearing a singlet in any temperature, and my senior rating was Leading Seaman Edwards, later a shipmate in *Vanguard* in '47 as an RPO (Regulating Petty Officer). A frequent operation was securing to a buoy in Gutter Sound, always under the approving observation of the resident seal. Mac initiated a swifter, yet safe, system, with the cooperation of our skilled buoy-jumper, Stan 'Shorty' Strange, also with 4 years sea experience, who, after the war, joined the Merchant Navy and became a Quartermaster in the P&O Line.

The usual drill for a destroyer coming to a buoy was, lower a boat, heave ahead, man on buoy and so on, taking maybe 30 minutes or more. Our practice was much swifter. Two men held a smooth spar, with padded base, over the side, placing it firmly on the buoy when under below. I made arm-signals to the bridge indicating the buoy's position, to help Mac manoeuvre the ship. Earlier, we had extended a length of cable, to water level, through the fair-lead on the nose and also passed the picking-up wire through there and back. AB Strange, fitted with lifejacket and life-line tended by other seamen, slid down the spar with the wire looped round his shoulder, landed on the buoy and hitched on. Then with the wire up and down, he shackled on the cable. When that took the strain, he let go the wire and scrambled up a rope-ladder, back to the fo'c'sle. Time taken, 5 to 10 minutes depending on weather conditions. If turbulent and the buoy swung about a lot, Shorty sometimes ended up in the 'drink' (slang for sea), but on such occasions he always received a large Scotch afterwards from the Fo'c'sle Officer (me).

Stan and I meet at the 17th DFA reunions in Portsmouth each year and the Merchant Navy Association (MNA) Christmas Party at Anchor House in Canning Town, London. Before the party we look in for a chat with the tallest of our torpedomen, always the 'marker' at 'hands fall-in', Tom Goddard. Now he is house-bound with emphysema, but in good spirits and we always have a tot of Pussers Rum. They both live in East Ham and when leaving Tom's place on 6 Dec 2001, I told Stan how much I admired him for picking up Tom's pension every week. He turned to me and said with great sincerity 'It's no trouble Ian, after all, he is a shipmate.'

PQ 16 was the largest convoy so far with 36 merchantships, 21 American, 9 British, 5 Russian and 1 Dutch, with the CAM *Empire Lawrence* in position No. 11, front ship in the extreme left column. They left Reykjavik on 21 May and we joined them, east of Iceland, on the 23rd with the cruisers *Kent, Liverpool, Nigeria* and *Norfolk*. It was becoming a regular thing, to provide close cruiser cover for convoys in addition to the distant cover from the Home Fleet and the US Navy. Air attacks from Heinkel 111s, some carrying torpedos instead of bombs, were frequent and heavy during these longer hours of daylight and I was thrilled to see our CAM in action. Flying the Hurricane was a South African Pilot Officer in the RAF, Alastair Hay, whom I had met in Hvalfjord. About 10 Heinkels were shaping up on the horizon ahead when off went Alastair who shot two down, for which he got a DFC later. Happily we saw him bale out astern to be picked up by the destroyer *Volunteer* with A.S. Pomeroy RN in command. Years later, I discovered that both Hay and Pomeroy had been trained as cadets in the *General Botha* at Simonstown, SA. Sadly Hay went missing in 1944. We screened PQ 16 to south of Bear Island and then came back with the QP 12 convoy. The enemy attacked the loaded convoy, PQ 16, sinking 6 with bombers and 1 by U-boat, whilst QP 12, in ballast, was left alone. Both convoys reached their destinations on 30 May and *Oribi* returned to Scapa.

In June, *Oribi* was taken in hand for repairs at Immingham, a few miles north of Grimsby, on the Humber Estuary, to reinforce the temporary repairs to her bow done at Rosta. We were there for a month and here's what happened. The ship went into dry dock and leave was granted, long term, 10 days to each watch and daily leave, over night, which meant a trip on the single line tramtrack to the nearest clubs and pubs in Grimsby. It was now that Spud and I set up a reputation for organizing Wardroom parties. First ashore, we would chat up the Wrens on the switchboard, thereby getting a free call home to our parents, in exchange for them having a gin onboard. Wren drivers were a close second, which guaranteed wheels in port. There can be no doubt, we thought ourselves the glamour boys of the navy, being destroyer types, dashing here and there, in the supposedly silent service. Anyway, it led to a marvellous moment for me, meeting one of the most charming and influential ladies in my life.

Pam was a 3rd Officer WRNS, attractive in all respects, great fun as a companion and rather than say we got on well, I would go further and say we fell in love, just like that. It was mutual and lasted about a year and a half when we lost contact and just drifted apart. Spud and I had shared the thought that marriage in wartime was a 'no no' for us and we would always tell our current partners so. When I suggested to Pam that we should have a week-end at the Lifeboat Hotel in Cleethorpes, she consulted her friend, mentor and boss 2nd Officer Jane, a few years her senior, who said 'Of course you must, you'll enjoy every minute, but let me tell you about this and that and so on', Jane having lived it up in the West End of London. I got the curtain ring and polished it with Brasso, an essential display on a lady's left hand when checking in to hotels in those puritanical days. Mac, my boss, knew what was going on and like Pam's boss, he approved, as did the rest of the Wardroom, so we didn't have to be secretive nor did we have to declare ourselves 'an item', we just carried on. Pam, who had studied art in Paris prewar, painted me a picture of the Immingham Naval Base, lots of barbed wire with a background of Nissen huts, to hang in the cabin. Also, she presented me with a pink cushion on which were hand-stitched musical notes amidst zs and the message 'Good Zizzing'.

Percy left *Oribi* in June and Mac appointed me Navigator on my 20th birthday, the 9th, when I was promoted to Sub-Lieut RNR, Acting, Probationary, would you believe it? In that capacity, my cabin at sea was the chart-house, under the bridge, where I slept on the settee in a bight of rope to prevent me from being thrown off by the rolling of the ship. For my meals, I went aft, to and from the Wardroom, which meant a hazardous trip along the upper deck, clutching a strop which slid along a jackstay and dodging seas sweeping inboard in rough weather. On the Russian run, I would remain in my clothes for about ten days, cosy and warm it was, to be sure. I carried two books in my battle-dress pockets when at sea, which fortified and comforted me during quiet spells between action, when I could read a bit, before 'zizzing'.

Palgrave's *Golden Treasury* was in the pocket on my left leg and my favourite bit was from Gray's Elegy:

> Let not ambition mock their useful toil,
> Their homely joys, and destiny obscure;
> Nor grandeur hear with a disdainful smile
> The short and simple annals of the poor.
>
> The boast of heraldry, the pomp of power
> And all that beauty, all that wealth e'er gave
> Await alike th'inevitable hour:
> The paths of glory lead but to the grave.

I don't remember feeling gloomy after reading this. Maybe it was my subconscious preparing me for the worst, should it ever happen. The other book, in the pocket on the right leg of my battledress, was Alice Duer Miller's *The White Cliffs*, written in 1941. I found this American lady's poem most uplifting and very much associated with Pam's loving support. She would be waiting to embrace me on my return from Murmansk, there was never any doubt about that. This romantic poem features a love story in WW1 and my favourite bit, often quoted by me over the years since, is:

> Lovers in peacetime
> With fifty years to live,
> Have time to tease and quarrel
> And question what to give;
> But lovers in war-time
> Better understand
> The fullness of living,
> With death close at hand.

It was 35 years later, mid seventies, when Tony Dixon and I were running a Management course for Conoco in the Frensham Ponds Hotel, that I told him about my old captain, living in Churt, now a retired Rear-Admiral and Lord-Lieutenant of Surrey. We called and invited him and his wife, the Hon. Jane, to dinner at the hotel, with our wives also present. Mac, sitting opposite, looked me in the eye and said 'Ian, I think that now it can be told.' I wondered what was coming. He went on 'Remember, we were anchored in Loch Alsh for a few days, before a Russian convoy in '42 or '43 and I decided to have a luxurious night ashore in the one and only local hotel. Well, I was welcomed at reception by the manager who, seeing my 3 stripes, said "Sir, you must be the captain of the destroyer out there" and I confessed to that. "Ah, well," said he, "I'm sure you will be comfortable with us; your Navigator and his wife are very happy here in the suite".'

Please note my discretion in never mentioning a lady's surname. However, I'll give a clue to posterity by saying that the given names of my lady love in full were Pamela Agnes Mary (PAM), so obviously she had parents as amusing, word-wise, as was she.

There could have been another budding romance at Immingham, but it was precluded by a signal from the Admiral saying that *Oribi*'s dog must come ashore only on a lead, with an AB in attendance. Apparently, Bastard had been trying to have an affair with the Admiral's wife's Pekinese and no way could this randy seadog be tolerated in this respectable shore establishment, even though treeless and composed mainly of Nissen huts.

The Admiral and the Chief Officer WRNS (Queen Bee) gave their approval to the Wren Officers, plus any officers' wives, coming to sea with us for a day, on trials, safely inside the boom defence of the estuary. It was Mac's idea that they should see and experience how a destroyer operates and we even had our respective lady friends doing our jobs, under close supervision, naturally. Pam loved being Navigator, giving wheel orders down the voice-pipe to the Coxswain, who enjoyed it too; then working with me on the charts. We had them hoisting flags, flashing signals, manning the guns and Dan Cawthra, who was now our Engineer Officer, had his wife in charge down the engine room. It was a great day and worth a mention, now that females are accepted afloat, all ranks up to Commodore, I believe, in the modern navy. No longer called Wrens I hasten to add. After Immingham, we needed further attention at Fairfields

on the Clyde before returning to Scapa in mid–September, where we joined
in the build up to Operation 'Torch', the Allied landings in North Africa.

Some grim things happened in 1942. In February, Singapore surrendered
to the Japanese. In July, the Admiralty unwisely scattered Russian convoy
PQ 17 on faulty intelligence, causing the loss of 24 merchantships out of
39 in total. In August, the raid on Dieppe by Canadians was a disaster from
which many lessons were learned and now, in October, it was estimated
that Admiral Donitz had more than 200 U–boats operational in the Battle
of the Atlantic. Operation 'Torch' was a light on the horizon, a dress
rehearsal for the invasion of Europe and the earliest example of combined
action by sea, land and air forces in which merchantmen played a prominent
part. It was the first time in the history of war that armies from two separate
continents were landed upon the shores of a third. It brought together the
greatest armada in history: some 250 merchantships with 100 naval escorts
from the UK and about 100 merchantships with 75 naval escorts from the
US; an overall ratio of merchant to naval (ships) of two to one
approximately.

Lieut John Lamb RN, a Gunnery man from the cruiser *Glasgow*, replaced
Bengie as No.1, in Scapa. When on the bridge, he seemed, to me, more
interested in exercising 'B' Gun, with strident voice over the canopy, than
taking over watch-keeping responsibilities and his laugh, like his voice, was
loud and to him obligatory. Tom Smith, a Glasgow gynaecologist, always
popular with our Wren guests, became our Surgeon Lieut RNVR. Before
leaving Scapa, we received three large wooden crates containing charts,
with instructions, 'Not to be opened until receipt of signal "Open Ton
One".' About mid-October we sailed for Northern Ireland and berthed
alongside at Lisahally, about 4 miles downstream from Londonderry in the
Lough Foyle estuary. All hands painted ship for the next few days, changing
our camouflage colours from dark to light grey, with patches of pink, in
wavy lines, all over the ship's side and superstructure. This would conceal
our presence, somewhere to the south, we knew not where. 'What's the
buzz?' was on everyone's lips. Some thought Dakar as a destination, others
guessed round the Cape to Suez, with troops for Monty (General
Montgomery) who had just taken command of the 8th Army (Desert Rats).
Nobody got it right.

Between painting sessions, daily leave was granted to Londonderry.
Wearing raincoats over uniforms, allowed us, in this disguise, to enjoy the
delights of Donegal by nipping over the border into the Republic. Spud's
ancestors came from the south, but he felt at home everywhere, regardless
of polarity. *Oribi* was close to the railway track, between the stations of
Lisahally (1 mile north) and Derry (3 miles south). On the way ashore, we
walked to Lisahally station and got a train to Derry, but on the return trip

at 11 p.m., Spud had a brilliant idea. Seeing a platform filled with fifty or more staggering shipmates, he shaped up to the driver and said in his best Irish brogue 'Would it be asking too much of a favour, to stop your locomotive opposite our ship, that's fighting the war for you?' 'No, indeed it would not, but it will mean you comin' on the footplate, to tell us when to stop,' Up we climbed and with a two-fingered mouth whistle, told the liberty men 'We're stopping at the ship, so when you hear the whistle blow, everybody out'. The Fireman let me shovel coal into the boiler and Spud had a go on the controls. We thanked them with some duty-free fags, and thought a railway journey like that could only happen in Ireland.

We departed from Lough Foyle, with *Onslow* and *Offa*, to escort one of the 'Torch' convoys, WS 24, on 29 October and received the signal 'Open Ton One'. Now that we were at sea, certain information could be revealed. The charts in our wooden crates were all to do with the North African coast, where the big landings would be in the Med, at Algiers and Oran, but we would be in the Atlantic, guarding the landing at Casablanca, in French Morocco. The date and time of D-day was still a secret. At sunset on 2 November, a signal from Admiralty, of top priority, said that the neutral Portuguese liner *Gil Eanes*, bound for Lisbon from America, should be intercepted, a certain radio officer removed as an alleged spy, and the ship prevented from reaching Lisbon for 6 days. *Oribi* was detached to search and next day, a ship was seen in the evening with the name clearly illuminated on the side, *Gil Eanes*. It took two shots across her bows to stop her, after which we lowered a sea-boat to take Doug over as Boarding Officer to bring back the spy and Dicky, with four sailors, to remain onboard and keep her at sea. The radio officer spoke no English and was obviously terrified, but we treated him reasonably and he ate with us in the Wardroom. Dicky had a tricky job. The *Gil Eanes* was only one day's steaming out of Lisbon, so Dicky had to go round in wide circles for 6 days. Every time he snatched some sleep, the Portuguese Captain tried to take charge and head for his home port, but Dicky's seamen were alert and called him to resume control. He succeeded in keeping the *Gil Eanes* at sea and we knew later, the significance of $2+6=8$, when the 8 November was declared D-day. On that date, Dicky and his team stepped ashore in Lisbon and rejoined us in Gibraltar about a week later.

We rejoined the convoy, but left again to refuel in the Azores at Ponta-del-gada. Radio man was locked in No.1's cabin, with matting over the port-hole to prevent him hearing the voices of local, Portuguese bum-boat men alongside and so become aware that he was a prisoner in his own territorial waters. We loaded lots of fresh fruit and vegetables, especially bananas and pineapples, both novelties now in the UK. On 3 November, Montgomery's 8th Army broke through Rommel's Afrika

Korps front line at El Alamein and on the 8th, the North Africa landings against Vichy France, by the Allies under General Dwight Eisenhower, were a success. Casablanca was quiet and capitulated early on. All I know about the place is what I saw later, in the film of that name, actually made in '42, when Bogart said to Bergman 'Here's looking at you, kid.'

We turned over the 'radio spy' (?) to the Army in Gib and never heard what happened to him. Dicky Gardner and company entertained us with their stories about the goings on aboard the *Gil Eanes*, as we sailed back home to our base. Scapa was very much home, because that is where our mail awaited us. The 15 November was declared 'El Alamein Victory Day' in the UK and church bells were rung throughout the land for the first time since the threat of German invasion in 1940. After a peal rang out from the bell-tower of bomb-shattered Coventry Cathedral, a radio announcer asked: 'Did you hear them in Occupied Europe? Did you hear them in Germany?' In the House of Commons Churchill said 'It is not the end. It is not even the beginning of the end. But it is perhaps the end of the beginning.' A glorious event at sea would occur on the last day of the year, but that's another story.

In mid-November the 17th DF were required by the Home Fleet for the new Russian convoy season and on the 28th Beaky Armstrong was relieved as Captain (D17) in Onslow, by Captain Robert St Vincent Sherbrooke DSO, RN. Another change in higher ranks, was the appointment of RAD (Rear-Admiral Destroyers), in charge of all destroyer flotillas in Scapa. The person doing this job was Robert (Bob) Burnett, a chubby, jovial mixer, who did well. I think he had quarters in either Tyne or Dunluce Castle when in harbour, but at sea, he flew his Flag in a cruiser. Soon it would be the *Sheffield*, but later it was usually *Belfast*, the ship that, after WW2 became a show-piece on the Thames and open to the public. Lamb said it was remarkable that a 'Springer' should achieve flag rank, explaining to us that it meant an officer who had specialized in PT. Spud and I thought 'good on him' and as Reserves we were aware of the snobbery amongst some RN specialists.

Russian convoy JW 51 was split in two halves A and B, each containing 18 merchantmen and the first to go direct to Murmansk, from Loch Ewe on the west coast of Scotland, just north of Loch Alsh, where I had a pre-voyage morale boost from Pam. JW 51 A sailed through from the 15th to the 25th without being discovered by the enemy. It was very different for JW 51B who sailed 7 days later, on the 22nd. The destroyers *Achates*, *Obedient*, *Obdurate*, *Onslow*, *Oribi* and *Orwell* joined the existing close escort, the corvettes, *Hyderabad* and *Rhododendron*, the trawlers, *Northern Gem* and *Vizalma*, and the minesweeper *Bramble*, on the 25th. Force R, the 6-inch cruisers *Sheffield* (with RAD onboard) and *Jamaica*, were the heaviest British units in the area, to the north-east, having seen JW 51A safely through to Murmansk. At that time of year we were mostly in darkness, with only a few hours of twilight each side of noon. The distant force, *Anson*, *Cumberland* and 5 destroyers, was distant as ever, to the south-west.

On getting a sighting report on 24th, the Kreigsmarine prepared for operation 'Regenbogen' (Rainbow) to intercept and destroy the convoy. Admiral Oscar Kummetz, in the 8-inch cruiser *Hipper* with 3 destroyers would attack from the north, whilst Kapitan zur See Stange, in the pocket battleship *Lutzow* with another 3 destroyers would approach from the south; thus forming a pincer movement. Meanwhile, on the 27th/28th, the convoy was broken up by bad weather and 5 merchantmen lost touch. *Oribi* and *Vizalma* attempted to round up these stragglers without success and neither we nor they ever rejoined the convoy.

We had accumulated about 100 tons of ice on our upper deck, which affected our stability, even though we had flooded our double-bottom tanks with sea-water as they were emptied of oil, until we refuelled again from a tanker, either at sea or in port. It was decided, therefore, to have all hands on deck chipping off the ice and in doing so, two men were lost overboard. Mac tried to turn the ship to effect a rescue, but the sea and swell were so steep, that when beam on, she went over to 55 degrees and hung there, with Mac and I clutching binnacles on the bridge and wondering whether she would come back. She did and we steadied on a safe course, sad at the loss of two shipmates. Despite their Mae Wests they would not have survived long in that icy arctic water. On later convoys steam hoses were fitted on deck for de-icing and Dan Cawthra had something to do with that invention.

Between snow squalls on the 29th, we exchanged a visual signal with *Bramble* (Commander Rust), who like us was searching for stragglers. We were the last British ship to see her. As usual, W/T silence was still imposed and our radar had become defective. Before the stormy weather abated, the ship pitched heavily and our gyro compass was put out of action, so we were in a bad way. Navigating on a magnetic compass in high latitudes (we were 73 N), is a tricky business, with the card swinging about erratically. We headed roughly south-east for Murmansk, hoping to sight the convoy en route. By guess and by God, helped by the stars and still independent, we made a good landfall on 31 December. When we judged we were close enough to land, we broke W/T silence and asked the Russians to switch on Tereberski Light, just to the east of Kola Inlet. All my life I have remembered with what relief I saw 'Flash Green every 10 seconds' almost directly ahead. 'Well done'' said Mac' 'and I'll tell the ship's company we have you to thank for our safe arrival here.'

It was at 0830, as we passed through the boom gate at Kola Inlet, that our Sparkers, Wireless Operators, heard the first 'enemy report' transmitted by *Obdurate*, having sighted 2 German destroyers. Mac was dismayed at not being with the others going into action and so was I, in a flotilla-mate sense. However, my feelings were mixed, navigating being my forte more than fighting. At about 0800, *Hipper* had passed 20 miles astern of the convoy from south to north and at 0930 was shelling *Achates*, as she laid a smoke-screen astern of the merchantships. Hearing gunfire to the north, *Onslow* led *Obedient, Obdurate* and *Orwell* at 25 knots in that direction and they opened fire on the *Hipper*, scoring many hits. *Hipper* retaliated (8-inch against 4.7-inch and 4-inch), but fearing a torpedo attack turned away. *Onslow* suffered six or seven hits, killing 'B' gun's crew and severely wounding Sherbrooke with a splinter in the face, leaving his left eye dangling out of its socket. He declined treatment for 20 minutes until everything was under control and only then did he go below, after ordering Lieut-Cdr David Kinloch (a relation maybe?) in *Obedient* to take over as Senior Officer. Lieut-Cdr Tom Marchant, Flotilla Torpedo Officer, took command of *Onslow*. JW 51 B eventually arrived at Kola Inlet on 3rd Jan without loss.

Bob Burnett in *Sheffield* with *Jamaica* arrived about noon unexpectedly and shelled *Hipper*, who broke off with her destroyers and headed for Norway. When they came across *Bramble*, the destroyer *Eckholdt* was detached and sank her, with all hands. On returning to rejoin *Hipper* in poor visibility, *Eckholdt* mistakenly joined *Sheffield* instead, who promptly sank her at close range. Marchant remembered seeing *Lutzow* at 1130 about 3 miles away, assumed she had seen *Onslow* and awaited her first salvo, but nothing happened. She came in sight and disappeared again, like a ghost ship, returning to Altenfjord without firing a shot. *Achates* had been badly damaged, her captain, Lieut-Cdr A.H.T. Johns, killed and her No.1, Lieut L.E. Peyton Jones now in command. He asked *Northern Gem* to take off his crew, but *Achates* sank suddenly, leaving 80 survivors afloat, with PJ, to be rescued by the trawler.

Sherbrooke received a VC for his valour and leadership in winning the Battle of the Barents Sea. Hitler was incandescent at the failure of 'Regenbogen' and said 'Scrap all battleships to make U-boats.' Gross-Admiral Erich Raeder resigned and Karl Dönitz (the Devil's Admiral) took over. Though pro U-boat, he persuaded his Führer to retain a few ships in Norway to tie down the British Home Fleet. It was almost a year before the Germans again sent out surface ships against a convoy, and this action too ended in defeat. Thus it was that the gallant action of five destroyers had consequences out of all proportion to the action itself. The tide was turning.

CHAPTER 10

HMS *Oribi*: part 3 – 1943–1944

WHAT BETTER WAY TO START THE YEAR 1943, than by looking ahead. Lots of good things occurred early on. Our resilient Russian allies in January, after heavy fighting, got Field-Marshal von Paulus to surrender his German Army at Stalingrad to a Red Army Lieutenant and after a 16 months' siege by the would be rulers of the world, Leningrad (now St Petersburg) was relieved. This was the beginning of great victories on land, whilst at sea, the U-boats would get the beating they deserved in a few months time. *Oribi* for the next 18 months would spend long periods at sea, on convoy duty, in the Arctic, then the North Atlantic and back in the Arctic before going south to the English Channel for D-Day in June 1944. During this time, there were many interesting developments in navigation that I want to talk about, but for now, let's go back to Murmansk. We were there for two weeks, until 14 January, and although we didn't know it at the time, we wouldn't be back for another year. The gyro compass was repaired. Skiing was fun indulged in by most of the ship's company. At the top of the sloping main street, there were stacks of skis for hire and the natives just loved to see jolly-jack having a go and falling all over the place. Little kids skating around on their mini-skis were most amused.

I suppose it could be called an antidote to the stress of war, that we played silly games in the Wardroom occasionally. A popular one we invented to play after dinner was called 'Night Action'. It was a simulation of an OOW on a blacked-out bridge at sea, in dirty weather, fighting an enemy surface ship and took place in half the Mess from amidships to ship's side. The scene was set in a darkened Wardroom, with a dartboard hung on ship's side and a dining-room chair placed amidships. We took it in turns being OOW, for 5 minutes, by sitting in the chair armed with 3 darts and a torch, being lifted and rocked about (rough sea) by 3 fellow officers. Others, on each side, squirted soda syphons (spray), threw rice (hail) and flashed a torch in the eyes (enemy searchlight), whilst OOW, with torch (own searchlight) and darts (shells from 'B' gun) tried to score hits on the dartboard (enemy). The winner was the one with the highest score, that is, if anyone hit the target, which wasn't easy. Lots of other things were hit including lamp shades, furniture and the panelling in ship's side. It was a bit over the top and we deserved what we got. Mac noticed the damage at breakfast and said to No.1 'OK, so everyone had fun last night. Now, the officers are to make good the repairs themselves, today by 1700, without any assistance from members of the crew.' We borrowed tools, did the job and it was

Oribi communications crew (1943 approx.) Back row, l. to r.: Coder Bob Howell, Walker, Mason, Henderson, Marsland, Smith, ?, Tarrant, Lewis, Gregory. Front row, l. to r.: Williams, Lake, Gill, Pritchard, Smith, Broad, McManus

never mentioned again. Everyone respected Mac for applying, what was agreed to be, the appropriate discipline.

Before setting off for home, I think it would be sensible to relate a few facts about navigation, making it as simple as possible. Keeping track of the ship's position at sea was done on a chart by drawing a pencil-line of direction forward (Compass Course) and marking the estimated distance (speed of advance) along that line, as the ship progressed, to give what was called a DR (Dead Reckoning) position. It was necessary to make allowances for winds, tides, currents and prevailing weather, which might affect the direction and distance run. A DR position is still used today, basically the same in detail, but with more sophisticated approaches. What has changed a lot, is the way navigators obtain their true and more precise position on planet earth, by pressing a few buttons.

Before the great technological advances after WW2, culminating in Satellite/Computers, the wartime navigator had to determine his true position with the aid of heavenly bodies such as sun, moon, planets and stars. This was known as Astro-Navigation. He stood on the open deck with a hand-held sextant, a simple device, with mirrors and a small telescope, for measuring the angle of the body being observed above the line of the horizon, known as the altitude. He, or an assistant, recorded the exact time by chronometer, GMT (Greenwich Mean Time) and also obtained a compass bearing of the body (between 0 and 360 degrees). Whenever this operation was performed, it was known as 'taking a sight'.

Now, armed with these 3 components, altitude, time and bearing, Vasco was ready to do a short calculation on paper, using a standard mathematical formula. This he would do in the relative comfort of the charthouse, with the aid of books providing astronomical data and log tables. The result of this calculation would give a point, on the chart, relative to the DR position somewhere. The more of these lines, from many bodies, crossing each other, the better, and that is all you need know to follow my drift. For me, it was a personally rewarding art form and I loved it.

Onslow remained at Murmansk for the month of January, being repaired. Lieut P.J. (Peter) Wyatt, Flotilla Navigator, who was a 'tower of strength' to Sherbrooke on the bridge during the action with *Hipper*, for which he got a DSC, sailed with us in *Oribi* on 14 January. I enjoyed his company immensely and he left the navigation to me entirely. What he loved doing was sitting in the chartroom, with pencil and signal pad, drawing cartoon sketches of me in various situations. They were good and I wish I'd kept some. We had some bad weather but no enemy action. The sky had been overcast since leaving Russia, which had prevented the taking of any 'sights', so we had been running on DR for 2½ days at 20 knots (23 mph), a distance of about 1,200 nautical miles. The memory was still fresh in my mind of convoy QP 13, six months previously, missing a landfall on Iceland with disastrous results. The minesweeper *Niger* (my flotilla-leader in the North Sea, 1940) plus 5 merchantships ran into one of our minefields along the north coast, struck mines and sank with great loss of life.

I was hoping that a heavenly body would appear and imagine my delight when a shout from the bridge came down the voice-pipe 'Vasco, the moon.' I grabbed my ham bone (sextant) and rushed up the ladder, shouting to Goody on the plot, who seized the chronometer-watch and stood-by to take the time. There it was, appearing through gaps in the cloud, at about 15 degrees altitude and providing a reasonably illuminated, clear horizon underneath. It was on the port beam, bearing south-east, with a distinct upper limb (rim) and just what I wanted. 'Standby Goody now.' I shouted and again and again, taking three good sights to be sure. After about 10 minutes of calculating, in the charthouse, with dear old Mac fussing about and saying 'You're sure it was the upper not the lower limb you took Ian?' 'Yes definitely Sir' I said, knowing that if I got my limb wrong it would put me about 20 miles out. Peter sat and sketched me, calm as could be. Because the moon's bearing was south-east, the observed (true) position-line, at right-angles, ran SW-NE and to my great relief it was bang-on my DR course line. How far advanced we were, was still in doubt, but radar would pick up land ahead and I estimated we were within 50 miles, so we broke W/T silence and requested the NE Point light be turned on. Soon, we sighted the light, right ahead, bearing bang-on 225 degrees (SW).

This moment I have always looked upon as my finest landfall ever during my seafaring life as a navigator from 1938 to 1956. Not only that, but I felt a tremendous sense of achievement, a responsible action resulting in a happy beneficial feeling to me, but also to my shipmates. The technology since has been magnificent and I approve, particularly the changes that helped us before the end of WW2. However, jumping 35 years ahead to the mid-70s, I realized the fun, or should I say sense of personal achievement, had gone away. You see, I was passenger in the *Conoco Canada*, tanker of 276,000 tons, occupying the owner's suite, under the bridge, on passage from Le Havre to Bordeaux, with the object of designing a Management Course for the officers, nothing to do with navigation. The Captain, knowing I was a Master Mariner, gave me free run of the bridge, which was enlightening. I asked the 3rd Officer where we were and he said 'Watch that box up there,' pointing to a small display unit in the corner of the wheelhouse. In a matter of minutes I had a digital print out of Latitude and Longitude, by courtesy of Satellite/Computer technology. When I asked if they had such a thing as a sextant on the bridge, he thought there might be one under the chart room settee, but he hadn't seen it lately. It is interesting to note, that for deep sea certificates of competency, including Yachtmaster's (Deep Sea), a practical knowledge of astro-navigation is still required. After all, you never know when all the fuses might blow, do you?

We went south down the east coast of Iceland, calling at Seidisfjordur for fuel, before continuing to Scapa. Our next job was to be part of the distant covering force for convoy JW 52, which sailed from Loch Ewe in mid-January. We destroyers, *Oribi*, *Obedient*, *Inglefield* and the Polish manned destroyer *Orkan* (ex M Class renamed) sailed from Scapa, at the same time, for Hvalfjord, where we rendezvoused the battleship *Anson* and cruiser *Sheffield*. There was always a bit of inter-ship visiting and of course liberty men from each ship met ashore. We were all chummy ships as a result and it came as no surprise when the C of E padre in *Anson,* one called Fulljames, rugby international who played for England pre-war, suggested that all ships in harbour came to the Sunday Service on the quarter-deck of the battleship. What did come as a surprise to everyone was when he approached his captain and said 'The RC priest, the Methodist Minister and I would like all denominations to attend a combined Service that we three would conduct in harmony. We feel that shipmates will want to say similar prayers, before sailing tomorrow and hoping to stay alive. Have we your permission Sir?' 'Yes indeed padre, carry on,' was the reply. Spud and I welcomed the idea. He, a conscientious RC, had often said to me, jokingly, 'You and your "State" religion seem to have a monopoly in HM ships.' It was a 'one off' and a great success. After 50 years or more, I paid an infrequent visit to Matins, where the church and services were shared and applauded as a tremendous break through. Hearing this, I couldn't restrain myself from saying 'We did it in Iceland aboard *Anson* in 1943, you know. Pity about the gap!'

During the third week in January we went north about to Akureyri, for two days, before rejoining the battle fleet east of Iceland a week later. First ashore as usual, Spud and I turned a corner in this isolated frozen town and, would you believe it (?), bumped into a group of American Nurses. The Yanks had established a hospital in that remote 'neck of the woods'. I have never forgotten the opening remark of the nearest nurse. She introduced herself by saying 'Hello, I'm Miss Cock from Milwaukee, where they make all the beer.' Needless to say, we organized an allied party in the Wardroom that ran into the wee small hours and left some of us nursing a hangover, if not a US nurse, next day.

There was quite a lot of U-boat activity around JW 52's 15 merchantmen, 10 British and 5 American, but they were driven away by close escorts, who also shot down 2 out of 4 torpedo bombers. The convoy arrived undamaged in the Kola Inlet at the end of the month. Close cruiser cover was provided by *Bermuda*, *Glasgow* and *Kent* for JW 52 and for the westbound convoy, RA 52 (in ballast) consisting of 10 merchantmen, 3 British and 7 American, one of which, the *Greylock*, was sunk by U-255, but her entire crew was rescued. We destroyers screening the distant covering force, for both convoys, about 120 miles to the south-west, were kept busy counter-attacking many U-boats in our vicinity, damaging some no doubt, but no direct hits. RA 52 arrived at Loch Ewe on 8 February, with just the one ship lost, but no lives.

The spring of 1943 was a season of many unexpected changes, both in movements of ships and shipmates. After February, convoys to and from Russia were suspended for the summer. The last home-bound convoy, RA 53, with 30 merchantships, lost 3, sadly, torpedoed by U-boats, but the last loaded convoy, JW 53, consisting of 28 merchantships, got through undamaged. They had a large close escort of cruisers, corvettes and destroyers, which included 6 'O' Class, *Obedient*, *Obdurate*, *Offa*, *Onslaught*, *Opportune* and *Orwell*, from the 17th Destroyer Flotilla. *Onslow* was having her battle damage repaired in Hull and would not be operational again until May. *Oribi* went to Hull, also, for a refit and repairs from mid-February, to mid-March. The 17th DF was now complete, with 8 'O's, all of which survived WW2. Long after the war, in the early seventies, Sue and I were with Spud and his wife, Marguerite, when she said to us 'old shipmates', 'Are you sure you've got the names right, 'cos they're not easy to remember off hand? I can certainly see you two serving with great distinction in HMS *Obstinate* !'

Before we left Scapa to go south, Mac was awarded his 'brass hat' and that meant being promoted to Commander. The outward visible sign of this was gold oak-leaves, (scrambled eggs), on the peak of his cap, as well as 3 rings, instead of 2½, on each sleeve. He obviously knew about this coming his way, before us, because Gieves Ltd despatched the necessary attire most promptly. He also knew that he was going to be made Commander of Chatham Barracks and told me so. He had already said he would recommend me for a permanent commission in the RN, if I so wished, but I declined. Regardless, he would like me to be his No.1, if we were still at war, about 2 years hence, when he anticipated going back to sea in command of a 'Battle Class' destroyer, being laid down at this time. Even the name was mentioned as HMS *Finisterre*. I agreed with this idea, we would keep in touch and I was sorry to see him go. Later, in the autumn of '44, he dined me, with two Wren Officers, in his quarters at Chatham Barracks. I remember well, about every half-hour a 'doodle-bug' (V1) droned over our heads, aimed at London, and we would pause to pray that it wouldn't cut out over us. When the motor of a V1 stopped, that is when it descended and exploded on impact. Quite apart from our lives being endangered, if such had happened then, Mac reminded us that there were also a few thousand men in the Barracks. When the noise, on each occasion, continued into the distance, we all heaved a sigh of relief.

Back aboard *Oribi* in Hull, during February '43, Mac's personal relief as captain was Lieut-Cdr J.C.A. Ingram DSC, RN. He was a short, sprightly figure, with sharp facial features and a tuft of hair on each cheek-bone ('bugger's grips'). JCA (often referred to by his initials) had a limited knowledge of navigation, mostly coastal. His ship handling was very good and we, Spud and I, thought it much better than his man handling, which tended to be punitive over trivialities. We got on well with him and he thought well of us. After many months sailing with him, he would listen to our opinions with interest and we, as Reserve Officers, had no hesitation in expressing them. He seemed to believe that it was necessary to reprimand people, in order to maintain discipline, whereas we believed that was a nineteenth century style of leadership. Which reminds me that the Articles of War were read aloud to the ship's company, every quarter, I think. Whatever the misdemeanour, all paragraphs referred to the accused like this – 'If found guilty, shall suffer death, or some such other punishment hereinafter mentioned.' Most times it would mean just a few days stoppage of leave, but the very sound of the word 'death' was obviously considered to be a strong deterrent.

Doug Little left the ship and Spud Murphy took on the job of GCO. Doug had the most wonderful wit and I shall always recall his turn of phrase when estimating distance at sea. He related it to yards on the fairway of a golf course before he selected the best club to use. Whatever other qualifications he got at Cambridge, it was his Blue at Golf that dominated. He was aware that Mac, also, was handy with a set of clubs, so when OOW on the bridge at sea and haled up the voice-pipe by Mac from his sea-cabin

Oribi Wardroom. L. to r.: John Lamb, No. 1; Thos Smith, Doc.; Cooper, Midshipman; Ian Bryce, Navigator; Macbeath, Captain; 'Spud' Murphy, Gunnery Control Officer; Doug Little, Asdic Control Officer; Dickie Gardner, Sub-Lieutenant; Claude Stacey, Torpedo Control Officer; Pratt, Canadian, Sub-Lieutenant engineer officer

'Doug are we in station yet on the *Onslow*?' he would reply 'Yes sir, reckon I could put one on her quarterdeck, comfortably, with a No. 9 iron'. This meant nothing to me at the time, but I learned later that 200 yards or more (1 cable + at sea) was nothing to an expert golfer such as Doug. On another occasion, sitting on the club fender in the Wardroom, Doc Smith was asking his opinion about how many condoms to give a libertyman on 48 hours leave, thinking 2 would be adequate. Doug's response was emphatic 'Come on Doc, at least 4, 'cos I'm sure you like a bit in the 'dogs' (dog watches 4 to 6 and 6 to 8 p.m.) occasionally.' We missed his inimitable, sophisticated, dare I say 'Oxbridge' humour.

It was about this time, during the refit at Hull, that the Wardroom acquired two antipodean shipmates: Stan Jervis from Auckland, New Zealand, Lieut RNVR and Henry Hall, Sub-Lieut RNVR, from Adelaide, Australia. Stan was lucky to have his wife Peggy in the UK, working as a Governess with a family in Thame, Oxon. Henry was not so lucky, but we heard about his wife frequently. He was a good old faithful husband, whose standard remark, after a party with ladies present, was 'Listen you fellas, I'd back my wife's legs against anybody's.'

Stan and Peggy became very good friends in '43 and I saw them later in the '50s when world cruising in Cunard. Back in '43, they had a thing about staying for a few days at The Savoy Hotel in London, bit like Bob Swan insisting on going to The Ritz in '41, I guess, but when they did, I was asked to dine and met a charming NZ girlfriend of theirs, to whom I said, as we danced to Carroll Gibbons and the Savoy Orpheans, 'How about a date tomorrow and where would you like to go?' 'I'd love to go to a London theatre, if that's OK with you?' she replied. It sure was and I shall never forget taking her to the Haymarket Theatre to see John Gielgud as Hamlet playing opposite Peggy Ashcroft as Ophelia. Two young top performers, of their generation, at the time. Weren't we lucky and with a war on too?

Not the Savoy for me. Sometimes, nights in London during the war were spent at the Queen Elizabeth's Club for Officers, in Piccadilly, near where the 'In and Out' (Naval and Military) Club used to be. It was sponsored by Lord Nuffield, the man who invented and made Morris cars (Oxfords, Cowleys and Minors pre-war), a true philanthropist, which is why it only cost five shillings (25p) a night and why I used it frequently. Whatever income we received, and it was precious little in those days, five shillings (25p) a day as a Midshipman, increasing to just over £1 (say £1.10p) as a Sub-Lieut, it accumulated whilst we were at sea for long periods. This allowed us to live way beyond our normal means for short periods ashore.

Oribi and *Onslow* were fitted with High Frequency Direction Finding apparatus (HF/DF or 'huff-duff'), consisting of a small tower to enclose the operator, with a lattice type aerial mounted on it and situated on the upper deck, between the torpedo tubes and the 4-inch gun. This device listened, all round, for a U-boat's radio transmission and determined the direction, compass bearing, from which it came. U-boats surfaced to communicate with their bases in France and other U-boats, when intent on gathering a pack to attack a convoy. HF/DF was a great help to us in 1943, when in the Atlantic. Two ships so fitted and strategically placed around a convoy could co-operate and get a good fix on a U-boat's position. One or both could then approach at high speed along the line of bearing, hoping to catch the U-boat on the surface and destroy it by gun-fire, ramming, or depth charges if it crash dived. This was a successful tactic and happened quite often in the year ahead. Captain Sherbrooke VC, still recovering from his wounds, was replaced as Capt D 17, in March, by Captain J.A. (Bess) McCoy, who, with his Staff led the flotilla in *Offa*, relieving Alastair Ewing as captain, pending *Onslow*'s return to service.

Dönitz reckoned that if his U-boats could sink in excess of 800,000 tons of allied shipping per month, then he would win the war, in other words, Britain, without sufficient essential supplies, would be beaten. In 1942, the average tonnage per month sunk was 650,000 and in the months of March, June and November, it exceeded 800,000. Also, the number of operational U-boats in the Atlantic had increased from an average per month in '42 of 145, to over 200 in the spring of '43. To counter this appalling situation, every available destroyer was withdrawn from the Home Fleet and sent to form Support (Escort) Groups under Commander-in-Chief Western Approaches, Admiral Sir Max Horton. These groups could be switched from convoy to convoy in support, or be sent to areas where packs were concentrating and waiting for oncoming convoys. The 3rd Support Group, led by McCoy in *Offa*, included *Obedient*, *Onslaught*, *Oribi* and *Orwell*. It was during the Hull refit that I went to Liverpool for a week to attend a Tactical Course at Derby House, then part of HMS *Eaglet*, under the expert guidance of Captain Roberts RN and his team of Wrens. The delegates, about a dozen, were mostly navigators of convoy escorts, attending to learn the latest tactics to apply against U-boats.

The man who did most to win the Battle of the Atlantic was Captain F.J. Walker CB, DSO and 3 Bars, in the Bird Class Sloop *Starling*, leading the 2nd Support Group, with other sloops such as *Wild Goose*, *Woodcock*, *Magpie*, *Wren* and *Kite*. It was he who had developed most of the tactics we would be using and very few U-boats escaped the ultimate treatment from his Group. He died in July '44 of 'overstrain, overwork and war weariness'. He had driven himself beyond all limits. It is sad to reflect that between WW1 and 2 he had been eligible for promotion from Commander to Captain, but, as an anti-submarine specialist, he was excluded, as were other A/S specialists in favour of officers from branches of the Service that offered more glamour. It is the opinion of many of us WW2 veterans, that anti-submarine know-how didn't carry enough clout in the Admiralty, as it should have done, after our experience in the Atlantic in 1917. I feel sure the Merchant Navy was glad Walker returned to sea in 1941, after two years as Staff Officer (Operations) to Vice-Admiral Ramsay at Dover, with responsibility overall, for anti-submarine defences. A great leader recognized, at last, regardless of rank.

The scene in Derby House was practical and fun in the process of learning. A large central floor space was used to plot the movements of a convoy surrounded by U-boats and a dozen Close Escort, or Support Group, model ships, one for each delegate. Each of us was in command of our own ship, shut in separate cabins, forming a circle round the floor. We were unable to see the central arena and our only communication was through a two-way letter box, with our personal Wren messenger. Each cabin had a chart-table, with instruments on a blank plotting chart, a clock and a pad on which to write signals for despatch. Captain Roberts, with a small staff, was in complete control and would make signals, via the Wrens, to all escorts, or those selected, giving information on which we were expected to take action. I plotted away on the chart, movements of other ships, U-boat dispositions, huff-duff bearings, radar contacts and so on, from which I deduced the best thing to do. I then scribbled a signal saying, for example, 'To HMS Roberts: From HMS Bryce: Time 1015Z (GMT). My position, course and speed, such and such. Intend engaging U-boat on surface bearing 270 (West) from me. Please advise present course of convoy.' and posted this through the letter box.

My Wren was called Jackie. She took signals to and fro and plotted my ship's movements on the floor with chalk as directed by the Captain. The critique after the exercise, lasting about an hour, was always most instructive and not lacking in humour. We gathered in a large circle outside our cabins and listened to Roberts, like Walker, with Atlantic experience and ideal as Staff Officer for tactical training. He reviewed each ship in turn and then gave an overview, always producing new ideas. I recall him saying to me 'Bryce, you were doing alright, until you decided to engage a small iceberg, bearing 270, thinking it was a U-boat, which in fact was on a reciprocal bearing of 090 (East) on the other side of the convoy.' Oh yes, I learned a lot.

Naturally, Jackie and I got to know each other better, day by day. We worked well together as shipmates ashore and so on Friday afternoon I posted a personal signal in the box, saying 'RPC (Request the Pleasure of your Company) at dinner tonight, 2000, in the Adelphi Hotel.' Back came her reply pronto and in navalese 'WMP (With Much Pleasure).' We had a fun evening and went on to dance in the basement night club until about 0100. I was about to order a taxi when the air-raid sirens sounded a 'red alert', so that was that, no taxis. It was quiet in the centre and OK to walk, so that is what we did, all the way out to Allerton, some 3 or 4 miles. At about 0230, the front door of a large splendid house opened to reveal a lady, who looked distinctly displeased at daughter's late return home. It was no time to hang about, so I saluted and bade them goodnight, my duty as a close escort completed. On the walk back, luckily, I found a Police Station and looked in as the 'all clear' sounded. They were good lads and drove me back to my digs, without hesitation. Fraternity often happened, just like that, in wartime.

Next day, I got a phone-call from Jackie, who said 'Mummy was sorry she was so rude last night and she really wanted to thank you, for escorting me safely home. Also, Daddy wants to thank you and insists that we have dinner at the Adelphi on him, with my sister and her fiancé and also he has booked four seats for us at the Liverpool Rep.' It was Laurence Olivier and Vivien Leigh playing in something, much enjoyed, but I can't remember what. Anyway, I soon discovered that Jackie's father was the Architect for the City of Liverpool. I never met him, just enjoyed his generosity and thanked him by phone. It was a happy ending to a time in one of my favourite seafaring cities, which, by chance, extended my on-shore tactical experience as well as my off-shore, which was the original intention.

What lay ahead, was lots of seatime in the Atlantic, dashing from convoy to convoy and I shall tell many tales of action that I recall, but not always being specific about dates. It would be tedious if I listed all the convoys we supported from week to week, and besides it would be impossible, because I do not have that information. Our home base from March '43 to Feb '44 was in the Firth of Clyde at what was called the Tail of the Bank, with Greenock and Gourock, on the south side about 25 miles down the Clyde from Glasgow, as our two ports of call. As the 3rd Support Group we would go out round the Mull of Kintyre, pass north of Ireland and go where we were most needed. Sometimes we were at sea for two or three weeks, refuelling from oil tankers, with names like Brown or Black Ranger.

Many a time we picked up U-boat signals on huff–duff and two of us would follow up at high speed, only to see the bastard crash-dive on sighting us. Then we might apply a tactic learned. One of us would stand-off and 'ping' at a distance, knowing the enemy would pick up our Asdic on his hydrophone and realize we were a good way away and not attacking. Our sister support ship would not 'ping', but remain silent, at slow speed, being directed by us on signal lamp to the position of the enemy. The pilot in each ship co-ordinated the situation and when it was considered right, sister put on speed and dropped a pattern of depth charges on an unsuspecting U-boat. Also, about now, close escort ships were being fitted with 'Hedgehog', a cluster of twenty-four bombs, fitted in a framework on the fo'c'sle. These were fired, all together, over the bow and exploded on impact with the target, at whatever depth. This caught U-boats unawares and prevented them taking the avoiding action, normally used, against ships armed with depth charges only. Such ships were obliged to pass over the enemy before dropping the charges, over the stern, set to an estimated depth of target. This short period of time gave a U-boat commander the opportunity to dive and change direction, often with success. After two years in *Oribi*, witnessing hundreds of depth charge explosions, with only one recognized kill and a few damaged, I was inclined to back a skilled U-boat commander against his attacker on the surface, even though the latter had lots of experience.

A very big concern at the end of '42 was the 'mid Atlantic gap' in air cover at the height of the U-boat campaign. In December '42, after consulting a physicist, Prof J.D. Bernal, Mountbatten briefed Churchill about the possibility of a floating ice-island as a refuelling depot for aircraft and Winston after careful thought said 'What a good idea. We'll call it "Habbakuk", after a Book in the Bible which says "Behold ye among the heathen, regard and wonder marvellously: for I will work a work in your days, which ye will not believe, though it be told you".' This ice-airfield would be built in Newfoundland, 600 metres long, 90 metres wide and 60 metres deep. It would have 26 electrically driven propellers, a top speed of 7 knots, a crew of 2,000 and be made of a frozen, indestructible, substance composed of water and wood-pulp (Pycrete). A central refrigeration unit would keep the ice at a core temperature of 10°C. A model was built, which worked and it was discussed by Roosevelt and Churchill at Quebec in the summer of '43, but by then the 'mid Atlantic gap' was being covered most efficiently by RCAF and RAF Liberators, Sunderlands and Catalinas from Iceland, Labrador and Newfoundland. Consequently, 'Habbakuk' never happened.

It wasn't only us out there who won the big battle in '43. Bletchley Park (Station X), that fabulous place 50 miles north of London, where Alan Turing and his team invented the modern computer and cracked the German 'Enigma' codes, undoubtedly made a big contribution and shortened the period of the war by a year or two. Information about U-boat situations in the Atlantic was passed to C-in-C Western Approaches and helped his strategy enormously. Convoys were re-directed and Support Groups were concentrated where most needed. RAF Coastal Command were hitting more U-boats, not only in the Bay of Biscay, a happy hunting ground for them, but also in the north Atlantic. We picked up many U-boat survivors after they had been bombed and abandoned boat. On one occasion, the U-boat captain was a young arrogant Nazi, whose only comment when questioned was 'We will win, you will lose, Heil Hitler!' One of his seamen, mixing with crew members, was very different and told our Supply Petty Officer, Stan Meads, who spoke fluent German 'I wish this war would end. My wife has been bombed in Hamburg and I do not want to fight you fellows.' We landed many U-boat prisoners at Gourock, blind-folded and turned over to the army for safe keeping.

Sometimes we had to land survivors from our merchantships and the great personality that comes to mind is '2-ton Tess', Manageress of the Bay Hotel, Gourock. She was a large lady and the largest part of her was her heart. The doors of the Bay Hotel were open to everyone, regardless of rooms being available. The public rooms were full of survivors, on chairs, settees and sleeping on the floors; she fed them too and there was no charge. Just as well, because if a sailor was lucky enough to survive his ship's sinking, when he went over the side into a lifeboat, or the sea, to be picked up, his pay stopped from that moment until he signed on another ship in the UK. Being in the RNR, I didn't know this until many years after the war, but a lot of people in high places, like the MOT (Ministry of Transport) must have known and this tells us, now, about their attitude then towards the 'Fourth Service' in our fighting democracy. It would certainly have hastened them to join another ship (back on pay!) and continue supplying food and fighting materials to the UK. Makes me think that if the 'powers that were' had drawn up an 'Article of War', as a code for all

Merchant Seamen, it might have sounded something like this: 'If alive, after being close to death, by enemy action, shall, if rescued from the sea or a lifeboat, suffer some such deprivation as loss of pay and any other amenities thus affected, until such time as signed-on another merchantship-of-war.' How's that for terms of reference?

At the end of March and in early April we had long periods at sea in very heavy weather, going from convoy to convoy, at speeds that put the ship under stress as well as the personnel, and caused cracks in the upper-deck plating. These were detected by the eagle-eyed Jock Graham, crawling round on his hands and knees, so we went into Belfast for repairs. Spud and I nipped ashore and organized a party with the Wren Officers. We soon saw that our No.1, John Lamb, whom we considered somewhat naive, was immediately smitten with a 2nd Officer WRNS, daughter of an Admiral it transpired. When next day he told us he was going ashore to meet her, we took a chance, in his absence and piped 'Make and Mend' (half holiday) to the ship's company, to celebrate the 1st Lieutenant's engagement. Cheers all round. The amazing thing is, that No.1 on his return said he had proposed to the lady on the top of a tramcar and been accepted. Some months later, in the autumn of '43, they were married at St James's, Spanish Place, in London, because she was RC, and Spud, who was likewise, agreed to be best-man. I was there with my latest girl-friend June, a driver for the American Ambulance Corps (AAC), down from her base in Glasgow, where we first met and staying at the Mayfair Hotel. All I know about the AAC is, that the US supplied the vehicles and the UK the drivers, volunteers, without pay, daughters of wealthy parents who looked most attractive in their quality khaki uniforms, with a crossed flags, US and UK, insignia, on each arm.

It was during April and May '43 that the U-boat wolf-packs were heavily defeated in a series of great convoy battles in the Atlantic. In those two months the enemy lost from all causes a total of 56 U-boats (41 of them in May). The epic battles in the spring of '43 climaxed in the struggle around the outward-bound convoy ONS 5, escorted by B7, one of the most successful groups in the Atlantic, led by the celebrated Peter Gretton in command of the destroyer, HMS *Duncan*. Fought in gale-force winds and fog banks over several hundred miles, the battle lasted 10 days. There were as many U-boats, hunting in packs, as there were ships in ONS 5, and four and a half times as many U-boats, around the convoy, as there were escorts. 12 merchant ships were sunk, but 6 U-boats were destroyed and 2 more lost by collision. 5 U-boats reported severe damage and 12 more reported lesser action damage. Making good use of radar, the well trained escorts made some 40 attacks. *Oribi* and *Offa* were in on the action, the others of our 3rd Support Group having left to refuel.

On 3 May, Commander P.W. Gretton (later Vice-Admiral Sir Peter Gretton KCB, DSO – 3 times, OBE, DSC) was faced with an appalling dilemma, because his ship, *Duncan*, had only enough fuel left to make Newfoundland at economical speed. The convoy crawled on into heavy seas, with no sign of improvement, making fuelling at sea impossible and also such weather would not allow boat work, nor his transfer by jackstay to another vessel. After much heart-searching he decided *Duncan* had to go and therefore Command of the Escort was handed over to Lieut-Cdr R.E. Sherwood RNR in the River Class Frigate HMS *Tay*. *Duncan* reached St John's with only 4% fuel remaining.

On 5 May the weather moderated and the enemy attacked, during the day, with much success. Providentially, the convoy entered fog at dusk, which was a blessing for the escorts, now reduced to only 7 in total, 5 close, plus 2 (*Oribi* and *Offa*) in support. All ship's crews were worn out after many days of bad weather and a running fight which had already lasted more than a week. Dönitz had ordered his packs to remain on the surface and continue attacking, before the convoy came under the protection of an air 'umbrella' from Newfoundland. That night, the enemy, about 30 U-boats, made 24 attacks, all of them driven off, without the loss of another merchantship. Sherwood reported later 'All ships showed dash and initiative and the enemy was heavily defeated by a combination of skill, luck and sheer guts.'

Oribi's moment of triumph came in the small hours of 6 May and where was I? Dozing on the settee in the charthouse! Over many days, the captain and I had spent long periods on the bridge and as we were in a state of relaxed action stations, we gave each other short spells of rest. It was during a lull in the middle watch that JCA said 'Pilot, go and put your head down for a bit,' so there I was. Suddenly there was an almighty bang, followed by a violent shaking of the hull, which made me wonder if we'd been torpedoed, until I heard a voice, coming through the bridge voice-pipe, shouting 'There's half a U-boat going down the port side.' Because I was not involved directly, I shall tell the tale as related to me by shipmates later, supported by information researched elsewhere.

Spud was OOW and the captain was sitting in his high-chair. Everything happened very quickly, in poor visibility and it seemed that the target was picked up almost simultaneously and reported by the operators of radar, Asdic and huff-duff as a surfaced U-boat on the port bow, closing fast. JCA leapt from his chair to the wheelhouse voice-pipe and shouted 'Hard a-port.' *Oribi*, doing about 22 knots (25½ mph), swung away to the left and as the captain put in his report after the action, 'the U-boat more or less impaled itself upon my bow'. With the U-boat cut in half and sinking, JCA shouted down the voice-pipe to the W/T (Wireless/Telegraphy) office 'Report this to *Tay* on R/T (Radio Telephone) in plain language.' Don Pritchard was the duty Operator and what he said was 'To *Tay* (code-word not remembered) from "Mighty" (*Oribi*), at 0315 rammed "Hearse"

(U-boat) in position 52.40 N 45.30 W.' It was Signalman Doug Gowland, on the port side of the bridge who shouted what I had heard in the charthouse and added afterwards that he was sure he saw two of the U-boat's crew on deck smoking. There were no survivors from our victim, which we discovered later was U-531 (*Neckel*), rammed and sunk in a position some 400 miles north-east of Cape Race, Newfoundland and 440 miles south of Cape Farewell, Greenland. I still have the book in which all my DR and observed positions by astro-navigation were calculated at that time and throughout the war.

Oribi received 6 awards after this action, not just for the moment of ramming but taking into account overall service throughout this protracted battle. I now list the names of my shipmates who received such distinction.

DSC (a Bar) . . . Lieut-Cdr J.C.A. Ingram DSC, RN
DSM . . . Able Seaman Bernard Blowers (Radar)
        Able Seaman Frederick Smith (Asdic)
        Ordinary Telegraphist Francis Williams (HF/DF)
Mention in Dispatches . . . Lieut John Murphy RNVR
                    Able Seaman William Goodacre (Plot)

It needs to be said, for me anyway, on reflection long afterwards, that sending about 70 submariners to a common grave in the Atlantic, did not engender a happy, glorious, victorious feeling, but rather one of regret that it was necessary. However, it was the fearful realization that it was them or us in this fight for freedom and we felt such extreme action was justified. Our determined reaction had the desired effect, because after the ONS5 action, Dönitz ceased pack-attacks and told his U-boats to withdraw. His son had been killed in a U-boat a month before, just south of where we were and who knows whether this future Deputy and ultimate Fuhrer of the 3rd Reich in '45 was influenced by personal feelings? Did the heavy loss of life at sea change his attitude? After all, basically, he was a submariner and had been all his life.

For many years I have taken that excellent monthly paper called *Navy News*, to keep me in touch with naval affairs past, present and future. Imagine my surprise when browsing through the May edition 2002, while writing this account, I spotted a bit about a commemoration service being held in Liverpool Cathedral the following Sunday morning, the 5th. Serendipity perhaps or just a weird coincidence; I certainly didn't plan it that way. The *News* went on to say that it was to mark the 59th anniversary of this, the longest single battle of WW2. Later, I spoke to Lieut-Cdr Phil Russ at HMS *Eaglet*, Liverpool and he promised to keep me informed about the following year's event, the 60th anniversary. When I mentioned the Tactical Course at Derby House in '43, he said it was no longer part of *Eaglet* but was now a museum.

CHAPTER 11

HMS *Oribi*: part 4

THE DAMAGE TO *ORIBI* WAS CONSIDERABLE. Her bow was pushed back about 20 feet below the 12 ft water-line, the port propeller was lost and the Asdic dome gone, but she was seaworthy and able to steam on her remaining screw to St John's, Newfoundland, where she arrived three days later. This meant shoring-up No.9 bulkhead and doing about 9 knots, zigzagging furiously to avoid being fished by one of many U-boats still at large. We were docked there for a few days undergoing a temporary patch-up, before sailing on to Boston, Massachusetts, for full repairs to be carried out. During our stay, Spud introduced me to Lieutenant Ludovic Kennedy RNVR, who was ADC (aide de camp) to the Governor General. Ludo, as he was known to most people, had been an officer in the Tribal Class destroyer *Mishona* when Spud was a makey-learn seaman, about to be a CW candidate and I had read with interest and much enjoyed Ludo's book *Sub-lieutenant*, published in the war and selling well on railway station bookstalls. I have a very high regard for Ludo, as a person, philosopher and writer, having read many of his books. Knowing about him and his sensitive, sensible attitude to life, after a similar sea-going experience to mine in wartime, has helped me to write these memoirs. After editing a few of my paragraphs over and over again, I say to Sue, my most understanding wife, 'You'd better read this again and comment, because I've done a Ludo.' He said somewhere, that sometimes it took him a forenoon to compose two paragraphs and I know just what he means.

Wasn't I the lucky one to be in Boston, Mass, for my 21st birthday? Forget about that divisive tea-party way back in 1773, the citizens, even the Irish element, couldn't have been kinder to us all. The hospitality in Boston was really magnificent. The ship went into dry-dock to be repaired and whilst the crew still lived on-board, they were accommodated and entertained ashore for long week-ends, most lavishly, during our stay from 4 to 27 June. The hub of this social generosity was the Union Jack Club, presided over by Mrs Lawrence, a very wealthy widow, about my mother's age, early fifties I guess. She came aboard to organize our crew to stay with members of the Club, and because she did it mainly through Spud and me, we found ourselves invited to her home as her personal guests.

Mrs Lawrence lived in a large stately home at Groton, in typically English countryside near Boston, inhabited by her family for many generations and surrounded by lots of other wealthy families. FDR (Franklin D. Roosevelt), the then President, lived and was at school in Groton as a youth and a close neighbour was a partner in J.P. Morgans (big financiers); so the place was loaded with millionaires, whom we found mingled easily and without ostentation. Living with Mrs L were her fun daughter, Marion, of our age, whose husband was in the US Navy fighting in the Pacific, and a long established friend from London, England, Mrs Foster, who was staying for the duration of the war. Then there was a cook and housemaid of Irish origin which brought out the 'emerald green' voice in Murphy. We were surrounded by splendid oil paintings of ancestors, one rather special of a gentleman who had been Ambassador at the Court of St James in the nineteenth century. This caused my intellectual brother officer to adapt that well known rhyme:

> And this is good old Boston,
> The home of the bean and the cod,
> Where the Lawrences talk only to Cabots,
> And the Cabots talk only to God.
>
>   J.C. Bossidy
>   *On the Aristocracy of Harvard.*

One week-end we went to New York by train and everything was paid for by our American hosts. On arrival in NY we went to a hotel on Park Avenue, the centre for Services hospitality, where we were given tickets for rooms at the Hotel Commodore, for night clubs around town, and introduced to a hostess each, who would accompany us throughout our visit. Don't get me wrong, they weren't 'call girls', just lovely young folk, intent on giving the guys in uniform a good time for free, before they went off to the war. We visited the 'Stage Door Canteen', where Hollywood Stars ran a continuous floor-show, then on to the high spots, literally, like the top of the Empire State Building and licentiously, like a night-club in down-town Manhattan.

The return journey by train to Boston was unusual to say the least. We got to Grand Central Station on Sunday evening, humming 'Chattanooga Choo-Choo' and thinking about 'dinner in the diner' and so on, only to find masses of service men heading the same way. Extra travel space was provided by what was most readily available, in the shape of cattle-trucks. We did as we saw others doing, laid newspaper on the floor of the truck and prepared for a hard night's sleep. Suddenly, we were hailed by a Captain in the US Navy who said 'Hi there you guys, call me when you sight Bunker Hill!' as he spread his *New York Times* alongside us and settled down for a chat before we all dozed off. That night we got to know what it was like for folks back home, sleeping in the London Underground Stations during air-raids, but mercifully, for us, without the bombing.

Back in Groton for week-ends, Marion managed our movements magically by car, with music as we motored along the highways. Benny

Goodman's clarinet gave great counterpoint to the natural countryside concertos. She had lots of young friends, in their twenties, like us, intent on 'cuttin a rug' frequently, at parties. I can recall a typical introduction of us to others was 'I'd like you to meet with John and Ian from London, England, here after combat in the Atlantic with Hitler's U-boats.' We kept our egos reasonably under control, but indulged a bit now and then, why not, remembering that for one year we had stood alone? Spud, who spoke without affectation on board ship, would sometimes put on the voice of a 'BBC Announcer' of that era, rather 'posh' and without the slightest trace of any provincial dialect. This was always well received by his US audience, with the usual response, 'Gee John, say that again, please do, 'cos we just love to hear your English accent.' He needed little encouragement to fulfil this request, before ending with a few words in Cockney or Glaswegian for fun.

We dined each evening, all of us, in formal attire, John and I donning bow-ties, with our uniform jackets, which was all we had, but which delighted the ladies. Unbeknown to me, John leaked to them that my 21st birthday had happened on 9 June. Within the week, a big surprise party day was organized, with champagne and a cake displaying 21 candles, in the afternoon at Groton, followed by a fabulous party at one of Boston's top night clubs, for the younger guys and dolls, that went on 'til dawn next day. Spud was Marion's escort, 29, she 24 and it seemed to me, they took a suitably restrained shine to each other, from then on. I was happily paired with a tall top teenager, who took off her shoes to dance with me in bare feet, putting us on a more amicable footing, I guess. Needless to say, Mrs Lawrence picked up the tab, but delighted in so doing, as expressed in her letter to my mother, soon after.

I still have the original letter sent by Mrs L to Mrs B, way back in '43 and I am quoting it here and now, as a tribute to all mothers in WW2, with sons away in the fighting forces. This letter is from a US Mum to a UK Mum under such circumstances:

Mrs Richard Lawrence, Farmers Row, Groton, Massachusetts June 18 1943.

Dear Mrs Bryce –
Ian has just been staying with us over the week-end, and I thought you might like to hear of him as well as from him. He is very well and we enjoyed so much having him with us.

By 'we', I mean myself, my daughter, Mrs Cutler, aged 24 and a friend of mine Mrs Foster. We discovered Ian's birthday and although it wasn't the exact date, we gave him a party with a cake and champagne, on Saturday. We thought a 21st birthday should be properly celebrated and it was great fun.

My daughter's husband is in our Navy in the Pacific and my son in New Caledonia with the Parachute Troops. I must say I wish he wasn't!

I am interested in the Union Jack Club in Boston and through them often have English boys for a week-end. But we have never liked any of them as much as Ian and his friend John Murphy. They are dear boys and I am glad we will see more of them before they go.

We live 40 miles out of Boston in a large old house with plenty of room. So I have asked them to come any time they can.

with best wishes,
sincerely yours
Margery Lawrence

My mother, I know, valued very much this letter with its sharing of trans-Atlantic emotions and I was always aware of her courageous support during the war. However, it wasn't until much later that I appreciated what courage and control she had practised for my benefit. Time and again, Mum saw me off from Central Station. A happy hug and a brave wave sent me on my way to war. Always a cheer, never a tear, but I'm sure some were shed after I'd gone, knowing Mum rarely smothered her feelings. I feel sure we were all helped in those traumatic times by Gracie Field's song 'Wish me luck as you wave me goodbye' and the optimistic words of Vera Lynn (Sweetheart of the Forces) 'We'll meet again'.

Vera's words came true 32 years later, in 1975, when, once again, I met Mrs Margery Lawrence, my surrogate mother, in the US of A. I was then employed by Conoco (UK) Ltd, subsidiary of Continental Oil Co, Ponca City, Texas with HQ in Houston. Tony Dixon and I, as Management Trainers, were over there to develop ideas on a new Seminar and that took us from Houston to Harvard University in Boston. We stayed at the Sheraton Hotel for a few days and hired a car, or should I say an automobile. With time to spare, I suggested a trip down memory lane for me, which I was sure Tony would enjoy and so we drove to Groton. The scene was the same as in '43, when we knocked on the door of the Lawrence family seat. A young Mum with a couple of kids answered and I said 'Is Mrs Lawrence still living here?' She replied 'No, not now, but we know where she is and you guys must be English, by your accent. Come on in, you're welcome and I'll put you in touch with Mrs Lawrence.' Over coffee and cookies, she told us that Mrs L had moved into the old school house nearby and the ancient family residence was now split into four apartments. Our young hostess phoned Mrs L and said, mischievously, 'I've got a man here from your past who wants to talk to you.'

The sound of my voice was enough for her to identify me. 'Ian!' she said. 'How wonderful to hear you again, I'll get a chicken out of the freezer right now and you and your friend must dine with me this evening.' A memorable dinner it was, with Ambassador ancestor looking down on us as we ate. In her eighties, as she was then, she still motored to Florida each year, in the fall, to spend the winter there. On bidding us farewell, she said

'Go down the road from here and at the main highway it's easy to turn to Boston.' We did that, with Tony driving and me as co-pilot. We turned at the T junction, we thought correctly, but with my innate sense of compass direction, from seafaring days, I felt uneasy, especially when looking up to a clear sky and seeing the pole star ahead. 'Stop Tony,' I said, 'We're going north and Boston is south'. We had joined the 'Reciprocal Club', like me, on the Tactical Course in Derby House, Liverpool, back in '43. After turning round, we steered south on a steady course for the Sheraton Hotel, to conclude a very happy occasion with another lovely lady in my life. When we got back to the UK, we both, Tony and I, fitted compasses in our cars.

After those peaceful three weeks in Boston, we sailed for Bermuda and berthed in Hamilton on the last day of June '43. We enjoyed lots of swimming and practised an 'abandon ship exercise' in wonderfully warm water, so different from the Arctic, in which, happily, we were never immersed. I recall that one of the ABs removed a dental plate from his mouth before diving in and realized, only after we had sailed, that he had left some of his teeth on the jetty.

On 2 July we left Bermuda escorting the battleship *Queen Elizabeth*, the cruiser *Phoebe* and four BDEs (British Destroyer Escorts – Lend-lease ships built in the USA), *Bentinck*, *Bickerton*, *Duff* and *Stayner*. The BDEs were called Captain Class Frigates, whilst serving with the RN until 1945. Our speed of about 20 knots (23 mph), kept us out of trouble from U-boats on the eastbound crossing of the Atlantic and we arrived at Plymouth/ Devonport on 8 July. This fulfilled one of Jack's popular expressions, 'What's the buzz?' We're going to Guz!' and I want to quote the amusing reason for this from a book called *Royal Navalese*. Guz (short for Guzzle) was the nickname given to Devonport, with HMS *Drake* (stone frigate), purely naval in origin and use. It is said to have arisen from the West Countryman's inordinate love of cream teas with jam, clotted cream, fresh bread and lashings of anything else available. However, going to 'Guz' in '43, did not provide a happy sight. Those Nazi bastards had flattened large areas with their bombs and I shall never forget the contrasting image it gave us, to the wholesome US coastal port of Boston, still fresh in our memories. The visit was a short one and we were back in our home from home, Scapa, on 11 July.

The next six months were packed with incidents and I have selected the most significant or unusual. Later in July we escorted the Aircraft Carrier *Furious* down to Greenock, which gave us a few days alongside the jetty before returning to Scapa. A run-ashore in civilization was always welcome, with a chance to phone home and meet characters from other ships in harbour. A person with whom I struck an immediate rapport was a

Sub-Lieut RNVR, in a destroyer berthed nearby. He was called Count Hussary Bessoni (spelt phonetically) from Hungary, educated in the UK, whose spoken English was excellent and who had decided to stay and fight with us. He told me a lot about himself and jousting, his favourite pastime when at home on the family estate. How exciting it was to get saddled up as a well protected knight, with shield, and charge with blunted lance at another jouster, similarly mounted, attired and armed, with the object of unseating him. I found it quite fascinating to hear about it, over a gin, in the *Oribi*, but perish the thought of getting involved, should he ever think of inviting me home as his guest, after the war.

Over lunch Hungry Bee (my name for him) said 'How about attending a Court-Martial this afternoon, there's one on in Greenock?' We did that and it was most instructive sitting in the 'naval gallery', as it were, witnessing the procedure. I thought afterwards, let's hope I never see a sword on the table, with the blade pointing at me, indicating that the Board had found me guilty. Happily, I had a lot of luck in my naval career and so never suffered that indignity.

The anti U-boat sweeps continued throughout the summer, into the autumn, with *Oribi* and *Orwell* operating in the north Atlantic as the 10th EG (Escort Group), under C-in-C WA. The other ships in the group were *Musketeer* (Senior Officer) and the Polish manned destroyer *Orkan*, actually an 'M' Class, *Myrmidon*, but renamed by request. During August and September we used Skaalfjord in the Faroe Islands as our base, ideally situated, midway, between Orkneys and Iceland. Also, at this time, there was a noticeable increase in air activity by Coastal Command Liberators and Sunderlands.

One day we saw a Sunderland dive into the sea about ten miles ahead and on getting closer, we were amazed to find two groups of survivors, squatting in their life-rafts, about half a mile apart, shaking their fists and shouting abuse at each other. Apparently, our bomber had sunk the U-boat, a 'milch cow' (larger boat used to refuel others in mid-ocean), caught on the surface, but had been shot down at the same time. We picked up the 6 Sunderland survivors and *Orwell* rescued about 30 survivors from the U-boat. The result might best be described as 'Quid pro quo', or 'Tit for tat'. As a management consultant in the eighties, I might have said it was a win-win situation, but the survivors then called it something very different!

In September the 10th EG sailed out into mid- Atlantic, west of Ireland, to go from convoy to convoy, in support of the close escorts. About this time, Dönitz introduced a new weapon to the sea war, hoping to reverse the disastrous losses earlier in the year and regain supremacy in the Battle of the Atlantic. It was called the T-5 'Gnat', an acoustic homing torpedo fired from a U-boat and aimed mainly at escorts, in order to destroy the perimeter defence and make the ships in convoy more vulnerable to attack.

It was in October that a terrible tragedy took place within our Escort Group and I can see the scene clearly as I write this, 58½ years later. All four of us, in the 10th EG, joined the 39 ships of convoy SC 143, eastbound, in mid-ocean, on 6 October and carried out wide sweeps in response to HF/DF bearings from U-boat transmissions, which indicated about 8 or more in the vicinity. On the night of the 7th/8th, we dropped astern about 20 to 30 miles, to create a diversion, which we did by firing star-shell into the sky, dropping depth-charges frequently, talking on R/T and giving the impression the convoy was being attacked in our position. It worked well. The U-boats talked to each other and began to assemble around us. The convoy now was a good 40 to 50 miles ahead, so we became inconspicuous and followed it, at high speed in a flat calm sea.

At about 0600, we were in line abreast, from left to right, *Orwell, Oribi, Musketeer* and *Orkan*, 7 miles astern of the convoy, when suddenly *Orkan* was hit by a 'Gnat' torpedo, causing her to go under in less than five minutes. With great presence of mind *Musketeer*, next in line, put the wheel hard-over and went alongside *Orkan's* port side. This allowed 44 crew members of a total 190, to jump from ship to ship, 1 officer and 43 ratings. Commander Neville Currey, in command of *Musketeer*, was awarded the Polish Gold Cross of Merit with Swords, for his prompt action to save the *Orkan's* crew. It was a sad end for many heroes who came out of Danzig in '39, when the bully-boys of Europe moved into their country. They had fought with us for four years, before this tragic moment and their loved ones, who were far away in occupied territory, might not hear of their fate for a very long time. I'm sure *Orkan* lives on in the minds of many WW2 destroyer survivors who served in the Arctic and north Atlantic.

Later on 8 October, an RAF Liberator and an RCAF Sunderland sank three U-boats and damaged a fourth. One of these was believed to be U-378, which sank the *Orkan*. Next day, Pilot Officer John Wright RAF, in his Liberator, 'R' for 'Roger', bombed and sank U-419 close to us and we rescued the sole survivor, the captain, Oberleutnant Giersberg, with a leg broken in two places. We admired him for his courageous survival and his attitude, which was more Kreigsmarine, that of a sailor, than a Nazi. The convoy SC 143 had been well protected by the close escort led by the destroyer *Icarus* and lost only one ship (a 'straggler'), torpedoed.

A trip to Iceland and back to Scapa in very heavy weather caused another tragedy to occur. In a fierce gale, with mountainous following seas, the ship 'broached to', frequently. This meant the bow going down and the ship swinging suddenly to right or left, at right-angles to the course being steered. The stern was lifted, making the rudder ineffective, until submerged again, and control was regained by the man at the wheel. It was on such an occasion, off the most northern point of the Outer Hebrides, the Butt of Lewis, that *Oribi* 'broached to' once again and shipmate 'Bastard' went overboard. Normally he was well guarded and kept between decks in bad weather, but somehow he must have slipped out, onto the upper deck. His loss caused considerable grief throughout the ship.

In February 1944, during my penultimate stay in Murmansk, we held a ship's concert as usual, when our poetic shipmate, 'Paddy' Bourke, the CERA, rose to the occasion, as always and presented an ode he'd composed, for our four-legged shipmate, called 'The Bastard':

> Tarry awhile there — shipmates,
> If only for a short spell.
> Think of the Bastard — gone by the board,
> And never a bark o'farewell.
>
> He's down in Davy Jones' locker,
> Where so many old shipmates reside,
> Waiting to give us a welcome,
> Whenever we catch that tide.
>
> Gone to a doggie's heaven,
> Where great guys like him congregate.
> Guess he'll know all the *Oribi* boys,
> If it means an eternity's wait.
>
> From Malta to Rosta he cheered us,
> Keeping our spirits on high.
> Davy Jones has laid claim to his body,
> But his memory with us cannot die
>
> So think back on the chum we have lost boys,
> Yes, only a 'Bastard' by name:
> Guess you'll agree it's a pity,
> All life's bastards are not quite the same.
>
> Then goodbye you cheerful old shipmate,
> You went without saying adieu,
> But from fore and aft of your dear old craft,
> We're all wishing a goodbye to you.

When 'Paddy' finished this timely tribute there wasn't a dry eye in the audience. Each of us, stiff-upper-lipped warriors of the war at sea, was seen to 'pipe the eye', the sailor's way of saying 'to weep'. What proved to be 'Bastard's Memorial Service', allowed us to express our feelings about many other tragedies dormant in our minds.

A boiler clean in Greenock allowed me 5 days leave for a brief nip home to Cardiff and on return, Spud and I wined and dined our American Ambulance Corps girl-friends, Alec, always called Temple Bells, a corruption of her family name and June, at Roganos Restauraunt in Glasgow. The Lobsters Thermidor, with Chablis, were somewhat superior to the 'Herrings in tomato sauce' and coffee, served aboard *Oribi* and the girls endeared themselves to us by producing 'fivers' (the big white jobs of old) to help pay the bill. This was unusual in those days, when gentlemen were expected to pay and felt socially inferior if they did not do so. Spud and I were exceptions to this rule and happily rejoiced in our gift relationship with the opposite sex. Roganos in '93 (50 years later), had retained its character, which is when I last dropped in to place an order and you can guess what that was.

Sometime in the summer of '43, June took me home for the week-end to her parents farm in Rutlandshire. It was large and magnificent with a moat round the homestead, and provided a peaceful pause in my life at war. Before boarding the punt on the moat, in the heat of the day, I remember shedding my under vest hurriedly and popping it under the grand piano in a roulette wheel. Prior to playing contract bridge, after dinner, that evening, Mum searched for the cards and came across my ghastly garment. To my huge embarrassment, she held it aloft for me, June and father, a lovely earthy man, to see, saying 'What have we here?' When we left to return to Scotland, Mum gave June a few fivers for treats en route and two-dozen eggs for the man at Euston, which would ensure two 'sleepers' on the night train to Glasgow. June told me she was almost engaged to a Wing-Commander in the RAF, who was overseas, so we agreed that a fond friendship would suit us, meantime. Must say, there were moments, over the week-end, when I fancied mother more than daughter. Maybe, this was because when bidding, as bridge partners, we had a good rapport, or perhaps it was to do with her finding my 'intimate insulation', under the piano, that gave us something in common?

In November, *Oribi* was temporarily attached to Plymouth command and on 27th, a few miles west of the Scilly Isles, we collided with LCI (Landing Craft Infantry) 178 returning from the Mediterranean. This put us in Falmouth for a third new bow, repairs which lasted into January, 1944. February saw me promoted to Lieutenant and *Oribi* back on the Russian run with JW 57 (43 merchantships) and a new concept in escort routine. A light cruiser as flagship, HMS *Black Prince* and an escort (aircraft) carrier, HMS *Chaser*, a converted merchantship, operated within the convoy. Also, ships with greater A/S (anti-submarine) experience, from the Western Approaches, were involved much more in the escort. On this occasion, we were one of 17 destroyers and 6 corvettes, to deal with 14 U-boats deployed against the convoy. Enemy air shadowing was dealt with by *Chaser's* Wildcat fighters and all the U-boats were repelled by the escorts, U-601 and U-713 being sunk. No merchant ships were lost, but U-990 sank the destroyer *Mahratta*, close to us. She blew up and left only two survivors.

Oribi's radar improved greatly when the Type 271 set replaced the searchlight, now considered redundant. Bernard Blowers, on radar, told me that he could locate and identify very small targets like U-boats on the surface, at night, which enabled us to illuminate with star-shell and shoot at them before they could dive. He even reported fall of shot (shell splashes) which appeared on the radar screen.

Our next job, after returning with RA 57, was with outward bound convoy JW 58 (50 merchantships, 80% US), The naval force with JW 58 consisted of the cruiser *Diadem*, 2 escort carriers, *Activity* and *Tracker*, 16 destroyers (including us), 5 corvettes and the redoubtable Captain Walker in *Starling* with 4 of his 2nd Escort Group from the Atlantic. On 3 April we attacked 3 U-boats on the surface and probably destroyed one, though not confirmed. Six shadowers were shot down by fighters and 4 out of 16 U-boats were sunk, U-961 by *Starling*, U-360 by *Keppel* with 'hedgehog' plus U-355 and U-288 by Avenger A/S aircraft from the carriers. The convoy arrived unscathed at Kola Inlet on the 4th. The return convoy, RA 58, left three days later with the same escorts as the outward one and again no losses were incurred. There were a few skirmishes with U-boats on this, the last voyage back from Murmansk for me, personally. *Oribi* survived two more convoys, out and back, after D-day in '44.

Since resuming Russian convoys, we had received orders not to stop and pick up U-boat survivors, for fear of putting ourselves at risk. I can still see some of those submariners, in distress, waving and shouting, as we left them to their fate in the Arctic, and it is an awful memory. How sad it was, realizing that in peacetime sailors rescued each other, regardless of any conditions, other than the cruelty of the sea, common to both.

It was mid–April, in Scapa, when a WRNS Officer came aboard with three packing cases and asked to see the navigator, me. With the assistance of our EA (Electrical Artificer) she set up a new device in the SDO, near the plot and introduced me to QH (a meaningless title), that Goody and I called 'Mickey Mouse' when we saw it switched on. In fact it was magic, a radio navigation system operating over long distances. Synchronized pulses were transmitted from widely spaced radio stations to aircraft or shipping, the time of arrival of the pulses being used to determine position. This system had already been used with success by RAF bombers over Germany and after WW2, went under the commercial names of Decca and Loran. The pulses appeared on separate calibrated scales A, B, C and D on a monitor screen and these numbers being noted were transferred onto Admiralty Charts. These normal, navigational, charts were overprinted with numbered curved lines, each a different colour, according to the pulse, which when observed at their mutual crossing point, gave the ship's position within yards. Knowing that soon we would be in the English Channel, for D-day, in all weather conditions, QH was just what we needed and I kissed the sextant good-bye for the rest of the war.

The 17th DF went south to operate in the Channel during the build up to D-day and would remain in the area throughout the summer. We all took part in 'Exercise Tiger', the name given to a full scale dress rehearsal for the forthcoming Normandy landings. This was held in the area of Start Point, Devon, with landings being carried out by fully equipped American troops, in LCIs and LCTs (Landing Craft Infantry/Tanks), on 27 April at Slapton Sands. The craft went from Portland across Lyme Bay, and German E-boats, similar to our MTBs (Motor Torpedo Boats), cleverly infiltrated at slow speed into the assembled mass, then broke loose, at high speed, and torpedoed craft around them, before escaping to the south. This was a disaster that cost about 600 lives and was kept under wraps for 50 years, until someone in Devon recalled seeing lots of bodies being cast into a communal grave, in a field near Slapton. We, in *Oribi*, on the south side of the force, knew nothing, but our sister ships on the north side had seen the action and were sworn to secrecy. It would have been unwise to release this news prior to the big event for morale reasons, but sadly it was forgotten after victory, when it should have been made known to next of kin.

The spring of '44 around Portsmouth was full of adventures. Spud and I did a few short Courses, one at Whale Island, HMS *Excellent*, the home of gunnery, in gaiters, where you didn't walk, you didn't run, you f . . . g-well flew. All ranks did everything at the double. Then, along the coast at Brighton we were billeted at the posh girls school 'Roedean' taken over by HMS *Vernon* (stone frigate, Pompey), for Torpedo Control Courses. We slept in dormitories with signs over the beds, near bell-pulls, which said 'If you want a mistress during the night, ring three times.' It was dancing in the Brighton Pavilion that I met the glamorous VAD, Thelma, who told me that originally it stood for Voluntary Aid Detachment but now its meaning had changed to Virgins Awaiting Destruction or for those past that stage, Volunteers After Dark. Our affair was like the film, a 'brief encounter', only we went much further with our embraces than the censors would permit Celia Johnson and Trevor Howard to go on screen.

The Queens Hotel, Southsea was a great rendezvous for naval officers and some of us were aware that the Head Night Porter had a few room keys available, for a reasonable tip, at any hour. I remember staying overnight with an Army General's daughter, who said, like President Clinton 'No penetrative sex, please,' so we didn't and just enjoyed each other's company differently. I also recall meeting Sub-Lieut Wallop about then. Funny name, I thought, until a mutual friend told me it was the family name of the Earl of Portsmouth and that he was also known as Viscount Lymington. Later in life, as a Regent Oil Rep, I visited places in Hampshire named Nether Wallop and Little Wallop, which meant more to me then, having known him.

On 27 May, *Oribi* moved from Stokes Bay in the Solent and anchored off Yarmouth, Isle of Wight, for about ten days, awaiting orders for 'Operation

Overlord' to commence, amidst masses of other ships assembling. We awoke on 6 June to the sound of Glen Miller's band on radio playing 'Sunrise Serenade', as landing craft full of troops streamed past us and out through the Needles channel. D-day had arrived and our job was to screen the western side of the invasion force channel across to France from attacks by U-boats and E-boats. A trawler marked the entrance to this channel and displayed a large notice, painted on canvas for all the sea-sick soldiers to see as they heaved about on a choppy surface, heading for the Beaches in the Baie de la Seine. It said 'Buy your programmes, chocolates and cigarettes here!'

We established ourselves on a patrol line off Cap Barfleur, the north-east point of the Cherbourg peninsula, and it is interesting to reflect that it was from here that William the 1st, bastard son of a tanner's daughter, eventually known as 'The Conqueror', sailed to fight the battle of Hastings in 1066. This day, it was an invasion the other way and I remember looking up and seeing the sky full of aircraft, from horizon to horizon, all of them OURS!

We were shelled occasionally by German shore batteries, without being hit, and had several fights with E-boats from Dieppe and Cherbourg, being helped by long-range radar on Portsdown hill, north of Pompey, homing us on to them. On 27 June the German garrison at Cherbourg surrendered and we moved round the coast to the Channel Islands. Here we worked with a US frigate acting as control vessel for US and British MTBs, trying to prevent E-boat and other enemy traffic between the islands. One fine day, a few miles south of Guernsey, I was on the bridge with JCA, when we heard a whistling sound overhead and shells splashed into the sea on either side of us. We had been straddled by a shore battery and JCA shouted 'Full ahead both and hard a'port' down the wheelhouse voicepipe. Another lucky day.

Lieut. Peter Scott RNVR, son of the South Pole Scott, was liaison officer aboard the US frigate until landed sick in Cherbourg, and I was seconded from *Oribi* to liaise on behalf of our MTBs and destroyers. A US patrol boat came alongside *Oribi* to transfer me and when below decks I was handed a large dish of ice-cream and heard 'Birth of the Blues' on clarinet coming out of a speaker. 'What's that about' I asked a big black seaman. 'Oh, that's Joe trying to demoralize the Jerries, I guess. More ice-cream boss?' was his response. Aboard the frigate, in the operations room, everyone moved around looking like Humphrey Bogart in *The Caine Mutiny*. Seems they hadn't heard of 'relaxed action stations', until I suggested it and after an uneventful week, I was relieved to rejoin *Oribi* in Cherbourg.

Before stepping ashore for provisions in that recently recaptured port, the Petty Officer Steward, Haylor, asked me what he should buy. 'Camembert, lots of camembert cheeses' I said and he got about sixty, I think. Back in Portsmouth, in July, I went on leave for a few days to Cardiff, taking some twenty or so of the cheeses with me in a canvas zipped bag. It was a very

17th Destroyer Flotilla reunion. Seated round table, l. to r.: Ian Bryce, Don Pritchard, Jack Grieveson, Bill Goodacre, Stan Meads, Tom Goddard

hot day as I placed the bag on the overhead rack and settled in my 1st Class compartment, which rapidly filled up with fellow passengers. Soon, sniffing commenced and curious glances were exchanged. I became aware that such a delightful smell as this had not been appreciated in the UK for 5 years and so, magnanimously, I got the bag down and gave a camembert to each companion who possessed a similar epicurean taste to me. A happy journey ensued and my father, particularly, enjoyed my return from fromage France.

More E-boat chasing in August, when we forgot where we were on one occasion and almost ended up in Dieppe harbour, still occupied by the enemy. On 22 August I left *Oribi* in Portsmouth after 3 years, 74 days, and so ended my 'fighting' war at sea. I feel it sensible, now, if asked what are my basic memories of WW2, to say 'The fighting was fearful, the friendships were fabulous and the fucking was fun.' If some of my memoirs shock some people, then I think it tells those people more about themselves than it does about me. I was encouraged to be candid by reading Barbara Windsor's autobiography, *All of Me*, cover to cover, on the Emirates Airline flight to Australia in 2001. It was given to me for my 79th birthday by my beloved daughter Peta, the one who got me doing what I'm doing now.

CHAPTER 12

More mistresses in grey – 1944–1946

TOWARDS THE END OF A MONTH'S LEAVE, at home, in Cardiff, I received the usual letter, 'By Command of their Lordships' which, much to my surprise, read as follows: 'THE Lords Commissioners of the Admiralty hereby appoint you Lieutenant in Command of His Majesty's Ship *Goathland* and direct you to repair on board that Ship at Portsmouth on 21.9.44.' This letter from Admiralty, SW1, went on to say that I was to acknowledge the receipt of this Appointment and report on the said date to Commander-in-Chief, Portsmouth. Imagine my delight, receiving my first command, a Hunt Class destroyer, at the age of twenty-two. Polish up the silver knobbed cane indeed and bone the leather of my half-wellington boots. There were more surprises to come, however.

The duty officer at C-in-C Portsmouth told me that my ship was anchored in the Solent. I was to relieve Lieut-Cdr Goteley RNVR, who as 1st Lieut (No.1), had assumed command of a skeleton crew when the *Goathland* had returned from the Normandy beaches recently, having been Oyster mined (a new type reacting to hull pressure) and put out of action. Her main engines had been shattered and her guns were inoperative. A diesel generator provided auxiliary power for essential services and she was due to be towed round the coast to Loch Fyne, where she would await facilities to be scrapped on the Clyde. This information was not only a surprise, but a severe shock to my system and particularly my social stature. I suddenly became aware that my current mistress was not only legless, but toothless as well.

I had a succinct turnover from Goteley (a peacetime barrister) ending with the good news that there was still one case of duty-free Gordon's gin left over in the Wardroom wine locker. My No.1 was a Welsh RNVR Lieutenant called Griffiths, from Cardiff, whose father had been Lord Mayor of that capital city. We had a Sub-Lieut RNVR plus 15 crew, which included deck and engine room staff, a cook and a steward. Next day, a senior Master Mariner from the Ministry of War Transport came aboard to brief me fully on the towing arrangements involving a merchant ship. I got a feeling that as RNR, having served in Merchant and Royal Navies, I had been chosen for this job because of my extensive practical experience in both. This amounted to my year pre-war in cargo liners working with derricks and winches, my time on the sweeping deck of a minesweeper in 1940 dealing with heavy wire-rope gear and being in charge of mooring with wires and cables on the fo'c'sle of a fleet-destroyer. Also, a greater rapport was likely between the MN Master and me, as men coming from a similar background.

Two tugs from Portsmouth arrived at dawn one day and towed us in the *Goathland* westward through the Needles Channel to the middle of Christchurch Bay, south of Bournemouth, where we rendezvoused the merchantship *Empire Gauntlet*. This splendid ship of 7,000 tons, with a speed of 18 knots, was one of thirteen, built in the USA in great secrecy during '43 and '44, designed for carrying troops, rather than cargo. Many other 'Empire' named cargo ships were built previously under lease-lend, and in fact 45 participated in Russian Convoys. Trained with selected Masters in command, the special 'Empires' landed thousands of men on the beachhead during Operation Neptune, the naval part of Operation Overlord, on and after D-day. *Empire Gauntlet* was one of these gallant vessels under the command of Captain Jeffers, a quietly spoken, verbally persuasive Irishman, who spoke to me, frequently, on R/T (radio telephone). By binoculars, he appeared, on his bridge, to be a tall, muscular, middle-aged figure with a happy countenance, and our chats were always easy going, yet seamanlike. I wonder now, was he related to my friends, in Grimsby 1940, but stupidly, I never asked him.

A six-inch, or was it an eight-inch wire from the 'EG' was made fast to the end of my starboard cable, which I paid out through its normal hawse pipe, with anchor still attached, to give it catenary (curve) and prevent tautness and strain twixt EG's stern and *Goathland*'s bow, during the coastal passage. The weather was fine and the sea flat calm, about noon, when we were ready to go and the 'EG' gently got us moving, around St Albans Head, down the English Channel. Jeffers was explicit on R/T and behaved like a caring trainer with a frightened filly on a long rein. Must say, I was a bit scared when, suddenly, I realized our predicament if the tow parted. As a dumb-tow with no engines, our last resort, to keep off the rocks, would be to let go the one and only port anchor, hoping it would hold.

All went well, with our Quartermasters on the wheel, getting used to steering a ship under tow. Giving Portland Bill, with its tidal race, a wide berth, we experienced a rapid deterioration in the weather as we approached Start Point, about thirty miles east of Plymouth. Up came that comforting Irish voice on the R/T saying 'Hello Lieutenant, Jeffers here. With a westerly gale developing, this is no time for me to be taking you round the Lizard and Lands End 'cos you might easily end up adding to the vast number of wrecks already on this infamous coastline and that would never do. I think we should take shelter somewhere now, what say you?' Without hesitation I replied 'Aye, aye Captain, I share your summary of the situation and I shall make a signal to C in C Plymouth seeking shelter and assistance.' This I did and a big tug, with paddle-wheels each side, secured alongside *Goathland*. When the tow was disconnected, we were taken inside the breakwater and moored to a buoy in Plymouth Sound. The *Empire Gauntlet* anchored in Cawsand Bay nearby.

Jeffers and I met a few times ashore and swapped many salty yarns, during the two days we waited for the gale to subside. We were thankful that bombing in the West Country had stopped, but our hearts went out to the citizens of London, when we heard they were now enduring more Nazi terrorism. In September, a second Battle of London was being fought, four years after the first, with a new and terrible weapon. V-2s, long range rockets, 15 tons in weight and carrying one-ton warheads, were being launched from Holland and Germany, adding to the havoc caused by the V-1, doodle-bugs. When the tow was re-established between *Empire Gauntlet* and *Goathland*, we proceeded, in fair weather, round Lands End and north through the Irish Sea to the Scottish coast. Off Campbeltown, a large ocean-going tug took over and I waved farewell to my wise and trusted adviser and guide, Jeffers of the *Empire Gauntlet*. An unusual experience in my seagoing career, but, I felt, a job well done.

Goathland was moored to a buoy at the head of Loch Fyne, close to Inveraray, which was the base for training Combined Operations Forces. I reported to NOIC (Naval Officer In Charge), a four-ring Captain, called back from retirement, probably in his 50s or 60s. I cannot recall his name but I do remember him greeting me with 'Welcome Bryce. What do you know about the *Goathland* hunt?' 'Well sir, it's in Yorkshire,' said I, feeling very pleased with myself. 'Oh is that all?' said he and went on to say that before being recalled to the RN, he had been 'Hunting Correspondent' to the *Daily Telegraph* and proceeded to tell me about all the hunts associated with the destroyers named after them, which was fascinating. Incidentally, the name *Goathland* recently became famous, in the '90s, as the location of a popular TV series called 'Heartbeat'.

Life was lovely, peaceful and idle for the next two months, until I was discharged from *Goathland* and returned home to Cardiff on 17 December '44, to spend my first Christmas at home since '39. Me and my crew had little to do except keep the ship tidy, so we sailed boats and went for long walks ashore. Autumn in the Highlands was beautiful to behold. One of my favourite walks was beyond the Castle to the north, following the river up Glen Shira, where I watched the salmon leaping upstream. The old Duke of Argyll was said to be somewhat eccentric; slept in the kilt and welcomed visitors to his Castle. I regret not calling, but some of my crew did and said they were served tea by the butler at a card-table, with the Duke, in the middle of the Main Hall. South of Inverary was bristling with Commandos, covering a vast training area, ashore and afloat, now, mainly with the Far East in mind. I met many such types in the local pub called the Argyll Arms.

'You must lunch with me at my home, on the other side of the loch and meet the family,' the Captain (NOIC) said to me one week, when I reported to him. Sure enough, next day, he picked me up in his boat and we landed at St Catherine's. When we entered his house, I was amazed to be greeted by a glamorous thirty-year-old lady, as the Captain said, 'Darling, meet the Commanding Officer of the Hunt Class destroyer, *Goathland*, one of the ships I'm always going on about.' I was even more amazed when my host said 'Come and meet my son', taking me aside and holding up a two-year-old. His concluding remark will live on in my memory forever. He slapped me on the back as he said 'We destroyer types, you know!', which was explained later when he told me he was in destroyers during WW1. Living through these contrasting times, I thought, sometime, I must read Tolstoy's *War and Peace*.

Playing Father Christmas to niece Christine, who was now five, was fun for Uncle Ian, acting as her surrogate father whenever home on leave. Her real father, my brother-in-law, Malcolm Carpenter, was Territorial Army before the war, granted a commission in the Welsh Regiment and sent to North Africa in 1940. After surviving action in the Libyan Desert, Greece, Crete and Tobruk, he was promoted to Major on the Staff of General Wavell in India. There were many kids, like Chris, who didn't see their Dads for four or five years during the war and this gap, in lots of cases, adversely affected their relationship in later years. Only last week, July 2002, my young cousin, Anthony Musitano, confirmed this sad state of affairs with his late father, Peter, who had been in Syria with the Army for the first five years of Ant's life.

The big celebration, to Scottish folk anyway, at this time of year, is of course Hogmanay. Happily for me, my friend John Nicholl, Squadron-Leader in the RAF, Coastal Command, was at home on leave in Cardiff and his Ma and Pa, both Scots, always had a big New Year's Eve party at their capacious home in Bryn-gwyn Road, Penylan. John and I met, because our sisters were members of the Cardiff Little Theatre and they persuaded us to attend a 'play reading' at the house of Mrs Darby, the Director. They thought it would be good for us and indeed it was, for I believe it sparked off my liking for live theatre, which continues to this day. Mrs Nicoll insisted that I should be First Foot on the night; that is, the first dark haired man to cross the threshold in the New Year after midnight and present the lady of the house with (a) a piece of bread – for health; (b) a piece of silver – for wealth and (c) a piece of coal – for warmth, saying 'Lang may yor lum reek', which, for the 'Sassenachs' amongst us, means, 'Long may your chimney smoke.'

I accepted this formidable invitation, having sufficient hair to comply, in those days, and having got the gifts organized. John and I, with our sisters Joyce and Betty, went to warm up at the Cardiff Golf Club in Cyncoed. As honorary members, the regulars did us proud, mainly congratulating John on his recent award of the DFC (Distinguished Flying Cross) for sinking a U-boat with his Liberator aircraft in the Bay of Biscay. At about twenty to twelve we drove back to the Nicholl's house and sister Betty walked me round the lawn a few times to make sure I was sober enough to do the necessary. It was a magic moment, that I shall never forget, as I received a huge hug from the hostess, when I stepped from darkness into light. We sang 'Auld Lang Syne', after which I took the liberty of embracing every 'lassie' within sight. John drove us home in his father's large car, which I think he tried to get airborne like his Liberator. My mother, good old Zill, in the back, with Betty, said, when we got home, 'That was a fantastic party, wasn't it and didn't we fly home?'

In mid-January, I got orders to attend lots of refresher courses for about three months, obviously preparing me for being No.1 of a destroyer. So it was, I did a succession of one, two or three week courses in: Damage Control, Torpedo Control, Gunnery Control, Navigation and Asdic Control, the last of which was the most important. Remember, that Asdic was an antisubmarine device for detecting submerged U-boats. My tutor for the anti-submarine course, lasting a fortnight at Dunoon, was an old chum, 'Dicky' Bird, Lieut RNVR, who had been Specialist Asdic Officer on the Staff of Captain D in Onslow, our 17th DF leader. He did an excellent job in preparing me for my next appointment, which came as another stimulating surprise. On 26 April '45, in Birkenhead, I joined HMS *Wildgoose*, one of the famous 2nd Support Group, described fully in Chapter 10, as Anti-Submarine Control Officer (ASCO). When Captain Walker died in '44, Commander Wemyss, my captain, assumed leadership of the group and so I felt greatly honoured to be in such a position of responsibility. Maybe my knees did knock a bit at the thought of maintaining their high reputation, or was it the name of my new mistress that made me tremble. Could I cope with a lady called 'wild goose'?

I need not have worried, because I never had to put my skills afloat into action. The ship was in for repairs and on 8 May, Victory in Europe (VE) Day was declared. I remember dashing ashore with other shipmates and dancing with the people of Birkenhead, in and out of the terraced houses, anyone grabbing anybody, singing, hugging and happy to be alive. That well known Cornish song the 'Floral Dance' came to mind, until radios took over with Glen Miller's 'Don't sit under the Apple Tree, with anyone else but Me'; as though anyone cared just then!

Wildgoose sailed round to Plymouth later in May and I left her at the end of the month. June, July and August, saw me in Barrow-in-Furness, preparing ships for going into Reserve Fleet or being returned to the US after lease-lend expired. Skeleton crews remained aboard, first, *Tanatside*, a Hunt Class Destroyer, followed by *Manners*, a Captain Class Frigate and in terms of a mistress analogy, it was rather like a 'one night stand', ashore, with each. A surrendered German U-boat, one of the first driven by hydrogen peroxide, was berthed nearby. It was closely guarded and visited frequently by senior Allied naval staff, who were most interested in a submarine that could remain submerged for very long periods of time. A forerunner to the nuclear powered boat of today.

It was on the evening of the 14th that church bells rang out and ships' sirens hooted in the dockyard, announcing that VJ Day would be 15 August. Victory had been achieved by dropping Atom-bombs on Japan and WW2 had ended, suddenly, to everyone's amazement. Next day, I led a party of sailors from the ship as part of the Mayor's Victory March around the town, finishing with drinks and dancing in and around the Town Hall. The end of hostilities in the Far East meant most to those with kith and kin out there, either fighting or as prisoners in Jap hands, and this included lots of US forces billeted in the UK. Peace at last, worldwide, was greeted with great relief and rejoicing, despite the horrific manner in which it was achieved.

On 18 September '45, almost six years after being mined in the *Kittiwake* off Dover, I joined HMS *Comet* in Plymouth, one of 32 'C' Class destroyers built between 1943 and '45, with a very different accommodation lay-out to the old 'O' Class. Most sensibly, the Officers' Wardroom was now forward, under the bridge and some Crew Messes were situated down aft, where the Wardroom had been. It is interesting to record that 8 of the 32 were modified as frigates in 1966, one of which, the *Cavalier*, was restored and is now berthed in The Historic Dockyard at Chatham. She is open to the public, as an example of a destroyer in WW2.

When I crossed the gangway of the *Comet*, under the command of Lieut-Cdr Fitzroy RN, I discovered that, as a Lieutenant RNR, I was the third in line of seniority and as a result, found myself in charge of the Ship's Office. This was not to my liking then, but in retrospect, I think it was good for me, because it got me dealing with correspondence and coping with administrative matters, which, years later, I appreciated when I left the sea and became a manager in industry.

Having *Comet*, a celestial body, as my mistress, took me 'out of this world' and my curiosity gave me further delight. The dictionary definition showed that her name came from the Greek 'kometes', meaning 'long-haired', an obvious way of depicting a lengthy trail in the sky, which, probably, persuaded those ancient philosophers to choose such a sexually stimulating word.

Mentally, I may well have drifted out of this world, but, physically, *Comet* took me to Wilhelmshaven, the chief German naval port until '45, as guard ship. The natives were friendly and treated us with due deference, realizing that the Third Reich, which had existed as the Nazi dictatorship from 1933 to '45, was defeated and at an end. Also, they were aware that, in November, Hitler's associates would be taken to the Palace of Justice at Nuremburg, to answer for their crimes before a tribunal formed by Britain, America, Russia and France.

All amenities were ours at a minimal cost or for nothing, to which we responded politely and in a friendly way. An order had been issued stating 'no fraternization', which meant, strictly speaking, do not associate on friendly terms, but this was difficult to abide by under the prevailing circumstances of peaceful reconciliation. It became a regular thing for members of the ship's company to meet local people in a graveyard at night and barter provisions, such as butter, sugar and tea (some even dried-out after brewing), for items like cameras, watches and bits of jewelry. An AB approached me and said 'Sir, you mentioned going back to the MN soon and I wondered if you would like a Plath sextant from the German destroyer astern of us?' 'You bet I would. Who do I see to get it?' I replied. 'You don't see anyone,' he said 'they won't talk to officers, just leave it to me, Sir.' 'How much will it cost?' I asked. 'A carton of 500 Players cigarettes, worth 12/6d [62½p],' he replied, grinning cheekily and the deal was done.

That sextant was envied by all my brother officers in whatever merchant ship I sailed in post war. It was easy to handle, with large mirrors and a visible 'swastika badge', indicating previous ownership, which didn't bother me a bit.

We used the Officers' Club in Wilhelmshaven dockyard and drank gallons of superior vintage champagne, undoubtedly filched from France during the last five years, for a token payment of a few marks. Word got around the Wardroom that any officers who would like horse riding lessons would be welcome at the army stables, near Wilhelmshaven. This was to be free of charge and furthermore included a pair of riding breeches, made to measure, if so desired. About four of us took lessons on a daily basis for an hour, over a period of ten days. The horses were large, cavalry size and our instructor, who spoke good English with wit, did us a lot of good. After walking, trotting and cantering with care, he drew our attention to the slogan carved in wood over the stable door. He said 'Now, you will understand the meaning, which translated into English says "First learn to ride the horse and then the woman".' We got the message, especially when he added 'You know now that the pelvic thrust is similar, ya?' We did! I only wore my breeches once again, through the vineyards of Stellenbosch, in South Africa, in '47 and fifty years later gave them to my son, Charles, who had taken up Polo.

In November, I rejoiced when I left *Comet*, as office-boy and joined *Southdown*, a Hunt Class destroyer, as No.1, First Lieutenant. My captain was a senior Lieutenant RN, Norman Macpherson, who was happy to leave the running of the ship, mainly, to me. I admired him for his sense of direction as regards his future when he said 'Between you and me, No.1, now that the war is over, I'm doing a correspondence course, in my spare time, in order to leave the Navy and become a Chartered Accountant.' I felt, that his father-in-law, an Admiral, would probably take a dim view. Most of his time was spare and I carried on without interference. However, he was always available when needed and we had a very good understanding.

Southdown was despatched to Londonderry to take part in Operation Deadlight. I can only describe this activity as totally wasteful, because it meant towing all the surrendered U-boats out to the north-west of Ireland, beyond the 100 fathom line, where they were scuttled and sank, deep down into the Atlantic. This operation took place out of Stranraer, Scotland, as well as Lough Foyle. Wasteful, because a lack of trust between the US, USSR and UK, ruled out a division of these spoils of war. Each was capable of supplying sufficient energy to illuminate a city, but they had to be destroyed and we were one of many ships involved.

Towing was second nature to me after *Goathland* and we did many trips taking U-boats to their destiny. When in position, we took aboard the skeleton crew after they had slipped the tow and opened the sea-cocks to scuttle. It was interesting having a few Reporters from the Press (Media) with us on one of these excursions, but when at sea, they soon got bored and preferred the warmth of the Wardroom to seeing what was happening from the open deck. Knowing they were easy going and not having seen them for a few hours, I felt like a bit of fun, so phoned down from the bridge and said 'This is the Off-Shore Editor of the Daily Explosion (nickname for *Daily Express*) speaking, put my reporter on please.' When I got him, I said 'I've just heard from another source that your U-boat has sunk and the sun is about to sink in the west. Can you confirm this please?' My question was answered by a deathly silence for a moment, then by a lot of ribald remarks that I cannot repeat. As a result, we had lots of laughs and some lively conversation together, over a few gins, when back in port.

The end of January saw the end of Operation Deadlight. Those devilish U-boats had been dumped deep in the ocean they had terrorized for six years. Recently, I noticed that on 1 January 1946, the first civilians took off from a new airfield at Heath Row, the future terminus, west of London, for all long distance flights, many of them over the same deep ocean. Change was rightly taking place and for us in *Southdown*, it meant sailing to Portsmouth, where we would become part of the Reserve Fleet. When heading south through the Irish Sea and about 50 miles west of

Aberystwyth, early on 4 February, we received a signal from the Admiralty, to go to the assistance of HM submarine *Universal*, in distress in Cardigan Bay. I shall tell the story mainly from memory, but enriched considerably by details, provided recently by Brian J. Wead of the Royal National Lifeboat Institution (RNLI) at Poole.

Late on the night of 3 February, on her way to the breaker's yard at Newport (Mon) South Wales, the *Universal*'s engines broke down and she sent out a distress call. The coastguard passed the call to the St David's lifeboat station and at 0015 on the 4th, the motor lifeboat, 'Civil Service No. 6', was launched. The submarine was found nine miles west of South Bishop Lighthouse, with the Irish steamer *Lanahrone* standing by, in a moderate westerly gale. By means of her line-throwing gun the lifeboat connected the *Universal* with the *Lanahrone* and the steamer started to tow, but the submarine broke away. Another wire-rope was then connected, but this also broke.

At 0845 we arrived in *Southdown* and the *Lanahrone*, no longer needed, went on her way. A third attempt was made and with the lifeboat's help we were able to get *Universal* in tow. The lifeboat sheltered for a time in the lee of Ramsey Island and then returned to her station at 1615 that afternoon. The towing went well as we headed north, away from the land, in order to ride out the gale, before proceeding round the coast. Standing with Norman on the bridge at 1300 with the one o'clock news coming through the bridge speakers, we heard the announcer say 'The destroyer HMS *Southdown* has now got HM submarine *Universal* safely in tow.' We felt pleased with ourselves and thought, who better for this job, with all our recent experience in towing U-boats. The gale was increasing in strength and I was down aft, minutes later, when there was an almighty 'bang' and the towrope parted. The next thing I remember was hearing Norman's voice through a megaphone from the bridge saying 'Number One – we must get another tow on before the six o'clock news.' 'Aye-aye sir.' I shouted ineffectively into the wind.

Getting a tow aboard a submarine in a howling gale in the open sea was vastly different from passing a tow to a U-boat in the calm, sheltered waters of Lough Foyle. As a vessel on the surface, we were drifting much faster in the sea and wind, than the submerged hull of our submarine and we tried, for hours, without success. The *Universal*, having drifted 25 miles along the coast, needed more help therefore we made a signal to shore. The Fishguard motor lifeboat, *White Star*, was launched and reached us at 1530. She stood by until 2245 that night, when she left to refuel and rejoined next morning at 0850, by which time the *Universal* had drifted a further 30 miles into Cardigan Bay. The lights of *Southdown* and *Universal* were seen from New Quay and at 0620 on 5 Feb, the pulling and sailing lifeboat, *William Cantrell Ashley*, was launched and was standing by when the Fishguard lifeboat returned. Aberystwyth had heard from the coastguard that the *Universal* was approaching and at 0825 the motor lifeboat, *Frederick Angus*, was launched. All three lifeboats were now standing by.

It was a sight never to be forgotten, witnessing these lifeboats in action and particularly the *WCA* from New Quay, with a well-reefed lug-sail, going about from tack to tack in the gale and I recall that one of the crew was wearing a butcher's apron. *WCA* returned to New Quay at 1100 in a moderating gale and fifty years later I heard she was the last of the 'sailing' lifeboats. The *William Cantrell Ashley* was taken out of service in 1949 and presented to the Outward Bound School at Aberdovey. Subsequently she went to Cardiff and the Lifeboat Enthusiasts' Society say she is stored now at Nantgarw in Cardiff for future display at a Museum there.

The officer in command of *Universal* had let go both anchors, which began to hold, off the coast, near Aberaeron. As the gale abated, the crew members were taken off, 16 in the Fishguard and 11 in the Aberystwyth lifeboats. The former came alongside *Southdown* to put the commanding officer of *Universal* on board and that person was none other than Bill Mayne, met by Dad and me in '35, when he was 3rd Officer of the Canadian Pacific flagship *Empress of Britain*. Now, he was a Lieut-Commander RNR, recently returned from Germany after three years as prisoner-of-war, having been captured off the Danish coast when navigator of HM submarine *Seal*. I cannot say there was instant recognition, because our meeting was eleven years earlier, but after exchanging names, our world was smaller. Three years later, in '49, we sailed, Bill as 1st and me as 3rd Officer, under Captain Grant in the *Empress of France*. A remark we shared and often quoted, with glee and a wicked Welsh accent, was 'Cardiff's my home'. A tug towed *Universal* to Newport and I'm glad some good came from her misfortune, in the shape of this tribute paid to the RNLI. A lifelong contributor, I became a Life Governor in 1989, when my cash flow with Kinloch Bryce Associates (KBA) permitted.

On arrival at Portsmouth, Norman left the *Southdown* and I reported to the Senior Officer Reserve Fleet (SORF), having assumed command, to prepare the ship for acceptance at a date to be decided. SORF was a Rear-Admiral, whose name escapes me, but after discussing what was required of me and my ship's company, we agreed a date about six weeks later, say the beginning of April. Returning on board, I cleared lower deck, meaning all hands on the upper deck, to hear the news. Being aware that the men had not been home on leave for many months I said, 'Right, we have six weeks to do the job and that means a lot of hard work. I am prepared to give one week's leave, consecutively, now, to each watch (port and starboard), if, when you return, you are prepared to work all hours.' There was an immediate, positive reaction.

About an hour or so later, I was in the Wardroom and heard the conversation between two officers' stewards, through the hatch to the pantry. One, who hadn't been on deck, said to his mate, 'Well, what did Jimmy have to say then?' The reply he got was 'You work with me and I'll work you to fucking death, but he is giving us a week's leave before that.' It worked out well. I had to turn them to late into the night and pipe them up again early next day, but I cannot remember a single shirker. The boys didn't let me down and only later in life, ashore in the oil industry, did I realize that the practice, of openness and trust in man-management forms the essence of good leadership.

Did I, perchance, witness signs of a future behaviour style, in the person of Prince Philip of Greece? He was then a Lieutenant RN, who was putting a ship into Reserve, up Portchester Creek, next to Fareham Creek, which is where *Southdown* was stationed. In that capacity, he attended the weekly meetings of SORF with lots of us lesser lieutenants and we noticed with what tolerance the Rear-Admiral endured his verbosity. Did the Prince's superior uncle, as a Signals Specialist in the Service, encourage such excessive communication and, if so, did that contribute to his nephew's cultivation of a purposeful gift for 'gaffes', later in life?

To assist me aboard *Southdown*, I had as my No.1 and only other officer, a Lieutenant RNVR called Ken Spivey. He was a competent jovial fellow with two great assets, a car, which he kept in the Dockyard and an ability to play contract bridge. We played frequently, with my cousin Cecily Lowther and a friend, both of them Marine Wrens, stationed at Eastney Barracks and equally keen on bridge, after having had dinner on board, as our guests. The rubbers would often go on until midnight, when we would land them by motor-boat near the 'Still and West' pub in Old Portsmouth, to grab a taxi. If we told other naval types about these evenings, they wouldn't believe us, but our priorities, at times, differed from theirs, I guess.

I almost forgot, but I'm glad I didn't, that the Southdown Bus Company, operating along the south coast to the east, at least as far as Brighton, had adopted the ship *Southdown* long, long ago, and before the crew paid off, they gave us a very big party at their Cosham Garage, just north of Portsmouth. Drinking directors and dancing clippies gave us shipmates a good time and we gave them some souvenirs from the ship, in return. Over the previous years, any sailor showing a letter addressed to him in *Southdown*, would get a free ride, anywhere, on their buses. He had to do this, because the ribbon round his cap showed only HMS, in wartime, for security reasons.

Southdown went into Reserve on time and I will not bore you with the details of what had to be done to achieve that. It was a lot of work, manual and paper, but SORF was pleased enough to give me a few more frigates in Fareham Creek to sort out. It was sometime in the spring, say May or June, when I went into Haslar Hospital at Gosport for two days, to have a wisdom tooth removed. It was my good fortune to be visited there by a lady-friend, Pat, 2nd Officer WRNS, who gave me a much treasured book to read and signed it 'With love from one of the females of the species.' The book was *Portsmouth Letters* by Admiral Sir W.M. (William) James, just published recently in 1946. These letters, commenting on the progress of the war and other current events, were written from 1939 to '45. For the first three years he was Commander-in-Chief (C-in-C) Portsmouth and later Chief of Naval Information and MP for Portsmouth North. Pat and I much enjoyed thumbing through the book together. We knew that he had been a much loved and admired C-in-C in Pompey, during those grim years, but we also knew about his fame as a little boy. He was always known as 'Bubbles', after a portrait painted of him by his famous grandfather, Sir John Millais (1829–1896). This, showing him blowing bubbles through a clay pipe, became, through the Pears Soap Advertisement, a household name and one of the best known Victorian childhood images. Pears Transparent is still my favourite soap to this day. Sir William's letters captured the mood of the moment and contributed much to the history of that period. He had a mop of curly hair through life from 'Bubbles' to C-in-C.

In mid-July, I was drafted from Portsmouth to Harwich for similar work, putting a group of six frigates into the Reserve Fleet and living in the River Class Frigate *Waveney*. In this harbour, with many happy memories from 1940, SORF was more remote, because my group came under the command of Stannard VC, a Commander RNR, who got his gong in Norway. He acted as my liaison and being an ardent Freemason, seemingly seeking promotion, he would depart on a Thursday, with case containing apron and other accessories saying 'Carry on No.1, I'm off to London, back on Tuesday and I've told SORF that you will send a working party to save the sinking pontoon at Parkstone Quay.' 'Aye-aye sir,' was my response, happy to receive such delegation. I rigged jungle ladders between the ships, much quicker than boats, for getting to and fro and I coped with any situation Stannard let me in for, with SORF.

In October, unexpectedly, I was called to the 2nd Sea-Lord's Office of the Admiralty, responsible for personnel appointments, by a Captain Bell RNR. Being aware that I intended to return to the Merchant Navy and knowing that I had no qualifications as a MN officer, he advised me to get a 2nd Mate's Ticket now and he would give me the necessary leave to do so. He went on to say that he would also arrange more sea time for me in the RN, so that I could skip 1st Mate's and go straight for a Master Mariner's Certificate, when I was demobbed, in about a year's time. What valuable advice that was and I took it. With a month's leave, I got my 2nd Mate's in Cardiff which necessitated getting a doctor friend to give me the St John's Ambulance lectures in one go as opposed to over six weeks, because that First Aid Certificate was as necessary as any nautical qualification, it seemed.

Wondering where I would go to get more sea time as promised by my mentor Captain Bell RNR, I was indeed surprised and delighted to receive the customary letter —

> By Command of the Commissioners for Executing the Office of Lord High Admiral of the United Kingdom, etc
>
> To Lieutenant L.K. Bryce DSC, RNR,
>
> The Lords Commissioners of the Admiralty hereby appoint you Lieutenant of His Majesty's Ship *Vanguard* and direct you to repair on board that Ship at Portsmouth on 1.1.47.
>
> Your appointment is to take effect from that date.
>
> You are to acknowledge the receipt of this Appointment forthwith, addressing your letter to the Commanding Officer HMS *Vanguard* c/o GPO, London, taking care to furnish your address.
>
> By Command of their lordships,
>
> H.V. Markham
> 10.12.46

Well, there I went, determined, as a small ship man, to show big ship men how to have fun.

CHAPTER 13

HMS *Vanguard*: Royal tour of South Africa — 1947

THE NINTH *VANGUARD*, WHOSE CREST carried the words 'We Lead', was a product of WW2, ordered in March 1941, to be built by John Brown of Clydebank, in the same yard where the giant Cunard liners *Queen Mary* and *Queen Elizabeth* were built a few years earlier. She was the largest and the last of Britain's battleships, proudly displaying the names of 14 Battle Honours on her quarterdeck, from 1588, the Spanish Armada, to 1916, Jutland, although never seeing any enemy action herself. Launched by Princess Elizabeth, aged 18, on St Andrew's Day, November, 1944, her name was kept secret until the end of the Japanese war, the following year. When it was eventually made public, the humorous magazine *Punch* printed, 'Wouldn't it have been more appropriate to name her "Guard's Van", now that we know she is the last of a long line?'

My intention, in recalling this unusual voyage in my life at sea, is to tell about events that I found most interesting and amusing. The last thing I want to do is bore you, my readers and myself, by spelling out everything in diary form. So, I shall dart about, as the only RNR officer, with distinguishable crisscross stripes, in those days, amongst the majority of Dartmouth trained characters with ordinary straight stripes. I did share this difference in apparel with three RNVR officers aboard, who wore wavy stripes, which gave them the nickname of Wavy Navy. Soon after WW2 ended, all Reserve Officers, both RNR and RNVR, converted to straight stripes with an 'R' in the curl of the upper stripe, a democratic move if ever there was.

During the war, the three categories of stripes were often described, as: RNRs are seamen trying to be gentlemen, RNVRs are gentlemen trying to be seamen and RN, depending on the company at the time, or what stripes you were wearing, were either, neither, or both. All in good fun, naturally and we had a very high regard for each other without studying stripes to supply background information. We Reserves were sometimes cheeky enough to tell our shipmates in the RN that, in reality, they were only the caretakers in peacetime.

The peacetime crew of this vast vessel totalled about 1800, of which 100 were officers. This was one of the last ships to have three separate officers' Messes. The Wardroom contained 53 people, made up of: 6 Commanders; 16 Lieut-Cdrs; 2 Majors (Royal Marines); 1 Chaplain and 28 Lieutenants, of which I was the second youngest, aged 24. The Commissioned & Warrant Officers' Mess held 17 in total, 9 of the former and 8 of the latter and the Gunroom had 4 Sub-Lieutenants plus 26 Midshipmen, 3 of them Canadians, making a total of 30. The month of January was devoted to settling in and getting to know my fellow officers in the Wardroom. I shared a cabin up in the bridge superstructure with Bill Pakenham, recently promoted to Lieut RN and two years younger than me. We got on well together and discovered through our cabin port-holes we had a good view of the way ahead.

The Commanding Officer was Rear-Admiral W.G. Agnew, CB, CVO, DSO★, serving as Captain, wearing 4 rings, because, it was said, there was nowhere to fly his flag aloft, what with the Royal Standard and the flag of Lord High Admiral. The next most senior officer was Commander W.J. Lamb, MVO, OBE, Executive Officer, a similar position to that of No.1 in a destroyer. I cannot think of any other similarities. As Officer of the Watch on the quarterdeck gangway, lying alongside Railway Jetty in Pompey, I had a Midshipman and Quartermaster in company as I paced about with a telescope, neatly tucked under my left armpit. Not having a telescope of my own, I used the communal one, kept in the Wardroom lobby and discovered it was short of one or two lenses. It didn't matter, because this telescope was never used as such, but just carried as a badge of office to indicate who was OOW. Something that came as a complete surprise, was the stamping of feet on the deck close by, as a Royal Marine (RM) reported something to me with a military salute. I had never been shipmates with marines before but soon got used to them and admired their high standard of dress and discipline.

On the main deck of *Vanguard* was a large board covered with keys, to all compartments in the ship, and a marine sentry standing guard. The drill was to note the time of withdrawal and return of whatever key against a signature in the book, supervised by the sentry. To this day, whenever my wife, or I, mislay our housekeys, usually put on a tray near the front door, I will say 'Sue, pity we haven't got a marine sentry in the hall!' My early friendships, for a run ashore, were formed with Bill Packenham and Robin Graham, a Lieutenant RM. We knew Pompey well and would often visit the back room of the Osborne pub in Southsea, where a parrot, hiding behind the water-jug on the bar, would pop its head out and shout 'Ahoy there.'

Our last port of call, before returning on-board, was always the bar in the Keppel's Head Hotel, on the Hard, near the Dockyard Gate, where we could be sure of finding other groups of officers going back to the ship and thus able to expand our friendships. One of these was renewed with David Shaw, Lieut RN, who had been at Dunkirk with me in '40 and who was now the Commander's Assistant. He introduced me to Gordon Bevis, Lieut RN, the only one of the 28 senior to him and both of them became lifelong friends of mine. I still drop in to the Keppel's Head annually, when I attend the 17th DFA Reunion at the Royal Sailors' Home Club. It lies half-way between the Club and Portsmouth Harbour Station, my point of arrival from London and is only five minutes walk from each.

It was at the Harbour Station, in the afternoon of 31 January, that the Royal Family, King George VI, Queen Elizabeth and the Princesses Elizabeth and Margaret arrived with a Royal Party containing 38 persons, made up of: Ladies-in-Waiting and Equerries; Secretaries with Clerks; Dressers, Maids, Valets and Footmen; Hairdressers; Press correspondents with cameramen and a BBC commentator plus engineer. When 'Good King George the Sixth' looked out, on the eve of sailing, he saw deep snow lay round about in a climate cold prevailing, just as it had been for 'Good King Wenceslas', in his time. It was said that the King was reluctant to leave for warmer climes, with his people suffering such conditions, especially realizing that a poor man in the UK '47 couldn't gather winter fuel, because it was still rationed. The wartime feeling of wanting to share hardship with his subjects lived on in his mind, no doubt, but he was persuaded to carry on.

Wing Commander Peter Townsend, DSO, DFC, Equerry to KG VI, remained at the Station to oversee the luggage procedure after the rest of the Royal Household had departed for the ship. I was baggage officer from *Vanguard* and he and I liaised amicably in shifting 127 pieces of personal luggage from train to ship. Frankly, it was Mr Evitts, Sergeant Footman, well known to Peter, who did the job, whilst the Wing Co and I chatted on the side. I liked Townsend, Spitfire hero of the Battle of Britain Boys in '40, instinctively, a no bullshit personality, of whom the King thought most highly and whom I met, on and off, for the next 50 years at *Vanguard* reunions. Later, in the fifties, I thought, pity he and Margaret didn't get spliced but later still, having met his Belgian wife, I thought otherwise.

At 1730 that day, all officers were assembled in the Wardroom and formally presented to the Royals. From this moment on, for me and many more, the Queen was the most charming and captivating character in the family. She seemed to be different from the others and having read her life story since, I think I can understand why. As a teenage girl in WW1, at Glamis Castle, the Bowes Lyon Scottish home, she nursed and nurtured troops from the trenches, of all ranks, which I believe gave her the common touch and sensitivity, which she never lost throughout her long life, despite other inclinations. Before sailing, the ship's Entertainment Officer wanted to know how many of us had got civilian dinner jackets and tails, presumably an advantage in South Africa (SA). Happily, I had both, on loan from my brother-in-law Malcolm. C-in-C Portsmouth, now Admiral Sir Geoffrey Layton, an unknown quantity to me, and Lord Louis Mountbatten, always one not to miss an opportunity of influencing the monarch, came to dinner with the Royals on their first night aboard and the last night before we sailed on 1 February.

The Trinity House yacht *Patricia* led us out of harbour and to my delight, the destroyers *Offa*, *Obedient*, *Opportune* and *Orwell*, from my old 17th DF and now the Portsmouth Destroyer Flotilla, escorted us into the Channel, where we passed through an assembly of battleships and cruisers. The Commander told Bevis to organize a ship's concert and liaise with the BBC Commentator, Frank Gillard and his Engineer, Stanley Unwin, who would record it for broadcasting at home. This liaison led to Gordon and me being invited to the Recording Room, where we listened to Frank's broadcast of the day's events and then recorded our personal views, which were played back. It was quite weird to hear my voice for the first time.

As the Wardroom's contribution to the ship's concert it was decided to form a choir under the vigorous baton of Major Vivian Dunn, MVO, ARAM, Director of Music, Royal Marines. I was a tenor, 2nd promoted 1st and it was inspiring to be coached by Vivian seriously, yet in an atmosphere of fun. On 2 February, early morning, we entered the Bay of Biscay in a howling gale, our cabin was a shambles and this big ship was moving considerably for her size. The Portuguese Navy sailed out to salute us off Cape Finisterre. The Queen in oilskins and south-wester hat turned out on the bridge to acknowledge them, being the only member of the Royals capable of doing so. We were escorted by a cruiser or aircraft-carrier down to Freetown, when *Nigeria*, an SA cruiser took over. The ship's concert, or should I say 'command performance', with the Royals present, was a great success, recorded by Unwin, edited by Gillard and sent home to the BBC for broadcasting on the Light Programme.

We sailed across the equator into the southern hemisphere on 10 February and the ceremony of 'Crossing the Line', a fun event for all on board, was held in the forenoon. King Neptune (Lieut P.J. Odell RN), with his Queen Amphitrite (Chief Petty Officer Brynly Hale, DSM) and 96 members of Court, consisting of Trumpeters, Pirates, Doctors, Barbers, Bears and Police, assembled on the quarterdeck, in fancy dress, to be welcomed aboard, as it were. The rig of the day, for the rest of us, was 'Skylark' and anything was worn. A large canvas pool, with ducking-stools and surrounding platform, had been erected on the fo'c'sle, where Dolphinius, Clerk of Court to His Oceanic Majesty, would call all novices to be initiated. Before the fun began, the Captain walked the Royal Party forward along the upper deck and the King agreed to notice a frayed rope. 'What's that rope Captain Agnew, it's in a sorry state?' said the King. 'It's the "main brace", Sir,' replied Agnew. 'Well, have it spliced,' said HM, and bosun's pipes heralded 'Splice the main brace,' an extra tot of rum to all the ship's company, which was issued later. This was my first crossing, so I would be summoned soon by Dolphinius.

The procedure that followed is best described in the address made by King Neptune to the two Princesses, who were excused a drenching and repeated duckings by the Bears in the pool.

A hearty welcome to you, Princesses
Your lot is not one which distresses;
For we've decided in consultation
To modify your initiation.
We seldom make a special case,
For fear of serious loss of face;
But on this day Queen Amphitrite
Put in a plea to treat you lightly.
You've been excused the ducking chair,
Which throws its victims through the air;
Razor, brush and lather, too,
Have been debarred for use on you.
Elizabeth and Margaret Rose,
Accept some powder on each nose;
And after this my doctors will
Administer a little pill.
These rites admit you to our real-um,
For which we hand you proof on vellum.

Frank Gillard incurred King Neptune's severe displeasure by avoiding him in the past and having actually Crossed the Line by air. For this heinous offence., he went through the ducking chair twice and the punishment meted out by the Bears was more rigorous than usual. Must say, he appeared to enjoy every minute, as did we all. Captain 'Jackie' Broome, DSC, RN, well known in the Navy for his artistic ability, offered, in '46, to produce a Crossing the Line Certificate. This he did, with a wealth of beautiful detail, Neptune enthroned on the sea-bed surrounded by masses of mermaids, some on dolphins and two waving at *Vanguard* on the surface. Everyone present got a copy and the original went to Princess Elizabeth.

To stress the size of the crew is important, before relating an event that happened about thirty years later. We moved from Stourport to St Albans in the '70s and one Saturday, when Sue was paying our friendly milkman at the front door, he glanced over her shoulder and saw my 'Crossing the Line' Certificate, framed and hanging in the hall. 'I've got one of those, because I was in *Vanguard* on the Royal Tour to South Africa in '47,' he said. 'Come in and meet my husband,' said Sue, and thus started a friendship of many years.

The milkman, Dennis Spicer, had served as an AB, Able Seaman (Radar) and as we were two amongst 1800, it's not surprising that we hadn't met before. Many's the time, from then on, that Dennis came in for a tot and we went round the Cape again and again, with my photos to assist us. Whenever we looked at the photo of the whole ship's company, Dennis would point to a small dot of a person on 'B' turret and say 'That's me.' He never lost his seaman's sense of fun and when Sue told him, one day, that the previous night I'd been carried on to Bedford by the last train and spent the night there, on a station bench, his response was, 'If you believe that, you'll believe anything!'

The *Vanguard Daily News* of that same day, Monday, 10 February 1947, published the following – 'Mr Frank Gillard has informed us that the Director of Outside Broadcasting for the BBC, yesterday, telephoned him to say how much the broadcast of the Ship's Concert was appreciated. He offered his congratulations to all concerned and said that it had helped the people of Britain to forget the great freeze-up.'

I feel sure that the informality engendered by Crossing the Line brought about a sort of sea change in attitudes between the Royals, their Household and the Wardroom, of which I was part. I cannot speak for others, but the regal family seemed more like shipmates now and mixed more casually with us on the quarterdeck. The Princesses found great happiness visiting the Gunroom for tea and often stayed an hour or two playing games. The fun and frolics of midshipmen, in the Gunroom, was a scene they liked to share, with parental approval, of course, rather than risk being bored by those geriatrics in the other two officers' Messes.

Life was not all social, elbow bending activity, we did have a job to do and I was fortunate to be Assistant to Lieut-Cdr Raymond Hart, DSO, DSC★, RN, who was officer in charge of 'Tween Decks, that is, everything below the Upperdeck, and also proved to be most efficient as a Chief Bear in the pool. I want to give some of his nautical background, because I think it explains why we worked so well together. He, like me, but 9 years older, went to sea in the Merchant Navy, aged 16, in the Royal Mail Line. When discharged in the shipping depression of the 1930s, Hart was a lumberjack in Canada for three years, before being accepted into the RN, in 1937, as a Sub-Lieutenant, having been in the RNR since 1933. He was one of the so called 'hungry hundred' converted from RNR to RN at that time.

We hadn't met before, but we had been in close proximity in the Atlantic, where he had been one of the most successful destroyer captains. Our ships, his, *Vidette* and mine, *Oribi*, had exchanged signals in the big battle around Convoy ONS 5 in '43, but when aware of this, we didn't talk about it. The war was over now and such memories, then, were best forgotten. He retired as Captain and died in 1999. I read the obituary of that man I had admired greatly and agreed with the remark made by his shipmates, at a reunion, which went 'He was the best admiral the Navy never had.'

On 14 Feb (St Valentine's Day) we saw a shoal of dolphins leaping lovingly about in the ocean and later that day we welcomed a shoal of Royals, to dine in the Wardroom Mess. It was a special occasion and Lieut Phillip Higham RN, 2nd Gunnery Officer, who was now more interested in wine than guns, included 'Veuve Clicquot 1934' and 'Cognac Louis Philippe 1830', with and after the meal. The King got the Princesses to sing a couple of cowboy songs and 'My Grandfather's Clock' to the sensitive touch of Margaret Rose on the keyboard. Then followed a general sing-song, with words on printed sheets provided. The Queen turned to me and said 'How about "Goodnight Sweetheart"?' To which I replied, 'Isn't it a bit early for that Ma'am?', and she agreed. It was last on the song-sheet, she didn't know that, but the Commander knew that it was her favourite song and so that's how we ended the evening.

The Royal Family entertained groups of us to cocktail parties, in their quarters, from time to time. As Their Majesties (TMs) circulated among us, I remember saying to my close company 'Fancy, actually being at sea with a Queen Elizabeth as we are now. Those pirates, Drake and Raleigh never experienced that, did they?' The Queen told us how much she had enjoyed the Line Crossing activity and acclaimed Queen Amphitrite's, in reality Chief Petty-Officer Hale's, curtsey, as most daintily performed and quite the best formal gesture of greeting she had ever received. I thought afterwards that she might well have curtsied to Amphitrite, as she was, at that moment, in the presiding Oceanic Court of King Neptune.

Two frigates of the South African Navy, *Nereid* and *Acheron*, saluted us with their guns at 1100 on 16th and took up escort stations, in company with the cruiser, *Nigeria* as we got ourselves organized for arrival at Capetown the next day. It was sensible of the Captain to speak to the crew over the intercom, giving a few last words of advice about how to cope with the culturally different scene in SA and what to be aware of as regards black and white segregation. He asked them to avoid conflict, keep out of trouble and behave as British sailors had always done, over the centuries, with great regard for the welfare of the local population.

The day before our arrival at Capetown, the *Vanguard Daily News* had this to say: 'If tomorrow dawns fine and clear, look ahead at about 0540 and catch a glimpse of one of the most distinctive mountains in the world – Table Mountain (3,549 feet high). At 0630 we are expecting HMSA Ships *Good Hope*, *Natal* and *Transvaal* to join the escort and by the time we enter Duncan Dock, we shall have steamed a distance of 6,000 miles from Portsmouth.' A platform had been built on the top of 'B' gun-turret, just below and forward of the bridge, for the Royal Family to show themselves and wave to the welcoming crowds. It could be considered the seaborne equivalent of the balcony at Buckingham Palace.

When the King, Queen and Princesses disembarked, on 17 February, they were met by His Excellency, The Governor General, Mr Brand van Zyl and the Prime Minister, The Rt. Hon. Jan Christian Smuts, with members of the Union Cabinet. Smuts, born in Cape Colony 1870, settled in the Transvaal and commanded the Boer forces during the South African War, at the turn of the nineteenth and twentieth centuries. He then worked for reconciliation between Boers and British and led a united South Africa

HMS Vanguard *in Table Bay, Capetown, Royal Tour, 1947*

on the Allied side in both World Wars. Churchill valued his advice throughout WW2 and it was Smuts who told him that SA would pay for a destroyer. Hence, my wartime mistress, *Oribi*, whose crest, an SA antelope's head, was under-written by the words 'Nulli Secundus', second to none, strangely similar to *Vanguard*'s.

It was known that there was still quite a lot of anti-British feeling in SA and the hope of alleviating this, was, I believe, the reason for the Royal Tour. In other words, to try and keep SA within a Commonwealth that was gradually replacing an anachronistic Empire. After the opening of Parliament on the 21st, the Royal Party departed, in a white train, on an extensive tour, returning to Capetown on 20 April.

I do not wish to get involved with politics, but two events, of worldwide importance, are worthy of note, during 1947/48. The first is, that on 20 Feb '47, in London, the government announced that Britain would quit India by June 1948 and appointed Lord Louis Mountbatten to preside over the transfer of responsibilities. The second is, that Field Marshal Smuts OM, leader of the mainly English-speaking United Party and SA Prime Minister since '39, lost his seat to a candidate of the race segregationist Nationalist Party, which represented Afrikaans-speaking whites, in May '48. I'll say no more.

Having delivered our VIPs, the time was ours as a ship's company and was mainly devoted to leisure activities, for the next two months. The hospitality was stupendous and SAWAS (South African Women's Auxiliary Society) were up front in providing that, for all of us. On board ship, the most important officer was Lieut-Cdr Western, labelled Gunnery Officer, but now, far more important, functioning as Entertainments Officer. The social pressure from on shore was such that we officers were expected to volunteer in response, or Guns, Western, would exert pressure, gently but persuasively.

We soon learnt to play with the right hand and drink with the left. This for me and Gordon meant tennis at Newlands Club, Kelvingrove, a lot of the time, where we were made honorary members. We also became friendly with Leslie and Shirley Summers. I met Gillian (Gill for short) who became my steady Capetown girlfriend and her parents, who came on board, often as my guests, when we held mammoth cocktail cum dancing parties on the quarterdeck. Gill's father was editor of the *Cape Argus* newspaper and he showed me round his domain.

The band of His Majesty's Royal Marines, Portsmouth, was undoubtedly one of the ship's finest assets. They counter-marched on the foreshore, each evening, behind Drum-major Louis Beer and before a large local crowd. They played such tunes as, 'A Life on the Ocean Wave' and 'Sarie Marais' (a well-known Afrikaans folk-song), always finishing with Vivian Dunn's arrangement of 'Sunset', with the band playing in counterpoint to the well blown bugles, as the ensign was lowered slowly. Not just a band, they were all accomplished musicians, who could cope with any occasion from a string quartet to a jazz group and did so, many times.

One day, some of us went up in a plane of the Royal Flight to fly over and around Table Mountain. The bird's eye view of Capetown was magnificent, *Vanguard* was tiny and the ride was quite bumpy, as we were affected by changing temperatures, winds and air-pockets. By way of a thank you, we entertained the RAF boys on board afterwards. Lots of organized groups of visitors were shown round the ship and, without a doubt, the two most hilarious days were when the whole ship's company gave afternoon parties to the children of Capetown. We, the crew, had as much fun as the kids, as we took them on swings, roundabouts, slides and an aerial railway, all constructed by us for the occasion. They went on boat trips, entered caves full of live pirates, heard voices and saw balloons coming out of the barrels of our 15-inch guns and were given frequent breaks to consume ice-creams and chocolates. Now, as I write this, fifty-five years later, the thought has just crossed my mind, what better use could there have been for 15-inch guns at that time?

The magic moment for each youngster was when they stepped from the gangway onto the deck, to be greeted, vocally, by a diver, actually an unoccupied diving-suit, large and imposing, with helmet closed and hand outstretched, rigged for speaking and hearing any response. Wires, hidden from view, crossed the deck to a fatherly Petty Officer, hiding in the superstructure and peering out through a port-hole, wearing ear-phones and clasping a microphone. The dialogue went like this, for example, as a small girl stepped aboard – Diver 'Hello, that's a lovely red dress you're wearing. What's your name' – 'Oh, I'm Mary and this is my little brother Tom. Who are you?' – 'Well, I'm the diver and I go over the side, now and then, to look at the ship's bottom and so on . . .'

It was a pleasant and most unexpected surprise, on the quarterdeck of *Vanguard*, to meet two old wartime shipmates from *Oribi* days, Benjie McCleod, the first No.1 and J.C.A. Ingram, the second Captain. Benjie was now a Lieut-Cdr, sailing in the *Nigeria*, so presumably seconded to the SA Navy and JCA was in the Cape visiting family, who had bought a house from Shirley Summer's family. Benjie and JCA just turned up at one of our large parties and were equally surprised to find me, a destroyer man, serving in such strange surroundings. We reminisced and refreshed ourselves under the biggest canvas awning we three had ever seen, completely covering the quarterdeck and a source of anxiety to any OOW, who feared a sudden 'southeaster', a fierce wind, whistling round Table Mountain from that direction and lifting the whole lot sky-high. The answer was to slope the awning at alternate places around the ship's side, whenever in doubt, but happily we were OK most days and such a disaster never did happen, much to the relief of the Mate of the Upper Deck, Lieut-Cdr Michael Kyrle-Pope, MBE.

From 7 March to 11 April we sailed round the coast of South Africa, visiting Saldhana Bay, Simonstown, Port Elizabeth, East London and Durban before returning to Capetown. We received great hospitality everywhere we went and returned it as best we could, with our 'duty free' facilities. Anchored at Saldhana, we held rowing races and met the SA frigates *Transvaal*, *Acteon* and *Good Hope*. Lieut. Hogg, No.1 of *Transvaal*, was an old chum of mine from minesweeping days in Harwich 1940 and we entertained a big party of Voortrekker type farmers, who spoke very little English. I had a good rapport with a wizened, toothless old boy, who kept smiling and raising his hat to me, as I was kept busy topping up his glass, until a large lady, his wife, came and took charge. The visit was a great success.

At Simonstown, then a British Naval Base, we played tennis at Admiralty House and Vice-Admiral Sir Clement Moody, C-in-C South Atlantic, joined in, wearing tropical rig, that is, white shirt and shorts with long stockings to the knees and one of those soft white hats with a red lining, not part of the rig, but suitable top-gear for any flag-officer to hoist. The climate in SA was such, that when in port, we often worked to 'Tropical Routine', which was hands turn to at 0500 and finish work for the day at 1100, or noon. This meant the afternoon was free for leisure, in naval jargon, a 'make and mend'. On we sailed to Port Elizabeth, where the heavy ocean swell made it unwise to operate ship's boats and so the tug *Harry Escombe* did yeoman service, taking libertymen and others to and from shore.

At most ports of call the ship arranged fixtures with local clubs for cricket and football teams. In the former, Mid. Upfill-Brown was the best player and easily topped the batting averages. In recent years at reunions, I call him 'Uppers Fillers', because, I tell him, that is what Brian Johnston, the famous cricket commentator, would have called him, if under his observation. Gordon and I stayed with our social tennis and in Port Elizabeth, the high spot was being taken to the 'Snake Park', a circular area covered with masses of poisonous vipers and a few gaitered keepers, separated from us by a moat inside a low wall. Having been lunched, most lavishly, at the City Hall and well fortified with 'Van der Hum', an SA liqueur meaning 'Old Chap', I was bold enough to reach out and touch the body of a serpent, when presented to me by a keeper. Two hospitable citizens, Charles and Peggy, took us home to their Felsted flat where we slept the night on their 'stoop', SA for verandah, and on the last day of March, we sailed for Durban.

Whilst in PE, I was most happy to receive a cable from my father, announcing the birth of a nephew Paul, born on 28 March to my sister Betty and Malcolm Carpenter. Now demobbed, he was getting involved with his uncle Al Bowley, as a peacetime butcher, rather than return as a clerk to the Westminster Bank, his pre-war job. Quite a change from being a Major on the staff of Lord Wavell, but he was a most adaptable person. Malcolm told me one thing he recalled about Durban when his troopship called there to refuel in 1940. A certain operatic lady, dressed exclusively in white, stood at the entrance to the harbour and sang patriotic British songs as his ship arrived and departed. She did this throughout WW2, being known as the 'Lady in White' and she was there, by special request, to greet the *Vanguard* in 1947.

Memories of Durban, for me are, firstly, the superb appearance of Zulus everywhere, as happy smiling people, of splendid physique and many of them in rickshaw harness, providing transport without pollution, before it became an issue and talked about. Secondly, thunderstorms were frequent, being in a sub-tropical latitude and evening quarterdeck parties were sometimes threatened with cancellation, indicated by the ship hoisting a large black flag before sunset. My great pal in Durban was a gorgeous girl called Claire, seen first in the Stardust night-club, with her uncle, a big-game hunter, with whom she lodged. They both came to a party on board before he went off on safari, which suited Claire and me. We were well matched in all respects, so, after escorting Claire home, we exchanged feelings on the settee, under the mounted heads of uncle's trophies on the walls. It was natural to wonder which species were looking on, and only after thirty years, in the era of Flanders and Swan singing their comical songs, did I realize that the face I had seen, smirking from above, must have been a 'Gnu'.

I'm a G-nu, I'm a G-nu, The g-nicest work of g-nature in the zoo – so they sang and I guess that's how I felt when I left Durban. Back in Capetown, it was hello Gill and then SAWAS organized a weekend for me with the Hagens family at Camp Bay, just round the corner from Lion's Head, to the west of Table Mountain. They made me feel really at home, Ma and Pa, with daughters Brenda, 19, Bunty, 13 and son Graham, 5. Ma, with SAWAS, had done a lot for troops passing through Capetown during

WW2. Pa's hobby was making models of ships, and he took me to the home of Mr Juritz who did likewise and also painted pictures of ships in oils. Juritz's house was full of nautical books, magazines, pictures and models, made with a minute eye for detail, including one of the *Cutty Sark*. He was intrigued when I told him I had actually sailed in that famous ship, and even more so by what happened next. He said he was going to paint the Finnish 4 masted barque *Passat*, which had just arrived at Capetown, and how about going aboard to look around, he could fix it. When I told him about passing the *Passat*, anchored in the English Channel as I steered the *Cutty Sark* under tow from Falmouth to the Thames in June 1938, well, that made our day and off we went to visit the *Passat*.

The Hagen's dog used to bark early every morning and on the Monday at breakfast, I asked why? 'Oh, he barks at the Cape cobra when it comes out of its cave in the garden and it soon goes back again,' said Ma Hagen. Much as I liked the family and had enjoyed the weekend, the 'PE Snake Park' scene returned to my mind and I was glad to be rejoining *Vanguard* later that day. As a parting gift, the Hagens gave me the song 'Sarie Marais' in Afrikaans with the English translation, which I treasure to this day. It was sung during the Boer Wars, about 1900 and one line, in the third verse, calls the English a crocodile pest, which, at the time, must have seemed appropriate. 'Sarie Marais' was, to the troops then, like 'Lili Marlene' was in WW2.

Lieut. John Coker RN was listed as Fighter Direction Officer, which was really a non-event now and he will always be remembered in his secondary listed job as Laundry Officer, which he fulfilled most efficiently. The laundry was a vitally important hive of activity, dealing with a massive, continuous throughput of white uniforms. John and I became good friends, as we both did with Lieut Desmond Hunton RM, which got the three of us going to the top of Table Mountain in the cable-car. Here, we relished the view and the company of little lizards leaping about on the rocks. We descended by wire and remember hearing that Jan Smuts never used this facility, but always walked up and down from his house on the lower slopes.

The opportunity that I had hoped for, to meet and talk to this distinguished man, happened when I was one of thirty people, including the Royal Family, as a guest of the Governor General at Westbrooke, Rondebosch. This was to attend the dinner party celebrating the 21st birthday of Princess Elizabeth, on Monday 21 April. It was by sheer good luck that I was there. Two officers from each Mess, Wardroom and Gunroom were invited and the fairest way was declared as putting all names in a hat in each Mess, and the first two drawn in each would go. Lieut Browne RN and I, plus Midshipmen Bell and Clarke were driven to Westbrooke, at high speed, by a Marine Driver in the ship's Jeep, to the cheers from crowds en route, who must have thought we were the Royals. We felt obliged to respond as if we were.

After being presented to Their Excellencies, an army major took me to meet Prime Minister Smuts. A fit, slimline, 77-year old, he confirmed that he always walked to the Table top and back, daily, if possible and how he loved the open country. I mentioned *Oribi* and yes, he remembered them paying for a British destroyer back in '41 and was glad to hear I got the benefit. The Royals arrived and after the presentations of others to them, the King, a shy man, spotted our naval uniforms and joined us to ask about the ship's activities. The Monarch was in a merry mood and chaffed his daughter, Elizabeth, before she blew out the 21 candles on her cake, saying, because there had been a lights failure that evening when they were dressing for dinner, 'I suggest we share your candles round our rooms tonight, in case the lights fail again. Will you arrange their distribution later, please?'

During dinner I had been sitting next to Lady Margaret Egerton, Lady-in-Waiting to the Princesses and chat came easily to us, having met before on board. The dinner plan in my scrap-book has a pencilled scribble opposite the name of a young lady called Winsome, at the other end of the table. All I wrote, by observation, was 'Smashing blonde,' which has raised a smile ever since. Afterwards, we went on to a big Birthday Ball at Government House where I was pleased to see so many friendly faces, including Benjie with his Swedish wife Ural, Leslie and Shirley Summers and with great delight, danced with Gill and Brenda Hagens. For me, it was a form of personal farewell, before the public send-off three days later. My final date with Gill was on the 23rd, celebrating her 21st at the Cafe Royal and then on to the Bohemia nightclub, which was full of *Vanguard* officers enjoying their last run ashore in Capetown.

At noon on the day of departure, 24 April, I received a personal farewell, in the shape of a Poskantoor Telegraafdiens: Lt Ian Bryce, *Vanguard*, Docks, Capetown; *Totsiens en alles van die beste*, love, The Family Hagens. That happy signal sits in my scrap-book to this day. The public display as we left Duncan Dock at 1600 that afternoon was most moving and impressive. A well balanced choir and band, on the dockside, struck up with 'Sarie Marais' and 'Auld lang Syne', as the sun shone on Jan Smuts in front of them and Table Mountain behind. With the Royals waving from the quarterdeck, the singing and the music was mingled with many shouts of '*Totsiens*' (Cheerio) from ship and shore, alike. *Vanguard* was homeward bound, leaving a South African autumn and heading for an English spring.

Five days later, on Tuesday, 29th, we anchored off the island of St Helena for the Royals to land and meet the inhabitants. The most important of these was an ancient tortoise, who had kept company with Napoleon until his death in 1871 and so was over 126 years old. Apparently, Bonaparte's buddy had disappeared before our visit and the total population of the island, about 5,000, had been ordered to search and had succeeded in finding this special subject to be presented. I wondered, did this remote reptile, perhaps, hide deliberately, because it would have preferred a republican rather than a royalist government?

There was a long standing tradition as regards toasts in Wardroom Messes when dining at sea on a Saturday night. After the port had been passed, the 'loyal toast' was proposed and drunk, in a sitting position, which was a naval privilege granted by a previous monarch, having witnessed officers strike their skulls on the low deckheads of old. The President of the Mess would then hammer with his gavel, a second time and stand to announce 'Gentlemen, I propose the toast to sweethearts and wives,' after which most people muttered the words 'And may they never meet!', as they sipped their port. Then, the youngest member of the Mess was called upon to respond with a suitable, usually saucy, speech.

As second youngest in the Wardroom, it was my turn on Saturday, 3 May, Bill Pakenham having already been committed. This was my first ever composed utterance to an audience of any size and I took some trouble with it, running to 400 words and considering about five minutes to be enough, without rushing it. My main objective was to point out to the majority of my messmates how I had pitied their plight, at being precluded, by their age, from attending The Young People's Ball at Government House in Capetown.

I opened with, 'We are now once again under the influence [pause – to sip my port] of the northeast trades [trade-winds], just about half-way home when our thoughts, now, should be turning towards the wives and sweethearts we have left behind and the choice is ours [pause], those in the UK, or those in SA, or maybe for some, those in both!' My closing sentence was 'Let us prepare ourselves for whatever welcome we may receive at Portsmouth and remember too, that it is spring, a time of year, when sweethearts and wives usually have great expectations. *Totsiens* to you all' It was insisted, by my messmates, that I stood on my chair throughout this much interrupted oration, but happily nothing was thrown at me!

Next day, in the evening, the Homeward Bound ship's concert took place on the quarterdeck, which could be called another command performance. The Wardroom act was busy and required lots of rehearsing, which we had done daily, hilariously, under the baton of Vivian Dunn. Lieut-Cdr Brian Gallie, DSC, Communications Officer, had composed a parody of the words of a popular song, telling of our stay in SA, which was memorized by the cast of eight.

Four of us were impersonating different ranks of officers and four of us different ranks of ratings, portraying extreme behaviour in all categories, no holds barred. Each four alternated on stage three times to sing words appropriate to what they were wearing, which went from day rig, to evening dress and finally to sports clothes. No wonder the show was called '*Totsiens*' for a cast of eight lightning shifters, with a footnote – in quite a number of cases most of Rig No. 3 can be worn under Rigs Nos 2 and 1. That's what we did and the cast was as follows: the 4 officers were Lieut-Cdrs Butler and Hart with Lieuts Browne and me, whilst the four ratings were Lieuts Murphy, Odell and Pakenham with the Chaplain The Rev Tiarks MA.

On Monday, after taking fuel oil from the tanker, *Brown Ranger*, an old wartime convoy chum of mine, we were joined by escorts from the Home Fleet, the aircraft-carrier *Triumph* and the cruisers *Cleopatra* and *Diadem*. Late in the afternoon of Tuesday, 6 May, I got a hard white card, about 6 × 4 inches in size, from The Equerry in Waiting, saying that he had received Their Majesties' commands to invite Lieut I.K. Bryce DSC, R.N. to Dinner at 7.30 o'clock that day and requested a reply should be sent, which I did most promptly and in similar formal style. Now, it was my turn to dine with the Royals and I enjoyed the prospect of a closer encounter.

At dinner, I sat next to Princess Margaret and found her conversation lively, amusing and most sophisticated for a seventeen year old. We talked about atoms, Germany post-war, Winston's speeches, Agatha Christie's novels, New York (me), Windsor (her), London (us) and the Navy in general. I mentioned the importance of salvage during wartime, when it was customary to remove iron railings from all parks and public spaces to make munitions, and I shall always remember her response, which was, 'Oh yes, that was a very good thing to do, but we were so glad they didn't take the ones in front of our house (Buckingham Palace), or what would we have done on VE Day!'

The film shown after dinner was *The Ghost Goes West*, a favourite of the Queen's, because it was shot in and around Glamis Castle, her childhood home in the Highlands of Scotland. She turned to me and said 'Come on, let's go up front and sit in the "fourpennies",' so I did that, sat between the Queen and Princess Elizabeth and occasionally they exchanged remarks, across me, in a natural way, mother to daughter and vice versa. I felt quite at ease and in no way out of place. A night-cap and a chat about our respective goings-on in SA rounded off a delightful evening, which was much less formal than I had expected from the tone of the invitation.

Having passed Finisterre, the north-west point of Spain, now in blue uniforms again, to cope with a cooler climate, we crossed the Bay of Biscay and dined the Royals in the Wardroom for the last time, a few days before our arrival at Portsmouth. This was a form of farewell party with singing and dancing after the meal. The Queen led a Conga Line round the quarterdeck, with the Commander next, then the Princesses and all of us behind. The Hoky-Coky was followed by a 'Strip the Willow' and because of the paucity of women, some of us pulled out our shirt fronts to identify us in a feminine role. The King thanked us all for our efforts afloat and ashore and we replied by singing 'We are the King's Navee' as we marched round the Wardroom in great disorder, climbing over any chairs and tables that were in our way. The next day photos were taken of Royals with each of the officers' Messes and one big one of them, with the whole ship's company.

Mum and Dad came down from Cardiff to welcome us into harbour, on Monday 12 May, amongst hundreds of others on Railway Jetty and the picture on the *Daily Mirror's* front page, next day, showed the scene well. The Royals paused halfway down the gangway, turned and waved goodbye to their recent shipmates, bye and large. In our absence the UK had suffered a severely cold winter, but now by contrast a scorching summer lay ahead. Many senior officers and a large part of the crew left the ship after the Royal Tour, but I was one of many more junior officers who remained. I expected to be demobilized by the end of the year and meantime, I was content to carry on with normal shipboard duties in *Vanguard*. The greatest pleasure came from being officer in charge of organizing visits to the ship, alongside in Portsmouth and later in Plymouth.

My cousins Ann Lowther and Ted Evans came aboard, but the big memory of visitors, in Pompey, is operatic. The Sadlers Wells Opera Company was performing *Carmen* at the King's Theatre, Southsea, nearby and being aware of our presence, promoted by the Royal Tour publicity, they wanted to come aboard. This I arranged and gave them a personally conducted tour ending in the Wardroom with some shipmates to help with the entertainment. I decided then that a certain gorgeous girl in the chorus was worthy of further attention, but now was not the moment. A number of us were invited to a performance of *Carmen*, which was sensational and suitably erotic as always, with an added thrill for me, in seeing and hearing my selected beauty in action. Afterwards, we went back stage, where gorgeous girl became Diana and the moment seemed right. I said 'How about a date on Sunday?' and she agreed.

It was a sunny Sunday, so we decided to take a Southdown bus along the coast to Arundel, where we walked in the lush fields around the castle and after a picnic lunch, got into a laidback position in the long grass, on the edge of a large pasture. Diana, by my request, sang snatches from *Carmen*, to my delight and being in such a state of repose, I closed my eyes. When she stopped singing, I sat up, with a jolt, to discover that we were surrounded by a herd of cows, all happily chewing the cud and looking at us, as much as to say 'more please'. We hugged each other and laughed aloud.

Talk about history repeating itself, well it did, exactly that. Two weeks ago as I write, when Sue and I were at Glyndebourne, as guests of Neil and Mary Jephcott for a performance of Bizet's *Carmen*. The procedure, on arrival, was to bag a place in the spacious grounds, weather permitting, where we set up table and chairs, with food and drink, ready for the forty-minute interval. After the explicit eroticism of Anne Sofie von Otter as Carmen, we returned to our patch, which was near the ha-ha (a perimeter ditch) to see a dozen heifers, facing us, on the other side. They all had contented expressions similar to those I had seen on the cows at Arundel. After relating my 1947 story, Neil's comment was, 'Now, I do believe that the milk yield can be improved by the medium of music.'

I think it was in June that we sailed for Plymouth, to lay up for the summer, for what else can you do with a battleship, when a war is over? This period was idyllic for Gordon Bevis and myself. We took the Saltash Ferry to swimming coves on the Cornish coast frequently and always visited a pub on the cliff above, where the landlord's reply to whatever was said, was always 'Well, the size of it, then!' To what he was referring was left to the imagination. Cousin Bill Musitano, ex-Glider-Pilot on D-day, came by car and took us back for happy times, with wife Pam, living in the 'White House' at Par near St Austell. Most evenings, we looked after her, whilst he went off to play contract bridge, at which he was an expert.

Captain Parham became captain of *Vanguard* in the autumn of '47 and Lamb was replaced by Commander Desmond Dreyer. My most vivid memory of them was when I played as wing forward in a *Vanguard* rugby jersey and they paced the touchline, giving continuous vocal encouragement. I think we were playing Devonport Services at the time, probably their 4th or 5th team, who beat us decisively, despite the captain's and commander's vociferous support. In October, I received the news that I would be demobilized, as a Lieutenant RNR, at the end of the month, but before concluding my naval service, I want to mention the many reunions, associated with *Vanguard*'s Royal Tour, in the years ahead.

The first reunion of *Vanguard* officers was in 1972, the 25th anniversary. It is all a bit hazy how it happened, but undoubtedly John Lamb, our Commander way back, managed to assemble a small committee, which included Ian Petrie, a Warrant Telegraphist in *Vanguard* '47, but in '72, Chairman and Chief Executive of Piggott Bros, Ongar, Essex, renowned for their flags worldwide and their marquees at the annual Chelsea Flower Show. He had better facilities than the others, whatever their rank, to cope with the role of Secretary. Ian thinks that they were aware of his rank in '47, being the most junior and therefore, all eyes focussed on him as they volunteered him for the job, which he did with the greatest efficiency for the next twenty-five years and enjoyed doing it. He and I became close friends when I joined the committee in '87.

The 25th was held at The Senior and Royal Aero Club in Pall Mall, now the IOD, Institute of Directors, attended by 66 officers plus wives. The 35th and 40th were at the 'In and Out', Naval and Military Club, then in Piccadilly and the 45th and 50th were in the Caledonian Club, attended by 38 officers and wives, with the Piper from the London Scottish Regiment present. The Queen Mother, whose party it really was, and the Queen came to all the reunions, with members of their Households who were on the Tour and sometimes Princess Margaret. During a mid-day drinks session, the Royals circulated, individually and my favourite memory is of the Queen Mum, at the 50th, looking round the group that I was in and saying 'My goodness, don't you sailors live on to a great age?', to which we replied, with one voice, 'Well yes, but you're doing pretty well yourself Ma'am.' She was, at that time, in her 97th year and enjoying her gin and dubonnet as she chatted with some younger *Vanguard* shipmates.

CHAPTER 14

More mistresses in peacetime colours – 1948–1956

I WAS DEMOBBED AT COSHAM GARAGE, commandeered for the purpose and just north of Portsmouth on 31 October 1947. Wearing the uniform of Lieutenant RNR, I entered this vast building and selected my civilian clothes, such as a sports jacket, grey flannel trousers, socks, shoes, a shirt with collar detached and a pork-pie style hat. At the exit, a supply rating gave me a cardboard box in which to place my chosen clothes and I shall never forget his farewell remark, as he tossed a front and a back stud into the rim of my hat. He said 'Good luck sir, in civvy street,' and suddenly, that made me think, seriously, about where my future lay.

Looking back on that moment, I did have a strange feeling of insecurity as I left the RN. I knew that Canadian Pacific Steamships (CPS) would re-employ me, but should I trust my future to them? What sort of fleet would they have after a war in which more than 2,000 merchant ships had been sunk? Before WW2, there were no contracts for officers with a shipping company, it was sign-on at the beginning, then sign-off and be paid at the end, voyage after voyage, the same as other crew members. Officers' contracts came in at the end of the Forties. I remembered the words of Basil Ball, Lieut-Cdr (E) and Damage Control Officer in *Vanguard*, as we stood at the bar one day: 'You know Bryce, the Royal Navy is a very good club to belong to, don't you think?' He was right in that it provided a secure background, usually until retirement.

Good luck in civvy street came my way during the first week in November, when my mother said 'You must meet Brenda Pearce, a charming girl who lives only five minutes away and she was in the WRNS you know! Elsie and Frank, her parents, are coming here, with her, for drinks this evening.' Thus were the seeds sown by our extrovert, intuitive Mums, which led, eventually, to our happy marriage, not exactly arranged, but seemingly sponsored by them. In 1945, aged 60, my father had retired and my parents had moved from Lake Road West to a bungalow, 56 Bettws-y-Coed Road, which was now my home. Around the corner lived the Pearces at 28 Llangorse Road, both addresses being in the suburb of Cyncoed, Cardiff. About this time, my brother-in-law, Malcolm, disliked being a butcher and bought 'Devonia', a general store with Post Office included, also in Cyncoed, which meant sister Betty, niece Christine, now aged 8 and nephew Paul, a baby still, were nearby. Dad's job in retirement developed into helping in the shop, especially rising early to sort daily newspapers for distribution. With daughter Peta and husband Derek living at 30 Llangorse Road right now, in 2002, Cyncoed is and always has been a focal point in my life.

Brenda, in my eyes, heart and mind, could best be described by the words of a song from a film with Fred Astaire dancing with Ginger Rogers and which I sang to my beloved:

> You're lovely to look at,
> Delightful to know
> And heaven to kiss,
> A combination like this,
> Is quite my most impossible scheme come true
> Imagine finding a dream like you . . .

and so on . . .

Her figure was exquisitely shaped and probably enhanced by her favourite pastime, swimming. A happy face, with beautiful deep brown eyes, expressed an adventurous attitude to life and was crowned by naturally wavy, auburn hair. She was tactile at all times and mixed well with all types of people. As time went by, our empathy grew as we became good lovers and good friends. Today, a celebrity can imply lesser value to the latter, with the remark 'No, we're not really lovers, we're just good friends.' However, we heeded the advice on marriage by the poet and philosopher Kahlil Gibran in 'The Prophet' :

> Give your hearts, but not into each other's keeping.
> For only the hand of Life can contain your hearts.
> And stand together yet not too near together:
> For the pillars of the temple stand apart,
> And the oak tree and the cypress grow not in each other's shadow.

Now, the romantic me hates hearing two lovers refer to themselves as a single 'item'. I believe that happiness comes to people who love, but never try to possess, one another. Brenda had a mischievous sense of fun, visual and verbal. Sometimes, she would wear her old WRNS hat and pretend to be a girlfriend whom I had mentioned, from my past.

The Admiralty gave me a meagre grant of pay for three months, to cover the period of preparing for and sitting the examination to obtain a Certificate of Competency as Master Mariner. Happily, my parents allowed me to live rent free and just contribute towards the housekeeping. Brenda and I wanted our growing love for each other to be lasting and started to make plans for the future. Meantime, in my impecunious state and studying throughout the week at the Nautical College of Cardiff University, this was no time for gadding about. Influenced, no doubt, by our mutual background of Senior Service discipline, we had one night each week,

Saturday, whooping it up at either the Church Inn, Llanishen or the Unicorn at Llanedeyrn, walking both ways, regardless of weather and limiting our alcoholic consumption to two pints of beer for me and two halves for Brenda. In the present day (2002) of hyper-indulgence, by me and others, it is amazing how much happiness we achieved then with so little material wealth.

Brenda and I had many interests in common, one of which was Rugby Union, which took us to Cardiff Arms Park on Saturdays (now the Millennium Stadium and turned arse about face). We stood in those days at the Taff River end, the cheapest of tickets, aware of people, possibly, peeing on us from behind. Because in my Orals for Master I had to repeat, word-perfect, all 31 Articles of Rule of the Road at Sea, the period waiting for the game to start was used by Brenda testing me, with text-book in hand. The Barbarians played Australia on 31 Jan '48, and included such renowned players as Haydn Tanner (Capt.), Cardiff and Wales, Steele Bodger, Edinburgh Univ and England and C.B. Holmes, Manchester and England, whom we met many times later, in Warsash, Hampshire. A magnificent game it was, with good scores by both sides. Earlier, I did well quoting Article 9 or was it 10, the longest of the 31, without fault and the boyos behind us were considerate enough to pee in their empty beer bottles.

The examiner for my Master's Certificate was Captain Logan, himself a Master in the Mercantile Marine (now MN) with an office in Cardiff Bay. At the south end of Bute Street, turn left and there it was, still is, a large red brick building on the left. It has been preserved, during the recent development of the area, as has the Pier Head building, almost opposite, with its conspicuous clock-tower. The written part lasted four days and included two extra papers about chartwork and cargo-handling, because I was skipping Mates and going straight for Masters, as already explained. My mates at the College, with MN experience in tankers and cargo ships, whose minds I had explored to great benefit, teased me by saying that this examiner, a fiery Scot, was renowned for giving RNRs a tough time. He would focus on cargoes and ship stability, remaining upright, without a list to port or starboard and with reasonable trim, the draft fore and aft, the whole being affected by positioning and shifting of weights in the hull. Officers in naval ships were less familiar with such changing factors.

Feeling nervously confident when facing my Orals on the fifth day, I soon discovered that Captain Logan had a fair-minded, candid, approach as he fired his questions at me. I satisfied him about my written work and Rule of the Road, before we engaged in a most interesting exchange. He asked me to 'clear hawse', a turn in my cables, placing two coins on his desk as my anchors. I described how I had done it on a destroyer in Iceland using an RN joggle shackle. He got me to draw one, starting a fascinating chat about shackles and their different applications. With a clear hawse and head, he said – 'You've passed. Well done.'

It was 9 February 1948, exactly three calendar months after meeting Brenda for the first time, and I had invited her to be at the 'Steam Packet', an ancient pub near the MM, at the noon hour. Round the corner we went, into St James's Street, to a jewellers, where she chose a ring and we became engaged to be married. The £35 for the ring was my biggest insurance outlay for the future so far in my life, but I never regretted it. Both our parents were kept in ignorance, until I had done the right thing, in those days and approached the bride's father, to request the hand of his daughter in marriage. This was a ritual we were happy to continue, although any serious thoughts, of tribal, material and possessive implications, rankled.

When I went to 28, Llangorse Rd, the following Sunday morning, Elsie, with her feminine intuition, guessed why I wanted to see Frank. Whilst I waited in the living room, he was busy hoovering the carpets upstairs and seemed reluctant to descend in answer to Elsie's request. She succeeded eventually by shouting – 'Frank, will you please stop hoovering because Ian wants to talk to you and it's something important.' Down he came, and happily his acceptance was forthcoming when he heard what I had to say. My parents were invited round, the ring was now displayed on Brenda's finger and celebrations commenced. Both our fathers were 1914–18 army veterans and Frank (wounded five times in the trenches) told us he was responsible for getting rum up to the front-line for the 'tommies' before an attack, therefore providing liquor was a purposeful duty for him then and he proved to us that it was still so.

Brenda when demobbed from the WRNS had taken a Secretarial Course in London and now, living at home, she got a job with United Dominions Trust (UDT) in Cardiff. I joined the Canadian Pacific liner *Empress of Canada* as 4th Officer, in Liverpool on 23 March. My Empress mistress suited me fine, but when we reached St John, New Brunswick, after a stormy outward crossing, I heard a mature Canadian passenger say 'They don't kid me, no Sir. She rolled like a "drunken Duchess". They've just painted her hull white like the pre-war Empresses and upped her social status, that's what!' He was so right, because she used to be called *Duchess of Richmond* as was the *Empress of France* called *Duchess of Bedford*, before WW2 when they got their rolling reputation. I went to the *Beaverglen* as 2nd Officer for 6 months in '48, sailing out of the Royal Docks, London, before rejoining the *Canada* as 3rd Officer in Jan '49. It was good to get back to a gourmet menu, after cargo-ship grub.

Sailing as we did under Captain Shergold, Shergs, as we called him, was fun, for passengers and crew alike. He was an excellent seaman and would in no way hazard his ship, but if conditions were OK, then why not go 3 cables (600 yards) off Cape Race, the south-east corner of Newfoundland, for everyone to exchange greetings with the lighthouse keeper? This novel experience was appreciated by all, ashore and afloat. Shergs was a showman and loved showing passengers round the bridge in fine weather, which relieved my loneliness as 3rd Officer and Officer of the Watch (OOW) on the 8 to 12, Forenoon Watch. He had a good eye for the ladies, which gave me personal enjoyment when he said 'My 3rd Officer will take you into that darkened space at the back of the bridge and show you how the radar works.'

Homeward bound to Liverpool, on a clear day, we would make a landfall on Malin Head, the north-west extremity of Eire, to give our Canadian cousins a glimpse of the Emerald Isle, before entering the North Channel by navigating through the 3-mile gap between Rathlin Island and the north-east corner of Ireland. We would broadcast through the ship's speakers, a bit of geography and history, such as 'Scotland is only 12 miles from Ireland and Rathlin Island; on the port side, is where Robert the Bruce, King of Scotland, in the fourteenth century, was prisoner in a cave and was inspired to try, try, try again by watching a spider making its web. Who hasn't had that taught to them, as a moral example in life, during a history lesson at school?'

Of course, having a steam whistle mounted on the forward funnel of two, was a great source of entertainment. With good visibility and no other vessels in sight, who might misinterpret our sound signals, I can see Shergs surrounded by passengers on the bridge and hear him saying 'Who hasn't had a go, then?' as they took it in turns to create such a wonderful sound from that highly polished brass instrument, usually associated with fog. How dull by comparison is air travel today! For me, adjusting back to the MN from RN, I couldn't have been with a better skipper. He was not RNR but survived the war as captain of a merchant ship throughout and after the period I am talking about, he was promoted to General Manager of Canadian Pacific Steamships in Liver Building. CPS were unusual in that respect. Most shipping companies had accountants or financial whizz-kids put in charge but CPS always selected a reputable captain/seaman for the top job. In my time with them it was Captain R. N. Stuart VC, RD, RNR.

Draw a line around a globe and you have what's called a 'great circle'. The shortest distance between two points on planet earth is along a great circle and therefore it made sense, when crossing the Atlantic, going from north of Ireland to north or south of Newfoundland to follow such a track and vice versa, depending on the time of year. Track 'G', north of Newfoundland, through the Strait of Belle Isle, was used in the summer from, say, May until October, to reach Quebec and Montreal, when the Gulf of St Lawrence was free of ice. In the spring icebergs would break away from Greenland to the north and progress south on the current to the east of Newfoundland, gradually melting away in more southern latitudes. Because of the *Titanic* disaster in 1912 an Ice Patrol was established in this area, broadcasting frequent situation reports to shipping and after WW2, radar was a great warning resource for coping with this menace.

From about November to March/April, the ports of Halifax, Nova Scotia and St John, New Brunswick, were reached by Track 'F', south of Newfoundland, round Cape Race and across the Grand Banks. Field ice stretched south in winter, from the Cabot Strait, between the southwest corner of Newfoundland and Canada, when it might be considered wiser to use one or other of two Tracks 'E' or 'D', even further to the south, to avoid the ice-edge. Thus it was that in March '49, an incident occurred, which I consider worth recording, because it illustrates an occasion when I made a sensible decision under unusual circumstances which received a reasonable reaction from my commanding officer, with his astute sense of leadership.

It was a clear horizon, with me on the 8 to 12 p.m. watch, heading south-west, well clear of the ice-edge on the Grand Banks, south of Cape Race. Shergs said 'It's a fine evening so I'm going down to dinner at my table in the restaurant,' and I said, 'Aye, aye sir.' About half-an-hour later snow squalls occurred every now and then, but I wasn't bothered, nipping in to look at the radar screen frequently, which assured me that no ice was ahead of us. Then, after a prolonged and more severe squall, I went from the radar to the open wing of the bridge and saw a white object ahead, fine on the starboard bow. Without any hesitation I shouted 'Hard a'port' to the man at the wheel and he responded instantly. The ship heeled over and passengers hung on to their plates and chairs in the restaurant, whilst Shergs dashed up to the bridge, expecting to deal with an emergency. 'Midships, meet 'er, come back on course,' I said to the quartermaster, having avoided a small berg, or growler, as I thought.

When we had resumed our course I discovered, to my dismay, that the white object was still there in the same position and then I realized that it was snow that had settled on top of a post on the fore deck, just below eye level, and this had deceived me. Shergs was up in no time and all I could say was 'Sorry Sir, thought it was a growler, but it was only snow on top of a starboard samson post.' 'No need to be sorry, you acted promptly and appropriately at the time.' (pause). After glancing round to see all was well he said, 'I'm going down to resume my dinner. OK?' 'Yes sir.' I said, and that was that. The incident was never mentioned again, but my confidence increased as a result of his reassurance and obvious trust placed in me. On reflection, it was quite a responsibility being on the bridge of a liner with six to seven hundred passengers depending on the aptitude and judgement of the officer on watch, especially when passing through the Atlantic ice-track. Memories of the *Titanic* lingered on almost forty years later.

The round voyage of my 20,000-ton mistress was about a month; 7 days outward bound from Liverpool, 7 days approx in either Montreal or St

John, 7 days homeward bound and 7 days approx in Gladstone Dock, Liverpool. The distance between terminal ports was similar, about 2,800 miles and the slogan adopted for publicity was 'the seven-day comfort way'. This was most apt during the summer when we steamed up and down the picturesque St Lawrence River route to Quebec and Montreal, respectively 850 and 1,000 miles from the open sea. Any spare time was often devoted to the card game of cribbage (crib), at sea and in port, the keenest players being the two Marconi Wireless Operators and the ship's doctor.

There are three things I remember most about St John. First of all, it was renowned for having a 'reverse water-fall' on the river, up harbour, before entering the sea. Because the Bay of Fundy has the biggest rise and fall of tide in the world, about 30 feet, the height of tide at times would cause the water in the river to flow upstream over the ridge or fall, as opposed to downstream, which was normal. It had to be seen to be believed. The second thing was witnessing the Scottish game of 'Curling' on an indoor ice-rink. Heavy stones with handles (curling stones) were spun across the ice towards a target (tee) and other players in the team would warm the ice by brushing with a whisk ahead of the stone to enhance its progress, this way or that. I loved to watch this uncommon sport as a spectator.

The third thing is uppermost in my mind and deserves a separate paragraph, because my taste throughout life has always given it priority. I bought my very first oysters in St John at a cost of one dollar for two dozen! I had difficulty trying to open them in my cabin wash-basin with a seaman's knife and appealed to the Chief Steward, who arranged a tutorial for me under the Fish Chef in the galley, homeward bound, opening dozens of oysters for the passengers' menu. In no time at all, I was prodding the shell in the right place with a proper oyster knife, giving a twist to sever top from bottom and flipping the flat shell over my right shoulder. Like riding a bike, you never forget the knack and years later in the seventies and eighties when on cycling holidays in Brittany, Sue and I would sit by the roadside at lunchtime, with me showing-off my expertise at opening oysters and passing pedestrians would say 'Bon appetit, Monsieur et Madame,' never supposing for one moment, by our behaviour, that we were 'roast beefs'.

I want to pay tribute to Liverpool, as our sustained gateway by sea to the New World for over a century, and in particular to the stevedores in the docks, spread below the Overhead Railway in those days, from the Pier Head to Blundell Sands. As casual labour, they were selected day by day, at the dock gates, with no thought of security or a minimum wage and relying on a large merchant fleet in future to provide their employment. It is said that these dockers in WW2 handled about one third of the UK's vital imports. Respected by me as a reliable link in my job, I was sad to see them so under-valued nationally, much like the MN. As Cargo Officer in the *Canada*, I was responsible for the small cargo we carried, the most important being the 'Registered Mail' which had to be tallied in and out by me. Brenda, as my fiancée, liked chatting with the stevedores when waiting at the side of Gladstone Dock. In broad scouse (Liverpool's fun dialect) they said 'Don't worry love, we'll fix his mail and he'll be ashore in a jiffy.' To me, they said 'Don't take her to Southport or she'll spend your money in the posh shops. Take her jitterbugging in the Lighthouse Club at Formby.' What sound scouse sense that was.

Brenda and I were to be married at Llanishen Church, Cardiff on 23 April 1949, a date already celebrated as St George's Day and William Shakespeare's birthday. A month before that, B came up to Liverpool for the *Canada*'s period in port and my fellow officers, led by Chief Officer Scallan, suggested we got married, then and there, secretly, before 4 April, the end of the Income Tax year and to our financial advantage. If we did this, they would act as witnesses at a Registry Office and our relatives need never know. The church wedding could proceed as planned at the end of the *Canada*'s next voyage, when I was being given a month's leave, but the great benefit to us would be a Tax Rebate, which in those days was given on the earnings of the previous year. The idea had immediate appeal to me, with thoughts of the rebate paying for our honeymoon, but Brenda quite rightly asserted herself and said very firmly 'No way'.

I bade farewell to my Empress mistress, who had introduced me to and often seduced me with dozens of aphrodisiacal oysters, on Wednesday, 20 April, in Liverpool, and in the words of a song from *My Fair Lady*, got myself to the church on time, three days later. Guests from a distance stayed at the Royal Hotel in St Mary Street where the reception would be held and from where Frank organized a coach to and from Llanishen Church. In transit, my mother's brother, Don Musitano, quite the funniest man in my life, acted as conductor cum master of ceremonies (MC) by passing up and down the coach and introducing all the guests, one to another. A large man, 6 ft 4 ins or more, weighing about 18 stone (250 lbs), he distinguished himself by his flamboyant dress and personality, but in an acceptable way. Consequently, on arrival at the church, the guests of both bride and groom were behaving as one big happy family and after the return journey they entered the hotel reception as if it were a reunion.

The evening before the wedding, Don allowed Bill, his eldest son, to drive his precious new Jaguar car, which would accommodate the five additional members of the 'stag party', on a visit to the 'Unicorn Inn' at Llanedeyrn, a few miles east of Cardiff. My group consisted of Gordon Bevis (*Vanguard* shipmate) as best-man and four ushers, John Murphy (*Oribi* shipmate), Peter Humphrey-Baker (husband of bridesmaid Stella), Bill Lalonde (husband of bridesmaid Jean) and Bill Musitano (first cousin). I felt very singular indeed, knowing that the rest of them were already married. Brenda was supported by three bridesmaids, Stella and Jean, who had been with her in the WRNS and my niece Christine Carpenter, almost ten years

Brenda and Ian on their wedding day

old. Christopher Hawkins, about four years of age, was her wee page-boy in the kilt, who ate what he could and what he couldn't he put in his sporran.

At the wedding, Gordon and I wore our uniforms as Lieutenants, RN and RNR respectively, with swords and gongs. After the ceremony, with typical naval efficiency, he amused me when he said 'For your information, you uttered the words "I will" at precisely fourteen minutes past noon on British Summer Time (BST).' Undoubtedly, he set a precedent, because Sue says that to this day, whenever we attend a wedding she notices that I always glance at my wristwatch when I hear the groom supposedly forfeiting his freedom, but more likely finding a friend who can discover a pair of socks in a drawer where there aren't any?

It was a sad moment when we had to leave such a splendid assembly of loved ones, relatives and friends, but such was the custom fifty years ago. Brenda and I sang our song 'Much Splicing in the Church' (see Chapter 1) and the speeches were fun. My mother, 'Good Ol' Zill', got a standing ovation after her totally erroneous opening remark 'Being a woman of very few words,' which was all anyone heard because the cheers and applause took over, but this immediate response told her that she was loved by everyone for her inimitable verbosity. The young ones today have got it right, I do believe, by staying on for one or maybe two nights to mix with their guests, especially those from overseas. Having a screw before marriage, in the fifties, was still considered a tabooing matter for most, if not for some, whereas today, the media makes celebrities' screws, before and after marriages, all too-boring, for some, if not for most. When we got married, most people in the UK rejoiced with us, because sweets ceased to be rationed on the day after. I can't say what instant effect, if any, that had on screwing, but the easy availability of chocolate 'After Eight' mints may have helped some, at a later date.

Off we went by train to the Raven Hotel in Shrewsbury, now demolished and replaced by a supermarket, I'm told. Then on Sunday by train to Holyhead, to catch the steam packet to Eire in turbulent weather which we both quite enjoyed, being good sailors. Docking in Dun Laoghaire we went to Dublin, where we hired a Ford Prefect car for a fortnight and drove to the Marine Hotel at Howth on the north side of Dublin Bay. Elsie had arranged our booking there by writing to her uncle, Frank Bethell, a wealthy owner of many hotels in Eire, now living as a widower in County Wicklow, with his eldest of three daughters, still single, caring for him. We spent a happy day in the company of this elegant, upright man, who spoke with an English voice and entertained us well on his lavish estate. We felt there was a warm family feeling in his reception and this came naturally to him, no doubt, for only he, at the time, knew that he was meeting his grand-daughter, Brenda, for the first time.

It was a decade later, that Elsie, in her sixties, obtained a passport and discovered that Frank Bethell was in fact her father. She was born in 1895 before her parents were married and farmed-out to relatives on her mother's side, a customary move in those hypocritical times to avoid any social stigma to an upper class family. It was a shock to Elsie and to us all, but we admired the way she accepted the news, not allowing it to change her affectionate attitude towards cousins who were now her sisters, of whom she was the eldest. She continued living comfortably with her Frank, well provided for financially and thus never raised the issue of a possible inheritance when the old boy died. As a result, the generation of second cousins, from the four sisters, are all in touch and maintain a friendly relationship to this day.

One of four friendly RC priests at the the next table in the Marine, over breakfast, said to us 'Would you be liking a day at the races as our guests, with Baldoyle Course being just across the way from here?' I thought to myself, they fancy my Mrs, but believing celibacy to be their code of conduct, why should I worry? We went and they were lovely people to be with. All of them, during the day, were seen by us frequently at the 'Tote Pay-out' after we had witnessed them being given tips by locals, who, we presumed, were their parishioners. They passed on some tips to us and we won £8 on a horse called 'New Pyjamas', which more than paid for our day out. Later, in the bar, when we told the fathers that my new pyjamas, bought for our honeymoon, had yet to be worn, they laughed a lot and bought me another Guinness.

We explored Dublin extensively, eating Galway oysters ad-lib at our favourite place, where the bar was made of empty champagne bottles, and going on to the Protestant Cathedral where we shook hands with the skeleton in the crypt. After that, we decided to tour the south-west of Eire by car for four days, with Brenda driving because I hadn't mastered the art at that time. We booked in overnight wherever we happened to be and our first stop was Tipperary, made famous by troops in WW1 singing about it being a long way to go to get there. That evening, sitting on a bench in the Town Hall, next to our hotel, we roared with laughter at the hilarious dialogue dished out by two typical Irish comics, taking the mickey out of the south and north of their island home, regardless. On to Cork (Cobh) where we visited Blarney Castle and kissed the famous 'stone'. In doing so, we were obliged to see the surrounding rural scene upside down, which probably accounts for my topsy-turvy eloquence in subsequent years.

Some of the loveliest country and coastline we had ever seen was revealed to us, as we glanced down Bantry Bay from Glengarriff, en route to the lakes of Killarney, where we stayed for two nights at the Muckross Hotel for £4.50. The happiest memory is that of hiring ponies, or was it donkeys (?) and relaxing in the peaceful perimeter of Muckross Abbey. We returned to the Marine Hotel, Sutton, on the Howth peninsular for a few days, where Miss Geraghty, the Proprietess, wecomed us back. She was a close friend of Frank Bethell and rumoured to be one of many mistresses managing his many hotels.

At the Marine, an anonymous letter awaited us, addressed to Mr & Mrs I.K. Bryce (Honeymoon couple) in an envelope covered in confetti. Inside, was a story about the Great God Thor, in human form. Being curious about man's lusty life on earth, he took a busty beauty to a Celtic hotel on a bay. After three days of heavy indulgence, with not a word uttered, he thought it time she knew who he was. Taking a deep breath he said 'My dear, there's something you really ought to know.' 'Well,' said she, 'what is it?' 'I'm Thor . . .' 'Tho'm I,' she said, 'but I'm thatisfied!' This, we guessed, came from lifelong friends Dave and June Pither, who had been a Wren with B. They had filled a suitcase with confetti plus a few condoms, in the foyer of the Royal Hotel, thinking it was ours, until a strange, mature female voice from behind them said 'My husband will be amused.'

We had a couple of quiet weeks at home in Cardiff, with our parents, before Brenda went back to UDT and I went to Liverpool to sign on the *Empress of France* on 23 May, as 3rd Officer, with three shipmates already known to me. The captain was Ben Grant, my god-father's son-in-law, a Commodore RNR; 1st Officer was Bill Mayne, a fellow Cardiffian, met twice before, and the 2nd Officer was Jan Bezant, last seen when we reported to Chatham Barracks as RNRs, from CPS, ten years before. These floating friends provided good company and prevented a feeling of anti-climax after a very happy honeymoon.

Robin Gillett, sailing as 4th Officer, immediately made it apparent that the food in the *France* appealed to him and a close friend enormously. Every time he sat down at our table, he said 'A menu like this, always makes me want to eat with gusto,' going on to explain that 'Gusto' was the name of his pet worm. It became a habit to enquire about the welfare of this close chum, even when Robin shifted to a 'Beaver' cargo ship, when we communicated by radio over the Atlantic. After a successful career with CPS, Robin went ashore in 1960 to become an Underwriter in Lloyds of London. In 1977 he was made Lord Mayor and inherited a Baronetcy. His procession that year, seen by me on TV, contained a float resembling an Empress liner, with the words painted on its side saying 'Come back Robin, all is forgiven!' He is now President of the Merchant Navy Association, (MNA), Greater London Branch and I was pleased to meet him again in 2001 at the Xmas Party in Anchor House, Canning Town, near where the Royal Docks used to be and where we docked in the post-war Beavers.

My happiest moments in the *France* were when I was doing a weather prognosis for the passengers. I pinned up a chart, daily, near the ship's shop, showing isobars with low and high pressure areas and indicating what I thought lay ahead of us en route. This was eight years before 'sputnik', the first earth satellite, so my information came through the Marconi Wireless operators who recorded reports mainly from shore stations surrounding the Atlantic. Also, at that time, there were a number of old wartime corvettes stationed at strategic points in the ocean, for the sole purpose of reporting weather data and I can remember seeing them on their lonely vigils and being thankful it wasn't me. Jan Bezant came alongside me and helped with the forecasts and when we met annually in the seventies and eighties, on Remembrance Sunday, in Trinity Square, we joked about getting it right more times than Michael Fish on BBC.

I sailed for seven voyages in the *France*, with Grant as my captain, running to Quebec and Montreal, until November '49, and during this time I did some serious thinking about my future and sought the advice of both Grant and Mayne. Having been back in the MN for over a year now, it had become obvious that CPS had no programme for building any replacement passenger ships, whereas I knew that Cunard had already launched some and had plans for many more. When I disclosed my thoughts to these two senior shipmates, they listened and advised me wisely. They said 'The decision must be yours, but we have discussed the matter and agreed that if we were your age our thoughts would be similar to yours.'

I checked out the situation in Cunard with my old *Oribi* shipmate in '41, Mike Hunt, by visiting him, in a new Cunarder, in Huskisson Dock, travelling on the overhead railway from Gladstone Dock. He said 'Come on in, the water's warm, promotion's good with plenty of ships, so go and see our Marine Superintendent, Captain Pollitt,' which I did, and he said 'Let me know when you're free, and you're in.' I wrote my letter of resignation to CPS and got a personal reply from the General Manager himself. I had stated my case candidly, saying what I intended to do and his response came back in green type, which indicated that R.N. Stuart VC, had used his own typewriter to say 'I had similar thoughts after WW1 and decided to stay, you should do likewise. I shall hold you to your Contract until March 1950.'

I told Pollitt of Cunard and he said 'Keep in touch, we'll take you next year, whenever you're free.' Bill Mayne said 'Ian, you silly boy, you were too honest. If you'd told him you were going to join your brother-in-law in his Cardiff grocery business ashore, he'd have let you go pronto.' In November I was promoted, beyond my seniority, to 2nd Officer of the *Canada*, which hinted that CPS wanted me to stay, but my mind was made up. The pompous attitude, adopted by my remote boss, gave me an example of how not to behave as a boss or parent, in later life. With this incident in mind, I have never suggested that any progeny of mine should follow in my vocation, and in the light of their various subsequent successes, I have never regretted that decision. I wonder how younger 'royals' feel about their future, being expected to follow in the hereditary role set by their forebears and the constitution? Maybe, metaphorically, they'd like to 'run away to sea', as many freedom seeking subjects did in previous generations.

When accepted by Cunard, Brenda and I moved from our home, living with her parents in Cardiff, to a place of our own in Warsash, Hampshire, on the south side of the Hamble River, about halfway between Southampton and Fareham. The Jordan family, friends of the Pearces, owned properties in Brook Avenue. John, with wife Gegg, ran a large market-garden bordering on the river and his sisters, Phil and June, managed 'Naut Guest House' on an adjoining plot and were known, naturally, as the 'Naughty Girls'. John and Gegg's house, St Leger, was large and more than they needed, so they converted the top half into a semi-furnished flat for us, which was ideal. A 5-minute walk to Brook Lane, a 20-minute bus-ride into Woolston, 5 minutes crossing the Itchen by Floating-bridge (on wires) and a 10 to 15-minute walk to the docks, got me to my ship in reasonable time. In those days, collecting items for a home was fun, with very little cash and no credit cards. We bought a Belling cooker, but kitchen and

Cunard RMS Caronia, *the 'Green Goddess'*

bedside cupboards were grocery boxes, on end, with chintz curtains for respectability.

On 1 April 1950, I joined the *Caronia*, 34,000 tons, in Southampton, close to where I had visited the *White Empress*, 42,000 tons, with my father, in 1935. Sadly, the *Empress of Britain* was the largest merchantman to be sunk in WW2, bombed by a Focke-Wulf aircraft off north-west Ireland in October 1940 and finished off with torpedoes by U-38. As I walked up *Caronia*'s gangway, my thoughts went back fifteen years and I felt glad to be carrying on a world-wide cruising tradition, in this new ship built for that purpose. Painted pale green overall, with hull a darker shade, it was easy to see why she was known as the 'Green Goddess'.

Historically, it was 110 years before, in 1840, that Samuel Cunard established the Atlantic Mail Service out of Liverpool, to Halifax, Nova Scotia (where Sam was reared on the waterfront) and Boston, Mass-achusetts, with 4 paddle-steamers of 1,200 tons, the first being *Britannia*. Soon after this came the tragic potato famine in Ireland, when out of a population of 8½ million, 1 million starved to death and 1½ million emigrated to the USA, mostly in Cunard ships. They travelled at a very reduced steerage rate of £6 and landed in Boston, where most of them remained. Alistair Cooke in one of his 'Letters from America' recently reminded us that the Irish in Boston aspired to greater dominance in the mid-20th century. J.F. Kennedy became a Senator in 1952, displacing one of the patriarchal Lowells, who spoke only to the Cabots, who, in turn, spoke only to God, according to the well known Harvard ditty.

During WW2 Cunard's ships carried 91.4 million tons of cargo and a total of 21.4 million troops, of which 11.4 million were in the *Queen Mary* and *Queen Elizabeth*. Each could carry 15,000 troops at a time across the Atlantic and Sir Percy Bates, Cunard chairman, said this achievement of the Queens shortened hostilities in Europe by a whole year. Hitler offered the equivalent of £100,000 to any ship or U-boat that could sink one of the Queens. Of the 18 passenger ships owned by Cunard in Sept '39, only 9 survived to May '45. In the post-war years, the two Queens set up a weekly service across the Atlantic from the Ocean Terminal in Southampton (So'ton) to Pier 90 on the West River in New York (NY) and this was the main form of travel in the early fifties. Smaller liners, like us, provided a support service from So'ton, when the Queens were refitting and others linked Liverpool (L'pool) with the Canadian ports.

Before spinning a few yarns, I feel it would be wise to spell out, briefly, my career in 10 ships, during my 6 years with Cunard. Half of the time I was in *Caronia*, as 3rd and 2nd Officer, 2 years from '50 to '52, plus 1 year from '54 to '55. From '52 to '54, as 2nd Officer, I was mostly in *Georgic* and *Scythia*, but between times, I did two trips in *Queen Mary* one in *Mauretania* and one in *Saxonia*. As Chief Officer, in '55, I did one trip in each of the Atlantic cargo-ships *Alsatia*, *Andria* and *Asia* and finally sailed in that capacity aboard the Mediterranean cargo ship *Lycia* until April '56. This completed 20 years for me as a mariner, cadet to Chief Officer.

After 3 Atlantic ferry voyages in *Caronia*, from So'ton to and from NY, I was given two weeks leave before rejoining her in December '50 and doing the annual refit in Liverpool. The local brigade put a few firemen on the ship to keep watch and between our staggered rounds, each night, one of them taught me the game of chess. We set up a board, displaying those majestic pieces, in the wardroom, with a card showing his name on one side and mine on t'other, which we turned, after making a move, to indicate who went next. As I improved, the contest lasted longer and laid the foundation for a great love of the game. I have taught all my youngsters to play chess and cribbage, learnt, almost a decade earlier, from a crane driver in hospital. How thankful I am, looking back, to have met two such competent companions, each found during refits, one for myself and one for my current mistress, which helped, in both cases, to prevent the passage of time becoming tedious.

As an Atlantic ferry we had two classes, 1st and Cabin, say, 500 passengers in each, with the restaurants named Balmoral and Sandringham respectively, after royal estates in the UK, but when cruising, which was our priority, they were all one class and about 1,000. Now, the first thing cruise people did after checking-in to their cabins, was to book a table in one or other of the restaurants, and it was always entertaining for us to listen to those who were aware of the two class system as a ferry, saying 'Gee, I guess we want a table in the Bal-mo-ral,' with emphasis on the first and last syllables.

'Sorry, Sir,' the Purser might say, 'the Balmoral is fully booked, but the Sand-ring-ham,' with similar emphasis, to please them, 'is just as good.' In fact, the service and food was the same in both, so such snobbery must have been induced by personal attitudes, influenced by our superior nomenclature.

Our overall objective was to cruise out of NY and earn dollars for Britain, to help repay our lease-lend debt and this we did over the next few years. Sailing from So'ton before Christmas and knowing we would not be back until April was not a happy family prospect, but Brenda and I were resigned to this. We agreed to have fun socially and individually, she, happily, next door, in the company of guests at 'Naut', and me, with whoever I chose to associate amongst shipmates and passengers. We set a high standard of mutual trust, remaining faithful to each other, despite the distressing circumstances of being apart. If others got shacked up, that was their business and should not become the subject of in company chat, although most people were aware of such goings-on, in the intimate size of a ship's community. Rest assured shipmates, I may recall, but I shall not record any such arrangements in this narrative.

Donald Sorrell, the charismatic captain of *Caronia*, was short in stature, with a booming voice, when necessary. He was a superb seaman, with ship handling his speciality. Every crew member felt they knew 'Donald', as he was called, not to his face, naturally, because he walked about his ship daily. This gave a seaman, greaser, steward, stewardess or laundress (steam-queen) the opportunity to talk to him and helped to create a happy and efficient ship's company. Our first cruise was to the West Indies for 12 days, over Christmas and New Year. Leaving NY on 22 Dec '50, for La Guaira, Venezuela, Kingston, Jamaica and Havana, Cuba, returning to NY on 2 Jan '51. At places where Caronia was unable to berth alongside, like La Guaira, the 45-foot launches ferried passengers ashore from embarkation doors low in the hull of the ship.

On 23 Dec I got a cable 'GREETINGS JULY CONFIRMED LOVE BRANDY' (her nickname now), which declared the happiest news of the year, that an infant of ours was on the way. In Jamaica I joined an excursion, visiting a rum factory, which included sampling the end product. It was thought that comments from a sailor, after many years of naval rum tasting, would add to everyone's enjoyment on an already stimulating occasion. Calling at Havana was another rum event, going from dark to light, in spirit. When moored, the manager of a Cuban nightclub entered our wardroom and said 'Be my guests tonight and thank you for bringing all these rich Americans. They would not be here without you navigators, so please, come in your uniform mess-kit to drink and eat on me, for as long as you like.' We did that and I drank my first white rum in a 'Frozen

Daiquiri' cocktail, with a dash of lime, in a glass filled with snowed ice. Fidel Castro took charge of Cuba in Jan '59, but in '51 we were still welcome.

Before *Caronia* commenced her first World Cruise from NY on 6 Jan 1951, it would be sensible to look at the worldwide situation, politically and militarily. We were aware that the Korean War in south-east Asia may have caused some passengers to cancel their trip. US troops, under General McArthur, were part of a United Nations Army halting an advance by the Communist North across the 38th parallel into South Korea. Since the end of WW2, Communism had become an increasing threat to Western Democracy and Churchill in his speech at Fulton, Missouri, in '46 said 'An iron curtain has descended across the Continent of Europe,' which prepared us for the 'Cold War' to come. Another trouble spot was in the Middle East, where Egypt was demanding the 'total and immediate' evacuation of British troops from the Suez Canal Zone, but the effect of this was more noticeable a year later.

For me, it was a great thrill to be going through the Panama Canal for the first time. It was not a sea-level canal like Suez, which meant we had to climb, via three locks up to the Gatun, man-made lake, where we looked back, with amazement, at the Atlantic, 85 ft below. On we went through this beautiful lake and then down by locks to the level of Panama City on the Pacific Ocean, the crossing of 51 miles taking us about nine hours. Hal Henessey was sailing with us as Cruise Director for American Express, organizing the shore excursions for passengers in all our ports of call, and we became good friends early on. He did a lot for my pleasure and education by offering me first refusal on any excursion vacancies (no charge), and I usually managed to accept.

From seeing an iguana on a stick for sale in the market place of Panama, I saw the sensational humans high diving from the cliffs at Acapulco, before arriving at Los Angeles (LA) and seeing the impressions of Betty Grable's legs and Snozzle Durante's nose in the concrete forecourt of Groman's Chinese Theatre. A coach trip round Beverley Hills to view the homes of the Hollywood Stars was uninspiring. With no sign or sound of life, they weren't homes to me, but more monuments to the material wealth of movie moguls, which seemed to confirm and amplify the truth of an old Zen saying, that 'The treasures of the house do not come in through the gate'. Leaving LA on 18 January, our next stop was Honolulu in Hawaii, with grass skirts, surfing on Waikiki beach, pineapples galore and a glimpse of Pearl Harbour, almost a decade after the US Navy suffered severe damage from a Japanese air attack, which got the USA actually fighting with the UK and USSR against aggressors in WW2.

We had covered 2,200 miles west from LA to Hawaii (21N 158W), now we were going a similar distance to the south-west, across the equator to a place called Pago Pago in the Samoan Islands (14S 170W). Our cruising speed was 20 knots and therefore each of these passages had lasted 4 ½ days. Every day at sea, the ship's Pursers organized a lottery for passengers on the 'day's run', in miles, from noon to noon. The winner was paid out at lunchtime and our daily newspaper, the *Cunard Times*, kept people informed on this and other crucial matters, plus a crossword by arrangement with the *Daily Telegraph*. On 27 January we crossed the equator and the usual initiation of novices, passengers and crew, took place in a canvas bath rigged on the fo'c'stle. Having crossed the line in HMS *Vanguard* four years before, this time I was part of King Neptune's court, dishing out the treatment I had received, all in good fun. I wore the white top-half of a US Navy sailor's rig, provided by a friendly passenger, on which I had the words printed, back and front, 'From Davy Jones's Locker'.

Hal Henessey often had me to his cocktail parties and when we were south of the equator, some of his guests said to me 'How about you, as a navigator, telling us about the new stars we see when on deck each night, after dinner?' In accepting their request, I had to swot up on the star-globe, not being all that familiar myself, but the result was rewarding. Hal arranged a large audience down aft, two decks below me and out of sight. I had a microphone to overcome their murmurings and with my visual aids overhead, clearly visible in the night sky, I gave them the Southern Cross and much more, to rapturous applause. Later in life as a Management Consultant, running courses in Presentation, I would emphasize the importance of observing the audience, for body-language feedback, but when saying so, I would always recall this unique occasion, in my early speaking career, when it was impossible. Progressing from the islands of Samoa to Tonga, about 300 miles south-west, between 29 January and 1 February, we crossed the Date-Line and therefore lost a complete day, which was 31 January, 1951.

From dawn to dusk on 1 February *Caronia* was anchored off Nuku Alofa, a place on the south side of the Tongan group of islands, an idyllic, unspoilt haven of nature, with golden sandy beaches shelving into warm, clear blue sea and surrounded by coconut palms. Our captain, Donald, a keen swimmer, formed a group of us from the crew, about a dozen, to take a launch away and anchor off a quiet beach nearby. We entered a small bay to find twice our number of children swimming in the sea with parents watching from the shelter of the palm trees. Donald was in his element and with his booming voice soon organized races in the shallows for all ages of kids which they loved in a boisterous, rowdy way. Soon the parents overcame their timidity, trusted our natural behaviour and joined in the fun. One of the fathers indicated that he liked Donald's woollen swimming trunks so the captain changed into shorts and traded them for a few coconuts with this native negotiator. That day gave me one of my happiest memories of Cunard cruising. The scene was recaptured when I saw pictures of Queen Salote of Tonga, at our Queen's Coronation in '53, getting drenched, riding through London in an open carriage in the pouring rain, laughing and waving to the crowds, as only a child of nature would do.

On 3 February we reached Suva in the Fiji islands and Donald, sensing that the port pilot was scared by our size, maintained skilful control and took *Caronia* through the hazardous offshore reef safely into harbour for the day. What I noticed most was that the local men were giants with enormous bare feet, which probably explains how well they have developed as rugby players over the years since then. We got to Auckland, New Zealand, 1,100 miles to the south, on 6 February, where I made immediate contact with Stan Jervis, my wartime, destroyer shipmate, then sheep farming, combined with leisure keel-boat sailing, who took me to the Royal New Zealand Yacht Club (RNZYC). I remember little else about Auckland!

At that time, licensing laws were strictly limited and after 6 p.m. people made their own arrangements, which explains what happened next. I was made welcome by his friends in the RNZYC and we sat round a table with a bottle of booze in front of each member, produced from a personal locker. As their guest, with a known nautical background, they got me yarning and insisted that I should have a tot with each and every one of them. Two hours later, Peggy, Stan's wife, already met by me in the UK, was most understanding when we rolled home to eat and I stayed overnight. They suggested Brenda and I should emigrate and I could join the NZ Navy. A few months later, with B's approval, I went to NZ House in London with this in mind, but they only wanted airmen or engineers, not salt-horse surface executives like me.

After Auckland we steamed 500 sea miles round the coast to Wellington, capital of NZ, on the south side of North Island in Cook Strait, where we sighted a descendant of 'Pelorus Jack', a nineteenth-century dolphin, famous for giving incoming sailing ships a sense of direction. Once again, Donald demonstrated his seamanlike expertise by berthing the ship stern first alongside the Wellington jetty, without tugs. Captain Sorrell was never without his 'Bit of Wood', as he called it, which assisted him in all ship-handling manoeuvres. This gadget he had used for many years, in various ships, by placing it on the bridge rail and looking towards the bow or stern. It was a piece of level hard wood, with points accurately marked by luminous painted screws, indicating certain angles, which only he could translate into distance-off at each end of his ship. Later in the fifties, when he was captain of the *Queen Mary* (80,000 tons and over 1,000 ft long), he hit the newspaper headlines on both sides of the Atlantic, by taking her alongside Pier 90 in NY without tugs, during a strike, but with his ever handy 'Bit of Wood'.

I was fortunate to sail with two such spirited captains in the MN post-war, Shergold in the *Canada* with CPS and now Sorrell in the *Caronia* with Cunard. What happened next was typical. We were heading down the west side of South Island NZ to visit Milford Sound, the biggest of the many fjords on that coastline, when at 0630, Donald suddenly appeared on the bridge and said 'Let's look into a Sound before breakfast, just for fun.' We studied the chart for a suitable place with sufficient water and room to turn, found one easily and in we crept. 'Now,' said Donald, 'blow 3 short blasts and a long one, on the whistle, for 'hip-hip-hip-hooray.' The effect was instantaneous and hilarious. People poured out of their houses on shore and passengers rushed on deck in their nightwear. Both sides were staggered at being parties to this unexpected intercontinental 'hello', but it was a Sorrell success story for sure.

Before moving on, I must mention thoughts that have occurred to me, over the years, since sailing with those two splendid captains, who each had a wonderful war record in the MN. They attracted less notice, during and after the war, for their heroic activities in merchant ships, carrying troops and taking part in dangerous operations, because the MN, for security reasons, was made the more silent of the two most silent Services. Witnessing their post-war behaviour, my conclusion is, 'Those who take a reasonable, calculated risk, which comes off, are often called lucky and usually they are, because of an enterprising attitude.' I attribute some of my successful achievements since then to following in their footsteps, especially in training, to the benefit of myself and others too numerous to mention.

After a brief visit to Doubtful Sound, 60 miles beyond Milford on the south-west corner of South Island, known as Fiordland, we turned away from NZ and steered north-west for Sydney, Australia, 1,000 miles away. I have an uncanny feeling as I write this on 23 November 2002, because the BBC News keeps referring to 'green goddesses', which are emergency fire engines driven by the Army during the present Firefighters' Strike. I am recalling different days, in 1951, when embraced all the time by my Green Goddess mistress and never had any intention of putting out the fire. Sighting Sydney Heads and passing under the famous bridge, is still a vivid memory. I saw koala bears up a eucalyptus tree and bought a stuffed koala for the infant expected in July. When in Fiji and shown a 'shrunken human head', I had resisted the sick idea of buying one, as a swinging pram toy, for whoever should be so unlucky?

From Sydney to Singapore by sea, the way we went, was about 6,000 miles to the north and west. The journey took us to three places, each with simple, lovely people living in equally beautiful island habitations. The first place, 1,000 miles north-east of Sydney, was Noumea, in the French island of New Caledonia. The second, another 1,000 miles north, was Guadal-canal in the Solomon Islands, the scene of much fighting in WW2, and the third, a further 1,000 miles to the west, was Port Moresby in Papua New

Guinea. The overall passage took ten days and we arrived at Singapore, 3,000 miles west of Port Moresby, on St. David's Day, 1 March.

On a first visit to Singapore, dinner at Raffles Hotel was a must, so a few of us did it. All I remember is looking up from the table and being fascinated by seeing my first ever chameleon, now and then, moving around the ceiling, catching insects. On we went to Colombo in Ceylon (now Sri Lanka), 1,500 miles westward, where on landing, I didn't get further than the Grand Oriental Hotel on the dockside. On entering the foyer I met David Shaw, quite by chance, a past naval shipmate in *Fitzroy*, at Dunkirk and in *Vanguard*, on the Royal Tour to SA. He was on leave from a frigate after patrolling in the Persian (now Iranian) Gulf and was staying in the hotel, which gave him the all too easy convenience of accumulating drinks on his room number for the next couple of days, which was fortunate for me.

Steaming north 1,000 miles, dodging unlit dhows in the dark, we reached Bombay on 10 March. The density and sorry state of the population in the streets appalled me, particularly when I went by taxi to the market to buy a parrot, whom I would teach to say 'Pieces of eight!' (my *Treasure Island* dream). However, before we got to Aden, 1,600 miles to the west, my forever noisy Capt'n Flint was interfering with my off-watch slumbering so happily I persuaded an unsuspecting engineer officer to adopt him.

I realize it is a particularity of mine to know how far it is and how long it takes to move between places, and I guess this is because, being a navigator at heart, I always need this reassurance. I shall stop giving this data now as we enter the more familiar areas of the Middle East and Mediterranean (Med), but I hope the habit, so far, has helped my readers to form a better picture around my narrative.

When we reached Port Sudan, we had a signal from the Sultan, a relative of King Farouk, saying he and his entourage would like a conducted tour, and the Staff-Captain delegated the honour to me. The Sultan, with his harem of about eight or nine ladies, in yashmaks, came aboard and his first words to me were, 'How is Stanley Matthews?' I had the presence of mind to reply 'A very fit footballer indeed, for Blackpool, when not playing for England. I'll tell him you asked.' The Sultan smiled and we progressed through the public rooms, where I was aware of the ladies behind us nicking souvenirs and concealing them in their robes.

From Port Sudan, halfway up the Red Sea, to Suez and through the Canal to Port Said was an interesting first time experience for me, but uneventful. At Alexandria (Alex), all excursions to the pyramids were fully booked and Hal had to say 'Ian, it's no go, I'm sorry, maybe next time round?' Until then I had enjoyed lots of shore excursions on American Express (Amex) and later in life, when using their credit card, for me it was always Hal providing the facility. I was more than compensated for missing the Pharaohs' tombs, by fitting in to an excursion at each of four ports-of-call, as we progressed through the Med from Alex to Gibraltar (Gib). We went to Haifa in Israel, then to Piraeus, the port for Athens in Greece, then Naples in Italy and finally Villefranche in France before exiting at Gib on 14 April.

At Haifa, of the many trips arranged to the Holy Land, I chose to visit Nazareth, the home of Jesus as a youth. Back on board I heard that lots of the older lady-passengers had bought bottles of Jordan water to be used for baptizing future grand-children back home in the US of A. I had to laugh when a local Jew told me 'They buy it in shops very nicely presented, but don't realize that it is contaminated by arab infidels peeing into the River Jordan, upstream from where the product is bottled.' A quick visit to the up-town Acropolis and the down-town Athens, showed me, close up, the vast contrast between ancient and modern.

Naples, sitting in the shadow of volcanic Vesuvius, offered two excursions and I did both. The first was to the immaculate discovered city of Pompeii, which had us pausing in a street when we saw the shape of a penis chipped in the pavement, pointing to a brothel, inside which were many sexually explicit pictures from the past. The second was in taxis on the Amalfi Drive, a high, narrow, coastal road with a precipitous drop on one side. The view was superb, but our speed and the fact that our driver assumed that the sound of his horn would dispose of any vehicles approaching round a blind bend, was terrifying. After consuming a large lunch of ravioli and chianti, with a family group singing soothing folk-songs, I found the afternoon ride less frightful. A feature of the group was grandpa producing resonant tuba-type bass notes by blowing across the mouth of a large urn, every now and then.

Villefranche was a lovely little harbour in a beautiful bay on the south coast of France, just a few miles west of Monaco. An excursion to the Casino at Monte Carlo was a must for most of our $ millionaire passengers. I went out of curiosity, not as a gambler and saw people playing out their particular systems in silence, which I found utterly boring. A shipmate had suggested I listen for the occasional pistol-shot in the grounds of the Casino, which would indicate that someone had just lost all they'd got. No such shot was heard that day. Five years later, in '56, the film *High Society* was made with Crosby, Sinatra, Louis Armstrong (Satchmo), music by Cole Porter, and Grace Kelly, appearing for the last time before she became Princess Grace of Monaco. It must be because of her marriage to Prince Rainier, combined with other memories at different times, that always makes me associate *High Society*, a favourite film, with Villefranche and the Côte d'Azur. I took a break from writing this chapter at mid-day on 28 Nov 2002 and another 'high' happened then, when I watched the film *High Noon* on TV, in which Grace starred, in '52, as the wife of Gary Cooper, playing the Marshal of Haleyville, to the melody of 'Do not forsake me, oh my darling . . .' etc. Let's call it serendipity, what else?

One week and 2,000 miles later, via Gib, Lisbon and Cherbourg, *Caronia* docked at Southampton, most fortunately, on Thursday, 19 April, four days before our second wedding anniversary. We celebrated by staying two nights at the Queen's Hotel, Southsea and went to the King's Theatre to enjoy *Winter Sport*, a new comedy by Anthony Kimmins, an ex-Commander in the RN, with a reputation, amongst seafarers, for naughty nautical dialogue, *The Middle Watch* being his best known production.

Brandy was feeling and looking good, at six months pregnant, with an insatiable appetite for oranges. Because I would be at sea in July, she would send a coded cable so that I should be the first to know the sex and weight of our baby. Being crossword fans, we chose names and worked out anagrams. If it were a boy, the words used would be 'horrible cans' preceded by the weight. If a girl, there would be three options, 'treacle piano', 'repeal action' or 'pale creation' (rejected!) followed by the weight. Right now, dear readers, you'll have to wait and see.

CHAPTER 15

North Cape Cruise and other voyages to end of sea career – 1951–1956

A FTER THREE WEEKS LEAVE, I rejoined *Caronia* for two 'over the pond' ferry trips to New York and back, during May and June, followed by a westward trip to New York at the end of June, to resume our dollar earning duty, by cruising, to help the UK's lend-lease obligation to the USA. The North Cape Cruise attracted a nicely balanced passenger list of parents, in their forties and fifties, along with their college offspring, say late 'teens to early twenties, on summer vacation. We passed Nantucket Light Vessel, just south of Cape Cod, on Independence Day, 4 July '51, heading for Reykjavik, Iceland and from there to the North Cape of Norway, a route well known to me as navigator of my wartime destroyer, way back in '41 to '44.

This time, at all hours, day or night, in the light of the midnight-sun, it was playing deck-tennis with friendly people instead of fighting-off terrorists in bombers, battleships and U-boats. When north of the Arctic Circle (Lat. 66 ½ N), in mid-summer (21 June) at which time the sun has reached the tropic of Cancer (Lat. 23 ½ N), daylight is continuous and our customers had to be persuaded to go to bed occasionally! North Cape was about 5 degrees of latitude north of the Arctic Circle (Lat. 71 ½ N), so when we landed them and they ascended to this promontory, they saw, through shaded glasses, the sun descend from the west to pass a few degrees of altitude above the horizon to the north and then climb away to the east for another day. This was literally the high spot of the cruise, after which we went south down the coast of Norway, visiting places of most interest.

To Third Officer Bryce 'REPEAL ACTION HALF SEVEN LOVE BRANDY' was what it said on the Radiogram handed to me by Bob Ibbotson, a fellow officer in the *Caronia*, when he came into my cabin and woke me up at 6.45 a.m. on 18 July 1951. 'Yippee Bob, it's a girl' I yelled and his reaction was to seize my right hand with his in congratulations, whilst with his left, he grabbed a bottle of Gordon's Gin nearby. I explained to Bob that REPEAL ACTION was an anagram of PETA CAROLINE, who had weighed in at 7 ½ lbs, so we toasted the health of mother and daughter as we entered the harbour of Trondheim, the ancient capital of Norway.

Bertie Thelwell was now captain of *Caronia*, a jovial, portly character, with the rank of Commodore in the RNR, which entitled him to fly the blue ensign in any merchant ship under his command, in keeping with naval tradition. He sent for me in the forenoon and said he had agreed with my colleagues' suggestion that they would cover my watchkeeping duties for 24 hours so that I could take time off to celebrate the arrival of my first born. 'Congratulations Bryce. It is good of your shipmates to give you the freedom to enjoy this great event in your life,' he said as he handed me a large goblet of brandy. Bertie had obviously been shown my cable. 'Thank you sir,' I replied, as I swigged the spirit, which put the name of my wife into my mouth and mind, coincidentally with my captain, who was imbibing likewise. Cables always said 'from Brandy', spelt out, but for fun, on my letters, instead of signing her name, she would draw a bubble glass with a little dancing figure inside, which was much more intoxicating.

Parties went on ashore and afloat during the day, and in the evening before dinner, lots of passengers, all ages, clubbed together and hosted a big champagne party in our wardroom, with non-watchkeeping officers from all departments included. I gave out copies of the cable 'Repeal action half seven' to see if anyone could crack the anagram. Nobody did, but everyone approved of the unusual first name, Peta. I feel I should tell you, now, that if it had been a boy, his names would have been 'Robin Charles' (from 'horrible cans'). We were out of the Arctic Circle now, so, only a short period of darkness, but it was hardly noticed that particular night.

After Bergen we went to Oslo, where I walked along paths in a large park, lined each side with beautiful statues of naked humanity, depicted in delightful postures, at all ages and expressing every emotion imaginable. This sensational scene was followed by the contrasting sight of a renovated Viking Longboat, the main transport, for generations, of those lifelike humans on display. In Gothenburg, Sweden, we entertained a group of Swedish naval officers on board. They came in a mini-bus and one seemed to be teetotal until he explained that they took it in turns to be non-drinking driver on mobile outings. Any alcohol in the blood of a driver, in Sweden, meant prison in '51, whereas in the UK, the breathalyser didn't appear until '67!

The most memorable sight in the harbour of Copenhagen, for cruise passengers and crew alike, was the magnificent mermaid curled coyly on the central rock. Waving her goodbye, we crossed over the North Sea to Queensferry, by the Firth of Forth bridge, where we landed our passengers to progress from Edinburgh, through Glasgow and the Western Highlands to rejoin the ship at Oban. *Caronia* sailed north-about through the Pentland Firth along to Cape Wrath, most appropriately named, and then south through the Minches, between the Outer and Inner Hebrides, to collect our US customers at Oban. They were now dressed in tartan clothes, with 'tam-o'shanters' on their heads and many proclaiming ancestral rights to wearing such attire. Dublin was next stop with a similar trip across Eire, kissing the 'Blarney Stone' en route and coming aboard again in the south-west, at Glengarriff, a 'wearin' o' the green', with similar ancestral claims. After taking the folk back to New York we docked in Southampton on 18 August and I saw my wonderful wife with our darling daughter for the first time.

Rather than drooling on about the many pleasures I enjoyed whilst cruising with passengers and trading with cargoes in Cunard liners, I feel it would be better to select stories from the next five years, before relating my series of short, most unusual, experiences as an 'Aide-de-camp' (ADC) for the MN, at Holyrood, Edinburgh, for 10 days each year, from '53 to '56, whilst still serving with Cunard, concluding with my traumatic departure from the sea, which I shall shape up in the next chapter. Two more North Cape Cruises and an Autumn Mediterranean Cruise were happy events, which followed a similar pattern of ports previously visited, so let us look at the longer voyages, starting with a Round Africa and India Cruise, in '52. Later, in '55, a World Cruise going from west to east, gave me two Saturdays, on 16 April, when crossing the date-line and compensated me for the lost day in '51, when going the other way.

Nowadays, in 2002, it is often said that most people's geographical knowledge of place location on our planet is deplorable, probably due to the current system of global travel, which is almost exclusively committed to transporting people, out of sight and touch, at 37,000 ft. Here then is the down to ocean route, from start to finish, of the Round Africa and India Cruise. NY to Trinidad, south down the east coast of South America to Rio de Janeiro, east across the South Atlantic to the island of St Helena, south-east to Capetown, around the Cape of Good Hope to Durban and on to Diego Suarez, on the north tip of Madagascar. From there to Mombasa, the port for Kenya, south to the spicy island of Zanzibar and then across the Indian Ocean to Colombo in Sri Lanka (then called Ceylon). North to Bombay, west to Aden, up the Red Sea, through the Suez Canal, west through the Mediterranean to Gibraltar, out into the Atlantic, across the Bay of Biscay and home to Southampton.

Two short cruises from NY to the Caribbean, of one week each, over Xmas day and New Year's day, preceded the long cruise and allowed us to fill our cabin wardrobes with cases of cheap booze purchased, duty-free, in Barbados, to see us through the three months ahead. I seem to remember Goddard's Gold Braid Rum at 2/6d (25p) a bottle and cricket enthusiasts may recall that the Goddard brothers, who owned the Company, distinguished themselves playing for the West Indies.

What happened when two charming and attractive ladies asked two junior deck officers to accompany them on a run ashore in Rio de Janeiro? I'm about to tell you. The dining table for eight executive, deck officers, from Chief Officer down to Junior Third, was situated in the forward, port-side, corner of the Balmoral restaurant. It was customary to chat with passengers at tables nearby and on getting to know them, as the cruise progressed, we would invite them to the wardroom for pre-dinner drinks. It was off the coast of Brazil, as *Caronia* steamed south from Port of Spain in Trinidad, that Wicksteed, 'Wicky' for short, and I were approached at table eating our breakfast 'May we sit with you and ask a special favour?' said one. 'Please do,' we replied. 'Well, you know already, that we two travelling companions have left our husbands back in New York City to make another million and the prospect of being in Rio tomorrow on our own is somewhat scary. Will you two be our escorts, and we'll pay for everything, of course? Please think about it and let us know later today. Forgive us for being so bold and believe us it took a long time to pluck up the courage to ask! Dining and dancing in the clubs of Rio would be such fun and we felt you two would understand and cooperate.'

Back in the wardroom Wicky and I simultaneously asked each other how we felt about being a gigolo, knowing only a little of what that meant. Being similar trustworthy married men who didn't sleep around, we agreed it would be fun, but what would the neighbours, our shipmates, think and say? I got a dictionary and read aloud that a gigolo was a man kept by a woman, usually older, paid to dance with and escort, coming from the French gigolette, a prostitute who danced, from gigue a fiddle. It was the thought of being a male pro that caused hesitation and an anxious discussion which was noticed immediately by our Chief Officer, Richard Conway. 'You boys seem to have a problem, can I help?' said he. He was a man we greatly admired for his code of conduct, both on and off the job, so we said 'Yes please,' and told him our story.

Without any hesitation old Conway said 'Accept their invitation, go and enjoy every moment, but don't mention it when you get home. I did something similar as a junior officer without any compromise, but told my wife and never heard the end of it! Now, I have met these ladies in question and trust them, as I know and trust you, to behave suitably, so fear not and treat it as an honour to be so chosen by them. If they just wanted you to screw them, they would have tried it before now, is my opinion.' We did as he suggested and had a fabulous time in Rio. As a foursome we walked along the world famous Copacabana beach before dining in the hotel of that name and moving on to a few top night clubs. What fun it was receiving $100 bills discreetly placed in the turn-ups of our trousers, under the table, if the ladies had given us too little, beforehand, to pay the bill when it was presented. This was a real gift relationship, with mutual pleasure provided. We could never have afforded a night like this on our Cunard pay and they needed us as escorts for their comfort and security in a strange place.

After a quick hello to the islanders of St Helena we reached Cape Town and shaped up a ship's cricket team when challenged by the Cape Brewery to a match on their fine ground. The form on both sides could best be described as fluid, with stewards producing trayloads of beer, between, I could swear, every other over. We were beaten by a strong brew imbibed in the outfield. Leslie Summers, my friend of '47 and now owning a frozen food store in the Cape, came aboard to see the Chief Steward who gave him a large order for the ship's stores. Les drove me to Hermanus on the coast, for a night out, to whoop it up with Shirley and friends.

Cricket cropped up again when we arrived in Bombay. A tall distinguished looking Sikh, in the usual immaculate turban, piloted *Caronia* into harbour and visited the wardroom afterwards. 'Do you have a cricket team and how good are you?' he asked. On hearing that we did have a team, but not much good, he said 'If you agree to a game, then I think it right to put you against the Pilots' 4th Eleven out of seven and I shall captain our side, to ensure fair play.' We accepted the challenge and the game was arranged on Bombay Common the following day. Never shall I forget the feeling of inflated importance walking out to bat in front of a crowd several hundred strong. The Common was swarming with spectators around our pitch and others in use. It was great to strike the ball and hear deafening shouts of applause, but not for long. Our Sikh pilot organizer, fielding at mid-off, took great delight in catching me out, but the team scores were fairly even and he had matched us well. My lasting impression was, don't these Indians love their cricket, which must be one of the many good things we bequeathed to them from the days of the British Raj.

As we entered the Suez Canal in March '52 we were aware of recent January riots in Cairo when 17 British people were murdered. The Turf Club, frequented by the British elite, and Shepheard's Hotel, founded before the Suez Canal was built in 1879, were both badly damaged. Therefore, when a gust of wind caused the ship to run aground with the bow on one side of the canal and the stern on t'other, we knew that we presented an easy target for terrorists of the day. However, British troops still in the Canal Zone were on full alert and immediately, on hearing of our predicament, we had a platoon of infantry on one side and a few tanks on the other. The passengers were then treated to a lively exchange between HM Forces. 'Call yourselves f . . . ing sailors,' said the soldiers, to which the reply was 'Pipe down you f . . . ing pongos, at least we're giving you something to do.' With the aid of ropes passed ashore, the ship was warped off and refloated to proceed without harm. We had been made aware that if a ship blocked the canal for 24 hours, then the Egyptians could demolish it.

After berthing alongside in Naples we heard the voice of our Chief Officer shouting from his cabin 'Wicky or Ian, one of you, nip up to the opera house and book a box for tomorrow night, in my name. Here's the money.' 'Aye, aye sir,' one of us replied and rushed to do his bidding.

A night at the opera was Richard's treat to his fellow officer shipmates whenever we visited that Italian port and the scene was colourful as well as musical with the attendants attired in frock coats and cocked hats to greet us in our evening mess kit. At the end of a performance Conway was on his feet shouting 'Bravo, bravo, bravo!' and had us all doing likewise. The last work we witnessed was Bellini's most beautiful and powerful opera *Norma*, which reminds me that we had a delightful telephonist by that name on *Caronia*'s switchboard. Many moons later my Cunard shipmate Bob Ibbotson was sensible enough to propose marriage to the said Norma and she was sensible enough to accept, thus forming an ideal loving couple. They live near So'ton and I am still in touch with them both to this day, by telephone, naturally.

I want to tell you more about Conway, because he was a man with whom I shared so many values in life. He had a passion for words and the plays of Shakespeare, to such an extent that his annual leave was always arranged, in those days, during the six weeks Festival at the Memorial Theatre in Stratford-on-Avon, commencing on the bard's birthday, 23 April each year. It was a joy to hear him quote with wisdom and wit; for example, when on the bridge and welcoming the officer taking over the watch from him at 8 a.m. or p.m., he might well say 'You come most carefully upon your hour,' followed by 'For this relief much thanks.' Once, I heard him cajole a wardroom guest, to good effect, with the remark 'We'll teach you to drink deep ere you depart.' All three quotations are from Hamlet, if you didn't know. He had been a submariner under steam in WW1 as an RNR officer and he attended a reunion of similar seamen, at HMS *Dolphin*, Gosport, once, when *Caronia* was docked in Southampton. He returned after four days away and it was obvious he had revelled in this gathering of submariners, who, in their day, he told us, had to lower the funnel and make things watertight before submerging and running on batteries. Well, 'Blow me down,' said I.

When I went away and Peta started to talk, she would ask her Mummy 'Where's Daddy?', to which she received the reply 'Daddy's gone.' Being an intelligent little girl she thought that Gone was really my name and from then on her question took the form of 'Where's Gone?' For many years after, this name became an in-family joke and sometimes, when I was absent, it would be said 'Gone's gone again.' From spring to autumn in 1953 I did many Atlantic crossings from Southampton via Le Havre, in the liner *Scythia*, as 2nd Officer. In August of that year I had three weeks leave and because Brenda and I decided to spend a fortnight of that in Brittany, Cunard granted us a free passage out to Le Havre and back from Cherbourg. We left Peta with her grandparents, Elsie and Frank, in Cardiff and so for that short period we were both goners!

Back in '52, when I left *Caronia*, I bought a Vespa Scooter and passed the formidable, hair-raising test, for a motor-cycle licence, in busy down-town Southampton. Made by Douglas in the UK, my Vespa was one of the early ones and being an unusual sight would attract an interested group around it when parked in the street. A year later, most people were familiar with this fabulous Italian created vehicle, having seen the magic movie *Roman Holiday*. This was about Gregory Peck, as an American newspaperman, propelling Audrey Hepburn, as a modern-day princess rebelling against her royal obligations, around Rome, astride a Vespa Scooter. Let's call the scooter excursion in France our 'Carnac Holiday', 'cos that's where we ended up, on a most beautiful, white, sandy beach, looking south over the Bay of Biscay.

We sailed out as passengers in the *Scythia*, which was fun, amongst the crew I knew and stayed overnight in Le Havre with Monsieur Forget, the Cunard Agent, before setting off next morning to the west through the province of Normandy. In the late afternoon we would stop at a cafe and over a glass of wine ask where we might stay the night. Never a problem, 'Madame en face will put you up,' we were told and it was always clean, cheap and we were warmly welcomed into the family circle. It wasn't as it was back home, bed and breakfast, but just the former and we grew to like this, because it allowed us to buy whatever we felt like in the market-place next day.

Our French improved as we progressed and I delighted in tasting my first globe artichoke, cooked over an open fire, by a grandma, during the evening, at one of the stop-overs. After one night in an hotel at Carnac we found a house close to the vast, golden sandy beach owned by an elderly mother and adult daughter, from whom we rented a large, sparsely furnished room over five nights for next to nothing. They obviously liked our presence because they treated us more like guests than lodgers. Every day, when we returned from the sun-drenched beach, or a visit to view the historic 'menhir stones', smaller but similar to Stonehenge, they invited us to drink a glass of Muscadet, the wine of Brittany, with them in the garden. On each occasion they would adorn themselves in the gorgeous lace head-dress, made famous by Breton ladies, which we admired and loved to see. For many years we exchanged photos and Christmas cards avec nos amies, les belles femmes de Bretagne, en France.

On our return to Cherbourg, we scooted through the middle of Normandy to the coast near the Bay of Mont St Michel, before entering the peninsula from the south-west, and en route I remember passing frequent signs saying 'prenez garde des crapauds', keep clear of toads crossing the road; the implication being that the toads, quite rightly, had priority. As we approached the coast, we heard a persistent, percussive beat, flippity-flop, flippity flop, which aroused our curiosity so we headed towards it and arrived at the world-famous 'Mère Poulard' restaurant on the island of Mont St Michel. The rhythmic sound came from chefs beating eggs for omelettes, before electric mixers became fashionable, and the subsequent feast was fabulous. We stayed the last night in a petrol filling station, being well entertained by the proprietor and his family. He wanted to improve his English and our cooperation was rewarded with calvados, the local apple liqueur, in abundance, until sleep became inevitable.

Reaching Cherbourg next day, we sat sipping champagne outside a cafe on the water-front. At the next table were an English family who had just arrived in their yacht and were having difficulty ordering drinks. Hearing the youngsters ask for lemonade and father floundering, I was forthcoming with 'Citronade is the word you want, mon ami anglais,' and at once we had rapport. Assuming that we were yachting types from the UK, like them, he inquired where our boat was for getting home. His question was well timed and my reply caused much merriment and surprise. 'Look to seaward and you'll see our boat, or rather ship, coming through the breakwater right now,' I said and he did this to witness *Queen Elizabeth I*, the largest liner in the world, entering harbour. After discharging US passengers and baggage, an enormous crane hoisted our tiny Vespa on board and Brenda and I, the only passengers to embark, went up the gangway to be welcomed by Chief Officer Woolfenden, who escorted us to our cabin. I had given Woolfy a suitcase containing evening clothes for us both beforehand, so we were well prepared to change for drinks, dinner and dancing, as we sailed, overnight, to Southampton.

After that lovely holiday in '53, I did a voyage to New York and back in the *Mauretania*, 35,000 tons, as Senior 3rd Officer, with Geoffrey Marr as Staff Captain, a fluent conversationalist in continual circulation. He was known, affectionately, as 'the egg with teeth', which perfectly described his large, rotund frame, topped by facially prominent dentures, revealed in an almost permanent smile. In September I returned to the smaller *Scythia*, 20,000 tons, as 2nd Officer on the Canadian run, with Captain MacKellar, a canny Scot, until April '54. *Scythia*, my beautifully furnished mahogany mistress, was a steadying influence on me, her lover, of a similar age, having been launched a few years after I was born in the 1920s.

The procedure for promotion in Cunard was by moving from a passenger liner, as a junior officer, to a cargo liner in a more senior rank, then back again and so on. Seniority was based on a list of when a person joined the Company and most officers kept a copy in the inside pocket of their reefer jacket, which would show them at a glance their chance of becoming Commodore one day. This list was kept updated as people retired, swallowed the hook, or were dismissed for some excess, such as alcohol or sex. Most lists had pencilled remarks alongside names, judging on present behaviour, which way anyone was likely to depart. Everyone had a substantive rank, below which pay would not fall, but often, in order to facilitate leave arrangements, an officer would sail in a higher rank, to his financial advantage. So it was that I switched ships many times during '54 and '55 as I ascended the Cunard Line's ladder.

Another North Cape cruise in *Caronia* from June to August '54 was followed by my first trip as Chief Officer in the *Alsatia* with Challoner as my captain, a previous shipmate, admired by all and called 'Happy', because his countenance always displayed that feeling. When we got to Norfolk, Virginia, he said 'Ian, come ashore and dine with me tonight, I'm told the seafood here is rather special'. I didn't realize then, that something else in his mind was also special, but that would be revealed later, when we went ashore. As we walked along the dockside 'Happy' paused as we passed the bow, patted our mutual mistress on her nose, with affection, like any rider might pat his mount and said 'Thank you *Alsatia*, my first command, for getting us here safely.' Now that I knew it was his first captaincy, I was touched by his expression of gratitude realizing that he, like me, had made dozens of successful Atlantic crossings, in many different ships. However, this one was very special for both of us and he thought it right to celebrate.

When ready to sail with our homeward cargo from Norfolk, I received a final visit from the foreman in charge of the stevedores who had loaded the ship. He and I had worked well together regarding weight distribution and the use of dunnage, loose material, mostly wooden battens, purchased by him and used for packing the cargo. As Chief Officer I had to sign the bill paying for the dunnage and relied on the foreman ordering a sufficient quantity, without feeling obliged to tell me what he had, in fact, used. The Company's grape-vine had already made me aware that as I shook the foreman's hand over a farewell drink in my cabin, an anonymous brown envelope, containing dollar notes, would be placed discreetly on my desk nearby. This was never to be acknowledged openly, just accepted without comment and pocketed as the Mate's perks, no doubt contrived, with the dunnage acting as a delusion.

Alsatia berthed in Victoria Docks, London, on 17 August '54, where I was relieved as Chief Officer. After a week with Brandy and Peta at our Warsash home, I joined *Caronia* once again on 25 August and sailed for New York, to commence an Autumn Mediterranean cruise, through September and October. Most of the ports on this cruise I had visited before, except for Genoa in Italy, Catania in Sicily and Malaga in Spain. In Malaga we marched round the promenade deck with local visitors, singing a Spanish folk-song with a lovely melody, which I can still hum, learning the words as we went, which I've since forgotten, except for 'Canta, Canta', at the beginning of each chorus. Another spell at home for two weeks with my loved ones, during the refit in Liverpool, before sailing, in early December, for New York and more dollar earning cruises. I cannot be certain, but I think the minimum annual leave entitlement in those days was three weeks. Peta, now three, and her Mum were saddened by my absence, especially over Christmas, as I was myself.

Following the two short West Indies cruises over Christmas and New Year, we sailed from New York for a World cruise, going eastabout, on 21

January, with a few regulars amongst the passengers, one of whom was Lady Oakes, widow of a past Governor General of the Bahamas, with her lady companion. They greeted us happily and we knew from past experience that we should be seeing them frequently at exchange parties either in their suite, or our Wardroom. Dottie Davis (Mrs), a millionairess in her own right, with husband still working back home, was another regular, who wandered up to the Wardroom, provided drinks and flirted for fun, in the nicest way, with whoever was off watch. A glamorous mid-forties, at a guess, reputed to own 49 evening gowns, her movements could always be detected by the trail left behind her, created by the forceful fragrance of her exotic perfume. Was it called 'Youth Dew', by Estée Lauder, who produced exclusively in the USA? I can't be sure. When Dottie ascended after dinner in the evening by elevator, her aroma was still present, in that same elevator, when I descended for breakfast next day. I was indeed stimulated as I moved from a fresh sea-breeze on deck into the scented light-airs of Dottie down below.

Our circumnavigation was as follows. Down to Rio, then across the South Atlantic, via Tristan da Cunha, that lonely island, with lovely, unspoiled people, to Cape Town and Durban. Then the Seychelles, Bombay, Madras and Singapore, before Bali in Indonesia. Up the west coast of Borneo to the Philippines, then Japan, followed by Hawaii, LA and Acapulco, eventually descending from Panama, through the canal to the Caribbean and back to New York.

The big memory for me, on this cruise, was on the beach at Bali, Indonesia, quite by chance, but which had a lifelong lasting effect on my self assessment and attitude to others. The immortal words of Robert Burns sum up what happened, most appropriately:

> That man to man, the world o'er
> Shall brithers be for a'that.

We anchored off the island of Bali early one morning and coming off watch at 8 a.m. I walked aft to see a dead shark, about 10 feet long, caught, earlier, by the crew trailing a baited butcher's hook astern. I examined this splendid, but frightening, specimen closely, and particularly the teeth around the open jaws, with the greatest respect. In the afternoon I walked ashore alone in sun-hat, shirt and shorts, with swimming trunks under. Heading out of town, I found a lovely, long, beach, with trees skirting the sand and providing me with shelter from the scorching sun. Feeling like a swim, I shed my outer garments and entered the sea, which was like a hot bath, but as I paddled, I remembered those jaws and went no further.

Lying back under the trees, I then witnessed a remarkable sequence of events. A native man came out of one of the few huts along the beach, armed with a short barbed spear, dropped his loin cloth at the edge of the sea and swam, naked, out into the bay, obviously without fear of sharks.

For about twenty minutes, he circled the bay on the surface, dived for long periods and reappeared each time with an extra fish on his spear. Four was presumably enough for the family meal, because he stepped ashore, donned his garment and having seen me, gave a friendly wave as he approached and squatted down beside me. We sat in silence, admiring his catch and staring out to sea, until, between smiles, he made hand to mouth gestures of someone smoking. I got the message, produced a packet of fags and when lit up, we had something in common at last. It was a time of true tranquillity, sitting with a stranger, who lived close to nature and had just demonstrated qualities quite beyond me, with all my supposed, superior, western, civilized background. As we brothers, for all that, sat on the sand, the simplicity of our meeting in such surroundings gave birth to my first serious thoughts about 'humility', which I have worked on developing, ever since. My definition is, 'no better and yet no worse than any other person on planet Earth', encouraging assertiveness, rather than being 'ever so humble', as many people think. I am wearing the MacFarlane kilt as I write this on Burn's birthday, 25 January 2003, the 144th anniversary and with humility, I'll soon be eating haggis, neaps and tatties, with a glass of claret, prepared by that bonny lassie, Susan.

Caronia was back in New York on 10 May and next day I was transferred to the *Queen Mary* as Junior 2nd Officer, to get me back to the UK in time to perform my annual duties as ADC at Holyrood, for the third year. The goings-on in Edinburgh as ADC, from '53 to '56, come to life in the next chapter. After an Atlantic ferry trip out of Liverpool in the passenger liner *Saxonia*, 22,000 tons as 2nd Officer, between July and Dec '55, I did one trip as Chief Officer, from London to the USA and back, in each of the cargo liners *Asia*, *Andria* and *Alsatia*.

Would you believe it? I actually had Xmas and New Year at home, before joining the cargo liner *Lycia*, 3,500 tons, as Chief Officer in Liverpool, on 9th January '56. Cunard had a few small ships, like *Lycia*, that carried cargoes out and back from the UK and tramped round ports in the Mediterranean. To give my landlubber readers some idea of relative ship size, the *Caronia* of 34,000 tons was about ten times bigger than *Lycia*, the tonnage being measured by cubic capacity, 100 cu.ft to the ton. I cannot remember details of all the goods we carried, but from Liverpool, with general products, we went to Swansea to embark a large cargo of steel. It was from Port Talbot, nearby, that I tramped, 20 years earlier. Off we went to Casablanca, Algiers, Palermo, Naples and Piraeus, near Athens. Piraeus brought misfortune to the ship, but good fortune to me, personally, because we ran aground in the harbour and couldn't be refloated until our vast cargo of tinned tomatoes in cases was discharged into lighters alongside and reloaded again later. Using the ship's derricks, this operation took about ten days, which gave me the opportunity to visit Greek classical monuments, such as the Parthenon and other temples, besides a run ashore in down-town Athens. More good fortune came my way in the shape of 'ouzo', the strong aniseed flavoured spirit, a bottle of which was left in my cabin daily by the foreman of stevedores. I revived the taste for 'ouzo' in 1992, when Sue and I visited Parga on a painting trip, with that charismatic American tutor, Bill Whitsett.

CHAPTER 16

Holyrood and ship to shore – 1953–1956

IT WAS IN MARCH '53 THAT Angus Letty came aboard *Scythia* in Southampton especially to see me. He was an officer about seven years my senior and his name I had heard associated with a special job in Scotland that he had been doing for the last few years. When he said 'Ian, I'm here to tell you that the Company has chosen you to succeed me in my role as an ADC, Aide-de-camp, to the Lord High Commissioner at the General Assembly of the Church of Scotland, in May this year,' I was flabbergasted and speechless. He went on to say 'Soon, you will receive a letter from Sir Edward Stevenson, the Purse Bearer at Holyrood Palace in Edinburgh, who is in charge of all arrangements, and he will tell you all you need to know, what clothes to take and so on. Don't look so concerned, you'll do it well, I'm sure, with your past experience in the RNR and you will meet a great variety of people, many of whom are considered to be very important and therefore known as VIPs.'

My confidence returned and my curiosity was aroused, so, I asked Angus how Cunard came to be connected with the Church of Scotland. He told me that after WW2, Lord Mathers, when Lord Provost of Edinburgh, attending the Assembly, noticed that the Lord High Commissioner had three ADCs, representing Navy, Army and Air Force, and thought the Merchant Navy should be represented. He discussed this idea with Lord Inverclyde, then Chairman of Cunard, who agreed and fixed it through the Marine Department, hence the appointment of Angus. I confirmed this later, when I met both gentlemen in May over an aperitif at the Palace.

When I met Sir Edward Stevenson, for the first time, in May, he was wearing the army uniform of a Lieut-Colonel, long since retired, from his Scottish Regiment, with black leather gaiters and a tartan forage cap. He welcomed me as Commander Kinloch Bryce, considering the word Lieutenant before Commander as superfluous, and when I told him I was usually known by the single surname of Bryce, he replied 'Remember you're in Scotland now and the Kinloch tells people more about you,' and so it was. He always used my RNR rank, as upgraded by him, when introducing me to others, even though in '56 I wore my uniform jacket with two stripes, as 2nd officer in Cunard, which caused curious expressions on the faces of some I met.

Having been reassured by Angus, I accepted my selection gladly. Thus it was, that four short periods in my life, each of ten days, revolved round the General Assembly of the Church of Scotland, which took place annually and seemed to me like stepping into another world. Before transporting you to this wonderland and telling you about what happened spiritually and socially, I thought it would help your understanding and enjoyment if I provided some background details of why, when and where it all took place and still does.

The Church of Scotland was founded in 1560, after the Reformation. In 1636 Charles I ruled that the Scottish Church should be governed by bishops, but this was successfully rejected and there never has been a hierarchy. An elected Moderator assumes leadership for a year and then reverts to being a minister, unless re-elected. With the King south of the border, in London, since 1603, it was considered prudent to appoint a person, representing the monarch, to preside over the Assembly, but not to participate, and this person was called a Lord High Commissioner (LHC). The Assembly Hall, on the Mound in Edinburgh, was the focal point for the clergy, with their agenda, whilst the LHC, with supporting staff, took up residence in The Palace of Holyroodhouse, to accommodate guests, from home and abroad, to meet the ministers, and also provide entertainment such as lunches, dinners and a garden-party.

The Lord High Commissioner to the General Assembly of the Church of Scotland, as the Queen's representative during this period, takes precedence immediately after the Sovereign and occupies the State apartments of the Palace. An ADC, in such royal circumstances, is known as an Equerry (from the Latin equus, horse) and wears his badge of office on the right shoulder as opposed to the left, used by ADCs to Senior Officers in the Armed Forces. The badge, called aiguillettes (from the French for needles), consists of two intertwined, gold-braided loops, each with a similarly adorned spike at the end, resembling a tent peg rather than a needle. Before mechanization, ADCs used them to tether their horses in the field, with the loops round a horse's neck and the spikes into the ground. Happily for us ADCs, in 1953, it wasn't household horses but a fleet of Daimler cars that provided transport and that meant our aiguillettes never left our shoulders. Another badge of office was for the Purse-Bearer and took the shape of a large, dark green, velvet bag, which he carried slung over his right fore-arm. Sir Edward confided in me, a week or so later, that its contents, in reality, were a packet of cigarettes and a box of matches.

The Palace of Holyroodhouse was completed by James IV in 1503, built on the site of a twelfth century abbey and since then has been associated with Mary Queen of Scots in the 1560s and Charles Edward Stuart the Young Pretender, better known as 'Bonnie Prince Charlie', in the 1740s. Holyrood consisted of a range of buildings round a grass quadrangular Inner Court, surrounded by cloisters, which gave easy access from the Main Entrance to all parts of the Palace. It stood at the eastern end of the Royal Mile, facing west, towards the narrow, uphill streets and ancient buildings of Canongate and beyond, to Edinburgh Castle, with its Esplanade, at the western end. The front of the Palace, with two towers at each corner, overlooked a large forecourt, protected by formidable gilded gates, and the other three sides were mainly surrounded by lawns, with the grass sloping up to the top of a perimeter wall, which had an 8 ft drop the other side. This gave the impression that the garden was endless, stretching out and up the grassy slopes of Arthur's Seat, a famous hill nearby. The well preserved ruins of the original Abbey Kirk could be seen at the rear of the Palace and were used as background for a household photo in 1953, Coronation year of Queen Elizabeth II, when the Duke of Hamilton, Hereditary Keeper of the Royal Palace, with a permanent suite of rooms therein, was Lord High Commissioner.

The front towers on the right facing out, contained the closets and bedchamber of Mary Queen of Scots. It was here that her Italian secretary Rizzio, also an accomplished musician and allegedly her lover, was murdered. He was stabbed many times at the top of a spiral staircase, and X, literally, marks the spot. The towers on the left were named after Charles II, who may have used the Palace in 1650, when he was crowned in Scotland, before being defeated by Cromwell at the battle of Worcester and fleeing to France a year later. However, it is probable that he visited Holyrood between 1660, when he was recalled to the throne in England, and his death in 1685. Guests were entertained on the first floor, approached by the widely curved Great Stairs, with claymores, large two-edged broadswords used by Highlanders, displayed on the walls. The south side, from front to back, was divided into West Drawing Room, Middle Drawing Room and Throne Room, each ideally spacious and decorated with massive oil paintings and tapestries.

The Picture Gallery, also called the Banquet Hall, on the north side of the Palace, was huge and contained 100 portraits of Scottish kings by the seventeenth century painter De Wet. Many were drawn entirely from his imagination. This is where dinners were served. Up to 120 guests sat at a candle-lit table running the entire length of the gallery. On it lay the handsome collection of silver presented by Sir Alexander Grant to King George V in 1934. The loyal toast was followed by a procession of 12 pipers round the gallery, after which the Lord High Commissioner poured a large measure of malt whisky into a loving cup and handed it to the senior piper. He proposed a toast in Gaelic before downing the cup in one and leading his pipers away, playing 'Over the Sea to Skye'.

Coming down to earth in the Palace was most important. On the ground floor, the south cloister passed a couple of lifts and went into a corridor, with a door to the garden at its eastern end. On the right of this corridor was a room about 30 ft square, known as the 'Equerries Waiting Room' (EWR), overlooking the garden and resembling the leisure half of a naval wardroom. It was fitted with easy chairs, for forty-winks between times, a TV set and discreetly in the corner behind the door a large table loaded with bottles and glasses available to us, house guests and other guests of whom Sir Edward approved. Tony Stevenson, ex-Captain in the Scots Guards and assistant to his father, kept the bar topped up. This most refreshing facility was open all hours, help yourself and no charge. On the opposite side of the corridor were the offices of Sir Edward, Tony and Sir Edward's essential and efficient secretary, a young lady called Maureen Younger, one of the brewery family, who came in daily and was always the best source of information about people and procedure. When a Palace function was in progress, a body of gentlemen known as the High Constables of Holyrood would position themselves at prominent places throughout the building, to assist the flow and presumably act as a form of security. I understood that they were locally distinguished men, professionally or in business, who dressed for these occasions in splendid uniforms, with top hats and batons, to add to their authority. I enjoyed a chat with many of them and learned a lot of local history.

The next most important person in the household, after the Purse Bearer, was the Chaplain, the Rev. Alexander Campsie, a round faced, jovial character, who conducted prayers every morning in the Middle Drawing Room. He had been a soldier in WW1, a padre in the Navy for twenty years between the wars, and his livelihood at that time was as minister of the kirk at Crathie on the Balmoral estate. At all the dinners in the Banquet Hall, the Purse Bearer would sit at one end of the long table and the Chaplain at the other, often with an ADC on either side of them. Campsie couldn't bear the sound of the bagpipes at close quarters and sat with fingers pressed over his ears during the pipers' performance, before rising to exercise his privilege and propose the toast to Her Grace, the Lord High Commissioner's wife. This was the signal for two ADCs to rise and precede Her Grace, followed by all the other ladies, to the Middle Drawing Room to partake of coffee distributed by the Maids of Honour, with us, ADCs, close at hand, to circulate and contribute to the conversation when and where considered desirable. Meanwhile, the gentlemen passed the port and smoked before rejoining the ladies.

A man who deserves a special mention, as a vital link in the chain of activities, is Mr Aitken, always seen near the Main Entrance, immaculately clad in lounge-suit, with trimmed moustache and umbrella at the ready, organizing the Daimler fleet of cars officially and sometimes informally. He and I became good friends, which resulted in him letting me have a chauffeur-driven Daimler occasionally to take me wherever I wanted to go in my off-duty moments. I indulged once or twice and felt frightfully posh, parking off Princes Street near that fabulous shop, Jenners, almost opposite the statue of my Kinloch grandmother's cousin, James Young Simpson, who discovered chloroform.

I think that is enough background, and now I shall tell you about the most memorable occasions until my last appearance in 1956.

For three years I was ADC to the Duke of Hamilton and one year to Sir Walter Elliott. In April '53, I received a friendly letter from Sir Edward Stevenson which said 'I am informed by His Grace The Duke of Hamilton, Lord High Commissioner to the General Assembly of the Church of Scotland, that you are to be one of his Aides-de-Camp during the time that the Lord High Commissioner and Her Grace are in residence at the Palace of Holyroodhouse between Monday 18 and Thursday 28 May. I will have a batman detailed to look after you at Holyrood. If you meet Lieut-Cdr Angus Letty, meantime, he will be able to tell you all about your duties, but if not, I will put you thoroughly in the picture on the Monday afternoon. I can assure you now that there is nothing that need cause you any concern. With regard to clothes, you will require full dress uniform with sword and medals, plus modified mess dress and miniatures. I'm afraid you will not have much time off, but you will have a bit, so do bring up ordinary clothes for golf, etc.' Obviously, but erroneously, Sir Edward presumed that I played what was north of the border the national sport, but the etc indicated other opportunities no doubt.

I went by train from Southampton to London on Saturday, 16 May and stayed overnight in Golders Green with John (Spud) Murphy, my *Oribi* shipmate in WW2, his wife, Marguerite and their young family. John, plus family, in his large Lanchester car, drove me to King's Cross station on Sunday, the 17th, to catch the 'Night Scotsman' on which I had booked a sleeper. On the way, he braked suddenly and my suitcases, on the roof rack, jumped up, slid over the bonnet onto the road ahead and came to rest at the feet of a policeman standing on the kerb. Spud got out to retrieve them, expecting a reprimand, but the officer had observed that the labels were addressed to the Palace of Holyroodhouse, Edinburgh and saluted Spud, with the comment 'Please carry on Sir.' The Murphy youngsters were most amused and never forgot that incident. After a good seven hours sleep I arrived at Waverley Station, Edinburgh at 0715, parked my bags in the cloakroom, then took a walk to the Castle and back, before breakfasting in the grill. At 0915 I took a taxi to Holyrood.

At the Palace, two porters grabbed my baggage, took me by lift for three floors and thence on foot to a room on the 4th, attic, floor, where a card stuck on the door said 'Lieut-Cdr I. Kinloch Bryce.' The room was large, sparsely furnished, with a black tubular steel bed, a large water jug standing in a larger basin on top of a marble-topped table and two bell registers, marked Queen's Bedroom and Dressing Room, over the door, indicated that its inhabitant was usually a maid, who could be summoned. Facing east from the window, I overlooked the ruined abbey to my left below and Arthur's Seat in the distance to my right. Happily there was a plumbed bathroom nearby, which I shared with three other ADCs on the same floor,

Squadron Leader Forrest RAF, from the Duke's old 602 Glasgow Squadron, Flight-Lieutenant Reece RAF and Lord Fintrie, grandson of the Duke of Montrose, whose father was the Marquis of Graham. After unpacking and reporting to Sir Edward Stevenson in his office, I crossed the corridor to the Equerries' Waiting Room, where Tony Stevenson assembled the five ADCs, including me, all of us in civvies, and four Maids of Honour, for an initial briefing and walk-about.

The Senior ADC was Commander Eddie Edmonstone RN, a long standing friend of the Duke of Hamilton and of a similar age to the Duke, who was in his fiftieth year. Forrest, Reece and I were in our thirties, with the young Lord Fintrie, a mature eighteen, who always dressed in civilian clothes, sometimes with the kilt, and therefore was without aiguillettes. The Maids of Honour, in their twenties, were by name, the Misses Elizabeth Carnegy, Jane Drummond-Hay, a niece of the Duke of Hamilton, Delia Reid and the Hon. Fiona Campbell, related to the Duchess of Hamilton's Lady-in-Waiting, who was the Lady Stratheden and Campbell. Tony introduced us to Maureen Younger, the secretary, who organized printed hand-outs for everyone. One sheet of paper listed the names and rooms of house guests staying at the Palace throughout the Assembly period, with expected times of arrival and departure by car, plane or train. Another sheet gave the schedule of events, stating times and places, with car arrangements and was distributed daily, in advance, usually on the previous day. By now dear readers you should have a good idea about the composition of the household team and its state of preparedness whilst supporting The Lord High Commissioner and his wife during their first year in office.

After an informal lunch, Tony talked us through the overall programme of the Assembly, start to finish, and told us what drills and procedures to expect, both inside and outside the Palace, and how to conduct ourselves, particularly towards house guests and others, making sure they knew what was happening next and where they should be. We rehearsed a few aspects of certain ceremonies, especially the slow march, with pauses, which we three junior ADCs, that is Forrest, Reece and I, in dress uniform, had to perform often, when preceding Their Graces, for example when Sir Edward was presenting 100 plus dinner guests in the Throne Room. This required a frequent glance astern, with perfect poise to stay on an even keel. Mid afternoon we gathered at the Main Entrance, with Sir Edward, to be presented to the Duke and Duchess of Hamilton on their arrival, after which we called each of them 'Your Grace' and cultivated an ability to bow the head only and walk backwards when leaving their presence.

Before dinner on the 18th, the Ceremony of the Keys took place in the Throne Room, when the Lord Provost of Edinburgh, then Sir James Miller, presented the keys of the city to the Lord High Commissioner. The Duke returned them, promptly, saying 'I gladly return the keys of your city, knowing that they could not be in more trustworthy keeping.' Another

General Assembly of the Church of Scotland. The Palace of Holyrood House May 1953. Back row, l. to r.: Flight Lieut. B.H. Reece, AFC; Lt. Commander I. Kinloch Bryce, DSC, RNR; Squadron Leader J.A. Forrest; Lieut. Colonel Carnegy of Lour, DSO, MC; The Rev. A. Campsie, CBE, MC, DD; Lieut. Colonel Sir Edward Stevenson, KCVO, MC; Mr W.R. Milligan, QC; His Excellency Dr A.L. Geyer; The Rt Hon. Alan Tindal Lennox-Boyd, MP; Commander E. Edmonstone, RN; The Lord Fintrie; Captain A.R.G. Stevenson, MC. Front row, l. to r.: Mrs Carnegy of Lour; The Hon. Mrs E. Edmonstone; Lady Patricia Lennox-Boyd; Mrs Geyer; The Rt. Hon. The Duke of Hamilton, KT, GCVO, AFC, The Lord High Commissioner; the Duchess of Hamilton, Her Grace; The Lady Stratheden and Campbell; Miss Delia Reid; Miss Elizabeth Carnegy; Miss Jane Drummond-Hay; The Hon. Fiona Campbell. (Photo taken by Churchill of Edinburgh)

208

splash of colour was added to this mediaeval scene by the presence of Lord Lyon King of Arms, then Sir Thomas Innes of Learney. On our first public appearance, we ADCs slow marched ahead of His Grace to fulfil this ancient ritual. Guests for the banquet on Monday consisted mostly of the Scottish peerage and long established ministers, which included many past moderators in the Church of Scotland. Dinner guests circulated in the Throne Room and after the presentations, Sir Edward called out the name of each gentleman to escort into dinner the lady whose name was called immediately after his. We ADCs had to make sure that people paired up as planned. Two distinguished guests, that first night, were Earl De La Warr, the Postmaster General and Miss Charlotte Whitton, the Canadian Mayoress of Ottawa. Next day, in St Giles Cathedral, guiding guests to their seats for the Service prior to the Assembly opening, I said 'This way Miss Whitton.' She was surprised and delighted to be addressed by name and said 'Gee, thanks for that, they always call me "Your Worship" back home.'

For the first time in the history of the Church of Scotland, the Lord High Commissioner to the General Assembly wore Royal Air Force uniform. The Duke of Hamilton became an Air Commodore during WW2. When I saw this in the newspapers next day, it occurred to me, that it must have been the first time, also, that a Merchant Navy uniform had appeared on the person of an ADC, such as me, because I left insufficient time for Gieves to change it to RNR, as I did in subsequent years. Sixteen hundred ministers and elders crowded into the Assembly Hall to witness the newly elected moderator, Dr J. Pitt-Watson, take the ring of office from the previous moderator, Dr George Jeffrey. In his opening speech, the Lord High Commissioner recalled that in darker days his forbear, the first Duke, descended from the mighty Red Douglases, held the King's Commission at the famous Glasgow Assembly of 1638. In his reply, Dr Pitt-Watson hoped that the Moderator's relations with the present Lord High Commissioner would be happier than in 1638, when a 'rattle of swords' was heard. 'Nowadays,' he added, 'our rustle of order papers would indeed be a poor substitute.'

I want to tell you about the Duke of Hamilton as I saw him then and through the next three years as his ADC, because, I feel that knowledge of his personality would improve the tales I tell about the people surrounding him throughout that period. I remember him as a quietly spoken modest man, with conversational charm, never dominant, but persuasive and always immaculately attired. I knew that he was one of the first men to fly over Mount Everest, 29,001 feet, in the open cockpit of a bi-plane, on 3 April 1933, On the few occasions when we were alone in a Daimler we talked about navigation, as airman to seaman and I got him to talk about the Everest flight, when he said they measured winds from 80 to 120 knots.

He was interested that I had sailed, recently, as a navigator in the *Queen Mary*, because she had been a great help to him, twenty years earlier. When she was the Cunarder No. 534, 1,000 feet long and 120 feet wide, lying in John Brown's shipyard on Clydebank, during the years of economic depression from 1931 to '34, she was the best navigational aid for those flying with 602 Squadron, Glasgow, as he was then, being a Volunteer Reserve with the RAF. I remember him saying 'When 534 was launched and named *Queen Mary* in September '34, we lost our main sense of direction.'

The most memorable and poignant of his remarks was forthcoming on Wednesday, 27 May, after the Assembly had closed and he had returned to the Palace, no longer Lord High Commissioner. When we, the household and family guests, gathered for drinks, before an informal dinner in the private dining room, the Duke said something like 'What a relief this is, now I can be myself again.' The speeches at dinner were spontaneous and we danced Scottish reels to Fintrie on the pipes 'til gone midnight. The following week on 1 June, the day before the Queen's Coronation, it was announced that Sherpa Tensing, a native of Nepal, was the first man to stand on the top of Everest, with his companion Edmund Hillary, a New Zealander. In fact, they performed that feat on Friday 29 May, a little over twenty years after the Duke of Hamilton's airborne achievement.

From the opening of the Assembly on Tuesday 19 May to the close on the 27th, there was a similar routine each day for household and guests except over the week-end. All our meals were taken at the Palace, breakfast at 8.55 a.m., after prayers at 8.45, luncheon at 1.15 p.m. and dinner at 8 p.m. The catering was contracted out to Donald Ross, who owned two restaurants in Edinburgh, the 'Aperitif' and the 'Albany', and who personally supervised the situation at Holyrood. At 9.45 a.m. a cavalcade of cars took people from the Palace to the Assembly and were then available for incidental trips throughout the day. His Grace attended the Assembly daily for most sessions a.m. and p.m., often, but not always accompanied by Her Grace, who went on visits to charities, hospitals, and other institutions, particularly in the afternoons. The Senior ADC, Commander Eddie, plus one other ADC, stayed with His Grace, whilst Her Grace always had her Lady-in-Waiting with her, plus two Maids of Honour and usually one ADC, if not two, depending on overall commitments. Morning and evening Services at St Giles Cathedral were attended on Sunday and there was a Garden Party at the Palace on Monday afternoon. Oh yes, I almost forgot to say that Saturday p.m. was a 'make and mend', in naval jargon and we had the afternoon off.

Now let me tell you about my personal associations and activities, within this daily schedule and beyond, into the leisure moments after dinner.

The Duke had married a red-headed Percy, daughter of the Duke and Duchess of Northumberland whose mother, Helen, was a house guest throughout the Assembly, as were the Earl and Countess of Selkirk, the Earl being a younger brother of His Grace. Jane's parents, Major James and Lady

Margaret Drummond-Hay, the Duke of Hamilton's sister, came to stay over the week-end and until the finish, in mid-week. They brought with them some other entertaining members of the family, namely four Chihuahuas. These Mexican canine companions were tame, well behaved and beautiful to behold. They caused great amusement, around the equerries waiting room, hiding here and there and on better acquaintance, for fun, it was possible to have one peeping from a pocket, to the surprise of a new house guest. Liz's parents Lieut-Colonel and Mrs Carnegy of Lour visited for meals. Seamus Fintrie's mother and sister, that is Isobel Marchioness of Graham, with Lady Fiona, came to stay on the 25th, when the Marchioness took over as Lady-in-Waiting to Her Grace. Commander Eddie had his wife, the Hon. Mrs E, as I always called her, living in full time, and their daughter, Antonia, came to lunch one day. Delia's parents also looked in one lunchtime and I had some interesting chat with her father, Rear-Admiral Reid, the Second Sea Lord, who was responsible for all naval personnel.

Lady Prunella, at one time married to a brother of His Grace, now deceased, and who, under her maiden name of Prunella Stack, became famous for starting the League of Health and Beauty in the '30s, stayed for a day or two. I escorted her in to luncheon one day and mentioned Rosemary, my WRNS girlfriend in Harwich 1940, whom I knew had been involved with this keep fit and look lovely campaign for ladies. She remembered her well, from pre-war days, as one of her loveliest and youngest team instructors. My Scottish dancing was improving and Prunella liked to join us after dinner in this gaelic health promoting activity. That was when Fiona Graham taught me the Petronella, with brother Seamus on the pipes and Lady Margaret with daughter Jane taking it in turns on the piano. I could feel a happy family atmosphere developing in the household at Holyrood.

A few days previously, Tony thought it was appropriate that I should take a Daimler to Turnhouse Airport to meet the First Sea Lord, Admiral of the Fleet, Sir Rhoderick McGrigor, GCM, DSO and his Lady wife. Having accomplished this, back at the Palace, Sir Edward, told Sir Rhoderick that I had agreed to be his personal ADC for their two day stay, in addition to my normal household duties. This was great fun for me, as they were such an easy-going couple and the Chaplain had sailed with McGrigor, way back, when he was then a Lieut-Commander. Addressing the Assembly next day, the Admiral stressed the fact that naval chaplains were without rank, unlike the other Armed Services. We had lots of naval chat between us, and Lady McGrigor told me about the Admiral taking horse-riding lessons before being mounted, with other Chiefs-of-Staff, in the Coronation Procession the following week. She said he was determined not to capsize when trotting through the streets of London and on Tuesday, 2 June I watched the event on TV, with my eyes fixed on the First Sea Lord.

Seeing the Admiral on horseback provided me with the most memorable sight in the procession. He coped well and although his facial expressions didn't exactly exude confidence, I admired his ability to maintain stability, under the continuous rain, which created a slippery situation under hoof.

Next day, my army batman Spalding called me early to go and meet the Lord Chancellor and Lady Simonds stepping from their sleeper at Waverley Station. I sat next to Lady Simonds at breakfast and we talked about the coming Coronation. She said that a number of her friends were having leg massage in preparation for their long stand in Westminster Abbey. Putting her remarks alongside those of Lady McGrigor's, I formed the opinion that certain anatomical stress was being imposed on some VIPs taking part in the ceremony. The next day, His Excellency the High Commissioner for South Africa, Dr Geyer (pronounced 'hair') and Mrs Geyer arrived and naturally, during their stay, we swapped a lot of memories about the Vanguard Royal Tour to SA, in 1947. Dr Geyer was delighted to join Major James D-H and myself, who were by now good chums, with similar tastes, imbibing our usual pre-prandial schooners of sherry from South Africa, before they were obliged to call it 'fortified wine'. Tony had obviously arranged the origin of bottles on the bar most diplomatically. The Earl and Countess of Home (pronounced Hume) stayed over Sunday night. Later in the '50s, he rejected his peerage to become Prime Minister. Saturday saw the arrival of the Transport Minister, The Rt. Hon. Alan Tindal Lennox-Boyd, MP and Lady Patricia, a member of the Guinness (is good for you) family and I thought, good for him indeed, remembering my captain, Reggie Forbes in *Fitzroy*, 1940: saying 'Mid, don't marry money, but marry where money lies.' I recalled that Reggie's wine bill, each month, was paid by his mother-in-law, who was a Lady in her own right, and I often say to Sue, in fun, that it must be obvious that I have fulfilled his advice.

A frequent visiting guest, but not to stay, because he was our next-door neighbour, was the Rev. Selby-Wright, the minister of Canongate Kirk and well remembered as the Radio Padre on BBC during WW2. I had listened to him whenever I could and I know my mother always gained greatly from his words of comfort and encouragement to endure the anxieties and terrors of those times. One of my greatest pleasures at Holyrood was meeting him face to face and hearing about his current welfare activities for all ages. Another great pleasure was having time off on Saturday afternoon to see my Scottish cousins who lived in Corstorphine, a suburb to the west of Edinburgh.

Charles Massie, who ran his own business as a Civil Engineer, came down to the Palace in his Ford V8 and drove me home to meet the family; Elsie, his wife, son Howard, aged 17 and daughters Rhona and Celia, aged 20 and 15 respectively. The last named was disappointed that I wasn't dressed in uniform with all the trimmings, because her teenage friends in the road wanted to get a close-up of an ADC. Later in the afternoon,

Charles, Elsie, Rhona and I headed east about 20 miles in the V8 to meet other members of the clan at Dirleton, a lovely place, with ruined castle and village green, near North Berwick on the coast. En route, near Prestonpans, we passed a Daimler with flag up front going the other way and I knew it was Their Graces returning from seeing their family of five sons at their stately home, Lennoxlove, near Haddington.

It was a happy reunion with Great Aunt Jean Massie, first met twelve years before in Glasgow, when I was a Midshipman joining *Oribi*. Now in her 79th year, she gave us a great welcome, with daughter, cousin Jean and husband Bill, who took us in to an enormous high-tea on a groaning table in their shared summer flat overlooking the famous golf-links. I liked all my cousins and particularly their sense of fun, when they teased me, a blown away Scot from south of the border, with leading questions about my views on Scottish Nationalism. Bill was a boisterous character with a 'blow me down' attitude, having bought an old life-boat and had it converted to a handsome cabin-cruiser. He showed me round the club room and sail-loft of the East Lothian Yacht Club, which was once a granary, built of local red stone. At 2100 we took our departure and Charles dropped me at my rather exclusive hotel, as he described it.

On Monday the 25th the weather was wet and windy for the Garden Party. However, during a respite in the rain, Tony escorted Their Graces and presented people brought forward by us ADCs. I picked out Captain and Mrs Higgins, USAF, from Kansas City and whilst waiting for Tony to do the necessary, Mrs H whispered an aside to me – 'Gee, do I have to curtsey to the Dook?' Actually, her curtsey was noticed and acclaimed as the best of the afternoon. Early next morning I had a braces button crisis on the front of my trousers, depending, precariously, on one each side instead of the usual two. I told Jane at breakfast and she gladly sent one of her maids along later to restore my confidence by replacing the missing items.

Into the second week, a good family feeling existed at the Palace and on Monday evening, after dinner, Donald Ross invited the ADCs and Maids of Honour, as his guests, to a restaurant, which continued as a night club beyond midnight. Whilst we wondered, Isobel Lady Graham spoke up, with words that filled my heart with joy. She said, quite simply, 'Of course you must all go. You'll be taken good care of I know, because Commander Kinloch will be there.' When dancing after dinner, she always trusted me to call time before midnight, so I feel that she initiated a remarkable change for the better in my social conduct.

After tea on Wednesday, the 27th, The Duke of Hamilton called his Aides, one at a time, by name, into his private sitting room and presented us each with gold cuff-links, engraved with our initials on one side and 'Holyrood 1953' on the other. He said 'Thank you Ian, Commander Kinloch Bryce, for what you have done, and I would like you to accept this gift from me as a memento of Coronation year.' The Maids of Honour received silver handbag pencils suitably engraved and when we shared our pleasure, over a tot, in the equerries waiting room, I remember Major James saying, jokingly, to his daughter Jane, 'Roughly how long is it going to take you to lose that much treasured memento?' Sir Edward was missing, because he went south the day before, to prepare for his role as Green Rod, Order of the Thistle, in the Queen's Coronation procession.

On the last morning at Holyrood, Thursday 28 May, I was up early and walking in the gardens before breakfast, talking to the gardeners, already mowing the lawns. When I reached the top of the perimeter wall and gazed at the world outside, my thoughts flew back over the past ten days. I appreciated my good fortune in meeting so many distinguished personalities, glad it had all happened, but equally glad to be returning to the world of reality out there. What a relief to resume being my normal self, a husband, father and MN officer in Cunard once again, a similar feeling to that expressed by the Duke of Hamilton at the end of the Assembly on the previous day.

In April 1954 I was delighted to receive a letter from the Purse Bearer, Sir Edward Stevenson, saying 'Dear Commander, I am so glad that once again you are to be on Their Graces' Suite . . .' The national press always printed the names of the Lord High Commissioner's suite in the Court Circular, which told me who was in the household team that year. Commander Eddie Edmonstone and Lady Stratheden and Campbell were in their previous roles, but the ADCs were now Lieut-Colonel the Hon. Ronald Colville, son of Lord Clydesmuir, employed in the family firm of Colvilles Steel in Glasgow and a member of the Royal Company of Archers, Flying Officer Duncan Simpson and me. The Maids of Honour were listed as Liz Carnegy, Jane Drummond-Hay and Delia Reid, all known from '53, plus Hermione Home and Diana Douglas-Hamilton. In fact Jane and Delia were both a few days late arriving, the former having been injured falling from her horse and the latter being in quarantine for measles. As before, Major James and Lady Margaret D-H, with the Chihuahua family, enriched the palatial company by their presence. Dear Delia would ask me what the Navy was really like at sea, because her father wouldn't tell her, and I enjoyed reciting a reasonably salty scenario. Ronnie Colville and I shared a similar sense of humour and soon became good chums, on the basis of Colonel to Commander and vice versa, so to speak.

Now, I'm aware that I could bore you, my readers, by naming all the VIP house guests for this and the next two years, so, I shall refrain from such a name dropping exercise and select a few in each year, whom I personally found most interesting and entertaining. After all, I'm not writing a history of the Assembly. My few words about these chosen people give a candid account of some fortunate and friendly encounters. Each year Brenda came north with me and stayed with the Massie cousins in Corstorphine for the ten days, attending several social events at the Palace, such as luncheons, dinners and the garden party. Meantime, Peta was taken to Cardiff to be cared for by grandparents Elsie and Frank. On Monday afternoon the Assistant Purse Bearer, Tony Stevenson, took the ADCs to St Giles Cathedral to discuss details for the Assembly Opening Service next day. The Scottish *Daily Express* took a photo of us, which appeared in the paper on Tuesday under the dramatic headline 'Five Meet to Iron Out a Problem of Pomp.'

One of the house guests attending the opening was His Excellency The French Ambassador, Monsieur René Massigli, GCVO (Hon), KBE (Hon), in his distinctive, colourful, regalia. That evening in the Palace, Sir Edward's secretary, Maureen, shouted across to me in the Equerries' Waiting Room, 'Ian, the French Embassy is on the phone, please get Monsieur to come down and talk.' I dashed up aloft and found the Ambassador half dressed for dinner, in a state of dire distress because his butler had omitted to pack a wing collar, but who was greatly relieved when I said I'd lend him one of mine. After dealing with the call, his valet and I wrestled with one of my collars round his bigger neck by enlarging the studholes with nail scissors and a bit of brute force. We three laughed a lot during the process, and throughout the evening, whenever he saw me, he said 'Merci Monsieur for saving my life.' He flirted charmingly with the Maids of Honour, as would be expected of any fascinating Frenchman such as he and next day, when I escorted him to the car for his departure, the girls lined the palatial staircase, with handkerchiefs to their cheeks, putting on a weeping act, which pleased him enormously. On the way to Waverley Station he confided in me, saying that his wife was in Corsica furnishing their new home and fairly obviously her absence had allowed Monsieur a few moments of flirtatious freedom.

On Tuesday, I was most excited by the arrival, as house guests, of the Rt Hon. Sir Alexander Cadogan, OM, GCMG, KCB, with his wife the Lady Theodosia. When I met them in the Equerries Waiting Room over a glass of sherry, I said to him 'Sir, I was Midshipman of the destroyer *Oribi*, in August '41, when we took you and others with Churchill from Thurso to the battleship *Prince of Wales* in Scapa Flow, on your way to meet President Roosevelt. In December of that year, we escorted an early Russian convoy PQ5 at the same time as you and Anthony Eden went to Murmansk in HMS *Kent*, sailing independently.' After that revelation, we had an immediate rapport, which led to many interesting discussions on a variety of topics, mainly over aperitifs and at meals, during his visit of two days. How fortunate was I to enjoy the company of so distinguished a character, in such salubrious surroundings.

Once again, it must have been serendipity, that I heard Alistair Cooke, on radio, in his 'Letter from America' recently, in March 2003, refer to the late Sir Alexander Cadogan as one of the most professional statesmen in modern times. He was Under Secretary at the Foreign Office throughout WW2 and the UK's first representative at the United Nations (UN) when it was formed post war. Currently, the US of A, the UK and Australia are at war with Iraq and Alistair said that Cadogan, who had witnessed the birth and failure of the League of Nations, had pronounced, when the UN started, that it too would probably remain impotent, because the five major powers had retained the use of the veto and might be inclined to act independently. Nobody agreed with him at the time. I'll say no more.

When Sir Edward brought two house guests into the Equerries Waiting Room and introduced them to those of us there, as the Lord Bishop of Derby and Mrs Rawlinson, the Bishop, with a mischievous glint in his eyes, said 'Yes, in fact we are married, although you might well wonder, by the style in which we present ourselves, whether I was living with another man's wife.' Both the Bishop and Mrs R were great fun and their conversation was invariably witty.

Having addressed the Assembly on Tuesday morning, the Bishop said that they wanted to tour the historical parts of the Palace, so, Liz and I took them there that afternoon. The regular guide told us a fascinating tale about the Holy Rood (Crucifix), after which the Abbey and Palace were named. In 1346, King David II, son of Robert the Bruce, invaded England with an army of Scots and took with him the Black Rood of Scotland, from the Abbey, as a symbol of protection. In the country west of Durham, they were defeated by an English army under the Archbishop of York, led by his warlike assistants, the Lords Neville and Percy. It was named the battle of Neville's Cross. The Black Rood was taken and kept in Durham Abbey, later, moved to the deanery, for security and eventually returned to its place of origin. On hearing this, the Bishop, who had been Dean of Durham Cathedral before his promotion, exclaimed to his wife 'Do you know Cuckoo, it is probable that the Holy Rood was kept in our old house.' Liz and I laughed a lot, later, at the thought of Mrs R being his 'Cuckoo in the nest'.

In 1955, once again, it was like a family reunion, for the Duke of Hamilton's third term as Lord High. This time, the Drummond-Hays included Jane's younger sister Annalie as a Maid of Honour, who in later years achieved an international reputation on horseback for show-jumping and dressage. There were many notable house guests for the opening; His Excellency the Ambassador of the USA, the Hon Winthrop W. Aldrich GBE; The Rt Rev. the Lord Bishop of Durham, Dr Ramsey, with the bushy eyebrows, who later became Archbishop of Canterbury and Lt Colonel the Hon Sir Michael Adeane, KCB, KCVO, whom I had met, many times, aboard *Vanguard* in '47 on the Royal Tour, and we chatted a few times during his stay.

Other American house guests stayed at the Palace, in addition to Mr and Mrs Aldrich. They were, His Excellency the Ambassador of the USA to the

Dominion of Canada, Mr. R. Douglas Stuart, with wife, and the world famous Evangelist Dr Billy Graham, also with wife. That occasional, itinerant, preacher of the Christian gospel, Billy Graham, was well received by the ministers when he addressed the Assembly and in conversation, back at Holyrood, he was an easygoing charismatic character, which was to be expected from someone of his vocation.

Imagine my amazement when I read the following information in the *Independent* newspaper, in February 2003. 'George W. Bush was a feckless near-alcoholic who rediscovered his Christianity after a long conversation with the evangelist Billy Graham in 1986, and went on to become a teetotaller, Governor of Texas, and finally one of the most relentlessly disciplined presidents of the USA in history.' In a more recent media disclosure, I read that when debating with Al Gore, in the presidential campaign of 2000, he said 'If we're an arrogant nation, they'll resent us,' speaking of American dealings with other countries in general, but 'If we're a humble nation but strong, they'll welcome us.' As I write this in April, 2003, after 12 days of war, the US Army's relations with the Iraqis can best be described as ambivalent.

In 1956 Sir Walter Elliot PC, CH, MC, MP was Lord High Commissioner, with Lady Elliot CBE alongside, and I was to be their Senior Equerry. Sir Edward's letter said 'Dear Ian, I am so glad you are at Holyrood again, from 21 to 31 May this year. The Elliots I have known for years and I know you will like them very much. My regards to your very charming wife and I hope we shall see more of her in Edinburgh.' On the dominant picture page near the front of the magazine *Tatler & Bystander* for May there was a large photo of the lovely Lady Colquhoun of Luss, who was to be Lady-in-waiting at Holyroodhouse. Kay Colquhoun and I worked closely together, admiring Their Graces, greatly for their altruistic, emotional reactions, when running the usual schedule, supporting them under the expert guidance of Sir Edward and Tony Stevenson. The ADCs consisted of Captain Micky Blacklock (Grenadier Guards), Lieut Angus Erskine RN, and Flt Lieut John Atkinson RAF. The Maids of Honour were Miss Davina Bowes Lyon (cousin of the Queen), Miss Alice Fergusson and Lady Arabella Stuart. This was the team, of which I was the only one who had done it before.

After the Assembly was over, Kay sent me a warm letter of appreciation from which I quote: 'My dear Ian, I want to thank you most sincerely for all that you did for me. For the maternal help and encouragement and the timely words of warning you gave. You made what for me was quite the most terrifying experience of my life a blissful memory. And if we ever are asked to do it again, I hope and pray it will be the same team. It must be a fairly unique event for eight people to get on so well together, and all strangers. Yours ever, Kay.' I treasure this letter as a tribute to my unobtrusive leadership and inspired teamwork, qualities developed, I believe, mostly, as a shipmate at sea. Forgive me for indulging my ego, but it's good for my morale.

Kay's husband, Sir Ivar and my wife, Brenda joined in a few of the functions when we were less busy, and I enjoyed a lengthy chat with Brigadier Sir Bernard Fergusson, Alice's uncle, when he came to lunch. He was second in command to the famous General Slim, during the Burma campaign against the Japanese in WW2. Lady Arabella Stuart had the same name as her ancestor, who was well known as a niece of Mary Queen of Scots and near in the line for succession to the throne, but who died in 1615 when confined in the Tower of London. 441 years later, it was this Arabella's birthday on the last night and I proposed the toast at dinner.

I believe it would be of interest to mention two representatives of countries in south-east Asia: The High Commissioner for India, Mrs Vijaya Lakshai Pandit and The High Commissioner for Pakistan, Begum Ikramul-lah, considering that it was only nine years previously that each nation established its separate status. Both ladies displayed their eastern culture with charm and distinction. For me, meeting the Lord Provost of Glasgow, Mr Andrew Hood and his wife was a pleasure and we talked about their predecessors in '41, the Dollans, whom we both knew. Their Graces with Kay, Davina and myself visited Glasgow next day. In June, I received cordial letters of thanks from each of the Elliots, expressing similar sentiments to Kay. Sir Walter said it was invaluable having me around, someone who knew all the ropes. How very nautical, which for me gave him the status of a shipmate, bye and large.

On Thursday, 31 May, Brandy and I returned to our lovely home in Warsash. Frank and Elsie brought Peta back from Cardiff at the week-end and I had two sunny days with the family before doing my RNR training. I had done periods of training since being demobbed in '47, but they had always been in shore establishments. This time it was different. The next three months, from June to September, are very vague in my mind. My memory recall was sporadic and a lot of details recorded here have been supplied by others afterwards. The following experience has been talked about occasionally over the years, but never written about, before now. However, I shall tell the story as though I was totally aware of the circumstances throughout and thereby, I hope, give you a better under-standing.

On Monday, 4 June '56 I joined the frigate HMS *Portchester Castle* at Portland to update my knowledge of anti-submarine warfare. I was now a Lieut-Cdr and this was the first time since the war that I was afloat in a small naval ship. The Captain of the frigate, like me, had two and a half stripes on his arm, but being about five or six years younger, had not seen any action in WW2. Next morning we went to sea to carry out exercises with one of our submarines and it was in the forenoon, on the open bridge, close to the Captain, that things started to go peculiar. After a gap of eleven years, once again, I heard the persistent 'ping' transmission, every few seconds, coming from the bridge loudspeaker, as the 'Asdic' searched underwater for contact with the submarine. That was the familiar, haunting, sound I had lived with, day and night, on the bridge of a destroyer, for four years, from 1941 to '45.

Suddenly, I heard the 'wop' sound of an echo, in response to the 'ping' and then I saw a submarine surfacing on our port bow. I dashed to the wheelhouse voicepipe and shouted 'Hard a-port, full ahead both, stand-by to ram.' The Captain of course was alarmed and cancelled my orders immediately. He looked at me calmly and said, 'Do you feel alright?, to which I replied 'No', rushed to the back of the bridge and threw up. I didn't feel physically ill and I had never been sea-sick in all my twenty years afloat. I was not anxious or depressed, but excited and confused by what seemed logical thoughts chasing through my mind. The Captain was kindness itself. He took me down to his cabin and said 'Something strange has happened. You seem unwell, so, we'll go back into Portland immediately and get a doctor to look at you.' Keen to know what was the matter with me, I thanked him and agreed.

There was no diagnosis at Portland, nor was there at Haslar Hospital, Gosport, which I visited by ambulance, so, I was sent to Netley, the Army Hospital on Southampton Water, which had a psychiatric wing for officers of all three services. There, I was put under the care of Lieut Colonel McQuillan, a friendly psychiatrist, who diagnosed my condition as 'hypermania' and commenced my treatment. He counselled me daily for about an hour and arranged ECT (electro convulsive therapy) for me as he thought fit and with my agreement. He got me talking about my war experiences at length and in great detail, from being mined, dive-bombed, wounded in an air-raid and seeing other ships being sunk. He listened attentively and popped an occasional question, but left the talking mostly to me. When I told him about the long periods at sea, escorting convoys, under threat of U-boats in the Arctic and Atlantic, with constant fear, but never showing it, of a torpedo bringing death by explosion, drowning or freezing to me and my shipmates, he nodded appreciatively. It seemed to me, at that moment, we both realized a possible reason for my behaviour aboard the *Portchester Castle*. The suppressed wartime stress had come back to me when I heard the 'ping', 'wop', from the Asdic causing a 'nervous breakdown' as it was called then, but which is now more readily recognized as 'post traumatic stress syndrome' (PTSS). In my case it was a gap of 12 years.

Confidence in the Colonel as a person, his treatment and my positive attitude was getting me better. After a month had elapsed, the Admiralty signalled that I was to be transferred to a civilian hospital as my training period had ended. McQuillan replied, through the Admiralty Liaison Officer, Southampton, Lieut-Cdr Derrick Mallinson, an OW and friend of mine, 'Over my dead body' and he refused to discharge me. In September I was fit again and went home to convalesce, but my saviour said it would be inadvisable for me to go back to sea and told Cunard so. They generously gave me six months, on pay, to find a job ashore, which I'll tell you all about in the next chapter. By this unexpected occurrence I had achieved my hidden agenda for the family, unconsciously. At last, I had moved from ship to shore for good.

CHAPTER 17

Regent Oil and Southern Batteries – 1957–1963

'I'VE SWALLOWED THE HOOK,' I said to everyone I saw, using the sailor's way of telling folk that I was now ashore permanently. Home was a three bedroomed house in Warsash, about half a mile from our original flat at St Leger, and had been since 1954. Back in '53 Brenda and I thought it would be sensible to own a house and we started looking around. On seeing some land, half an acre in depth, for sale as a building plot, we decided to buy it. My father-in-law Frank generously paid £200 for the land and gave it to us. Happily, we met a young student architect in the 'Rising Sun' pub, who was pleased to design our house, without a fee. In exchange we provided food and drink for him during our many sessions together and we negotiated a mortgage of £2,500 with the Woolwich Building Society. The plot had been an orchard to a large house nearby, with a quarter of an acre on each side of a stream, so, we had the apple trees removed from the side bordering Brook Lane, on which to develop our home, with the appropriate name of 'Pippins'. Brenda often called me the 'old Worcester' pippin, fruity to the core. An old hollow oak close to the road would hide the kids later, who pelted passers-by with acorns.

During the three months before Christmas I convalesced quietly and occupied my time making a scaled down model of 'Pippins' as a dolls' house for Peta. When presented with the finished work, whose base was a piece of mahogany from an old wardrobe door in the *Queen Mary*, she was thrilled, but soon compared the stairs in house and model to tell me that the latter was one short! I was somewhat sad to leave the sea, but glad to be home and excited at the prospect of a new career, with ideas about the oil industry in mind.

Frank, once again, was most helpful. As senior manager for National Benzole Petroleum (NBP) in Wales and South-west England he was a mine of information on his own company, which he'd joined in 1922, when they delivered petrol in 2 gallon cans, and on his five major competitors. They were Shell-Mex & British Petroleum, Esso, Mobil, Texaco and Fina, with Regent Oil Company (ROC) expanding and owned by Caltex (California/ Texas). He told me, frankly, an obvious pun, he felt sure that National Benzole would want to employ me, but if, as he expected, I was promoted swiftly, it might savour of nepotism, which was something he strongly opposed. Therefore, he suggested that I applied to Regent, who were advertising for Sales Representatives at that time and which I did in the New Year.

I realized that as a Sales Rep I would have to drive a car and as my licence, then, permitted me only to use motorcycles, which included scooters, I would need lessons to pass another driving test. Brenda gave me the necessary tuition in a car lent to us by our good friends, John and Anne Ingram, because at that time we couldn't afford to buy and run a car. I passed the test, but continued to use the Vespa scooter, until midsummer '57, knowing that if I got the job I wanted then a Company car would be provided. In the spring I was interviewed by Regent, who took me on as a Trainee Rep. The training period was three months, from March to June, most comprehensive and controlled by a man who would influence my career, immensely, both in oil and later in life as a management consultant.

T.R. Williams, always referred to as TR, was a distinguished, tall, white-haired, Welsh wizard, whose voice and looks suggested, to me, a prophet from the Old Testament. He had a wonderful way of developing skills in people and 'TR's boys' were recognized throughout the oil industry. He himself had progressed from being a Rep with Red Line in the thirties, a company no longer in existence, to a manager on the Board of Pool Petrol in South Wales during WW2. His postwar years with Regent saw him promoted up the marketing ladder to senior manager before switching to training. It became apparent that he exercised considerable power in Head Office, Park Street, London, where, as a dedicated Training Manager, he achieved outstanding results, by his discerning ability and a high standard of team discipline. It was he who decided, ultimately, which trainee candidates would work for Regent. I was one of a dozen trainees.

The training started with two weeks in Head Office, with us trainees staying from Monday to Friday in a hotel near Marble Arch. TR coached us in the qualities required by an effective salesman, such as listening, to assimilate the needs of buyers, then feeding back ideas about how our products and service might satisfy those needs more efficiently. Always a positive sell, never knocking competitors' products, because when facing a prospect that would mean insulting his intelligence in the past when he chose his current supplier. Caltex had produced a large book of selling techniques by numbers. If the buyer responded to your No. 3 opening with No. 5, then your best bet was to state No. 8 or No. 9. It may have had some merit, in the US of A, but we considered it unsuitable for use in the UK. TR stressed that success when selling was achieved mainly by personality, as a distinctive individual, thinking on one's feet and not reeling off trite remarks like a robot. His method of developing our negotiating skills was cleverly combined with learning about company procedures and products.

TR would arrange for a company director or manager to lecture us in the Training Room for 30 to 40 minutes, no longer, about his speciality, after which TR would nod his head at one of us. This was the signal for the person selected to rise and stand upright behind his chair. After saying his name, he would then give a summarized appreciation, not exceeding 10 minutes, of what he had understood, finishing with a vote of thanks, whereupon the rest of us applauded. It was a nerve wracking experience, but very good for us and we improved by helping each other. Every session followed this routine and when it was just TR up front talking, he would finish and nod at someone. As the chosen one spoke, TR would walk towards him as a sign of improvement, and back away from him if the reverse, always with humour and positive suggestions. This procedure set a superb foundation for giving a presentation. We all got better and TR made it fun, without detracting from the learning.

I was sent to the Regent, ship-fed, oil depot at Poole in Dorset for a month's operational training. During the week I was accommodated at the Dolphin Hotel on the harbour front, where I enjoyed a garlic-rubbed rump steak, most nights, for dinner, a reminder of Cunard feeding, and at weekends travelled to and from home, about 40 miles to the east, on my Vespa scooter. The training was most comprehensive. I discharged ships, dipped large storage tanks to determine quantity of product therein, loaded road tank waggons (RTWs) and accompanied drivers, as their mate, to deliver our products to customers' premises. Many evenings were spent, socially, with the drivers in Dorset pubs, playing real skittles in the alleys for which they were famous. This new life was very much to my liking. A great variety of interesting tasks, with friendly, capable, characters readily accepting me into their company and giving me the benefit of their experience. My health was excellent, with no backward thoughts to the nervous breakdown, which was never mentioned again. Ian Edwards, my GP and personal friend in Sarisbury Green near Warsash, was most helpful, over a scotch in the local pub, when he said, 'Ian, liken your break in nerves to a broken limb, now healed and that's the end of it.' I did.

The next period of training was a month in the field with Peter Newell, a representative living in a thatched cottage near Puddletown in Dorset. Peter and his wife Cynthia were happy to have me living with them during the weeks, for which they were compensated by the Company. Life with this pair was fun, with spontaneous role playing and theatrical quotes coming from each, frequently and usually in dialogue. They had built a worthy reputation in Amateur Dramatics and would often get me involved in their humorous exchanges. Peter had the personality to succeed in selling and his high monthy sales figures reflected his ability. I got a lot of useful tips from him about running an area which, in those days, covered both markets, Retail, consisting of Regent Filling Stations and Industrial, catering for bulk deliveries to haulage contractors, bus companies and fuel for heating premises. A Rep's car was also his mobile office, with customer files and records in the boot, along with incoming daily mail from District

Office thrown in. Peter's boot was chaos and horrified my shipshape mind, but no comment from me. He always seemed to extract the right paper, at the right time, with apparent ease.

For a few days I acted as a Forecourt Attendant on a Regent Filling Station, serving petrol before the days of self-service and always remembering to say 'Sir, or Madam, may I check your engine oil for safety?', knowing that lubricating oil was a lucrative form of profit. We original members of the Trainees Course, having completed our outside training in various places, returned to Head Office for a final week with TR. Meantime, we heard that his only son was killed in WW2. He never mentioned it, but we realized that we, his boys, provided some small solace. As a token of our love and respect for him, on our last night, we all took TR to 'The Crazy Gang' at the Victoria Palace, to see Flanagan & Allen, Nervo and Knox and Nosmo King.

Such was my way of life that I had graduated from a seaman to a salesman at the age of 35 and in June 1957 was appointed as Regent Representative on an area in the lovely rural county of Hampshire, bounded by Winchester, Andover and Basingstoke. The centre of my patch was Winchester, only 15 miles away, which meant I could work from home in Warsash, with an A40 Somerset as my company car. It had no heater or radio fitted in those days, but it had a handle to start the engine if the battery failed. Four wheels instead of two was a great family asset because I could make allowance on my monthly expense claim for petrol used on private mileage. Many filling stations in the fifties were shared by oil companies as indicated by the globes displayed on pumps, but the policy was highly competitive, persuading dealers to sign a 'solus' contract, that is sell one company's products only. Contracts varied from 5 to 20 years, in exchange for financial support, including maybe, the price of an ocean cruise, as perks. An alternative was for Regent to buy the site and retain the dealer as tenant.

My patch had a few Company owned sites and about fifteen mixed sites, with Regent globes on pumps, that I was working on to gain solus contracts, which was a challenging way to put TR's training to the test. Father-in-law Frank gave me a few bits of good advice from his past experience: 'On a day's trip, always return home by a different route to the outward journey, to give you a greater chance of discovering new prospects. Never miss the opportunity of a chat with a Regent tanker driver. Drivers often know more about what's happening in an area than the Rep. They meet other companies' drivers in transport cafes to chat over a cuppa. So, stop whenever you see a Regent RTW near a cafe. Besides, maybe, hearing some useful info, you'll enjoy the best cup o' tea you've ever had. Transport cafes have that reputation. Your driver chum may well tell you that the Esso site, up the road, is coming off contract soon and might be worth a call. Remember, some drivers may have a greater influence than you with some of your customers.'

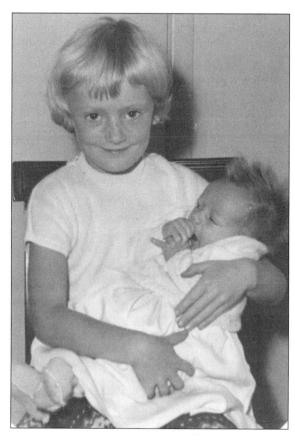

Peta, aged 6, holding baby brother, Charles

Dougie Rogers was my District Manager in the office at Woolston depot, Southampton with Stanley, his Sales Superintendent, who would meet me in Winchester, by the statue of King Alfred and accompany me on my calls occasionally. Brenda, happily, had become pregnant in the spring and we expected our second infant in October, to be born at home. Elsie came and stayed at 'Pippins' and early on 4 October, indications suggested the happy event would be later that day. In the forenoon I met Stanley and we went to Andover to clinch a big deal on two sites at Weyhill with father, the owner and his two sons who ran the sites, one on each side of the A303. The deal was soon done and after lunch, I put the foot down for home.

At precisely 4 p.m., a black cat dashed across the road in front of my black A40 Somerset and I pulled into the drive at 'Pippins' an hour later. Out rushed my mother-in-law, Elsie, shouting 'It's a boy, born at 4 o'clock.' 'Yippee,' I yelled 'Charles Kinloch, our son, has arrived.' Another big event occurred on that day in 1957. In the evening, I went to see the Hunts, Mike and Margaret, then living in 'River Barn' at Old Bursledon, to ask Mike, my old shipmate, to be a godfather to Charles and as he agreed, standing in the garden, we heard a humming noise above and cast our eyes to the heavens, as we had done so often in the past as astro-navigators. This time we saw something never seen before, the Russian rocket 'Sputnik', the very first spacecraft to orbit planet earth.

The two prime areas, out of six, in the Southern District, with the largest gallonage turnover, were Southampton and Portsmouth and in 1958 I was promoted to Rep in the former. I took over from a Canadian guy, Jim, who was leaving to become boss of Major Oil Co., in Yorkshire. When Rogers heard that I didn't play golf, he said 'You soon will. An important customer of yours called Creek will expect you to play a round and have lunch with him at his golf-club at least once a month.' I bought a set of clubs; Dougie and Jim coached me; I enjoyed it and became quite good. Jim, with his usual wit, suggested that as an old salt, I should select a 'paddle', from my golf-bag, when teeing-up to Ivor Creek. Dougie was ex-Shell, so, there was a wicked rumour in Regent that Shell only employed Sales Reps to play golf with their customers, from which it was assumed that the day would be spent talking business between holes, to be finalized in the bar at the 19th. Those were the days!

Living in Warsash meant keeping in touch with sailors and the sea, with the School of Navigation, part of the University of Southampton, just a mile down the road and the local residents being mostly yachting types. Those who knew my history would invite me to crew for them at week-ends. Thus, sailing, not golf, became my main leisure pursuit and I never had to buy and maintain a boat of my own. Those friends with keel boats, at moorings, were usually members of the Royal Thames Yacht Club and others, with smaller craft, kept them at the Warsash Sailing Club. It was about then that I got to know Neil Jephcott and we have remained lifelong friends to this day. We met through our wives, Brenda and Denny, who saw a lot of each other with the youngsters. They had two boys and a girl, David, Penny and Mark, the two boys being similar in age to our girl and boy and who likewise have kept in touch over the years. Neil had been in the MN as a Chief Engineer, but in '58 was ashore in Thornycrofts Shipyard, responsible for repairs and maintenance in Cunard ships. He told me his greatest achievement was fitting stabilizers in the *Queen Mary*, before which she could behave quite unpredictably in stormy weather.

Another attribute of Neil's was cricket. After going to sea in Shell tankers, he went to Cambridge to read engineering and played for his College, Emmanuel, before returning to sea with Norwegians, to go whaling in the Antarctic. Every summer, Cunard and Thornycroft played each other at cricket and inevitably Neil captained the shipyard's team. It was a rum event, with eccentric items produced by surprise. One year, Neil's team made a ball with a loose rivet inside to open the bowling, only to be faced by a man wielding a bat, made by a ship's carpenter, to the same width as the three wickets. Neil had a Folkboat with four berths for off-shore cruising or racing, after a Flying 15, designed by Uffa Fox, for very fast, wet and exciting in-shore racing. First time, crossing the line at Calshot, in the Folkboat, at the start of a Round the Island (Wight) Race, with about forty other boats, Neil said 'Reckon we're the only boat with a Master Mariner and Chief Engineer as crew.' With cricket in mind, I replied 'Yes, you're probably right, but unlike Lords, we professionals are not obliged to enter the Solent by a different channel to the amateurs.' I have always been amazed that the two categories in cricket weren't treated as one until the sixties, almost 20 years after WW2.

I was adapting to my new career, liking it and being successful. The most noticeable difference between working as member of a sales team spread over a District and being in a ship, with mates always at hand, was that it took longer to establish rapport and trust. My new area, centred on Southampton, can best be outlined by imagining a circle with a radius of about 12 miles from Lymington on the coast to the west, taking in Eastleigh to the north and finishing at Lee-on-Solent on the coast to the east. This embraced my home and all the coastal territory east of Southampton Water and south of the Hamble River. A startling move was about to be made by Regent's parent company Caltex. What they had in mind was establishing a large oil refinery, similar in size to the one on the opposite shore, further north and owned by Esso. At first they made an extravagant offer to a man named Mortimer, for his farm, bordering the south side of Hook Park, a residential area between him and the Navigation School, on the bank of the river. They did this on the understanding that he could rent back and continue to work the land, until wanted for the refinery. He was a customer of mine for lubricants and when he told me, laughing merrily at having clinched a good deal, that was the first I heard of it.

Within a few days, I was phoned by a top PR Manager with Caltex, staying at the Polygon Hotel, who arranged to visit me at home in a chauffeur driven Rolls and use my knowledge of the area and people to further his project, which was to persuade the population that a refinery in Hook Park was most desirable. He was a retired Commander RN and went down well with all the family, even teaching Peta to ride her bicycle on the grass at 'Pippins' in the weeks ahead. Yes, he used our home as a centre of operations when mingling with Council dignitaries and the yachting fraternity. Caltex wanted to get planning permission on the farm and extend it into Hook Park, where they would offer fancy prices for properties. My yachting friends were totally against the idea, but rather than take it out on me, with the wealth available to them, they decided to brief barristers to fight the Almighty American Corporation. The Jephcotts lived in Hook Park and I used to phone Denny, put on a US accent and say 'What's the real estate price you're putting on the ranch today?' It was about six months later that the Cmdr phoned to say 'It's goodbye, we're withdrawing and going to Milford Haven instead.'

Three miles up river from Warsash, at Swanwick, was one of the most prolific yacht builders in the UK, Moodys Ltd, a family business, expanding fast and gaining a great reputation in those days. My cousin Cecily Lowther, with husband Bruce Kilpatrick, MD of South-Western Tar Distillers, took me to see their very special new yacht, *Killiecrankie*, in the boatyard and I met old man Moody, still pedalling his bike around in a yachting cap, and both his sons. Imagine my delight when later, in '59, Alan Moody, the senior son, agreed to having a Filling Station, opposite their boat yard on the A27, then the main road from Southampton to Portsmouth and we decided on a Regent Company owned site, with Moodys as tenants. Another brilliant idea was to convert a drifter into a Floating Filling Station, with Regent pumps and globes, selling petrol, diesel and TVO (Tractor Vaporizing Oil) to yachts up and down the Hamble river. This mobile source of fuel, named Bo'sun, was moored in Moody's yard, opposite the 'Jolly Sailor', the pub that featured frequently in the TV series 'Howard's Way'. Both outlets did well for Moodys and Bo'sun was a joy for me to see, as a blown away sailor.

In 1960 I was selected to go to Head Office in Park Street, London as a personal assistant to the Managing Director (MD). At that time I met Jack Nolan, General Manager Marketing, who influenced my promotional prospects and whose name will recur in the future. My job was to review and present to the MD all deals submitted by Districts, with my recommendations, for his approval or otherwise. This move was preparing me for promotion to management and my first experience made me feel most important. The tea lady peeped round my office door with downcast eyes, then disappeared back to her trolley in the corridor. She returned, a few minutes later, with a smile and a remark I shall never forget, 'Here you are sir, you've got a carpet in here, so, you get your tea with a cup and saucer, not in a mug.' 'Thank you so much, how posh,' I said, with some sincerity. In the days of the British Raj, when going to India and back was solely by sea, superior nabobs always booked cabins on the shady side of the ship and this was Port side Out to India and Starboard side Home to the UK. This was expressed briefly as POSH, a word still used to this day by many people unaware of its origin. The MD was an American from whom I learned little except prejudice. We seemed to spend rather more time amending punctuation in reports, than examining the contents.

I filled this role for a month, travelling up weekly and staying in the 'Mostyn' hotel, where I had stayed when training under TR. By happy coincidence a naval chum of mine living in Warsash, Lance Bell-Davies, had just been made a Commander and was doing a period like me at Head Office, which, for him, was the Admiralty in Whitehall. Lance was a specialist submariner, with many commands under his belt. He had been at

HMS *Dolphin*, Gosport, training officers to take command of subs, known in the vernacular as the Perishers Course. Joan, his delightful Dutch wife, drove us to Southampton Railway Station on Monday mornings and met us there on Friday evenings. Meantime, we always managed to meet in London for a drink at the 'In and Out' (Naval and Military Club) in Piccadilly or the 'Senior and Royal Aero-Club' in Pall Mall, which he was now entitled to enter by virtue of rank. Being a relative junior amongst many seniors, in the latter club, he spoke in hushed tones, as did I, and when I recognized Phillip Higham, Vanguard '47, another recent 'brass hat', who had just returned from learning Arabic in the middle-east, we reminisced, sotto voce, in English, of course.

With Peta nine and Charles three, in 1960, Brenda and I were well aware of a complete, happy family life, now that I was ashore. Also, as a so called bread-winner, in those days, I was pleased that my alteration of course was providing better prospects ashore, in oil, than afloat, in the MN, because air traffic was taking over on the Atlantic. About this time, I was promoted to Sales Superintendent in the Southampton office at the same time as Dougie Rogers was replaced by Sydney Trott as District Manager. I liked Sydney, instinctively, because he had an adventurous spirit, but I soon learned a thing or two about being passed the buck in business. His background was RAF in WW2 and before that, in the thirties, he was flying Gloster Gladiator biplanes over Mesopotamia (now Iraq). He had 'duck's disease', which described a short man, who waddled as he walked, because his bum was too close to the ground. Sidney was a persuasive salesman, and a compulsive gambler by instinct, whose management style was inclined towards the latter. He and I had desks, facing each other and adjacent, in the depot office at Woolston and the daily routine, which follows, will amuse you, I'm sure.

I would arrive in the office by 0900 and Sydney about 0930, to see piles of letters on our desks, for individual attention, mostly from Regional Office, Brighton, already sorted and opened by Maureen, our mutual secretary. Initially there were always more letters on his desk, but not for long. Having dealt with much of my mail, before his appearance, I would sit back and watch Sydney deal with his. In silence he would glance at each letter, sometimes writing a comment, but not often, before throwing it over his desk calendar in my direction. For about an hour, my view ahead alternated between seeing Sydney through his horn-rimmed specs and then observing his missiles dive-bombing my territory. This form of delegation might have been common in the RAF, but it was new to me. After this airborne exercise ended, he would extract the day's *Sporting Life* newspaper from his brief-case and mark up his winners for the day. When that major managerial commitment had been completed, he would say, 'Ian, I'll be back to have lunch on you,' and depart up town to see his bookmaker. Which of us paid for lunch was always a gamble, decided by a round of spoof or a roll of dice and I lost, invariably.

In the autumn of 1960 Regent rationalized its marketing by dispensing with about 30 Districts reporting to 6 Regions, which showed great savings in many respects. This meant that in future Sales Reps would be responsible direct to Regional Offices and the positions of District Manager and Sales Superintendent ceased to exist. Sydney decided to leave Regent and I was approached by my new Regional Manager at Bristol, 'Ginger' Turlington, to move over to Operations for a few years. An abrupt, yet sincere, person, he said, 'Bryce, the experience gained would enhance your chances of promotion when you return to Marketing later.' I agreed, did three months training in the Depot at Portslade, near Newhaven, before being appointed Depot Manager, Southampton. My tanks at Woolston were supplied by ship and I had 20 RTWs to distribute fuel, within the old district boundaries, and a lorry for barrels and cans of Caltex lubricants. Regarding staff, I had six in the office under Eric Speller, the Chief Clerk, my No.1 and next in authority to me; ten in the yard under Foreman Angus and twenty co-operative disciplined drivers, most of whom had been in the forces, either in WW2 or in National Service. For me, it was like being in command of a small ship, whose crew I had met before, when in Marketing. I was happy ashore, but the sea was never far away. I was still a member of Southampton Master Mariners Club and in touch with old shipmates.

After the hogmanay party for 1962, Brenda complained of a terrible pain in her tummy and at first we thought it was part of a hangover, but it persisted and we called in Ian Edwards our GP and personal friend for a glass of sherry and a diagnosis. We were still treating it trivially but Ian arranged for B to go into Southampton General Hospital for observation and X-ray. Ten days later, on a visit, a nurse said the surgeon consultant wanted to see me and led the way. We met a tall white-coated man in the corridor and she told him who I was. He looked down at me and said quite briefly, 'Mr. Bryce, I have to tell you that your wife is suffering from cancer of the colon and has a life expectancy of ten years at the most. We shall operate of course and keep you informed.' With that he turned on his heel and was gone. The nurse took me into a side room, but I was stunned into silence and she was speechless.

This was a totally unexpected tragedy and as in wartime I had to muster my courage to face the consequences. I drove my car mainly by instinct back to the depot and crossed the road to a pub on the corner. After a very large scotch, I phoned father-in-law, Frank and shared the sad news with him. He replied calmly as I knew he would and said, 'Ian, old son, all is not over yet. I'll break the news to Elsie and we'll be down.' Because Frank had just retired, they were negotiating the purchase of a cottage near us in Warsash and I appreciated how this terrible shock would diminish their joy in that move. The medics didn't tell patients if they had a disease considered terminal in those days, so Brenda never knew and GP Ian said to me 'Whilst there is hope, and research can reveal new remedies from day to day, let's keep it that way.' Peta and Charles knew that Mummy was ill, but not how desperately, until things got worse and the liver was affected, allowing her an even shorter life span. When I was told this at the hospital, I returned to my desk at the depot and wept. The door opened quietly, Eric entered, sat beside me and put an arm round my shoulder. Of similar age to me, he was sensitive enough to realize that his presence, in silence, was the support I needed, and it was a great comfort. I thanked him afterwards for his careful behaviour and companionship.

Throughout the spring, Brenda was in and out of hospital, but we had a family holiday in Brighton, to give the kids some fun. Friends rallied round especially at week-ends and Joan and Lance often took Peta and Charles sailing with their three youngsters in the brig *Marjorie*, a unique square-rigged yacht, moored at Bursledon or Gosport and owned by Lance's father, Admiral Richard Bell-Davies VC, DSO (1886–1966). He was a naval flying hero in WW1, retired at Lee-on-Solent, close to the Fleet Air Arm base, HMS *Daedalus*, or 'Dead-loss'. Peta told me later that the old Admiral would stand on deck, piping orders to Auntie Joan, setting sails on the yard-arms up aloft! Also, Emmalina Anne, EA, would invite Peta to her Wendy House in the garden at 'Hollyhill', nearby. Still giving me constant support, Frank and Elsie moved from 'Pippins' into Brook Cottage, Greenaway Lane. In May Brenda came home, under my care, with District Nurse and GP. That is when Mike and Margaret, lovingly, had Peta and Charles to live at River Barn for three months. Jennifer Hunt was Peta's age and also attended Rookesbury School, whilst her older brother, Christopher, guided Charles.

The support I had from personal friends and company colleagues was immense. The Hunts, Ingrams, Jephcotts, Bell-Davieses, Phil Hawkins and June McDonald, plus the near neighbours such as the Kroons, Turners, Littledales and Powells, with many others, provided close assistance in every day chores. Anne Ingram came round daily to deal with the laundry, bless her. Regent were most understanding and generous in their response. My Regional Manager in Brighton, David John, a man from Penarth about whom I had heard many good things, but never met, phoned me and said 'Ian, I am aware of the situation, for which you have my sincere sympathy, and I am giving you indefinite leave to look after your wife. You can keep in touch with the job by phone and occasional visits. I know Speller is capable of managing the depot and will refer to you as necessary. Your priority must be your family, and please phone me at any time.' The trust and empathy expressed in his words confirmed my belief that leadership is best when based on mutual respect and personal contact between human beings.

Knowing our life together was limited I spent most of my time by the bed, reading to her and holding hands, but at night when she was sleeping, I sought solace in the garden. I walked for hours on the grass amongst the trees and on a cloudless night looked aloft to the stars and wondered. My thoughts would go back to night-times, alone, on a wing of *Caronia*'s bridge in mid-Pacific, when I became aware that I was like a grain of sand on a universal beach, but very much a single part of the whole, with a soul, or spirit, if you will. I would wonder then about what happened to souls if they were not saved by SOS. Maybe, at the moment of death, the spirit was released into space and found a purpose on another planet, in orbit round another star, or sun, if you will. Would Brenda's spirit find Aldebaran, an old sextant friend of mine, a star in the constellation of Taurus, the Bull, through which our sun was passing as I walked. Aldebaran, also, contained the message 'a la Brenda'. Often, I would look up and repeat the words of Jesus — 'In my father's house are many mansions: if it were not so, I would have told you.' The garden persuaded me to a more realistic view of God, who, ever since, in my mind, has been the 'Great Overall Designer' of everything, everywhere, and I feel sure such realization then helped me cope with the inevitable sequence of sorrowful things to come.

Brenda's bed was moved to a corner of the living room at 'Pippins' and I had a bed near the door. The District Nurse called daily to deal with the physical plumbing now attached to B and Ian Edwards came daily to administer ever increasing doses of morphia. I can say this now, because Ian went aloft long ago. As a naval officer in WW2, I carried tablets of morphine, issued by the ship's Doc, before going into action, to give to anyone seriously wounded. Ian knew this and said to me, 'I shall leave a few tablets with you and should my call be delayed and Brenda is in pain, then give her one or two.' I never had to do it, but the trust placed in me was appreciated and only now am I making this fact public. If Brenda suspected that she was on the way out, she never said so and we two Ians treated the daily visit as a social occasion, with cheerful chat and a glass of sherry. Friends continued to call and were admitted with discretion. Peta and Charles came frequently to see Mum, until the last desperate days, when I thought her skeletal appearance would upset them. At that time, Margaret advised me to tell Peta and Charles what to expect. My message was simple, such as, 'Mum will be happier at peace in space than living with anxiety on earth,' and we hugged each other in mutual support.

Brenda died on 16 August, 1962 and was cremated at Eastleigh after a funeral service at Sarisbury Green Church. As a single parent, with Frank and Elsie close by and surrounded by so many friends of mine and the children, I knew it would be unwise to stay with Regent, as my future promotion, already planned, would mean moving to strange parts. Fortunately, good friends Donald and Peggy Beswick, neighbours of the Hunts in Old Bursledon, offered me a job with them as a director in their motor factoring company, 'Southern Batteries Ltd'. This was a business, owned and run on the side of Donald's main practice as a solicitor in Southampton, I accepted gladly and when I told my Brighton boss, David John, he said 'Good luck Ian, I'd have done likewise in your position. Regent will miss you and I'm sorry I can't get away to give you a farewell lunch, but we may meet in future and I'll do it then.' We never did, but I will remember him always with thanks for his appropriate action – a manager in a million.

Peta, Charles and I continued to live at 'Pippins', with Elsie and Frank in Greenaway Lane, about ten minutes walk away, and I arranged a housekeeper to come in daily during the week. On one side we had our good close neighbours, the Kroon family, Claude, Leila, godmother to Charles, and their three daughters, Elizabeth, the eldest and the twins Marion and Katherine, with whom Peta had grown up. Claude and I had a lot in common. The same age, he was trained for the sea in the *General Botha* at Capetown when I was in the *Worcester* and in the fifties, as a 'Master Mariner', he captained British Rail's cross-channel ships between Dover and Calais. On the other side of us, the Littledales lived in the big house with daughters Carole-Ann and Suzanne. Brian was a Lieut-Cdr RN in submarines and Hazel his wife was a wonderful character, who managed well on one real leg, one false one and the aid of a stick, which she waved, as she gave a cheerful shout, whenever she saw me. Beyond them in a tiny cottage on the corner of Brook Lane and Brook Avenue, were Phillip and Kay Powell, with their youngsters Cathy and Peter-D. Phillip was a keen Territorial Army (TA) soldier and as a Lieut-Colonel in the Hampshire Regiment dined me at their Mess in Winchester a number of times. When not a soldier, he was an estate agent and we were helpful neighbours on each side of Hazel, in Brian's absence, sometimes even assisting her to refit the false leg.

   In the early years at 'Pippins', the Littledales at Littlebrook, the name of their large house, held big cocktail parties for lots of naval officers and their wives, to which we neighbours would be invited. I remember well standing next to Phillip in a corner sipping gin, as pinkers or gimlets, when he said, 'Ian, listening to the chat around me, I'm convinced that we are the only officers in this room who can say, honestly, that we didn't seduce our wives in Malta.' Hazel, with her candid sense of humour, told me that after enjoying sex with Brian, he would always offer her a 'Senior Service' cigarette. She said 'Brian believed that if *he* hadn't satisfied me, then *it* would.' Everybody knew the advert at the time, was 'Senior Service Satisfy!'

   On the opposite side of Brook Lane, lived another ex-seafaring 'Master Mariner' called Ron Turner, an Instructor at the Navigation School, and his Tasmanian wife Dorothy with their two small daughters Susan and Carole, of a similar age to Charles and who became his playmates. Over earlier years it also became obvious that the Turner home was 'open house' to anyone from 'down under' and it was fun for us meeting them. The Fox family deserve a mention here because they were very important people in the life of Warsash. They owned and managed Fox and Son Ltd, the only grocers shop in the village on the corner opposite the clock tower. Gerald and Hilda Fox, with son Tony, had been good friends of Brenda and me since 1950. Tony, when not running the 'off licence' side of the business (a bottle of Nuit St Georges burgundy was then 62½p), or driving his red MG, distinguished himself at the tiller or more often on the trapeze of a dinghy. He and John Oakley, whose father was a well known heavy-weight boxer, had crewed and won in the Olympics, at sometime during the fifties, sailing a 'Flying Dutchman' Class boat. The boat, called *Shampoo*, we saw, often, on the water at Warsash, and was easily recognized by its mast painted with red stripes like a barber's pole.

The word dinghy made me think of pram and that reminded me of an incident outside Fox's shop when Charles was a baby and I was some place else. Brenda was chatting to a lady friend at the bus stop and Charles was sitting in his pram surrounded by loose items of groceries just purchased. Suddenly he threw a tin into the road as a Hants & Dorset bus pulled in to the kerb. The near front wheel of the bus ran over the tin and Brenda's companion was smothered from head to toe in Heinz Tomato Soup! Our son, Charlie boy, had always been an adventurous lad from scratch. Just prior to the soup saga, he had escaped from his pram in the front garden of 'Pippins', crawled out into Brook Lane and headed for the village, on all fours, in the middle of the road. Along came a Hants & Dorset bus, which finding its progress impeded by this infant, stopped, picked up Charles as a passenger and fortunately found someone at the terminus, in Warsash, who recognized him and brought him back to base.

Returning to the scene in '62, further away at Exton, in the Meon Valley, the Fradgley family were friends indeed, when we were in need. Their younger daughter Diana, called Dilly, was a school friend of Peta's at Rookesbury Park and her mother Jo had Peta to stay, frequently, for long periods, during Brenda's illness. Whilst the girls were trotting and jumping ponies in their paddock, Jo and I would be drinking gin in the kitchen. Jo's husband, Tony, a quiet man and merchant banker in the City, would return home at week-ends, to sip a sherry before lunch on Sundays. For Peta, staying with the Fradgleys was like having a pony of her own, which helped to develop her into the excellent rider she became in her teens.

A Regent colleague Peter Rogers and his wife Margaret, known as Blag, did a marvellous thing at the end of '62, in harmony with her parents Bill and Peggy Boyd. Knowing Frank and Elsie as well as we three, they invited the five of us for Christmas at the Boyd's house in London. Bill was a senior engineering manager in Regent's head office and Peggy had been a Company secretary, so, the oil world was a popular topic of conversation. What a wonderful diversion that was and afterwards the Wills family, bless them, asked Peta and Charles to their home near Maidstone for New Year. Gerry and Madeline, a first cousin of Brenda's, with their four sons, Murray, Peter, Neil and Stephen had a sensational snowy time in that winter of '62–'63. It was great for all the cousins, tobogganing every day, for three weeks, not one, as expected, and for Mum, Madeline, drying their clothes and setting them up for the next day, came naturally to such a caring, loving person as her. Gerry, an equally caring and loving person, was obliged to manage his Barclays Bank each day!

With Southern Batteries I was in charge of the Portsmouth branch, centred in Southsea and the Isle of Wight depot in Ryde. I was now a buyer and seller of such products as Glasso Paints, Dagenite Batteries and Harmo Exhaust systems, as our main turnover and this taught me a lot of new skills. Unfortunately, the company was lacking in capital substance, at a time of economic depression in 1962 and things looked grim in '63 on the working front, but for me, much brighter on the personal front. After Brenda's death, I suffered a few weird experiences. As you should know by now, I'm a raving heterosexual guy, who focuses on lovely ladies. So, it may come as a surprise to you that I still saw lovely ladies everywhere, but in seconds they had withered away to nothing and that was how I saw my Brandy go from gorgeous girl to simple skeleton in eight months. It took time for me to adjust back to normal. Some of my lovely friends I have mentioned invited me to dinner with some distinguished single ladies included, possibly to create a second wife situation, done discreetly and accepted with pleasure by me, but without any conclusion.

The Jephcotts had moved to a house at Carnon Downs, near Truro, in Cornwall, because Neil had taken a job with Silley Cox Shipyard in Falmouth. For the school summer holidays of '63, Neil and Denny invited us three Kinloch Bryces down to join them in Devon. Neil's father, Sir Harry Jephcott, the boss man of Glaxo, who lived in Pinner, also owned a large house called 'Thalassa', on the foreshore at East Portlemouth, in the Salcombe Estuary. Kindly, he allowed family and friends to use 'Thalassa' as a holiday home, with the provision to keep the place spick-and-span. I could imagine old Sir Harry from his towering height of 6 ft 6 ins, telling Neil and Denny what to do at all times. 'Make sure the children wash the sand off their feet before entering the drawing room,' he would probably say.

It was during that sunny summer that I met the loveliest lady, with whom I am still living happily. Both our lives have continued to improve since our first meeting, which was off shore in a gale of wind. What better way to end a chapter than to keep you, dear readers, waiting to see how happiness returned to me.

CHAPTER 18

Devon and the Channel Islands – 1963–1964: including a bit of 1989

IN AUGUST OF '63, Peta, Charles and I motored down to Devon where we joined Neil and Denny Jephcott, with David, Penny and Mark, in their holiday home, 'Thalassa', at East Portlemouth. The five youngsters were looked after by a lively young lady called Libby Todd, their au pair from Southampton. Denny didn't like sailing, but had many friends in the area to keep her company, which allowed Neil and me the freedom to sail his Folkboat, named *Winwillow*.

Neil intended to sail *Winwillow* from Salcombe to Falmouth, then up the river Fal to Restronguet, which was close to their house, called 'Penvrane', at Carnon Downs, and where she would be berthed for the winter. He planned to do this in three stages before the end of August: from Salcombe to Plymouth, then Plymouth to Fowey and finally Fowey to Falmouth, using cars or taxis as appropriate for land transport. For the first leg, Neil suggested a third member of crew, who knew the ropes, would be handy and said he would phone a girl just returned from a holiday in Denmark who was staying with her parents nearby for the rest of the summer hols. Her name was Sue Balkwill. Of a similar age, they had grown up together, in and out of boats, whenever their parents, who were great friends, had been down in the seaside houses. They were both at Cambridge in the fifties and after getting her BA in Natural Sciences, Sue became a teacher ending up at Berkhamsted School for Girls in Hertfordshire. Neil phoned Sue and she agreed to crew.

The day of departure dawned to a southerly wind, Beaufort scale force 6, a strong breeze about 25 knots, which caused Neil to exclaim 'Good, we can tack out of harbour and get to Plymouth in under three hours on a long reach to the west'. Both of us disliked using auxiliary power when wind provided all we needed to go places. Peta came with us but David declined. At 0730 Thalassa's door-bell rang and Neil admitted Sue, a fascinating feminine figure closely clad in blue oilskins overall, with only the tip of her nose showing, because it was then squally and tippling down with rain outside. And that is how we met for the first time.

The four of us waterproofed people went out in the dinghy to *Winwillow* at her mooring and whilst I went forward to clear halyards round the mast and prepare to let go, Peta went below and Neil was with Sue in the cockpit sorting out the sheets and tiller. I was told years later about their conversation, which supposedly went thus. Neil inquired, 'How's life Sue, any interesting boy friends lately?', to which Sue replied 'No, I've found them all so boring.' 'Well, you know about him, up there?' said Neil, pointing in my direction. 'Oh yes,' said Sue. 'You told me about the sad loss of his wife last year, when it happened.' Realizing that it was top of high-water and we were ready for crossing the bar, Neil shouted 'Ian, stand-by, to let go' and I did as commanded, with the customary nautical response 'Aye aye captain,' not realizing that his helmsmanship would soon alter my course in life as well as that of *Winwillow*'s.

We were close-hauled into the wind tacking out of harbour and having passed the Blackstone Rocks Neil shouted the usual warning 'Ready about, lee-oh,' before bringing the bow through the direction of the wind from port to starboard tack. His cry was inaudible into the wind or was it intentionally subdued, we shall never know, because Sue and I, on either side of the foredeck, were surprised by this unexpected operation and she came charging across the deck straight into my arms. Legend has it, that had we looked aft, we might well have seen the face of our helmsman, over the canopy, displaying a large grin. So it was, that a short embrace on the deck of *Winwillow* in '63 led to a longer embrace at the altar of St Winwalloe's Church, East Portlemouth in '64, a year later. I'm sure it won't surprise my readers to learn that Neil was our 'best man' for that happy event

We picked up a mooring in Plymouth Sound and lunched at the Royal Western Yacht Club, just below the Hoe. Being divested of our oilskins, it was only then that I beheld the visible charm of shipmate Sue, which was accompanied by a well developed witty personality. Dear Peta was greatly relieved to be static again, because the boat's vicious behaviour on passage had prevented her doing what normally comes naturally. Denny came by car to return us all to 'Thalassa'. Soon, Neil had to go back to work at his job in Falmouth, so, Peta, Charles and I followed the Jephcott family by car to their Cornish home, 'Penvrane', at Carnon Downs.

Very sensibly and sensitively Denny asked Sue to stay for a few days, during which time we got to know each other better. Sue said that what she remembered most about sailing round from Salcombe to Plymouth in *Winwillow* was me repeatedly singing a catchy little French song, the first four lines of which we recalled recently as follows:

> Une chanson douce
> Que me chantait ma maman
> En souçant mon pouce
> J'ecoutais en m'endormant

As a translation, I feel sure my readers can imagine me as an infant in my mother's arms, sucking my thumb, as she sent me to sleep, with a sweet song. And as a statement of fact, my right thumb has been smaller than my left one ever since. I revived this tune four years later after our son Andrew was born in '67 and succeeded in sending him off to sleep when he was in my arms. My love for Sue grew at 'Penvrane' and I told her what I thought was sufficient about my past to please her and described my recent grief in detail, to which she listened with sympathetic patience and understanding. Another plus factor was that I was aware that Peta and Charles seemed to like having her around. However, I didn't want her to think I was mainly looking for a Mum for them, but I did believe she had the qualities to love and care for all of us and that this in time would be reciprocated, which has proved true.

Having formed such a favourable opinion, I popped the question at 'Penvrane', but Sue with her infinite wisdom said it was too early in our friendship to accept my proposal of marriage. There came a time when Sue had to return to 'The Port', her parents' house at East Portlemouth, in her Morris Minor. We agreed to travel in convoy on the A38, with me behind her in my A40 Farina, as far as the Victoria Inn at Roche on Bodmin Moor, then owned and managed by my cousin Bill Musitano and his wife Pam. Having received a negative reply to my verbal proposal and knowing that Sue had been both a Brownie and Girl Guide, I resorted to a bit of persuasion using the morse code. As we motored along, I flashed a signal in dots and dashes, many times over, with my headlights, to be seen in her driving mirror, which spelt out the words 'I love you.' Over lunch, Sue said she decoded it alright and appreciated my loving thoughts. I felt it brought us a bit closer and we laughed a lot at the novelty of sending such an intimate message in such a public way. Bill and Pam gave us a lovely lobster lunch, for which they were renowned, and after showing us their two caged monkeys, Ug and Og, in the garden, we went our separate ways, Sue to 'The Port' and me back to 'Penvrane'.

Early in September the Kinloch Bryces returned to Warsash where Elsie and Frank were pleased to welcome us back. At her parent's house, Sue found a favourite uncle, Arthur Harding, her mother's eldest of three brothers, staying with them. He was at the time Marine Superintendent of British Paints. When helping Arthur with his baggage from house to car, Sue said 'Why have you got your best suit down here?' and he replied 'Because right now I'm driving to Southampton to go aboard the liner *Canberra* and supervise the treating of the ship's bottom with our anti-fouling paint.' Noticing an enthusiastic glint in her eyes he said 'Would you like to come too?' and instantly Sue's answer was a very positive 'Yes please.'

Before continuing my memories, I feel it would be helpful if I gave you some history of the Harding family, which I didn't know when I first met Uncle Arthur. He and his wife Joyce had reared two sons, Peter and Barry, born in 1919 and 1923 respectively. In WW2, Peter went into the RAF and became a Spitfire pilot specializing in photo-reconaissance and Barry was serving his apprenticeship in the Merchant Navy as a cadet in the New

Zealand Shipping Company. In February '42, both boys were reported missing at the same time. Eventually Arthur and Joyce were relieved to hear that Peter had crashed his plane over Germany, but was alive and safe in a POW-camp, Stalag Luft 3. More about him in a later chapter. The news about Barry, however, was most distressing. He had perished when his ship, the *Opawa* was torpedoed by a U-boat in the North Atlantic.

Resuming my story, during their journey, Sue told Uncle Arthur about me and my seafaring background. When they arrived at the Polygon Hotel, he booked a room for Sue, and her voice by phone invited me to dine with them that evening. Closed up at the bar in the Polygon, with Uncle Arthur calling the drinks, for Sue a dry sherry and for him and me large pink gins plus tonic, he turned to me and said 'Sue told me today that you were trained in HMS *Worcester* and so I wonder whether you know Pete Luard?' 'Indeed I do,' said I. 'He was the same term as me in '36 and a particular chum in a small gang on board.' Arthur went on to explain that Luard had been a fellow cadet with Barry aboard the *Opawa*, and when on survivor's leave came to tell them the tragic story. Apparently two lifeboats got away from the ship, but only the one with Luard in survived, the other one with Barry didn't. Arthur admired Pete Luard's gesture as his son's shipmate and said that his other son, Peter, after the war, sailed a lot with Luard in the Medway. That evening I discovered that my beloved Sue was descended from a variety of nautical characters. The Balkwills owned the ships, the Evans family built them and the Hardings and Masters sailed them, out of Salcombe, for generations, as topsail schooners. Uncle Arthur would like to have gone to sea, but he was colour-blind and failed the eyesight test.

After I'd departed for home Sue asked Uncle Arthur 'Well did you like him?' and he replied promptly, 'Of course I liked him, very much indeed. He's a sailor isn't he?' When I heard about his appraisal of me, it was the start of a firm friendship for many years to come. Arthur was in fact the first member of Sue's family to know how we felt about each other, although many friends at that time had noticed our affection for one another. After the autumn term started and Sue was teaching again in Berkhamsted, lots of people helped us to see more of each other in September and October. Libby Todd, the Jephcott's 'au pair', for one, fixed it with her parents, Sandy and Thelma, for Sue to stay a week-end at their house in Southampton and this made it possible for me to introduce her to Frank and Elsie, who reacted in the kindest way. For many week-ends following they asked Sue to stay with them at their place, just ten minutes walk away from 'Pippins', which made it easier for her to get to know them and our many friends in the neighbourhood.

Some week-ends I would go in Sue's direction and stay on the fringe of Berkhamsted with Jim and Doreen Harvey, of similar age to Sue's parents, in their sixties, and long established friends from the days when both families lived in Stratford-upon-Avon, where Sue was born in 1930. Alan

Balkwill, Sue's father, had been a dentist in Sheep Street until he retired in 1961 because of ill health. He and Ella, Sue's mother, generally called Mrs B, then went to live permanently at 'The Port', one of two houses left to Ella and her sister Esme by their mother, Bessie Harding (née Masters), instead of using it just for holidays. Now, I hope you can begin to see how friendships and relationships were working to our advantage. Sue rented a tiny cottage, two up and two down, in Aldbury for £10 a month, which was most reasonable on her salary as head of a department, £1,500 a year, £200 more than me, then. Aldbury was a typical old English village, close to Tring and about 4½ miles from Berkhamsted, under the shadow of Ashridge Forest. Her address was 10 Stocks Road, the main thoroughfare through the middle past the pond with stocks beside it and opposite the popular Greyhound Inn.

It was at number 10, a trustworthy setting, without spin, that I suggested splicing to Sue for the second time and was accepted, to the accompaniment of a Mozart horn concerto. The Greyhound and I benefited from her wise decision. This was just before half-term and Sue suggested we went to Devon together to tell her parents. We did this and I insisted on going through the ritual of asking her father for the hand of his daughter in marriage, for fun, but naturally expecting him to produce a bottle of something, which he did. The next move was to Auntie Muriel's, one of Alan's sisters, married to William Grose, who lived in a large house, 'Swallows', opposite the Thurlestone Hotel, which they owned, and I was inspected by a mass of relatives, all friendly folk, whom I grew to love later. At the time I was terrified and like the sailor in Gilbert and Sullivan's opera *HMS Pinafore*, I felt like singing the line about 'Her sisters and her cousins and her aunts,' many times over. We made plans to get married in the summer of '64 and Sue said she would like Michael McAdam to conduct the Service. He was a close friend of Sue's at Cambridge in the fifties and at that time Chaplain and teacher at Hurstpierpoint School. I readily agreed and so did he. What I liked about him was how he wanted to get to know me before the wedding and came to Warsash for a week-end, at my invitation, to meet me and the family. It was very worthwhile. More about Michael later.

We went with the joyful news to Cardiff to see my Mum and Dad and also sister Betty with Malcolm and family. Dear old Dad we found was then breathing with difficulty due to his emphysema, but Mum was her usual sparkling self and both were delighted with their daughter-in-law to be. From there we crossed the Severn by car ferry from Beachley to Aust and stayed a night with Sue's sister Bridget and husband Jerry and baby Katy, living temporarily at Winterbourne, north-east of Bristol. Jerry was with Freeman Fox, designing engineers, busy building the first bridge over the Severn. Sue was one of three mistresses at Berkhamsted Girls School engaged to be married and leaving at the end of the summer term. This caused Miss Russell, an Edinburgh Scot and Head Mistress, to make reference to the Book of Judges in the Bible, on Speech Day, saying 'The hosts of Midian have encamped around my staff!' A lovely lady, her humour went down well as did her best wishes to the trio.

In July before Peta's thirteenth birthday on the 18th, when she was given a new bicycle, I sold 'Pippins' and bought 'Selbourne' in Greenaway Lane. This was a chalet type house, where the three of us lived, with only a cottage between us and 'Brook Cottage' containing Elsie and Frank. Down in Devon, before the summer of '64, Sir Harry had bought the two houses at the other end of the terrace from 'The Port' and after converting them into holiday homes he gave one to each of his sons, Anthony and Neil. This made it easier for them to relax, with no more anxiety about sand on Sir Harry's expensively installed floor in 'Thalassa'. Neil and Denny had the end house called 'Ferryside', next to the jetty used by the Salcombe ferry-boats, and that is where I stayed with them before the wedding, arranged for 29 August. Charles had mumps in August, but recovered in time not to be infectious and risk passing it on to others.

Michael McAdam stayed at the Rectory with the Rev. Baugham, Rector of St Winwalloe, on the top of the hill in the village of East Portlemouth. Baugham was a jovial cleric who hurried on foot from place to place in his parish, but found time for a chat when we met him quite often, out and about. He would always conclude the chat by waving his arms and saying 'I must fly, goodbye,' and it became a habit of mine to say to Sue, with an upward glance, 'He's off to Head Office again.' Sir Harry and Lady Jephcott, who were then in residence at 'Thalassa', kindly offered their house, with its large living room and spacious garden, for the wedding reception and the Balkwill parents accepted gladly. Peta, Charles and I stayed at 'Ferryside' with Neil, Denny, David, Penny and Mark, sand and seaweed everywhere, plus Libby and her boy-friend John Granger, making a full house. My mother stayed at 'Thalassa' and sister Betty with nephew Paul put up somewhere in Salcombe. Dad was not fit enough to attend.

Paul, aged 17, was an usher with Jan, Sue's brother, aged 26. The senior bridesmaid was Peta, in charge of Catherine Dinn, aged 6 and Diana Wells, aged 5. Catherine was the daughter of Sue's cousin Helen, the eldest of three daughters to Layton, Alan's eldest brother, and Myfanwy. Diana was the daughter of John and New Zealander Alison, and also Sue's god-daughter. John was the son of Philip Wells, the Balkwill family doctor in Stratford-upon-Avon. Alan well remembered going to collect Philip in the small hours of 2 May, 1930, to be present and assist at the delivery of Susan Elisabeth, because he was surprised at the intensity of the nightingales' singing over Stratford as he sat in the garden waiting for the doctor to dress. Thereafter, in his birthday cards to Sue, he said on that date he always heard those nightingales singing. Sue's cousin Anne Balkwill from Thurlestone arranged the flowers most beautifully in the church and Bridget's husband

Jerry volunteered to cover the day from dawn to dusk with his 38 mm camera. We have this now, converted to a silent video.

Sue, Neil and I did a lot of forward planning for the big day. We agreed that the location lent itself to an unusual departure of bride and groom, immediately after the reception, which was customary in those days. The guests could progress from 'Thalassa' to the sandy beach, after all it was summertime, and wave goodbye to us as we went away over the water. Sue and I packed suitcases with our clothes for the honeymoon, all except the instant going-away clothes, and put them in my car which we planned to leave in the Marine Hotel car park on the Salcombe side of the estuary. The hotel agreed readily, realizing that some of our guests would also be theirs for the week-end, so, quid pro quo.

Saturday 29 August was fine, warm and sunny throughout and Jerry was around at an early hour as promised. After shooting the Red Ensign flying at the Port flagstaff, his next camera shot was of Sue and Peta in *Varnish*, the Port's rowing dinghy, returning across the harbour from a hair-do in Salcombe. In the forenoon, Neil and I set off in separate cars, driving round through Kingsbridge, at the top end of the estuary, in order to leave mine at the Marine Hotel, Salcombe. Before returning in his car, Neil suggested we had a quick one at the Shipwrights, a pub in the middle of Fore Street and only a short walk from the Marine. To my surprise, but not his, four male friends were already there when we arrived just after opening time, at 1100. They had a mischievous plot in mind, requiring my co-operation, which after a few beers provided by the popular landlord, Edgar Foale, was not difficult to obtain.

The idea was for Jerry, in Fore St, to film us acting three separate exit scenes from the Shipwrights, obviously with breaks between for the cast to re-enter. The first, was me coming out swaying slightly and being steadied by one of them on each side. The second, saw me staggering and needing to be propped up by the same two. Jerry, at a discreet distance was not noticeable and by this time, the passing public were taking an interest to witness my third exit, incapable me, arms and legs outstretched, being carried out by all four of them. To show my gratitude for the aid received, I must mention the names of those who gave it. Apart from Neil, Jan and Jerry there were two ex-Merchant Navy characters who met in the P&O Line and married sisters who were first cousins of Sue, Gillian and Wendy, daughters of Ella's sister Esme and Bill Stockwell, retired Secretary of P&O. Wendy's husband Geoff Cosgrave, an Australian, was an engineer and Paul Doggrell, Gill's spouse, a purser. How apt it was for me, the supposedly malt-maimed Master Mariner, to have such salubrious support from two fellow merchant seamen on my wedding day. After all that, they got me to the church on time.

When Neil and I walked up the aisle to take station, passing ushers Jan and Paul at the entrance, I glanced around at the guests already assembled and thought how absolutely spiffing they all looked. Spiffing was a word I had loved since hearing grown-ups use it a lot during my 1920s childhood. I have learned since that it came from an old fashioned slang word spiff, meaning spruce or smartly dressed, which suitably described those attending the wedding. At 2.30 p.m. the organist struck up with Suite No.1 in F of Handel's 'Water Music' to welcome my beautiful bride, Susan Elisabeth and her handsome father Alan Balkwill. As they drew closer, the Hornpipe, with its familiar beat, filled the church, providing a nautical touch, and our much loved friend Michael McAdam, after tying the knot, blessed our union with some well chosen words.

The reception at 'Thalassa' was simply topping, another 1920s slang word implying splendid or excellent. John Wells, bridesmaid Diana's father, spoke on behalf of the bride's family, as was customary in those days, ending with a toast to the bride and groom. I replied briefly and after toasting the bridesmaids, turned over to best man, Neil, who regaled everyone with many salty allusions, in which *Winwillow*'s voyage to Plymouth featured prominently. A celebrity of the day was undoubtedly Cousin Ella, aged 92, and my new mother-in-law Ella's first cousin, who lived in a cottage, facing 'The Port', on the Salcombe side of the harbour. She sat in an armchair, chain-smoked cigarettes, consumed champagne copiously and with her inimitable chuckle, enjoyed every minute, chatting to all ages. Today, in 2003, Ella's cottage is owned by her great-nephew, Captain Michael Hodder, living in Salcombe, now a retired Master Mariner, like his grandfather, Ella's brother, before him.

Being still obedient to old customs, we departed before the evening fun started, with those who shall be nameless, on the terrace by the sea-wall at Ferryside. We heard later that this was a really 'ripping' party (more 1920s slang), or should I say stripping party, because a young, glamorous, naked mermaid streaked, then dived into the sea, swiftly pursued by an enthusiastic yachtsman seeking further seafaring experience, despite loud protests from a related lady onlooker. Our departure by dinghy as planned, at about 5.30 p.m., was quite a dramatic event. Guests had drifted down from 'Thalassa' onto the sands, already populated by lots of holiday folk, who asked if a film was being made. Bridesmaids held up their dresses and paddled in the sea, whilst Neil with the tails of his morning coat tucked into his swimming trunks, helped Sue and me into the boat, for the voyage across to the Marine Hotel.

There is no better way to start a honeymoon than by going somewhere special, and that we did. Not Barbados or the Seychelles, as is customary nowadays, but for us then, it was Branscombe on the south Devon coast, 15 miles east of Exeter, near Beer and midway between Sidmouth and Seaton. This area from 1700 to 1850 was renowned for its smuggling activities and we had booked a table for 8.30 p.m., to dine at the Masons Arms, Branscombe. Whilst sipping Remy-Martin after enjoying lobster, with a bottle of Chablis, we couldn't help wondering how this exquisite brandy had found its way across the Channel. After the meal, we went a further 40 miles east to Dorchester, where we checked-in to a previously booked room at the King's Arms Hotel. All the staff could talk about was how Mick Jagger and the Rolling Stones had stayed there the previous night and wasn't it a pity we had missed them. Peta and Charles would have reacted with much greater interest. Now, in July 2003, MJ has just turned 60, so he was 21 in 1964 and would have been celebrating his first year of fame.

Next morning we motored south to Weymouth, put the car into a long term car park and sailed away to Guernsey in the good ship *Sarnia*. We stayed at the Fermain Hotel, named after the Bay, about six miles south of the capital, St Peter Port, on the east coast and hired a Lambretta, for mobility, to scoot around this compact sunny island. Sue laughed at the sight of me, but said I looked very dashing in a black skid-lid, then required by law, to be worn by the driver, but not by the pillion passenger, at that time. Guernsey was good for us in all respects. Wonderful wild life surrounded us and in a behavioural sense we created some too. Soon we discovered La Bette, a tiny bay, down a very steep path, on the south coast, near Icart, where we remained undisturbed by others, on our daily visits. Here, we could skinny dip, sip champagne cocktails and snooze on the warm sand until awakened by the incoming tide. Usually we took lunch, with a bottle of Muscadet, our favourite wine, kept cool in a rocky pool.

The Lambretta lent itself to off the road travel, along many suitably safe cliff paths on the south coast. When we stopped to explore a concrete German observation point, I was reminded of shells straddling my destroyer offshore, in '44, which must have come from a battery near to where we were. On Thursday 3 September, the 25th anniversary of the start of WW2, a thought was spared for the endurance of people in the Channel Islands, as the only British territory occupied by the Germans in WW2. On that day we toured the west and north with its lower coastline and after a swim followed by a seafood, Muscadet lunch we attended the Point to Point Steeplechase Races at L'Ancresse Common. It was our lucky day, for we backed the winner, 'Red Ace', in the Guernsey Consolation Race, one of 14 runners. Some evenings we dined and danced at the Royal Hotel in St Peter Port, scooting back to the Fermain Hotel afterwards, and happily the weather was fine for most of our ten-day stay.

It was decidedly different on Friday, however, when we went to Sark, where it rained heavily all day. We walked uphill from the jetty to an open horse-drawn farm cart with seats, which took us plus ten companions to the Mermaid Tavern, motor vehicles such as cars and buses being banned on Sark. Here we dried out, partially, standing by a large fire and downing large brandies. After a snack lunch, we climbed back into the cart to be drenched again on the return journey to the *Commodore Queen*, which sailed for Guernsey just as the rain stopped. On Saturday we shopped around St Peter Port for presents to take home and treated ourselves to a Traditional Guernsey each, fitted at the Guernsey Knitting Box on South Esplanade, and advised to be worn loose, one size larger than normal. The rest of the weekend we spent exploring the St Martin's area especially the church of unknown age at La Bellieuse, with its well-busted stone statue of the Goddess of Fertility at the churchyard gate. Competent archaeologists had dated the stone at about 600 BC and said it was a statue menhir from the Bronze Age, of which there are many to be found on the continent.

Monday saw our last visit to La Bette beach, before turning in the Lambretta and going to see a very funny film at the local cinema, called *Bed-time Story* with David Niven and Marlon Brando. On Tuesday we sailed for Weymouth and shame on me, I cannot recall the name of the ship, but one owned by British Rail in those days, no doubt. Before continuing the tale of our life together in the UK, Sue and I thought it made sense, with Guernsey in mind, to include the story of our Silver Wedding holiday, when we returned there in 1989. So, here we go.

First of all, let me give you some background to our lives in 1989. We were living in St Albans with our son Andrew, aged 22 and daughter Fiona, 18, both of whom had jobs and could look after themselves. I had taken early retirement from my career in oil and been running my own company, from home, as a consultant, for eight years. Sue had resumed teaching part-time in '77 and was still doing so at J.F. Kennedy School in Hemel Hempstead. Also, it must be mentioned, that when we revisited the Channel Islands, for what we called our 'Silver Splice Holiday', we had more money at our disposal, which facilitated our movements through life, but didn't change our style. After staying with Ella, who was now a widow, at 'The Port', we rose early on Thursday, 10 August and set off for Torquay by car with both our Muddyfox mountain bikes carried on the roof. Having parked the car for our absence of two weeks, we boarded the *Devonian*, with our bikes, and sailed for Guernsey at 7.30 a.m.

We arrived in Guernsey at 1.30 p.m. and sailed for Sark at 5.00 p.m. after a bike ride round St Peter Port. The differences we noticed most between '64 and '89 were three, and all to do with density; people, peuple (!), everywhere, cars galore and keel-boats crammed in the harbour. Sue had booked a hotel room in Sark for five days and then a B and B in Guernsey for rest of our two weeks away, when we would be doing day trips to Herm and Alderney. We were pleased to have chosen thus and having enjoyed a 20-minute spray-drenched passage, with our bikes lashed on deck, we arrived at Creux Harbour on the east coast of that tiny feudal island. A bookmark purchased later summed up Sark most succinctly, by showing a drawing of a horse and cart, with the message 'A refuge from motor cars'.

Human beings could only go there by sea, as air travel was not allowed, which enhanced the poet Swinburne's appreciation of Sark as a 'Small, sweet world of wave-encompassed wonder.'

Our luggage was taken up the steep hill from the harbour to 'La Moinerie Farm' hotel, in a tractor-towed cart, this time, 25 years on. We followed with our bikes, walking or riding as inclined. The first meal was luscious and we were impressed by our room, the food, the staff and the service given, in this old converted farmhouse, run by Mr and Mrs Dewe. That evening, just after sunset, we walked through a dark avenue between trees for about 100 metres, close to the hotel, known as 'bat alley'. These excellent, elevated creatures, with their innate sense of sonar, flew in swarms around us, without colliding. It was a wonderful experience, by sight and sound, in no way frightening, and became a must after dinner throughout our stay. At the end of 'bat alley' was a five-barred gate on which to lean and catch a twilight glimpse of Herm, Jethou and Guernsey to the north and west.

La Moinerie was next to La Seigneurie, the seventeenth century home of the Seigneur, a Lord of the Manor, dating back to 1565. The most attractive feature of La Seigneurie was its large high walled garden, which was visited by us when open to the public on Saturday. For Sue, it was botanical bliss and when we saw a man tending plants, we presumed he was a gardener and she asked him a thing or two. He knew about everything and we realized that he was chief of all the gardeners, when he told us his name was Michael Beaumont, the then Seigneur, who had inherited the island from his grandmother Dame Sibyl Hathaway DBE on her death in 1974. She was known as the 'Dame of Sark' and we had seen a stage show by that name, some time before, at the Savoy Theatre, London, with Celia Johnson, who was superb playing Dame Sybil. It was about the German occupation and how the Dame succeeded in negotiating with the General in charge, helped by the fact that he was of the old school, 'nice' not 'nazi'.

Over the week-end we watched the fun and games generated by the Sark Water Carnival in Creux Harbour and visited a silversmiths where I bought Sue her 'Silver Splice' present in the shape of a bracelet made from silver mined on the island and hence without the usual hallmark. Most of our time was spent cycling and swimming all over the place. We cycled across La Coupée, the pathway to Little Sark down south, and swam daily at a bay on the west coast, Port du Moulin, a short walk from our hotel. On Tuesday we said a sad farewell to Sark and sailed away on the midday boat for Guernsey. After checking in at our B and B, the Kenwood in Allez Street, St Peter Port, we cycled to Fermain Bay for an evening's swim. The Fermain Hotel had changed and lacked nostalgic appeal, so we decided to dine at La Nautique, a restaurant overlooking the harbour, with beloved Sark as a soporific background.

Guernsey despite the three deterrent densities, based on our prejudices, was still offering many places of unpolluted charm and historical interest.

We found a quaint Victorian pillar-box, near Kenwood. The house of Victor Hugo (1802–1885), was closed for repairs, but I opened a bottle of Sancerre for lunch, in the shadow of his statue in Candie Gardens. We went underground to view the Museum of the German Occupation, from June '40 to May '45. We saw Sausmarez Manor, a place associated with a bygone naval admiral, and visited the butterfly centre, whose vast collection of colourful creatures settled on our hands and heads. La Bette beach was too popular for us to swim. One day, cycling through the streets of south St Peter Port, we were surprised to find people dancing and singing to a brass band. I asked a woman what it was all about and she replied, with a laugh, 'We are celebrating our victory over the English in 1066.' We joined in the merriment when we realized that Guernsey was an outlying part of Normandy until the thirteenth century and therefore Guernseymen had served under Duke William at the battle of Hastings. It was said, in fun, that England should have been called a Channel Island.

On the south side of the harbour's outer breakwater was Castle Cornet, where we witnessed the firing of an ancient cannon at noon, performed each day by men in ceremonial redcoat army jackets and black pill-box hats. Our happiest holiday discovery was the heavenly island of Herm, which lay only ten minutes away, to the east of Guernsey, by the passenger ferryboat, *Alouette*. In 1947 the States of Guernsey bought the island from the Crown for £15,000, after which Peter and Jenny Wood became tenants and made it their home in 1949. They changed a neglected wilderness into a scene of beauty and happily we met them by chance on a cliff walkabout and were able to praise their efforts in person. Their daughter Pennie returned to live on Herm with husband, Adrian Heyworth and their youngsters, to assist with the general management of the Island. Ten families lived and worked there all year round.

The Wood family own the island's lease until AD 2029 and every enterprise on Herm belongs to them. We visited the famous Shell Beach, on the north-east shore, composed entirely of shell fragments instead of sand. A cliff path round the island took a leisurely two hours to walk or longer if a swim and snack were included. Sue did a bit of painting sometimes and we always had a dip in Belvoir Bay, just south of Shell Beach. Herm was a delight to all the senses, a model of cleanliness, and rubbish bins were neither provided, nor needed. On the harbour quay a request greeted visitors, noticeably, but designed to fit unobstrusively into its natural surroundings, which said 'Please take your litter home with you and leave our Island clean.' From what we saw, this was done, which was wonderful to witness! Having fallen in love with Herm, we went there on our last three days, knowing that the boat trip always went close to Jethou islet, to show us the colourful Puffin birds who were breeding there. Very sexy!

One day we sailed to Alderney in a hydrofoil to make contact with the Duplain family, who had lived in 'The Port' from 1940 to '45 as evacuees.

Ralph and his wife Christine were then in their thirties, with son, David, aged five to ten. Fog cleared to sunshine as we entered Braye harbour. We tried the phone directory and enquiries without success, but after a few false leads in the lovely granite main street of St Anne we met a lady, by chance, who knew the name and directed us to their home through a passageway. Sue recognized Ralph, even though old and frail in his 70s, a widower, washing–up in his kitchen. He was thrilled to see her and called David, a confirmed bachelor in his 50s, whom Sue saw as a little boy during wartime holidays. We formed a happy foursome and they drove us round the island, complaining about the congestion, because there were then as many cars on Alderney as people. Two cricketing characters, John Arlott and Ian Botham, each had a house on the island, as also did singer Julie Andrews, famous for her role in the film *The Sound of Music*. A lot of lovely folk as well as a few celebrities lived on Alderney. Pity about the automobiles.

Saying goodbye to Guernsey in 1989, our Silversplice holiday over, means me reverting back to my memories in 1964, post honeymoon. We motored from Weymouth to East Portlemouth, collected Peta and Charles, then 13 and 6, and home to Warsash. As we entered 'Selbourne's' drive, a car followed us closely, containing Norman, my manager at the Portsmouth depot, who said 'Ian, I have to tell you that Southern Batteries Ltd is about to declare a state of bankruptcy.' Once again I was adrift upon the sea of life and wondering what course to steer?

CHAPTER 19

Changing jobs: Conoco and self-development – 1964–1971

WHEN NORMAN'S SHOCKING NEWS HAD SUNK IN, I was determined to share it with Sue only, not with Peta and Charles, whom I thought would worry about Dad being unemployed, which might affect all our expectations as a secure family group. This I achieved by mischievous, but I believe excusable, behaviour. After the kids had gone to school, I stayed at home, searching the newspapers for suitable job adverts and applying where appropriate, but before they were due home, I used to nip out and come back as though from work in Portsmouth. Donald Beswick, my MD, said how sorry he was, but I would have a month on pay to find another job. He was OK as a solicitor, but we agreed that I should try and return to the oil industry, so, I contacted lots of previous colleagues. My training and past experience in life caused me to be more confident than concerned, inspired by the old adage 'Grant me the serenity to accept the things I can not change; courage to change the things I can; and the wisdom to know the difference.'

I was aware that Regent had been split between Texaco and Chevron and many of my friends were working for new names such as Totale, Amoco, Murco, Gulf and Continental Oil (UK), from Ponca City, Oklahoma, USA, who spread internationally after finding oil in Libya and bought Jet Petroleum in order to market in the UK. Very few people knew about our misfortune and we kept it that way. Those who did, such as Frank and Elsie Pearce, Jan Balkwill and Neil Jephcott were naturally sympathetic, but our parents and the kids didn't know, until I had found another job. However, it is a month I shall never forget. Not only did I apply for jobs by post, but with my knowledge of industry in the area, I drove around and dropped into many businesses, on the off chance that there might be a vacancy. I remember a near miss, when I called on Polybond's head-office and saw the MD, who said 'Pity you didn't call earlier. I've just taken on a new Sales Manager this very morning.' Any spare time, I thought, would best be filled by creating something with my hands. I recalled the relaxation achieved when making the dolls' house for Peta, after I had left the sea and was searching for a shore job. Looking around for a likely task, I decided that our antique oak sideboard needed a substantial wooden shelf installed in the left hand side cupboard. I enjoyed doing that and inscribed thereon with a black felt pen, the following message for posterity: 'Made by IKB as therapy, (in 1964) when out of work, between Southern Battery and Continental Oil.' Frank from his senior contacts in the oil industry had said 'Ian, I hear that Continental Oil Company are recruiting personnel and going to build a refinery in the UK. That means they're likely to stay, whereas some companies are inclined to come and go. Also, I'm told that their Manager in London is Jack Nolan, who would remember you from Regent days, and so I suggest you write to him.' I did that and received a very positive reply suggesting I went through the usual procedure and applied to the Personnel Manager, Steve Lloyd, whose assistant was Brian Murray, a close friend to this day. After a plus interview in London I was recommended to Ricky Latham, the Western Regional Manager, based in Cardiff.

We left Peta and Charles in the care of Elsie and Frank in Warsash, whilst Sue accompanied me to Cardiff, which once again became the focal point in my life. I was seen by Latham with his Sales Superintendent, Keith Boyce, who would be my immediate boss and very soon a close friend. They agreed to give me the job of Sales Representative in Worcestershire, commencing on 1 November, 1964, and I told Sue the good news when I collected her from the Museum in the Civic Centre, where she had been during my interview. We stayed overnight with my parents, whom we made privy to the situation, and thus we celebrated my success at finding employment so soon. As my father said 'I'm glad you didn't have to go "on the dole" my son,' a 1930's expression that told of many poor souls, less fortunate than me, who were out of work and sometimes starving. My new job meant driving north from Warsash to my area on Monday morning and returning on Friday evening, until I found suitable accommodation for the family up there. My area included some of the loveliest country in the Midlands. From the south side of Birmingham, it covered the counties of Worcestershire and Warwickshire, parts of Herefordshire and Gloucester-shire, including the Cotswolds from Birdlip to Bladon. In the following year, 1965, Winston Churchill was buried in the graveyard at Bladon church, just round the corner from Blenheim Palace, where he was born in 1874.

I became an oil Rep again with confidence, drawing on selling experience with Regent, enhanced by buying skills gained with Southern Battery. This time as a Rep I was selling fuels into the Industrial Market only, appropriately called 'Direct to Consumer', in short 'D to C'. The Retail Market, supplying the public, was cared for by Company colleagues in 'Jet Petroleum', with whom we kept in close communication. Before our name was changed from Continental Oil (UK) to Conoco, a few years after I joined, the common reaction from prospects, when I said who I represented, was 'Tell us then, what part of Europe are you from?' At least it created curiosity and presumably my diplomatic response clarified the situation. I found lots of interesting prospects in my vast area, many of whom became customers and some close friends. However, my top priority that autumn was finding a home for the family. Thinking that a sensible place to live for schools and other amenities would be Malvern, just west of Worcester, Sue joined me for a successful weekend search. We decided to buy a new house building in Halfkey Road, Malvern Link, on the edge of farmland, which would be ready in the autumn of '65, and meantime we rented a spacious first floor flat in a block called Nether Grange, centrally situated in Great Malvern.

We moved to Malvern in April '65, with Selbourne still unsold, but happily a buyer paid our asking price a few weeks later. Peta went to the Convent School in Worcester and Charles to North Malvern Junior School. No longer able to sail dinghies on the Hamble, we thought camping would be a fun leisure activity in future. I spotted some second-hand tents on display in a field and paid just £30 for two ridge tents, each 9 ft by 6 ft, plus door-guards and a bell-end to act as a kitchen. They were last used by us as children's play areas at a garden party in St Albans, thirty years later. That must be my best bargain ever, for putting a roof over our heads, amortizing at £1 per year and no mortgage! The best camping country was to the west of a north/south line on my area from Ludlow through Leominster to Hereford and that's where I searched for a suitable site. Diverting from business one day, I drove along a grassy, leafy lane about ten miles west of Leominster and found an ideal field where the Lime brook entered the river Lugg, with a farmhouse on a hill nearby. I drove into the farmyard which contained a few well groomed horses outside their stables, on one side, a disused diesel jeep, on the other and in the middle a fine figure of a man, in his fifties or sixties, wearing breeches and a well-worn trilby hat whose brim suggested that his worthy steeds had used it for nourishment frequently. He must have wondered what I wanted. When I asked him if I could bring my family to camp on his field by the Lugg at week-ends his reply was instant and most memorable. 'Any time you like, you're welcome,' said Farmer Pritchard. 'It's good for you city folk to get out of the smoke.' 'What about rent?' said I. 'Oh, a box of cigarettes'll do me and we can have a good old chat, can't we?' Thus started a great friendship and many happy years at what we named Lugglime camp.

In Worcester, I revived my friendship with Ted Burnham, a shipmate in the training ship HMS *Worcester* from '36 to '38, who had left the sea post-war to become a co-director, with his father George and brother Eric, in 'Worcester Garages Ltd'. Their business was in a central square of the city opposite the King Charles pub, which was handy for meeting local celebrities. It was there that I met Dick Howorth and Syd Buller, both distinguished cricketers in their time, for Worcestershire County Cricket Club (WCCC) and because they lived over the river in St Johns, on my way to Malvern, I would often give them a lift home, after a pub session. Dick, a Lancashire lad, was a reputable slow left-arm spinner and Syd, after wicket-keeping, a famous umpire for many years. At his house, Dick would say 'Come on in for a drink and Ian can give us a tune on my inherited piano.' Dick, aware of the arthritis in his legs, would listen to me and say 'If I'd learned to play piano as a lad, rather than cricket, I'd be feeling a lot better now at my age.' Syd's reaction was 'Don't be daft Dick; you'd have missed playing in those Tests for England in the West Indies and running your sports shop, near the bridge, when you retired.'

After moving into 'Midships', the name we gave our house in Halfkey Road, with its easy access to the Malvern Hills for walking, we went to kennels in Herefordshire and bought a golden labrador pup, named Tarka by Peta. We already had a black and white cat of six years seniority as a pet, called Colonel Pinto from the 'Spycatcher' TV show in the fifties, who disliked Tarka's intrusion intensely. However, he soon accepted her playful company and they curled up in a basket together. In '66, after two successful years selling in the Midlands I was promoted to a new role, in the Western Region, as Rep in charge of Authorized Distributors (ADs), financially sponsored by Conoco and selling under our name, plus ex-tank buyers, who bought in bulk, which helped to keep our depot costs down, and sold under their own brand name. This elevation provided me with a regional office situated in the Depot at Cardiff Docks.

In December '66 I took up this job, which meant living away from home during the week. Happily I was able to stay with my parents in Cardiff, who were compensated by Conoco for my accommodation, until the family moved down, during the school hols, in April '67. We had found a suitably large semi-detached house in Insole Gardens, Llandaff and Sue, seven months pregnant, was able, later, to sing in Llandaff Choral Society at the Cathedral. Usually a home relocation was inconvenient for all family members, but this one was emotionally fortuitous for me, because I saw my father many times during the last few months of his life. In March, he died peacefully at Llandough Hospital about a week after standing face to face with me in the living room of his home, gasping for breath and saying 'Ian, my son, I think it's time I went to join the boys,' and I knew he meant his mates killed in Flanders in the 14–18 war. His will left money for his grandchildren Peta and Charles and being aware of Sue's condition, a similar amount for the wee bairn *en ventre*, as it was stated.

Peta went back to the Convent in Worcester, boarding for the summer term, to complete her 'O' Levels and Charles joined a local school in Llandaff. Our son, Andrew Kinloch, always called Andy, was born in St David's Hospital, Cowbridge Road, Cardiff, on 26 June '67. It was a first for Sue and also for me, in as much that I was present at his birth, in a building which no longer exists. Andy's arrival prompted me to name our house 'Spica', after a star I used when navigating at sea, whose letters indicated our family names, Sue, Peta, Ian, Charles and Andy. Betty and I arranged the sale of the bungalow, 56 Bettws-y-Coed Road, and moved mother into a rented flat in Mackintosh Place, with her own furniture, where she was well cared for by a widowed landlady, Winnie Hoyle. Winnie happily endured Zillah's constant chatter and enjoyed her piano-forte on the first floor. Lots of local kids called to get 'Ginny', the name given her by grandchildren, to play the latest pop tunes, which delighted her, and the minister from a Wesleyan Chapel nearby, of which she had become a member, looked in often for a chat.

Having an office in the Depot, beside Roath Dock, Cardiff, enabled me to meet many Conoco colleagues other than Sales Reps in the Region. Ray Whiteley was an experienced and efficient manager of the depot, with skilled tanker drivers, office and yard staff under his direction. Ricky Latham, Regional Manager, Keith Boyce and I had offices on the first floor and in Ricky's absence, one of us would assume control of the Region as convenient. Two staff characters that I remember well, were Len Hancock, a driver, who had always provided useful information when contacted delivering to my customers in the Midlands and Harry Bird, a senior driver and amiable 'shop steward' in the Transport and General Workers Union (TGWU), who would help me resolve a tricky situation two years later.

Relatively speaking, Aunt Darkie (Dorcas), my Uncle Harry's childless widow, of happy childhood memories for me in Paignton and Clevedon, was nearing her end in an old people's home at Devizes. We brought her to Cardiff for a holiday, where she was horrified to see Andy, about a year old, bouncing up and down, strapped in his swing seat in a doorway, a recent invention then, sold as an alternative to the boredom of life in a playpen. She repeatedly said 'Ian, you won't let me end up in a workhouse will you?' 'No Auntie,' I replied, 'you'll depart this life from the happy home you're in now,' but she refused to believe that workhouses, so prevalent in her youth as a nurse, were no more.

In 1963, my niece, Christine, had married John Stanley (always Jack to me) and in '67 they were living in Penarth, near my sister Betty, Malcolm and Paul, in the midst of creating a family of their own, exotically called Juanita, Manuel, Dominique and Giovanni. Jack was then with Guest Keen & Nettlefold (GKN), who had a steel factory and offices on the opposite side of Roath Dock. He was a big man, over 6 feet and weighing 22 stone. His shoulder length hair usually covered one eye, causing him to jerk his head backwards to see what went on. The biggest part of him was his heart and we were good friends until his untimely death in 2000.

Jack was born in '39, the same year as Christine, the son of a C of E Rector, and after graduating at Corpus Christi College, Cambridge, developed a successful career in Personnel Management, with the emphasis on Training, whilst moving through many large, notable companies in the UK. Such names as Cadbury, GKN, Dunlop, Rank Xerox and Ladbroke featured in his CV, before he established his own company called International Training (IT). His curriculum attracted senior executives from government departments and large multinational organizations, including Conoco, prepared to pay his proportionately large fees. I met many colleagues of his, including Barry Payne, Chris Glasson and Haydn Jones, all of whom I still see regularly, when invited by any one of them, or Jack's brother Mike Stanley, to be their guest at the Naval & Military Club, better known as the 'In & Out', St James's Square, London. Jack is always remembered as a good, generous man, who was never known to be mean, in fact to such an extent that ultimately he endured serious financial difficulties. He indulged himself often, but somehow, he looked right riding around in a Silver Cloud Rolls Royce.

Come 1968, Conoco changed the shape of its Industrial Market sales force in the UK from four Regions to eight Districts reporting direct to Head Office in London and after a collective selection interviewing session, I was one of eight promoted and became District Manager Midlands. It was during this procedure that I first met Tony Dixon, also promoted and who later became manager of Training in Personnel Department, where I joined him in '73. This time in the Midlands we settled in Stourport-on-Severn, where we found a lovely old reconditioned barn in Lickhill Road, opposite a spacious green-grass park, sensibly dedicated by the council in 1919 to those killed in WW1, with trees and tennis courts, much appreciated by all of us, including Tarka and Col. Pinto. Not quite all of us, because Peta, then aged 17, decided to stay on at Canton High School and happily was able to live with my sister Betty and family in Penarth. The Barn, with its walled garden, was a great joy for Sue to cultivate beds of shrubs and for wee Andy to play with Tarka, his cuddly chum. Also, we were close walking distance for shops and baby-sitters. Under the stairs in the Barn was my office; that's the way it was in those days; wives at home acted as secretary, without reward, but more about that later.

I established an immediate communication system that would not intrude on our private lives. My evenings in Regent Oil Co. as manager had been disturbed by phone calls from Reps who had an end-of-day problem they thought impossible to resolve. Now I said to my Reps, 'Sleep on it and phone me only between 0730 and 0800, no later, next morning, if you need to.' I received very few early morning calls, as a result of their subconscious activity. My team of eight salesmen was a pleasure to lead. In my mind, they were shipmates aboard an oil tanker called 'Conoco UK'. Who would have thought that I could adapt happily to an air-polluted life in the middle of England after a breezy life in mid-ocean? Also, I adopted a leadership style which I believed was right by having read Douglas McGregor's book on man management. He declared that motivation was not achieved by the usual carrot and stick technique. Instead, he was sure that it lay within each of us and could best be activated by creating a climate where people, like plants, used their own potential for growth. This would give greater satisfaction to individuals and the team overall, when going for their objectives.

During my tenure, from '68 to '71, a sales meeting occurred every month at various places such as the 'Mitre Oak Hotel', close to Stourport, a pub in West Bromwich opposite the football ground of the recent FA Cup winners, and the Belfry Hotel near Sutton Coldfield, but gradually we centred, regularly, on the Birmingham Chamber of Commerce, of which I was a member, at Five Ways in Brum. Over this period there were changes, but I always had 8 Reps from 13 names that I insist on recalling, under our title of – 'The Brew XI Team (Mitchell & Butlers beer) – The Men of The Midlands' – displayed in a badge showing hands, with exposed index fingers, pointing upwards, on either side of a Conoco crest, undersubscribed with the words 'Digiti Nobis Semper Extracti'; in the vernacular, 'We always have our fingers well out!' The design was by Allan Gardiner and amongst many uses was distributed as our Christmas card to colleagues and chosen senior managers within the Company. Let me list those Brew XI Beermates by name: Mike Burke, John Ellis, Roy Emery, John Fellows, Allan Gardiner, Mark Hulls, Arthur Leek, David Maxwell, John Nicklin, David Nurse, Dennis Rothwell, John Whatmore and David Whitehead. A distinguished collection of characters if ever there was.

Being mindful that training subordinates was a most important part of a manager's job, I introduced role playing at meetings. To develop our selling skills, half the team acted as buyers who gave the other half, in their normal role as salesmen, the most difficult time by asking diabolical questions about products and giving obstructive answers, within reason, such proceedings being presided over by me, as referee. Also, I gave each Rep in turn the opportunity to chair a monthly meeting, with me as a Rep in his team, at the end of which I would call upon another group member to conduct a constructive critique to determine what we had done well and what we might have done better. These occasions were fun amidst a lot of serious learning, which proved worthwhile during future sales encounters with the more professional buyers of such prospective customers as Dunlop, GKN, Rover and the Birmingham Corporation.

The most important deal during my time in the Midlands was the contract with Wimpey, who were building a long stretch of the new M6 motorway just north of Coventry. They set up a base camp from which to operate at Corley Ash and we provided large storage tanks for gas oil (red dyed, untaxed, diesel) and two bowsers (small tankers) to distribute this fuel to their equipment on site. It was big gallonage and required our constant and careful attention. We had to deliver from our small depot in West Bromwich, fed by road from Ellesmere Port, before a larger shared terminal at Kingsbury, rail-fed from our Refinery at Immingham, came on stream later in '69. From memory, Wimpey had about 10 Euclid earth-movers using up to 20 gallons an hour when driven flat out, which amounted to 2,000 gallons a day, and if they worked round the clock night and day it would be twice as much. I think their storage capacity, on loan from us, was 6,000 gallons, and so it usually meant a top-up delivery every day from us.

John Fellows was the Rep on whose area Wimpey was situated, a young conscientious Coventry born lad, who either called in person or phoned them daily to discover if any problems had arisen and kept me fully informed. I would call with him on Wimpey at least once a week, which resulted in an excellent rapport with the key man on site, a large loquacious Irishman called Mick Deasey. His manager trusted him to be in charge and we had Mick's co-operation and trust when difficulties occurred on the job. Off the job, he always appreciated a visit to the local pub for a pint or two of Guinness and so did we. John and I visited Corley Ash one afternoon and found friend Deasey in some distress. He said 'It's glad I am to see you indeed 'cos I'm low on fuel and your depot declared that they can't deliver today.' 'Tell us,' we said and listened. 'Well,' continued Mick, 'I phoned West Brom, just now and that's what they said, which is no good for us, we must have more fuel by this evening 'cos we're working all night and my manager has told me to get it from elsewhere if necessary and that would mean you losing our business as a result. So, can you get those West Brom bastards to deliver now, today, and save your skins as it were?' 'You bet we can Mick, we'll drive to the depot immediately, fix it and I'll see you get a load before sunset.'

On the way back to base, I should have realized the reason for this hiatus, but I didn't, until it was spelt out by Harry Bird, senior driver and shop-steward, together with the senior clerk who dealt with orders and was responsible for the smooth running of the depot. They said in unison that all the drivers had completed their legitimate driving time for the day. Harry I had known for five years since joining Continental Oil in Cardiff and it seemed we had developed a high regard for one another in our respective jobs. This is when it paid off. Looking back on what appeared to be an impossible situation, I believe I saw Harry as a Chief Buffer of a small ship in my past, with the initiative to 'take action this day'. Anyway, after seeking John's co-operation, I said 'Harry, are you prepared to look the other way whilst John, as my mate, and I, both in Conoco overalls, load a 2,000 gallon tanker and deliver the goods to Wimpey?' 'Yes Ian,' he said, 'for you I will.' What an adventurous journey that was. Me, without a Heavy Goods Vehicle (HGV) licence, coping with difficulty at first, but soon getting used to it and thanking heavens the police didn't intervene. I stopped the traffic on a main road north of Coventry for at least five minutes, as I couldn't change gear turning right for our destination. When Mick saw who was doing the delivery he danced with delight, our day was made and the business was saved. I had to thank my training with Regent Oil for helping me, but now, in the 21st century, apprenticeships seem to have vanished. At the end of day, a Guinness was good for all of us!

Don Booth was Fleet Engineer, stationed in Head Office and responsible for the condition and maintenance of all Conoco tankers in the UK. I didn't know him until '71, but I heard that he was an efficient operator who liked moving about and dropping in on depots without warning. His car was known as a mobile ashtray because its upholstery inside was stained dark brown from his chain-smoking habit. He could smoke freely in the car but not in a depot, which possibly accounted for his continuous countrywide circulation. One day he visited West Bromwich and was horrified to find one of his tankers on chocks, minus both front wheels and its gear-box. 'What is the meaning of this,' he shouted, at the depot mechanic, who replied, 'Well sir, Mr Fellows has been telling us to let Wimpey have any parts they want to keep their bowsers, similar models to this, operating on the M6 motorway.'

Back in London, Don saw Dennis Mackett, Marketing Director and said 'One of my vehicles has been cannibalized in West Bromwich Depot, by instructions from your local Rep, to help Wimpey, presumably with your approval, but why wasn't I consulted?' 'This is news to me Don,' said Dennis, 'but I'll find out why,' and he phoned me that evening. 'Ian, do you know anything about this vehicle being dismantled?' 'Yes sir, I do. I authorized it, to keep the show on the road, realizing that reference to HO, like the Admiralty in wartime, would mean indefinite delay.' I received a mild rebuke from Dennis, but he obviously liked what I'd done and I never heard another word. Dennis had been in the RNVR in WW2 and I believe that he, like me, approved of decisions and action being taken by the man in command on the spot.

> When phone bells ring;
> Then I get a feeling it's Wimpey;
> Come over to Corley Ash right away.
> Ring-ting-a-ling; I wonder what can be worrying Wimpey;
> It's not the bowsers this time, it's the fuel they say.
> Because those Irish noses keen
> Think they smell kerosene,
> But flash-point 159,
> Proves it's from the diesel line:
> So praises we sing, as the road-work resumes after respite;
> On the Conoco/Wimpey M6 Motorway.

These words I sang as a parody to Fats Waller's music, composed in 1929, for the song 'I Get a Feeling I'm Falling', in order to remember this five hour stoppage due to an erroneous sense of smell. Wimpey's staff thought the wrong product had been sent to them, their first delivery from the new terminal at Kingsbury, so, they stopped everything before phoning John Fellows and me. We dashed to Corley Ash immediately, took samples and got two independent laboratories to analyse, which proved happily that diesel had in fact been delivered.

I did many more parodies to the tunes of Thomas Waller, being a long standing fan of his. Sue, some years before, had sold her little-used Solo sailing boat in Salcombe and bought a mini-piano instead. For fun, in the Barn, I sat for hours recording what I called 'My Marketing Melodies '69', on a tape recorder borrowed from training department. I found a Recording Company in Birmingham who produced single discs, which I sent to selected Company colleagues for Christmas. Frequently, the bowsers at Wimpey had dirt in their fuel filters, when Mick Deasey always said 'It's sand from the desert, 'cos these waggons are old enough to have been with Monty fighting Rommel at El Alamein in 1942.'

On such occasions I called upon the skills of Dave Mackay, vehicle maintenance engineer at Immingham and Cleethorpes, who always came pronto and put things right. Dave as a lad in his 'teens played fabulous football for Grimsby Town when they were 1st Division, and his Dad wanted him to make it his career, but Mum said 'No way, he's got to have a proper job,' and he ended-up in Conoco's Head Office with Ron Perrin, in charge of terminals and traffic management countrywide. Both were determined to put all their subordinates through my training, when I switched jobs in '73, which gave us a lasting rapport and filled my courses. Dave produced a poem for those attending the 'Driver of the Year Contest', which appeared in the House Magazine *Conocoverage* October '69 issue. I include it here, because I believe it is even more appropriate in this day of the 'mobile phone':

> You watch the man who drives ahead,
> And the man who drives behind,
> You watch to the left and watch to the right
> And drive with a calm clear mind.
> But the man you really have to watch
> On the roadway, you will find,
> Is the man behind the man ahead,
> And ahead of the man behind.

Problems occurred frequently and most of you readers will appreciate that my dear wife Sue was often left wondering what time I would get home for an evening meal. Whenever possible I would phone and say. Once, when I called to inform her that it would be gone nine and I would eat something cold, I got a swift reply from Sue who said 'Oh, darling, that's terrible. You'll miss your favourite show on TV "The Troubleshooters".' My response is unprintable, considering the situation I was in, troubleshoot-ing, for real, with Wimpey on the M6. The TV show was topical and popular, based around a fictitious oil company called 'Mogul' with the Chairman and Deputy well acted by Geoffrey Keen and John Carson. What improved the viewing enjoyment for me, was knowing that these two characters, in their roles of Mogul oil chiefs, Brian Stead and James Langley, had earlier in the year visited a Conoco rig in the North Sea 'to get a bit of atmosphere,' whilst recording a new BBC series. Their picture was in a previous copy of *Conocoverage* entitled 'Mogul chiefs' first rig visit'.

On days without delays I usually got home by 8.00 p.m., after what became a regular, stimulating, diversion. A group of about eight or ten, under a similar time restraint to me, would gather, between 6 and 8 p.m., in a small very exclusive public bar, to discuss any topic that arose. The bar was in a fourteenth century pub, standing in the parish churchyard at Claines, a few miles north of Worcester on the road to Stourport. I was introduced to this haven of wit and wisdom by my old shipmate Ted Burnham, who said 'This bar, at this time of day, is only for very special people like us, and we try to keep it that way.' The pub was named 'The Mug House', because that was where the church plates and mugs were kept, for security, in olden times. Harvest Festival was still being celebrated in the pub, full of lovely locals and their luscious products, which were auctioned afterwards for charity. It was owned by the Wolverhampton & Dudley Brewery, who made and sold my favourite beers, Banks's mild and bitter. The tenant landlord and his wife, John and Joyce Trow, took the pub on as their home after they got married in 1938, over thirty years earlier. My most apt description of them must be, that this lovely couple could have fitted in with ease to that everlasting serial on BBC radio 4, 'The Archers', all about country folk, which originated in the Midlands anyway.

Each week, an amateur jazz group played in the lounge bar, furnished with a piano and opposite our public bar, from about 8 until 11 p.m. John Trow, affectionately called 'Wally' by us, had a mischievous sense of humour. He always knew who was present in our bar and one time, as I was about to leave, the young jazz band leader said to him 'Our pianist hasn't turned up. Do you know anyone in this bar who can play the piano?' Wally replied, with a twinkle in his eye, 'Go ahead and ask them,' knowing that one imbiber present was Christopher Robinson, the Organist and Choirmaster at Worcester Cathedral. 'Does anybody here play the piano?' said the leader. 'Yes, I do,' said Christopher, without revealing his identity. 'Do you read music?' said the jazzman. 'I do indeed,' was the reply, and that clinched the deal. I heard next day from Wally that Christopher Robinson loved every minute of the three hours he played until closing time, when the group knew who he was. When I told Sue, she was amused and amazed at the versatility of Christopher, who conducted her, each Monday evening, as a member of the Worcester Festival Choral Society.

Some weekends we resumed camping on farmer Pritchard's Lugglime field and Peta joined us to enjoy the horse-riding. He once said 'Peta, we should be in business, with me breeding 'em and you breaking 'em in.' However, one horrendous time, it rained for three days and nights, which made the river Lugg rise excessively with water from the Welsh mountains. Opening our eyes at daybreak, we saw water creeping towards our tent and only just got the car and camping gear out of the field in time. Sue and I can still recall seeing Andy, aged two, dressed in yellow oilskins and souwester, standing calmly in the sodden scene, with a puzzled expression on his little face. We drove home, avoiding floods, and phoned farmer Pritchard, who said, 'I wasn't surprised to see you'd gone, when I wandered down for a chat. They said, on radio, the Lugg came up 12 feet, the most I've ever known it.' I feel Sue's summing up should be recorded. When we had dried out, she said to me 'That was exciting, wasn't it?' I reckon she was thinking back to her off-shore Solo sailing at Salcombe, in a steep ocean swell, which scared me more than I'd ever been before, at sea. We didn't broach-to, as I expected, but I knew then that Sue's seamanship in that situation was better than mine.

In 1970, Sue was infanticipating again and her parents came to our support in November. Things were expected to come to a head on the 8th and I was advised to retire early, as Sue had done. However, I was determined to hear and see on TV, the intimate rehearsal, backstage, of Schubert's Trout Quintet in its entirety, with Jacqueline du Pre playing her cello and husband Daniel Barenboim on the piano. It was a memorable performance, which kept me up until midnight. Then, going upstairs to bed, I heard Sue shout 'I've got pangs, let's go,' and off we drove to Lucy Baldwin's Maternity Home, on the opposite side of the Park in Stourport. Fiona Kinloch, our darling daughter, was born, in my presence, during the middle watch, at 0340 on the 9th, an astrological 'scorpio', but to me always a musical 'trout'. I snatched a zizz at home, before dashing off for our monthly meeting. David Cole, our D to C boss, attended and arranged a floral tribute for me to present to Fiona and her Mum, later.

In '69 I had joined Worcestershire County Cricket Club (WCCC) and renewed my friendship with Dick Howorth. Also, I had made Charles, aged 12, a junior member and bought him pads and gloves at Dick's shop. Charles was a contemporary of Damian D'Oliveira, son of Basil, who was then a distinguished all-rounder for Worcestershire and England. Those lucky youngsters enjoyed the privilege of playing in the nets each week with the county's 1st eleven, captained by Tom Graveney, and Charles remembers well the fast bowling of Len Coldwell. When Worcester were at home on weekdays, I usually managed to watch the last hour of play. Charles, after school, got there too and would go into the ancient scoreboard to help the scorer change numbers, manually, in those days. It was a happy moment, when I walked underbelow, to see a head pop-out above and hear a voice shout 'Hi Dad.' Joe Lister was Secretary then and got me a signed copy of D'Oliveira's autobiography, for Charles. In June '71 a lovely picture of the Bryces appeared in the *Worcester Evening News*, headed 'Chance for a family outing'. We were watching a Sunday match with a picnic under the chestnut trees, the cathedral in the background and Fiona, aged 6 months, being spoon-fed by Sue.

The Chief Buyer at Dunlop in Birmingham, Maurice Pringle, was a cricket enthusiast like me, but supported Warwickshire, so it was that each year he would be my guest, for a day, at Worcester to watch his team play mine. We discussed business matters between overs and renewed the annual contract, during the lunch interval. On 16 July '71, whilst listening to willow and leather make frequent contact, we exchanged friendly views on exercise and what we did about it, both being of a similar age. I said that my brother-in-law, Jan, had introduced me to 'Canadian 5 BX', fifteen minutes of which on rising each day was vigorous and exhausting. My companion replied, 'I suggest you try Yoga, which I find leaves me with mind and body relaxed and reinforced.' I took his advice and the very next day bought the book *Teach Yourself Yoga* by James Hewitt, on 17.7.71. That was a palindromic date, easy to remember, a year before my half-century, and marked a turning point in my life, best described as the beginning of my late 'self-development'. I loved my Yoga exercises and meditation, any time of day, and was soon standing on my head with ease, to see my immediate environment very differently. After ten years, I changed into a gentler Tai Chi routine, which I still do to this day.

On Tuesday 21 September, 1971, at the Belfry Hotel in Warwickshire, my colleagues of the 'Brew XI Team – The Men of the Midlands', presented me with a 'digital clock' to commemorate my appointment to Manager, Consumer Sales, Conoco House, London. Roy Emery, the wittiest Rep in the team, spoke well and later I received a photo of the occasion, organized by John Ellis, the senior and most respected Rep in the team. I treasure this greatly, because it shows our crest with motto in Latin, which reminds me of three happy years, marketing in the middle of England, when everyone's finger was well extracted. I was promoted into David Cole's job, with whom I had worked well for a few years on developing a system of 'Management by Objectives' associated in industry, at that time, with the name of Drukker. David moved up into Dennis Mackett's job as Marketing Director and we continued our good working relationship. Sue and I did not rejoice at moving from the rural peace of the Barn in Stourport to the urban noise of the south-east, wherever, but we found happiness at 37, King Harry Lane, St Albans and named the house 'Halyards', a double entendre, nautical and historical, for Henry VII had his hunting lodge near where we settled. So, rural it once was.

CHAPTER 20

Training, self-development, GRTA, KBA, challenge of industry and young enterprise – 1971–1995

HERE WE ARE IN ST ALBANS in 1971, the place that suited us best for many reasons. Sue could resume singing in the Bach Choir at the Abbey; the price of houses was just within our reach and living north of the Thames was an advantage, because as UK manager, I could travel more easily about the country by train, to be met and driven around by colleagues. Watford junction, nearby, was handy for going north and I could use a First Class carriage as my mobile office en route. Fortunately I had six District Managers, well known to me, Hamish Cameron in Scotland, then coming south, Vic Morrison, Ted Wisbey, John Goodison, Dick Francis and Denver Thew in the south-west, all of them well experienced. Thus, I could delegate with trust and confidence, but each would still argue his point of view and they were in no way 'yes men', which suited all of us.

The most vociferous was Vic Morrison, a likeable lad from the North-East, who said to me one day 'Ian, I know I talk a lot and I think it might be better if I lost my "Geordie" accent, don't you?' My response was, 'No, I don't'. Happily, it was a time when most people were realizing that countrywide dialects added colour and character to life, as opposed to those who cultivated an unnatural accent, in the mistaken belief that a posh sounding voice would promote them in our class conscious society. Not until recently did I discover that to the trained local ear, Sunderland people, and he was one, have a different accent to those on Tyneside and feel insulted if called 'Geordies', which should be used exclusively for the latter.

One of my best gestures in marketing happened in 72, when my boss David Cole and I set up a combined operation, known only to us, which would satisfy a managerial training need and also reward wives for acting as unpaid secretaries, often taking messages at their homes in the various districts. With the co-operation of Tony Dixon, then Training Manager, I arranged a course to improve verbal presentations called 'The Floor is Yours' at the Cumberland Hotel, Marble Arch, where the District Managers and their wives stayed for three days and nights. The course, held in a spacious hotel suite, was a great success, whilst the ladies went out shopping and one evening we all went to see a suitably bawdy performance of Chaucer's

Canterbury Tales at Wyndham's Theatre, before a snack supper in St Martin's Lane.

The last night was the high spot of this few days get together. I ordered a table to seat eighteen, for a dinner-dance at the Savoy Hotel. In addition to my team of managers and wives, the party included David and Marion Cole, plus Tony and Judy Dixon as guests, with my wife Sue alongside me. Olivia Newton-John appeared in the cabaret singing 'Summer Nights', a song from the film *Grease*, in which she had become famous, starring with John Travolta. We were enchanted by her personality. This particular summer night was hot, so I removed my dinner jacket and danced in bow-tie and shirt sleeves. In no time at all, a young waiter approached me and said 'Sir, your jacket awaits you at the edge of the dance floor' and at a glance I saw the head waiter holding my discarded garment ready for me to reinhabit. I was impressed with the relaxed courtesy of their conduct and felt in no way embarrassed.

It was in the early '70s that a few other oil companies offered employees aged in their mid to late fifties the opportunity to take voluntary early retirement, and this triggered off ideas in my mind. Quite coincidentally, at this time, a job advert appeared on Conoco's noticeboard seeking applicants for a newly created position called 'Senior Management Development Advisor' in the Training Section of Personnel Department, working in parallel with Tony Dixon. I took the view that aged 51, if I got this job, I could acquire training skills and experience within Conoco. Then later, I could accept early retirement, if offered, and establish my own Management Training Company for the future. I got the job in 1973 and this pattern evolved to my benefit, as you will read.

On the family front, the greatest event in '73 was the wedding of Peta to Derek Ball at St Stephen's Church, St Albans with the reception at St Michael's Manor Hotel in Fishpool Street. Peta and Derek first met when students at Canton High School, Cardiff and when they married, she was a qualified teacher of Home Economics, whilst he was still studying Town Planning at Cardiff University. Charles, six feet tall and almost 16, was fashionable, with shoulder-length hair and wearing football socks in wedge shoes beneath his morning dress, whilst 6-year-old Andy was immaculate in shirt, tie and shorts. Fiona aged 2½ was a bridesmaid, who spent most of her time in the kitchens at the hotel and delighted everyone by describing herself as a barmaid. Alf and Joan, Derek's parents, came up with a large contingent of Welsh relatives and friends from Cardiff and Peta's grandparents Frank and Elsie Pearce were present. Zill's cousin Ted Evans, ordained after a career in Insurance, conducted the marriage in church, with the Vicar, Hart-Synott. At the reception, Gerry Wills, whose wife Madeline was a first cousin of Brenda, gave a great speech and proposed the toast to bride and groom after presenting them with a copy of the Karma Sutra. With Gerry and Madeline were their four splendid sons, Murray, Peter,

Neil and Stephen, to whom Peta and Charles were like a sister plus fifth brother, and they seem to have maintained that relationship to this day.

Another memorable guest was my old shipmate in *Oribi*, John Murphy (Spud) suffering severely from Parkinson's Disease, supported by his wife Marguerite, with whom Sue and I still keep in touch, I had renewed friendship with John, after a gap of 20 years, quite by chance, at Lords Cricket Ground in '72, after which I often took him out in the car from his home in Farm Walk, Golders Green. A frequent outing was to 'The Old Bull and Bush' pub in Hampstead, from which the famous music-hall song originated. It was sad to see Spud, who when younger was such a natural wit and mimic, struggling to say a word. Talking to Marguerite recently she said the wedding was the last social event he enjoyed and we recalled the sight of him lying in a bean bag at our house, roaring with laughter at being unable to get out. He died six months later in Feb '74. Last week, in April 2004, we met Aidan, 18-year-old grandson from Australia, living with Marguerite and working at 'The Old Bull and Bush'. Ain't life strange?

In telling you about the next 24 years of my life, I want it to be interesting, amusing and easy for you to understand. Therefore, I intend to keep it simple, without too much detail, because it concerns, mainly, my learning from experience working within and alongside groups of people, in a training environment. I have always found that the effect of any experience is very personal and to attempt an objective written description afterwards is unwise. However, I shall mention many points of personal learning and how I applied them later. Group work for learning in training was taking over from the old teacher-tell technique in most organizations.

The first time I became conscious of the word 'leadership' was when I was a cadet in the Thames Nautical Training College, HMS *Worcester* at Greenhithe, Kent, from 1936–38. Looking back on my career since then, afloat and ashore, I became aware that many managers in the hierarchies above me did not possess the personal qualities or skills that I associated with a leader. This was more clearly defined when, as a senior marketing manager in 1972, I attended a public course in the Savoy Hotel, Bournemouth, called 'Situational Leadership', designed and run by John Adair. His ideas about leadership in a group for any human enterprise were stated as satisfying three needs; to achieve the common TASK; to hold the TEAM together and to gratify the needs of each INDIVIDUAL. This was illustrated by three overlapping circles to be kept evenly balanced and as such an easy formula to remember. I enjoyed reading his career history and I'm quoting parts of it direct from the sleeve of his book *Great Leaders*, published in 1989.

John Adair was adjutant of a Bedouin Regiment in the Arab Legion at the age of 20. After a spell as a deckhand on an Arctic trawler he studied history at Cambridge University and then lectured at Sandhurst. In 1979 he became the world's first Professor of Leadership Studies at the University of Surrey and was internationally known as a consultant. The course in Bournemouth introduced me to a procedure I have used countless times since, especially with school pupils. In a team of 8, we divided into 4 action guys, who had to build a tower with lego bricks and 4 observing guys, given guidelines for peer feedback after the event. The exercise was repeated to give everyone a go in various roles and was competitive, between 6 teams, for highest tower, least time taken and least lego pieces used. Each factor was converted into profit or loss from tables provided beforehand, so, planning prior to action was also a key factor, which gave the whole process a feeling of reality. There was lots of learning shared in general sessions, confirming the basic value of the Task, Team and Individual theme.

At the time I moved from marketing into training my new boss was Brian Murray, Manager of Personnel, now named Human Relations (HR) and he and Tony Dixon were running a course called the 'Managerial Grid', embracing middle management of all Conoco companies in the UK. The 'Grid' was designed and produced by Blake and Mouton from the USA, with a third person in Austin, Texas who supplied all course material to selected and approved companies worldwide. Alan Marsh was their agent in the UK, with an office in London, who ran public courses, mainly to tutor and qualify managers to run the Grid within their own companies, using material supplied for an agreed fee.

The purpose of the course was to make a person aware of their management/leadership style from their position on a Grid, which was a diagram, shaped as an equal sided square, containing numbers from 00, bottom left corner, to 99 top right. The horizontal line 0 to 9 indicated attitudes/methods to complete the common objective and the vertical line, the attitudes/use of people, in doing so. The Grid was very structured, with multi-choice questions for teams to argue about, but for many brought up in a system where 'the boss knows best', it showed a new approach to decision-making. Naturally, everyone hoped to aspire to the top right corner of the Grid, between 5:5 and 9:9, showing a balanced attitude to team and task.

The Public Grid I attended at the Imperial Hotel at Hythe was unique. The team of six Alan Marsh put me in, called Purple for identification, amongst about six other teams, consisted of 3 senior UK managers from Gas Board, Post Office and Oil, plus two Europeans, an Italian psychiatrist who hoped to become an agent, and Carl from Denmark, whose English was splendid, as he proved frequently by saying to me, 'Ian, isn't it time we had another lager, on room service?' Our task as a team was to agree a sequence of 5 clauses, A to E, based on our pre-course thinking, to present in a general session. Vincenzio always had a clause F, to which we listened with interest and admiration, because it was often better than any of the 5, we thought, but we ran out of time and told him to stuff it. After dropping out of the group overnight, he empathized next morning and proved superb afterwards, when we assessed each other's position on the Grid. I enjoyed his company on the promenade and last remember him coming out of the hotel basement with an armful of cartons. He said, 'Ian, it is impossible to get cube sugar in Italy now, so I've done a small deal with the Head Chef. Arrivederci.'

For seven or eight years Tony and I ran the larger courses, such as the Grid, often attended by thirty or more people, at the Palace Court Hotel in Bournemouth. The manager and director was Jan Ronco, who was pleased to be introduced, by us, to a new form of revenue, catering for courses during weekdays, which filled the gaps between his ever popular bookings for week-ends only. The courses were frequent, sometimes every other month and always negotiated at a favourable rate with Ronco over a lunch. He and his staff became good friends over the years. Smaller courses we ran for convenience near our homes; Frimley Hall and Frensham Ponds, in Surrey, for Tony and Aubrey Park and Sopwell House in Herts for me. At all these venues we established a good rapport with management and staff.

The first person to greet a customer or guest at the PCH was the Hall Porter, Mr Holt, the only member of staff addressed by his surname with the prefix Mr, by tradition. His natural charming guidance made one feel important and most welcome. After a few months acquaintance and many chats on the side, he took me to his private office and we talked about WW2, being of similar age. It was then I discovered he had been a volunteer paratrooper and fortunately survived the Arnhem action. We called each other Alf and Ian after that, when not being overheard, and he told me of his embarrassment, as a private soldier in wartime, when he visited Dorchester HQ, to see his elder brother, who was Regimental Sergeant Major of the Dorsetshire Regiment.

After Mr Holt came the Chief Receptionist, Angela Hollins, an attractive, young, yet very experienced lady, who had mastered the art of proportional representation. By that, I mean knowing where to place what in whose account, as appropriate, for everyone's benefit and the continuation of our happy social and business relationship. Always available to us was the penthouse suite called Chevalier, because the great Maurice stayed there sometime in the past. Tony and I took it in turns to sleep up there and Angela decided whose turn it was. The Chevalier suite living room bar and balcony overlooked Christchurch Bay, and were used for happy hours during courses. In summertime box lunches and a swim on the beach were popular and refreshed us all for the sessions to come. Tony and I were keep-fit fanatics in those days and carried folding bicycles in the back of our estate cars, with the TV training gear which we transported from head office. Early each day we would cycle along the front and swim before breakfast, sometimes being seen by Ronco, exercising his dog, who would shout 'Now I know where my towels go; left around by my most generous guests for Father Neptune's clients, later in the day!' Santos, the Spanish wine waiter, was a great friend and decanted the very best wines into carafes and served them under the prefix 'house', which endeared him to us, throughout the '70s. He knew everyone by name and was well rewarded.

In 1975, Jack Nolan favourably influenced my life once again. He was now Senior Personnel Manager (Europe), having returned to the UK from being General Manager of Conoco's Company 'Ara-bolagen' in Sweden. In his Park Street office, he sent for Tony and me, having known both of us for many years and said 'I believe we need to move on from the Grid in training and knowing you two are capable of change for the better, I am asking you to go on a course in Houston, to bring back what's worthwhile and make adjustments to suit the climate you know so well over here'. We listened, we debated, but having faith in his sense of values, we agreed.

Another personality entered my life on 4 January '75, in the form of Oliver, third son of Tony and Judy and the youngest third brother to Thomas and William. Later, for fun, I used to ask the boys, when does TWO make 3? – got it? A remarkable coincidence occurred when Tony and I flew out in a 'Jumbo Jet' from Heathrow to Miami. Amongst 300 passengers Don Lee and I met in the gents toilet after a gap of 20 years. In the 1950s we were shipmate navigators in the Cunard's *Queen Mary*, on the surface of the Atlantic, just 37,000 feet below. He said he was Captain of a cruise liner based at Everglades and flying out to Florida with his exchange crew. 'We get better leave now, with two crews per ship,' he said, with a seamanlike smile.

At Miami we stayed overnight in an hotel whose back faced east over a beach to the Atlantic ocean. Early next morning we felt like a swim, but rather than in the hotel pool, we walked through the garden to the beach, dropped a few garments and entered the sea. The water was warmer than Bournemouth, but our human encounter was very different. On walking back to our clothes we were surprised to see two characters, with dogs, wearing stetsons and shooters on the hip, who turned out to be the Sheriff and his Deputy. As soon as we spoke, one said to the other, 'More limey funny business, I guess,' and the other nodded. We wondered at their reaction and only then recalled a much publicized recent incident. An English MP, named John Stonehouse had left things on the beach and tried to make it appear he had drowned in order to avoid an enormous debt in the UK. I think it was a year later before he was caught in Australia, living it up with a girlfriend.

In the forenoon we boarded a plane for Houston, Texas, owned by Continental Airlines, no link with the oil company, and were welcomed by Air Hostesses who gave us large glasses of Buck's Fizz – champagne and orange juice, for the uninitiated. Tony and I, with Jean Bekaert from Conoco Chemicals in Belgium, were 3 European delegates amongst 20 American guys and one lady, Betty Schwanke, on the Performance Management Seminar. The seminar was run by Stirling Institute of Boston, Mass, at the Sheritan Hotel, Clearlake, Nasa, close to the space centre and museum. Our Instructor was Pete Yensen, who guided us in group activities, assisted by J.D. (Dutch) de Haan from Conoco's training department in Houston. A hired Pontiac automobile was provided, which Tony drove mostly, whilst I navigated. We were scared by traffic density until advised by our Houston colleagues to buy a stetson each and wear them when mobile. This would cause others to keep well clear, as they would take us for a pair of simple cowboys from out of town, and it worked.

We stayed with the stetsons, they suited our style when seeking fun situations and besides, we looked better in such high quality headgear. Most nights after dinner we would walk across the road to the Holiday Inn, Nasa, where we formed a fantastic friendship with some young jazz players, specializing in Glenn Miller music. They were called the 'House Group', straight from the West Coast, that's LA, and providing a Fabulous Sound in the Sea Rebel Lounge from 9.00 p.m. to 1.00 a.m. every night. They sat around our table during breaks after playing our tune, 'There's only so much Oil in the Ground', popular at that time and could well be revived, right now. Some nights when arriving late, we would creep in and sit on high stools at the bar with our backs to the band and wearing our stetsons, of course. Soon we would hear our tune, then a pause and the sweet soprano voice of singer Jane saying 'Folks, let's welcome those cowboys at the bar for what they really are, oil men from London, England, named Tony and Een' and we always got a big hand.

One of the group that I got close to, instrumentally, was called 'Piano man' Tharp. He had a beautiful black girlfriend, who had been a Hollywood film extra and whom he had kept apart until the night he confided in me with a trustworthy request. He said 'Een, will you please dance with my girl 'cos she gets so bored sitting on the side just listening?' She and I jived and jitterbugged to applause and humorous asides, much to our delight, but surprise. Afterwards we were told that a tiny light was shining through the bottom of my left trouser pocket which everyone could see and was understood to show that I was really sexed up. The light was from my fountain-pen type torch being inadvertently switched on — I swear to that — and as for being sexed up, well why not? 'Piano man' laughed and applauded as much as anyone and said 'Thanks Een, you're my buddy, and my girl's too, right now, I guess.'

It was a great feeling at the age of 53 to be having such a happy time with these young musicians, making me realize that with music as a common factor, age doesn't matter. I want to record here the messages each of them wrote on a farewell publicity hand-out of theirs. 'Wish there were more people like you' – Bill (Guitar); 'Happiness to you' – Larry (Drummer); 'I'll see you in London '76' – Martin (Sax/Flute); 'Bloody good having you here' – 'Piano man' Tharp (Keyboard); and because I said my son Charles, then 18, would like their sounds, 'Hey Chuck, be cool' – Brady (on Bass); 'Charles, Howdy, wish you could be here with your wonderful Dad – he's great! and dances like Fred Astaire!! love,' Jane Miller (singer). Me giving my ego a boost once again. Finally, from the leader, 'You made us smile!' – Joe Miller (Trombone). I've lost contact, but I hope they read or hear about this tribute wherever they may be. Now, almost 30 years later, they'll all be about the age I was then.

It was good to meet our colleagues in Houston and see Bob Turvey again, our boss in London before being promoted to Vice-President, who sent for us to have a chat. Dutch de Haan drove us up the Colorado Valley to Austin, where we visited the Blake, Mouton Managerial Grid data base. On the way back to Houston we saw lots of bison by the river, in the valley, which was green in contrast to the rest of Texas.. Then off we flew to Boston, Mass for a few days to talk to Stirling Institute at Harvard University and gather further data on the seminar we had attended, which would help us to adapt it for the UK. Also we went aboard the eighteenth century USS *Constitution* and in a hired car visited Groton, where we met with Mrs Margery Lawrence, as described in a previous chapter. Then we enjoyed a lovely drive through New Hampshire to New York City, in order to fly home from JFK airport. It was fun being in New York again after about 20 years and with a few hours spare, I suggested to Tony, whose first visit it was, that after depositing the car at the airport, we take a yellow cab to the 21 Club on 52nd Street.

When I told the cab driver our destination, famous as 'Jack and Charlie's' during Prohibition, he raised his eyebrows and said 'I doubt if you'll get in unless you know someone there, 'cos it's very exclusive.' 'I'll get us in OK,' I said, showing him my club pass, a coin, about the size of an old silver dollar, precisely engineered, inscribed with the club's name on the down side when spinning and on the upperside was an arrow, saying 'All Right – You Pay', pointing at whoever, when it stopped. The guy on the door took the coin and let out a shout to his manager nearby 'Gee boss, take a look at this, it's one of the old ones.' I told them how I got it, when in Cunard and they said 'You're welcome any time you're over here,' and took us to the bar.

Very large Mint Juleps were a speciality, with a superior bourbon whiskey, and we were on our second when suddenly a calamity occurred. A percolator fell off a passing trolley and drenched my light grey trousers with black coffee. 'Go to the toilet fast and rinse them with cold water,' said Tony and I did that. The attendant, a guy called Otis, got a bucket and with frequent changes of water and immersing my legs, alternately, he did a perfect job, regardless of other toilet users wondering what was going on. I shall never forget Otis's final advice. After asking where I was going from there and hearing that I was flying the Atlantic, he said 'Well sir, if your pants are still wet when you arrive, you can always say the pilot lost altitude over the ocean and the plane shipped a few seas.' 'Brilliant idea Otis and thanks a million,' I said as I gave him what remained of my dollar bills. On the flight home, the movie was about the Titanic, which I could do without, preferring to imbibe some duty-free Southern Comfort and sleep thru' the time difference in longitude. At sea, in the *Queen Mary* we had 4 or 5 days to adjust, but in the air it was a similar number of hours, and hence the jet lag after arrival.

Back in London we began to adjust the Performance Management Seminar (PMS) to suit participants in the UK and we decided to change the title to the Development Management Seminar (DMS) as sounding more progressive. Working in groups, we wanted to find a creator of multi-choice questions appropriate to our needs and a Jet colleague gave us the name of Bill McEwen Young, Senior Lecturer at Loughborough University, with whom he had worked successfully in the past. When I phoned Bill to ask for his help in what we were doing, he agreed instantly and from then on it was Bill and Ian. Furthermore, he made a sensible suggestion that would affect our future for many years. In his delightful Scottish voice, he said 'Ian, if you and Tony agree, I would like to tell Professor Gurth Higgin about your ideas. He has recently come here from the Tavistock Institute to start a Centre for 'Continuing Management Studies', at the University and I'm sure he would like to be involved in your project. Let me know.' With hand over mouthpiece, I told Tony across the room and he gave his approval. 'Go ahead Bill,' I said and a formidable team of four developed as a result.

Gurth was a large New Zealander, both in stature and wisdom. He had a great presence and an inimitable wit, whatever the circumstances. About ten years older than me, in WW2 he had been in the NZ RNVR, a deck officer on the Russian run, which gave us a bit of extra rapport. He had since become a distinguished sociologist, best described as someone who studies the development and classification of human societies. In 1973, he wrote a book called *Symptoms of Tomorrow*, based on a series of letters to Swedish students, a copy of which he gave to me with warmest wishes. Who better to lead our training enterprise in the oil industry?

We designed the DMS during the summer of '75, at Loughborough University, where Tony and I made frequent visits for two days, staying in the college overnight. We four worked all hours in a spacious office on wall charts, but we always went out by taxi to a restaurant for meals at Conoco's expense. A few bottles of Gurth-chosen claret greatly improved our creativity. Back in the office, I can see Gurth relaxed, lying on the floor, and having kicked his shoes off, pointing, with right foot in sock, at the top of a wall chart and saying 'It's good to have a free circulation hour at the start of a seminar, so that people get to know one another. Sometimes we can pair them off and tell each to introduce the person alongside.'

The Seminar was shaped in four groups with one of us as Instructor in each and Gurth in charge up front, during general sessions. A group, ideally, consisted of six or eight managers from any level in any department, the greater the mix, the better. The emphasis was on developing inter-personal skills, such as leadership, negotiating, counselling and so on, with input from us, but each group deciding its own objectives. At the end of the four-day seminar everyone received a 'Certificate of Achievement', of paper-weight size mounted in acrylic, upon which to reflect when taken back to their work place. I quote you mine now as an example:

Certificate of Achievement
This certifies that – that bastard Bryce – has contributed towards the advancement of self and others during the MANAGEMENT DEVELOP-MENT SEMINAR.
Gurth Higgin   20–2–76
Director   Date

The DMS was a great success and we ran the seminars at the Palace Court Hotel, Bournemouth under the claret-conscious care of Santos, very much our wine waiter. After four or five successes, Gurth dropped out, Bill remained and Maurice Bailey, an Industrial Rep, joined the Conoco training team. I received three simple bits of advice from Gurth that I recall frequently, to this day:

1. Beware of the attraction of action; give a group (or person) a task and they will often be doing it in minutes, instead of planning for at least 50% of the time allocated;
2. When a speaker says 'but', give much more credit to what comes after than what came before that word;
3. Identify and prefer an intelligent person, who has the capacity to understand and develop ideas, rather than an intellectual, who knows lots of facts, without the nous to use them. It could be called common sense.

Eventually, with mutual respect, I called Gurth Prof and he called me Commodore. Bill, with a natural, helpful, flare for detail, was sometimes called Flight Engineer, having been one in an early Lancaster bomber of WW2.

One summer's day in '75 Gurth said to Tony and me, 'I would like you to be my guests next month at the annual conference of the GRTA, Group Relations Training Association, of which I am Chairman this year, and if you value the experience, I'll recommend you for membership.' He went on to tell us about the purpose of GRTA and we accepted his invitation, which introduced us to many new friends from all walks of life, who introduced us to new learning techniques. Gurth, whilst at the Tavistock

Institute, created GRTA, in '72, and initiated the idea of an 'Annual T-Group Laboratory' in January. T-groups started in the USA and were encouraged by the Tavistock Institute in the UK. The aim of a T-group laboratory was to provide participants with an opportunity to learn more about themselves and others. Without any prescribed structure, discussion developed, often with difficulty, until people felt inclined to give candid feedback to each other on behaviour and attitudes, which, in my experience, never failed to improve relationships.

The method of working was with participants in small T-groups, about four or five in a laboratory, each group consisting of about twelve members including two from the staff group. To support the work within the T-groups, general sessions were held with all T-groups gathered together, to interact and develop fundamentally democratic behaviour in a community or large organization. A laboratory lasted five days from Monday to Friday in rented academic accommodation, and I did two as a member, one at Alsager College in '77 and one at Pembroke College Oxford in '78, before being invited to join the staff group at Owens Park, Manchester from 6–11 Jan 1980.

Over the years with GRTA I had attended other five day and week-end seminars run by lovely people and learned lots of new psychological training techniques, which no doubt helped my selection to the staff. During this time I formed a firm friendship with Guy Wareing due mainly to us being in the same line of business. He was in Training with Gulf Oil and also in charge of their Public Relations, so, we were never at a loss for words. In fact at conferences we always sat together and were likened to the two old boys in the theatre box shouting advice to Kermit the Frog on stage in a popular TV show at that time called 'The Muppets'. Also Brian Nichol, then a Lecturer at Manchester University, and LouRaye Otterway, a consultant in group work, with skills as a jeweller and craft potter, helped me to understand GRTA workshops, when I stayed with them at their home in Didsbury, Manchester.

On the staff of eight in the 1980 Jan Lab, headed by Brian Nichol, was Steve Potter, a young and lively Senior Lecturer at the Manchester Polytechnic and Chairman of GRTA that year. The Lab was acclaimed a great success and a major contributory factor was the 'street scene' during most general sessions, created by Steve Potter. The 'street scene' required everyone to seriously enact a roleplay of some person or group who might be encountered in a public place, and interact with other role-players until the end of the session, when there would be a communal wash-up. I became a tramp with another man and we planned various approaches to others, begging, scrounging and selling, to be rejected by most, but helped by some. It definitely gave a real feel to being different and much learning was achieved. LouRaye played the role of prostitute, as did a few other ladies, and we tried our luck, here and there, but as tramps we were not worth considering as customers. My staff mate in our T-group of ten members was Gaie Houston, a charming independent consultant, who worked as a lecturer, teacher and playwright. She knew more than me about group work, but allowed me adequate space to comment and we agreed on ideas intuitively. I learned a lot from her and have admired assertive ladies ever since.

The eighth decade of the twentieth century started with the happy arrival of our daughter Fiona on 9 November 1970 and ended with a similar happy event, the birth of our first grandchild on 31 August 1979. Peta and Derek called their daughter Joanna Frances and she was in the uncommon position of having an aunt just 9 years older than her. Now, in 2004, aged 24 and 33 respectively, they have lots of contact, with jobs near each other in the captivating Cardiff Bay area. I love to visit the Bay and see the preserved building where I got my Master Mariner's Certificate 56 years ago. It still lacks the blue plaque it could display, to commemorate the many distinguished mariners who were certificated there before it changed its purpose. Looking towards Penarth I think I'm in Sydney Harbour, Australia; gone are the mud flats, with the tidal barrier now in place, but local character has been maintained, with the Pier Head building and the Norwegian Church, associated with the author Roald Dahl when he lived in Cardiff.

In the autumn of 1980, for the first time, Conoco offered voluntary early retirement to those over 55 years of age and as I was 58 I seized the opportunity without hesitation. It was just what I had hoped for when I switched from marketing to training in '73. Director Harold Liney, who was himself eligible, made sure the terms were most favourable. The Company would grant a pension immediately, equivalent to that to which a person would be entitled at the age of 65, plus a lump sum. All who qualified accepted when it became effective, at the end of the year. This move gave me the initiative to get involved with new activities of my choosing, both pleasurable and profitable, in order to maintain a reasonable standard of living.

In 1981 I registered my own Company as Kinloch Bryce Associates, Management and Personal Development Consultants, at my home address, which was then 37 King Harry Lane, St Albans, and also registered for VAT. Initially, I took over the dining room, until a visit from Peta who said 'It's such a pity that your beautiful oak dining table has lost its true purpose in life. Why don't you develop the spacious roof and use that as your office?' I did that and called it the 'Poop Deck'. It was magnificent, with plenty of light and vast book shelves; a phone, photo-copier and ultimately an Amstrad word-processor. I held training sessions for Fiona, being interviewed for a job, with my closed circuit Panasonic TV, and also rehearsed my seminar presentations and social speeches.

At a GRTA seminar in the seventies I had met a lively lass from Glasgow, called Irene Kightley, who worked for the Industrial Society (Education) in London. Early in '81 she invited me to be her Management speaker, at a school in Ealing on an event, called 'Challenge of Industry', the principle of which was to advise sixth form students what to expect after leaving school. Often a few schools combined for this two-day event under a Chairperson, with a team of volunteer employees from industry, about 10 or 12, to act as Advisors to each of many student groups. On Day One groups were given practical tasks to complete and on Day Two, they heard a Management and a Trade Union Speaker talk about their jobs, before asking questions in open forum. Recommended for the role of Chairman by Irene, who called me 'posh voice' for fun, I was accepted and did about four or five each year until '85, as far apart as Kings School, Canterbury and Pontypool Grammar School, with Jacqueline Palmer as my Society Organizer. As Chairman, on Day One, I always talked about and illustrated the three circles image of Task, Team and Individual as a basic theme for Leadership. Also I introduced student observers around action groups, to give candid feedback later, which proved very popular.

Some school governors benefited from Challenge of Industry activities and I give two examples. At Kings, Canterbury, a baronet farmer and governor was one of the Advisors and at the wash-up, afterwards, said to me 'I've learned more about this school in these two days than I have over the many years I've been a governor.' Then at Haberdasher's Girls School at Elstree, the headmistress asked me if the chairman and board of governors could meet me in the conference room during the coffee break. I welcomed the idea and was pleased that the groups of girls in the first session had listed, on flip-chart paper, extra subjects they would like to be taught, which were mainly about science and engineering. These were displayed on the walls and the front of the platform; for all to see. I explained the process and the board members read the flip-charts, approved and proceeded, muttering 'We must take heed, because this year is encouraging more 'Women in Science'. My management speaker was the pregnant lady Personnel Manager at British Airways, who talked about combining motherhood with a career, which went down well with my young female audience.

The London Borough of Havering ran its own show, on Society lines, for five schools, between 100 to 200 students, in July each year and invited me to be Chairman from '86 to '89, when I ceased, due to other demands. Over the years, I enjoyed every occasion, in which I created an appropriate climate for youngsters to develop their self-motivation. In '83 my business, as KBA, increased, with two courses for Conoco (UK) Ltd, Blackfriars working with Maurice Bailey and five for Continental Oil Company Ltd, Park St, (COCL), with Hazel Valentine and Tony Dixon, who had crossed the river Thames. Brian Slymon took over training in COCL at Park House when Tony left to go independent in '85, after which, Tony and I, with Hazel later, ran middle management courses for St Albans District Council for six years, from '86 to '92, under the guidance of Clive Payne, then Director of Personnel at the Council.

Alan and Anne Dale, also members of GRTA, created a commune in a large house and garden called 'Littlegrove', in the country near Chesham Bucks, where they ran workshops and rented out space for others to hold sessions. Sue and I enriched our lives by attending on many occasions throughout the '80s and I liked working with Ad Brugman, who taught me the ancient disciplines of Zen and T'ai-Chi as a moving meditation. My body posture and breathing improved, from which I got happiness and peace of mind, as I still do. I remember learning a lot about Transactional Analysis (TA) from Julie Hay, a TA specialist, living in Watford nearby, who ran a one-day workshop at Littlegrove with me as her assistant. TA, very simply put, is a means of changing communication between people, for the better. It assumes that each of us has three basic modes of personality in our speech and body-language. Any opening remark comes from either the Parent, Adult or Child, in short PAC. The response from another, likewise, comes from that person's P, A or C, giving a crossed or parallel transaction, hence its name. The best explanation is by giving an example and I do so now because awareness of TA has helped Sue and me, especially when talking to youngsters.

Mother, Sue: 'Charles, you're only 15 and I get very angry about you drinking in the pub.' (P)

Chas, son: 'Come off it Mum, the landlord's a friend and thinks I'm 18, 'cos I look it' (C)

Mum, Sue: 'How would you feel if your friend lost his licence because of you?' (A)

Chas, son: 'That would be terrible for him and the family. Maybe I should think again.' (A)

The analysis shows Mum coming out of critical parent (P) at first and Chas replying from his rebellious child (C). A crossed transaction. Then, with TA awareness, Mum tries the adult (A) and gets a reponse from his adult (A). A parallel transaction. It's not always that short and easy but it shows that the best results are usually achieved when both people eventually converse in the adult (A) mode. I hope my readers understand and find it useful.

In 1984, I met Charles Holme, whose company Management Organization Development Advisory Service (MODAS), formed a team with six Associates, including me, to design and run a five day Management Skills Course for the Health and Safety Executive (HSE). The aim was to improve relations between HSE Inspectors, be they Factory, Agricultural, Nuclear, Railway or Medical, with their clients, who might give them verbal or physical abuse. We developed their assertive speech and behaviour, and discouraged the extremes of being either aggressive or subjective. In TA terms, work towards an adult exchange as opposed to a parent or child. Charles organized about three a year until 1992, when the HSE abandoned training altogether. This was a retrograde step for the HSE and the public at large, I feel.

In 1987 my GP got me into the RAF Hospital at Halton for a double hernia, on the NHS. The ward contained a merry mix of servicemen, either ex or active and one joker, an RAF sergeant, called Tony. He came alongside my bed for a chat early on the day of operations and having seen the notice-board, he was able to say 'I see you're first in at 0900 and the surgeon today is Wing-Commander Stanley, named after the knife! They say with ex-navy guys like you, he always has a large piece of canvas placed under the anaesthetized body, so that in the event of mishap, a few swift stitches and a trip off-shore would resolve the situation. The best of British luck Ian, you old salt.' My visit to Halton ended happily for the Wing-Co and me.

CHAPTER 21

Summary of 1980s and 1990s until the end in 2004, plus Review

I N 1981, I STOPPED COMMUTING DAILY from St Albans to Blackfriars, when I wasn't away from home running courses, which gave me more time to develop a circle of friends and business associates locally. The focal point for me was the Goat Inn in Sopwell Lane. This was a Free House, with old oak beams and character, owned and managed by Peter Ransome and his wife Anthea, supported by well chosen amiable cooks and bar staff. During the seventeenth and eighteenth centuries, the Goat Inn and around the corner, the White Hart Inn, on Holywell Hill, were on the main coach route from London to Anglesey for embarkation to Ireland from the port of Holyhead.

In those days, the Goat Inn was often referred to as a doss-house for the hoi-poloi travellers to endure the night, whilst the White Hart, with superior accommodation, was where the more distinguished people slept in comparative comfort. It was at the White Hart, St Albans, that Simon Fraser, 12th Baron Lovat, spent his last night alive, in 1747, on his journey south from Scotland, having been captured after the battle of Culloden and found guilty of treason. Next day he was beheaded on Tower Hill, London, close to where the Merchant Navy Memorial Garden is today. It is believed he was the last person to be decapitated in such style. Almost 200 years later, the 17th Baron Lovat led the Commandos, on D-Day 1944, from the Hamble river to the British assault beaches in France, with great success – a good example of how family feelings can change over the centuries.

As time went by, I got to know the landlord of the Goat, Peter Ransome, and other regulars very well. We had many common interests, such as supporting the Abbey Theatre, listening to music, which Peter loved to compose on his guitar in the living quarters over the pub, and talking about cricket, which encouraged him to form a team. I think it was in the summer of 1982, when I had just turned 60, that Peter said 'Ian, how about you playing in the Goat Cricket Team?' I was aware that Peter had been educated at Aldenham School, just south of St Albans, which had a very high reputation for the game, to the benefit of several other friends of mine, such as Neil Jephcott and his brother Anthony, who were there at the same time as Dave Pither. I thought back thirty years to when I last played in Bombay on a World Cruise and replied 'Peter, I feel honoured to be asked, but I'm not up to your standard of play.' 'Nonsense,' he said, 'we play

'The Ancient Mariner': Ian at The Port; Salcombe in the background

another pub team on a Sunday afternoon and everyone sets his or her own standard. We insist that each team has at least one lady player in the side, so, how's that?' 'Aye-aye captain, I'll be your change off-spin bowler, medium pace,' was my immediate response. I played for many years and then resorted to umpiring.

The following summers were full of happy events, mostly in 'the dell at Verulamium Park', our home pitch provided by the Council and surrounded by grassy banks and tall trees for a bit of shade. Parents brought their young of all ages, with picnics, making it always a fun family occasion. Many names come to mind of characters whose friendship I enjoyed then and still do now, in Harry's Bar. John West – a good all-rounder – on and off the pitch, meaning an accomplished accountant to most imbibers at the bar and whose ultimate remark to me is usually 'Shall we have the one we came in for?' Chris Andrews ran an extensive family business in superior quality pens. A reliable opening batsman – he can still be heard calling in Harry's, not for runs now, but drinks.

Dick Brooks who became our family solicitor and legal adviser, was a great find at the Goat. He preferred bowling to batting and was admired by his lady partner, Sarah Burbridge, when we played for the Garibaldi. Sarah's father, Keith, had captained the Potters Bar team in the 1950s, when my *Oribi* shipmate, Bill Goodacre, played and I learned later that Keith and Bill put on a record 145 runs for a 4th wicket stand. Now, when in Worcester, I always see Dick Chicken, a chum of theirs who was fast bowler for Potters

Bar in those days. More naval, including cricket, stuff came from Dick Brooks, over the years, who discovered diaries, kept by his deceased great-uncle, which he passed to me for some fascinating reading. The old boy was a deck-officer in the RN, who had played cricket at many places and once on the ice at Spitzbergen. He fought at the battle of Jutland in 1916 and retired as an Admiral after WW1. Diaries are still being found, so, my readers, like you, I'm looking forward to more anecdotes.

Don Slade, tall, with long legs, also had a reputation for calling and causing his batting partner to be run-out. When not in the Goat he occupied an office on Holywell Hill from which he ran a world-wide business in compressed paper-products. As a teenager he was trained as a seaman on the Hamble river in the training ship *Mercury*, under the command of that celebrated cricketer C.B. Fry, so maybe he played the game then, on runs ashore? He served a few years in the RN, so he and I always used naval jargon, often to excess, whenever we met. Who better to help me sing a song I had composed and dedicated to the finest Lady Cricketer of the year, Fiona, from behind the bar, who boasted an English Mum and Australian Dad. We sang to the tune of 'Mud, mud, glorious mud' – the Hippopotamus Song by Flanders and Swann, at the Cricket Club Supper on 24 November 1984.

Here it is in full:

Title	The Goat Inners' Cricket Club Song
	Dedicated to Fiona, who now lives in Melbourne
Chorus	Balls, balls, inn-swinging balls,
	'Out, 'cos they're Open,' the Umpire calls
	So, off with the bails – on with Real Ales
	If you're a Goat Inner, it's all beer and balls!
Verse	A fair lady cricketer was batting one day
	And whilst guarding her middle and leg,
	The balls of a bowler she did stroke out of play,
	Now he can't tell his 6X from keg.
	When later an over she came on to bowl,
	A couple of swingers with pace,
	This lady all-rounder bowled bouncers at bounders,
	But did so with maidenly Grace!
Chorus	See above . . . Owzat?

Before the Sunday game started in the Dell, we were refreshed by Lee Roth, a clever conjuror, who never failed to produce a shaker full of cocktails from no ingredients whatsoever! Also, during the game, Nigel our wicket-keeper, a member of the Flying Squad, never objected to either batsman or bowler placing drinks behind the wicket for sips between overs. Sometimes after the main game, a quick 'Beer Match' was played to establish the losers, who would buy the first round of drinks for both teams, back at the pub. Such a match was eleven overs a side, with each man obliged to bowl an over, which provided indescribable performances. At the Goat, in the evening, our captain shouted out a fine, imposed on every member of the team, for some absurd reason. The money, a few pounds from each of us, paid for the pitch fee and ongoing maintenance of the club equipment. To give an example: 'Ian, fined £4 for taking four more wickets than his usual number, which is 0.' Two youngsters, now still in their forties, Pete Botsford and Geoff Baylis played regularly and since 1994 have taken me annually to Worcester, by car, to sit and watch, for two days, at the loveliest cricket ground in England.

I've just remembered that John West's wife Ann made the scoreboard for the Goat team and often operated it herself in the Dell and elsewhere. No wonder, because the eldest of their three sons, Gareth, was our best fast bowler – world class, no doubt. Peter and Anthea had a family and thought it wise to buy a house near the Goat in Sopwell Lane, leaving David and Alison to manage the pub and live in house. They did this with popular acclaim until D and A got their own pub, where we played them at cricket and lost! Peter sold the Goat and later became joint tenant, with Chris Andrews, at the Garibaldi Inn in Albert Street. A cricket team was established and a lot of Goat regulars moved to the Gari. John Kearins was one and his partner Judith Shone with her sister Abigail were keen supporters on the field and in the bar at the Garibaldi. With these three good friends in mind, I'll end my bat and ball memories.

During the decade from '85 to '95 I ran the last Courses as Kinloch Bryce Associates in an industrial setting and enjoyed them immensely. My pleasure was enhanced by working alongside Brian Slymon whose previous experience in industry, both at home and abroad, after graduating at Balliol College, Oxford, made him the ideal person to head up training aims within Conoco. He used my services, as KBA, regularly, for a reasonable fee, and the two of us concentrated on courses that managers needed most, such as Business Presentations, frequently, and Negotiating Skills, occasionally. Sometimes delegates would ask me where I had graduated, to which I replied 'Poseidon', followed by silence to cover their ignorance, until later, when I explained it was the Seven Seas University. We found the place that suited us best, overall, was the Imperial Hotel at Hythe, ten miles west of Dover, on the Kent coast. It was here, in 1973, that I did my public Management Grid Course, and in 1939, ten miles south of Hythe, I had survived being mined in HMS *Kittiwake*. Two turning points in my career.

The Hythe-Imperial was chosen because it provided all the background resources necessary to run an excellent course, where the tutors, or more aptly called coaches, plus delegates, could apply themselves fully to achieving their aims, without any distractions. All our courses were designed for an optimum number of ten or twelve delegates and ran from Tuesday to Friday midday. The first favourable feature on entering the hotel was the magnificent mahogany reception hall, and in no time at all the hotel staff in all departments gave us their unobtrusive care and attention to satisfy all our needs. Immediately, we felt residentially relaxed, which helped our speed of development throughout the course. For leisure moments there were about twelve sporting facilities, such as swimming pool, croquet lawn, snooker and scaletrix rooms, just to mention a few that Brian and I enjoyed, with mixed ability. We established a good rapport with two charming ladies behind the bar, whose mixed ability with a cocktail shaker we imbibed each evening. They said 'You are most welcome, 'cos creating cocktails is more fun for us than dishing out gins and tonics!' We invented some, with their help and called them 'Torpedoes' and 'Depth Charges', which described the explosive effect they had upon a human hull. Brian composed a 'Sizzling 70s' to celebrate my birthday in 1992.

Let me now give you an overview of a typical Business Presentation Course by spelling out the sequence of events. On Tuesday a.m., Video Equipment Hire Ltd set up cameras and playback gear in the main conference room and in four or five other rooms, in which pairs could critique and progress between general sessions. Carl and Paul were the guys who did this and also dismantled on Friday, so, over the years, we got to trust them well. They are still operating now, but known as Conference Craft Ltd., near Slough. After our arrival, about 11 a.m., Brian and I would always check audience seeing and hearing facilities in the conference room, with and without microphone, by me varying my position to give feedback and Brian up front, gesticulating and reciting Shelley's classic, 'Ozymandias of Egypt' quote; 'I met a traveller from an antique land Who said: Two vast and trunkless legs of stone Stand in the desert . . .' unquote. Sometimes he may have uttered the poem in its entirety, but all I remember hearing was his repetition of the first few lines, times without number.

At the first general session all delegates were given two pieces of flipchart paper, to be hung by blue-tac or masking tape, vertically orientated, with great care, on the wall, immediately behind a delegate's seat. The top sheets stated the skills that the delegates thought they already possessed and the lower sheet, divided by a vertical line down the middle, welcomed feedback from all course colleagues. On the left side, some skill that appeared as noticeably good; a positive statement. On the right side, something that came across as capable of improvement, always encouraging and never a negative observation. During the three days there were nine opportunities for each person to speak in front of camera and get feedback from fellow delegates, verbally and literally, with the one-liner comments on their flipchart papers always anonymous. This was possible because we trained the course members overall how to use the video–camera equipment in the conference room, which inspired confidence in each other and gave delegated control to the camera-man in our absence. This allowed Brian and me to deal with everyone on a one to one coaching basis, in separate side rooms, on days two and three and only depleted the conference room audience by a few, in transit, at anyone time. Many amusing presentations were made, not strictly business, from Nina's 'Support Bra Burners United', to David Quint's 'Snogging is Better than Jogging'. An Introductory speech by a young lady from Lancashire lives on in both our memories, for its courage and candour. She said 'Here I am, eager to learn and speak better, but mainly motivated to get away from a week of World Cup football on the Box at home, with my husband gorping at every game in the constant company of Greavsie and Saintsie, the two current commentators on that ghastly game. I was happy to be here, until I saw our tutors, who looked the spitting image of those two. There is no doubt that Brian is Jimmy Greaves's look-alike, so, Ian must be St John, and I might as well have stayed at home.' You can imagine the claps and cheers that followed, and to her credit, she had used pauses, with gestures, quite naturally, to good effect.

Most speakers said how they hated a pause; you've got to keep talking; it's what an audience expects; which usually caused ums and ahs. I used to ask delegates who appreciated music, how they would like to hear Beethoven's Moonlight Sonata played at the same pace as Chopin's Minute Waltz, or vice versa? I thought the analogy of 'rests' between notes in music and punctuation between words in speech, a good one to bear in mind. By Friday, the 'pleasure of the pause' was appreciated and any reference to the 'pain of the pause' had gone away. This reminds me that our big message, during a Negotiating Skills Course, was 'go for a win-win, it's OK to compromise'. In so many areas, to this day, it is a great pity that sides still go for a 'win-lose', regardless, rather than try to create more favourable circumstances, where a 'win-win' would be possible. On Friday a.m., each delegate gave a final presentation, standing in front of their flip-charts as a visual aid. It was a brief critique, 5 to 10 minutes, on their personal development from start to finish, and I can never recall a negative one. They enjoyed doing it and with sincere smiles, ours of gratification, the course ended with a group photo.

Sometimes we went to our Humber Refinery at Immingham to run Presentation Courses on site, which were always subject to frequent interruptions. Occasionally we flew to Belfast, hired a car and drove to Londonderry, to run Interviewing Courses at the offices of Du Pont Ltd, of which Conoco was a part at that time. Likewise, these were interrupted by office colleagues, which couldn't happen on a residential hotel course. Also, at times, we flew to Aberdeen, from Heathrow, to run a Presentation Course at the Tree Tops Hotel, for Conoco on and off-shore personnel in Scotland. It was at the start of a Tree Tops course that I noticed the name card, completed by a lovely young lady delegate, read, 'Kim Bryce'. 'Hello cousin,' said I, and so it proved to be, after discovering we shared Young and Simpson as family forenames, amongst known relatives, past and present. She helped me pronounce some Robbie Burns words on the Thursday night, when it was customary for each tutor to make an after-dinner speech. I had chosen the bard's 'Gie the lass her fairin', which goes to the tune: Cauld Kail in Aberdeen. The last line of every verse repeats 'An hey for houghmagandie!', and the translation of that final word I leave to the imagination of my readers from north of The Border.

It was in the spring of 1990 that we ran a Presentation Course in Head Office. Delegates got their length of speech better for time as the course progressed, and their last speech was expected to be accurate to within 5 mins. If over or under that limit, then a penalty was imposed, which, when at a hotel, would be to pay for the wine at dinner, that evening, but being in HO, this was not possible. John Bastin, Conoco's senior geologist and the only defaulter, insisted on upholding this tradition and suggested his own penalty. His proposition was to take one of the tutors, Brian or me, up in a Tiger Moth biplane from Headcorn airfield in Kent, where he was a qualified pilot and member of the Club. This was on condition that his tutor-co-pilot paid half the cost of fuel, £45, for an hour's flight. Brian declined, but I accepted gladly. So it was, by strange coincidence, on Sunday, 15 September, the 50th anniversary of Battle of Britain Day, that John and I became airborne in a 1933 Tiger Moth. Having checked that I knew, basically, how to control joy-stick, rudder and flaps from the front cockpit, he turned over to me, for twenty minutes, flying at 70 mph, at 2000 ft, with scarves blowing in the breeze. We gave Leeds Castle a wide berth, where a concert was in progress, and John took over for a gentle landing on this fine day. It was fun and being a goggled pilot in an open cockpit was similar to being pilot on the open bridge of a destroyer, in the Arctic, doing 35 knots – chilly.

Before saying goodbye, for good, to the Hythe-Imperial, I must say that breakfast was always a memorable meal. We tutors sat at a separate table for two and after our regular morning swim, at 0700, I would find Brian at the toast and marmalade stage, when I arrived for my grapefruit, about 0830. Invariably, he had completed that day's *Times* crossword and if not, I would express my surprise, which sometimes caused him to tell me the unsolved clue, but I was no help, thirty years having elapsed since I was a dedicated *Daily Telegraph* crossword fan.

Du Pont/Conoco diminished training in '93, which meant that KBA had only two courses that year and the very last course for Conoco in May, '94. This was regrettable in many ways, but it gave me freedom ahead, for other activities. Two worthy shoremates, a few years younger than me, had retired from Conoco recently and were living nearby: Ron Perrin in Watford and Dave McKay between Redbourn and Hemel Hempstead. Both, as managers, with good past reputations for training and developing them-selves and their subordinates, had decided to do something similar in retirement.

Ron and Dave had kept track of me and knew that my consultancy with Conoco was about to end, so, Dave phoned me and said 'Ian, you old rascal, I want to see you and tell you about something, I think, would interest you.' It was around the kitchen table at 37 King Harry Lane, with tumblers being recharged frequently, that we recalled the trouble-shooting foundation of our friendship on the M6 motorway in the 60s. Then, coming to the point, Dave said 'Ian, Ron and I have joined the North London Branch of Young Enterprise as Advisors, and it needs a Director of Training. I've told the Chairman you're the man for the job and he wants to meet you. He will tell you all about Young Enterprise and its aspirations, so, when's convenient?' After hearing Dave's brief description of his voluntary efforts, no pay, but much pleasure, I was sold on the idea and agreed to meet the Chairman, Tony Summers, who lived in Welwyn,Herts.

The meeting took place and Tony told me the purpose of YE was to get Lower Sixth Form students, prior to their A Level exams, to form Companies, which produced and sold a product or a service, whilst they acted in the roles of Directors on the Board and their subordinates, managing the whole process, for real. I believe the best way to give you, my readers, an overall picture of these voluntary efforts, is to quote Tony's letter to me, dated 5 January 1994, almost verbatim.

Dear Ian,

Following our conversation, I would like to confirm our invitation for you to join the North London Area Board of Young Enterprise, embracing Barnet, Enfield and Harringay.

There are a number of very good reasons for the invitation, but two stand out:

1) We have an on-going training need, not intensive but regular and very important, and we recognize not only your expertise in this field but also the fact that you have an immediate and obvious empathy with the youngsters. Your advice on training and your assistance in delivering it will be invaluable.

2) We need some wise minds on the Board to help steer us into what I think will be a very active period for Young Enterprise over the next few 'seasons', particularly active because of the fact that the Education Authorities are promoting YE for the first time as a means of delivering elements of much of the Curriculum for the General National Vocational Qualifications (GNVQs) which are just coming into all schools. Thus the teachers are asking us to assist in bringing in YE for the first time as a part of their courses in whatever vocational subject. There are a lot of schools not yet participating but the feeling is that there will be many more in the next few years.

All in all, I very much hope you will join us and I enclose a copy of our timetable which you may have seen anyway and which is overall more of a guide than fact since some of the events were included at the time of drafting more as an incentive to get things moving than anything writ in tablets of stone! However, the dates of the monthly Board Meetings are factual and the location of them is Legal and General Insurance Head Office in Cannon Hill, Southgate.

If you can make the next Board Meeting, that would be grand, but it may be a bit late to organize at this stage. No matter, we look forward to your presence on 9 February and I look forward to talking to you again before then. I will in any case send you a copy of the minutes of next week's meeting.

Best wishes and kind regards, Yours sincerely, Tony Summers. Chairman.

Receiving such a letter of praise in my 72nd year pleased me immensely and caused me to reflect on my good fortune that my career experience could still be used effectively in the present, with YE. My reply to Tony on 10 January stated my appreciation and said that without hesitation and a great deal of pleasure I accepted his offer of the job. With the Chairman's letter, quoted above, was a handout showing major Companies supporting Young Enterprise, which was founded in 1963. They were Midland Bank (HSBC group), British Aerospace, BT, GKN, Nestle and Laing, all of which provided materials and funds for the YE National Organization. Summers was Senior Personnel Manager at John Laing Plc, whose large conference facilities at their Head Office, between Mill Hill and Hendon, were used as my main training centre. For smaller exercises, the rooms of North London Polytechnic at Palmers Green were made available to me. Shortly after I joined, McDonalds told Young Enterprise, North London Area, they would be happy if we used their Head Office building in Finchley, with its large lecture theatre, for any of our staff meeting and training sessions for Advisers, which included a number of their managers. All was free of charge with plenty of good eats and drinks beforehand and at half-time. In no time at all, we called it the 'Hamburger University'.

These Organizations liked Young Enterprise because when students rose to the challenge of running their own YE Companies, it demonstrated their commitment, motivation and practical ability which would be available in future for our country's industrial success. At the same time, managers from these big business organizations were encouraged to volunteer as Advisers to YE Companies, which not only introduced them to the next generation of employees coming their way, but also helped them in their own development as team leaders. Young people, with good business knowledge and skills to lead our industries and create new businesses in future, will always be needed and YE is a great way to go about it. A handout to Lower Sixth Students helped recruitment, and the spoken words of recommendation from Achievers, already participating within their schools, would often give Young Enterprise a boost.

When a group of say 8 students formed a Company in which they adopted one or more roles each, it always raised an argument about who should do what, with whom and was usually influenced by in school friendships or otherwise. I suggested that there was a better way to determine personal relationships and introduced them to Meredith Belbin's advanced and proven skills to discover a person's inherent and dominant style, when working in a team. After completing and marking a multi-choice questionnaire, all participants had a profile of themselves in a team role, which would give useful self-perception in future under similar circumstances. Also peer observers were seated around a team in action, marking a checklist which recorded the behaviour roles used by the person observed throughout and given as feedback afterwards. For you to understand and then feel individually the interaction between roles, I am writing my condensed version of the 8 behaviour styles, not in order of precedence, but as given on an Observer Checklist:

1. Co-Ordinator Chairperson ... Seeks contributions and establishes systems.
2. Monitor & Evaluator ... Assesses others, analyses and clarifies.
3. Implementer (Company Worker) ... Turns ideas into feasible practice.
4. Completer Finisher ... Detects errors and pushes people to complete.
5. Shaper ... Sets limits with patterns and combines ideas.
6. Plant ... Proposes new ideas and directions.
7. Team Worker ... Pulls in and helps others overcome conflict.
8. Resource Investigator ... Broader vision to get ideas from elsewhere.

Belbin had developed this most effective team structure during many years at Henley Management College using delegates from the supposed intelligentsia of the UK's Industry, Government, Universities and other distinguished places. Having studied all members' self-analyses, he would select, say, 7 teams consisting of all 8 styles, and one, called 'Apollo', composed of those from the same or similar styles, who often, individually, fancied themselves, shall we say, as experts. Studying the previous paragraph, my opinion is, that the 'Apollo' team was made up, mainly, of 'Implementers', 'Completer- Finishers', 'Shapers' and 'Resource Investiga-tors'. Anyway, apparently they never got higher than 5th out of the competing 8 teams and I leave you, my most intelligent readers, to figure out why. Meantime, this must be my opportunity to define the word 'expert'. I thought everybody knew this critical humour, until recently, when I asked my daughter, Peta, if she was aware of the real meaning and she said 'No Dad, please tell me.' I replied 'Well, ex means a has-been and spurt, a drip under pressure.' You can agree or otherwise, depending on what you think you are.

To illustrate the numerous successes achieved by YE Companies, I have selected two schools, which, in my opinion, distinguished themselves most noticeably. The first, is Copthall School for Girls in Mill Hill, whose French Mistress, Jean Bate, was in charge of developing YE. This lady was a joy to work with. Her enthusiasm affected so many students that each time we met for a training session, there was yet another YE Company formed, until we had six. I believe it was one of them that made notice-boards, calendars, book-ends and many other useful items from corks, sliced in half and held in place by super-glue on wood and hardboard. They sold well and made a big profit for charity after covering expenses, which were minimal because they collected the corks, free of charge, from pubs and wine-bars. The Queen Elizabeth's Boys School in Barnet formed three or four YE Companies, supported by a team of very energetic teachers. One Company composed and published a comprehensive paperback entitled 'The Danger of Drugs', written with naive teenagers in mind, which sold well at their public stalls in shopping centres. I believe it attracted the attention of Waterstones, who subscribed to their publication and this boosted their sales considerably. The QE Boys School won the UK YE Top National Prize and later were awarded the Top European Prize for their superb achievement. The Bryce home still boasts a cork memo-board in the kitchen and a book about drugs in the living room, which remind us that there are still lots of good, enterprising, youngsters around nowadays, despite many modern deterrents.

Throughout the London Division Northern Area, a large number of schools were successful with their YE efforts, though many in poorer parts of Harringay were less privileged than those in Barnet and Enfield. We, the Board, ran, whatever the number of YE Companies, on a competitive basis, as did other Divisions in the UK. The year started in September and ran until April, when eliminating heats were judged by two chosen advisors and myself in Laing's training room. The finals were held amid great splendour in part of Alexandra Palace, with a stage, in front of three independent judges and a large audience of parents, teachers, advisers, scholars and other interested people from education and industry. YE Companies that reached the finals, usually six or eight, before making their presentations, would erect stalls, near the auditorium, to display and sell their products or services to circulating guests. A few Special Needs Schools joined in. They didn't have to make a presentation, but chose to do so and always did it extremely well.

Barbara Gandy was invited to join our Northern Area committee, in 1995, by her cousin Ron Newman, who was then Treasurer and Chairman, succeeding Tony Summers. She established the real role of Secretary, until then done haphazardly by an advisor, and the result was an immense improvement in team communication and operating efficiency. Barbara with husband Richard and daughters Karen and Jane, who went to the Abbey Primary School with Fiona, lived near us in St Albans. QE Boys School in Barnet was used regularly for meetings, and we were pleased to make Jason Dormieux, one of the keenest YE teachers, a member of our committee. Andrew Marr, who was YE Divisional Director for the whole

of London, appointed and paid by the National Board, attended some of
our meetings regularly. I got to know him well, especially after discovering
that his uncle, Geoffrey Marr, had been my Staff Captain aboard the
Cunarder *Mauretania*, way back in the 1950s. I saw a lot of Ron Perrin and
Dave McKay, my Conoco chums, and had some lovely chats with Ron's
wife, Lottie, at their immaculate house in Watford. A house so described,
because Lottie was a German lady, who married Ron when he was in the
British Army of Occupation after WW2. She was my age; had survived the
RAF raids on Berlin and had a brother who had sailed up the Humber
estuary in an E-boat, in 1940, so she said. 'Ian, mein freund, you must talk
to him next time he visits us,' but it never happened.

In 1997, after three delightful years with YE, happy days, I decided to
resign on my 75th birthday.

Looking back on my life, I realize how much I've changed and it's
impossible to name the times that caused it most, for the change was gradual
throughout, so, each reader can guess from reading my narrative. The love
and care received from, and given to, family and friends remained constant,
but my religious and philosophical attitudes shifted for numerous reasons.
Because I read lots of books and met many different people all over the
world, thoughts built on other thoughts and change happened over varying
periods of time. Today, my religion is 'To Do Good' thanks to Lao Tzu (old
boy) in the Tao Teh Ching (500 BC); Thomas Paine (1737–1809) and
William Blake (1757–1827). Also, my life is dedicated to GOD, meaning,
my 'Galactic Overall Designer', best described in the Chinese philosophy of
Yin and Yang, whose interaction is thought to maintain the harmony of the
universe and to influence everything within it. My mistress, the destroyer
Oribi (African antelope) shielded me from terror, U-boats under the sea, 60
years before 9/11. It was sometime in the nineties that I got in touch with
'Breadline Africa', a charity based on Capetown and managed by a local
lady, Edna Titus. Its aim is to help the poorer, often starving, natives help
themselves, especially the children, and Edna's illustrated Newsletters are a
joy to receive. Last year's donations bought olive trees, each given a donor's
name, and planted by children to form a large olive grove. I hope this will
give work and food to young enterprising South Africans in the years ahead,
similar to YE activities in richer parts of the world.

Before Christmas 2004 some charities and individuals suggested an
'unwrapped gift' to poorer people would be an acceptable link present to
those already self sufficient. The headline in Edna's Newsletter about the
olive trees, which said 'The gift that can grow for centuries', supported this
idea in principle and my mind was made up. I thought, it would balance
my book, nearly finished, if the wartime navigator of *Oribi*, coping then
with what could have been called 'Breadline Britain', helped Africa now,

Family group at The Port, East Portlemouth. Back row, l. to r.: Derek Ball, Andy Bryce, Craig Robson, Malindi Bryce, Charles Bryce, Joanna Ball, Fiona Robson. Front row, l. to r.: Sue Bryce, Ian Bryce, Peta Ball

in a similar state. I wrote to Edna using these words and saying I intend to give 5% from the sales of my book to 'Breadline Africa'.

Focusing on the family, I'm happy to say they all get on well and share a lot of time together. Peta is working part-time, after an excellent career in teaching, with textile skills foremost. Derek, still in Cardiff, now works for RPS, Rural Planning Services, which has a reputation for good enviromental compatibility, in a big way, countrywide. Fiona married Craig Robson, another worthy, Welsh, son-in-law, at St Albans Abbey in 2001. They live in Bryn Sadler, Mid-Glamorgan, and both have jobs in Cardiff Bay, only half-an-hour's drive away. Their house overlooks farmland beyond a good back-garden and with four bedrooms, it was a good move from the flat in Palmers Green, London, at a similar price! Andy now has a good rapport with a lady called Christine, whose presence we also find captivating. He has always liked an outdoor job and after the farm at London Colney, he now works for Coopers Landscape Contractors. Grand-daughter Joanna has become a most successful Estate Agent in Cardiff, and lives in a spacious Victorian terrace house, with a likeable local lad called Matthew.

Malindi, living with Charles in London, produced Scarlet Kiki Kinloch on Hallowe'en in 2000. Sue and I love her company on some Sundays, but she has other interests now, such as her own pony, stabled with Dad's numerous polo ones. On beating me at dominoes she said 'I hope you win the next game Grandpa 'cos it's so dull when the same side wins all the time.' Soccer celebrity Bobby Robson on TV expressed similar profound feelings when he said 'In the 1960s to lose was OK, but now, losing costs money!' Malindi's cousin Saffron is Charles's secretary running 'Gainsborough', a thriving design and office furnishing business, in Soho. When Charles and Malindi married in the summer of 2004 at Babington House in Somerset, Saffron's daughters, Poppy, Rosa and Holly, joined Scarlet, whom they treat as a fourth sister, to form a bevy of beautiful bridesmaids. Graham Head was great as best-man, and Malindi, much to her Dad David's delight, became my dear daughter-in-law.

Of regrets in life I have but few. After WW2 I did wish the UK had adopted PR, Proportional Representation, the Alternative Vote and also become part of a federal Europe. I have endured sixty years of 'first Party past the post', confrontational, government and in recent decades, policy seems to have come from a right or left wing political celebrity. There are never any doubts about who they want to run the Country, Commons and Cabinet. After being ADC at Holyrood, I believed that it would benefit most people if we changed our constitution. Thereby, all royals could be released from their unrealistic relationship with subjects and be permitted to pursue careers of their own choice, like any normal family. My patriotism was and still is less provincial.

When pedalling my bike with pleasure for 75 years, from 5 to 80, I regretted the increase in traffic density; most days, a car every 3 seconds along King Harry Lane. Now, every day, I pedal for a few miles on my stationary bike, whilst watching TV. I still regret the current obsession with speed; in speech, few, if any, pauses on radio or TV news; in transport, ignored limit signs and cameras instead of mobile police; on TV, most picture displays too fast to take in all features. And that's about enough regrets ed; as they say in *Private Eye*.

We downsized house in 2000, about a mile away from 37 King Harry Lane to 19 Antonine Gate, in a cul-de-sac, only 3 minutes walk through a cutting to Waitrose. What with friendly neighbours and staff at the shop, who are partners in John Lewis and change very little, it is like living in a lovely village, which suits our way of life. I have thanked Lloyd and his ladies in the Waitrose off-licence for their valued vintage support in writing this book. Now I'll say farewell to you my readers with a favourite poem of mine, and my love.

Leisure
by William Henry Davies

What is this life if, full of care,
We have no time to stand and stare.

No time to stand beneath the boughs
And stare as long as sheep or cows.

No time to see, when woods we pass,
Where squirrels hide their nuts in grass.

No time to see, in broad daylight,
Streams full of stars like skies at night.

No time to turn at Beauty's glance,
And watch her feet, how they can dance.

No time to wait till her mouth can
Enrich that smile her eyes began.

A poor life this if, full of care,
We have no time to stand and stare.

By me, for your contemplation:

What is this life if, full of care,
We have no time to stand and stare.

No time to heed thru' history's door
That both sides lose when waging war.

Glossary

Abeam   On a line at right-angles to a ship's length.

Aft   The back end of a ship.

Abaft   Aft of.

Acoustic mine   A mine which is triggered off by the sound of the ship's engines.

Barque   A 3, 4 or 5-masted sailing ship carrying square sails on all but its after mast, which carries fore and aft sails.

Buffer   The Chief Boatswain's Mate, a 'buffer' between No. 1 and the work done by ratings about the ship.

Companion Ways   Ladders between decks.

Ensign   The flag flown by a ship as the insignia of her nationality or the nature of her duties. Britain has 3 ensigns, each with the Union Jack in the 1st quarter: 1. The White of the Royal Navy, which also bears the cross of St George and may be flown by members of the Royal Yacht Squadron, 2. The Blue of the Royal Naval Reserve, 3. The Red of the Merchant Navy.

Fore, or For'ard   The front end of a ship.

Gig   A slim, 6-oared rowing boat.

Gun Room   The mess which houses all midshipmen and sub-lieutenants in a large cruiser or battleship.

Guz   A naval nickname for Devonport and Plymouth, said to arise from the West Countryman's inordinate love of guzzling cream teas.

Gyrocompass   This consists of a heavy disc, spinning at high speed, suspended in a ring. The axis of the gyro adjusts itself so that it always points to true North, and is unaffected by variations in magnetism. The gyrocompass is hung in the bowels of a ship and its reading is transferred to repeaters throughout the ship.

'Hands fall in'   A command instructing men to line up, with tallest on the right and shortest on the left. A 'marker', the tallest man, would indicate where others should line up.

Jimmy   The First Lieutenant or No. 1.

Master's Certificate   A voluntary system of examination was introduced for Masters and Mates of foreign-going merchant vessels in 1845. From 1850 onwards this was compulsory. Initially a certificate could be gained by long service, then was obtained by examination, containing both written and oral sections.

Midshipman   An officer in training in the Royal Navy, ranking below the lowest commissioned officer.

Mizzen Mast   The aftermost mast of a 3-masted ship or of a 2-masted ketch, yawl etc.

Mountbatten Pink   Camouflage painting of light grey with patches of pink, which broke up a ship's outline, and was used particularly on ships in the Mediterranean and in tropical waters.

Port   The left hand side of a ship when facing the front, or bow.

Starboard   The right hand side of a ship when facing the bow.

Stem   The front end of a ship.

Stern   The back end of a ship.

'Sound the Still'   When a ship sails past another, carrying an officer of flag rank, a signal would be ordered on bo'sun's pipe or Marine bugle to command all crew members on deck to stand to attention and face the ship carrying the senior officer.

Stone frigate   A stone or brick-built shore establishment duly commissioned with a warship's name.

'Sunset'   The bugle-call played while the ensign is slowly lowered at sunset.

Wardroom   The collective noun applied to the officers of a large warship above the rank of sub-lieutenant and to all the officers of a smaller ship; the Mess for these officers.

Yard   A cylindrical spar, with tapered ends slung across a mast to support a sail.

Yard-arm   Each end of the yard.

Yeoman   A senior assistant/rating; e.g. Bill Goodacre, as Navigator's Yeoman, helped the Navigator with work on the charts.

Index

Entries in italics indicate illustrations